CORPORATE GOVERNANCE

ICSA STUDY TEXT

CORPORATE GOVERNANCE

BRIAN COYLE

icsa.
Publishing

First published 2010
Published by ICSA Information & Training Ltd
16 Park Crescent
London W1B 1AH

© ICSA Information & Training Ltd 2010

Designed and typeset by Newgen Imaging Systems Pvt. Ltd., Chennai, India
Printed in Great Britain by Hobbs the Printers Ltd, Totton Hampshire

British Cataloguing in Publication Data
A catalogue record for this book is available from the British Library.

ISBN 978-1-86072-453-4

Contents

= 100

How to use this study text

ICSA study texts developed to support ICSA's Chartered Secretaries Qualifying Scheme (CSQS) follow a standard format and include a range of navigational, self-testing and illustrative features to help you get the most out of the support materials.

Each text is divided into three main sections:

- introductory material
- the text itself, divided into Parts and Chapters
- additional reference information

The sections below show you how to find your way around the text and make the most of its features.

Introductory material

The introductory section of each text includes a full contents list and the module syllabus which re-iterates the module aims, learning outcomes and syllabus content for the module in question.

Where relevant, the introductory section will also include a list of acronyms and abbreviations or a list of legal cases for reference.

The text itself

Each **part** opens with a list of the chapters to follow, an overview of what will be covered and learning outcomes for the part. Part openings also include a case study, which introduces a real-world scenario related to the topics covered in that part. Questions based on this case and designed to test the application of theory into practice appear in the chapters and at part endings (see below).

Every **chapter** opens with a list of the topics covered and an introduction specific to that chapter. Chapters are structured to allow students to break the content down into manageable sections for study. Each chapter ends with a summary of key content to reinforce understanding.

Part opening

Chapter opening

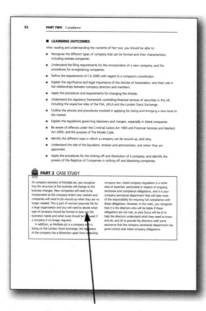

Part case study

Features

The text is enhanced by a range of illustrative and self-testing features to assist understanding and to help you prepare for the examination. Each feature is presented in a standard format, so that you will become familiar with how to use them in your study.

The texts also include tables, figures and checklists and, where relevant, sample documents and forms.

Case Examples
Case examples present short, illustrative case studies which look at how concepts are applied in practice.

Checklist

Sample wording

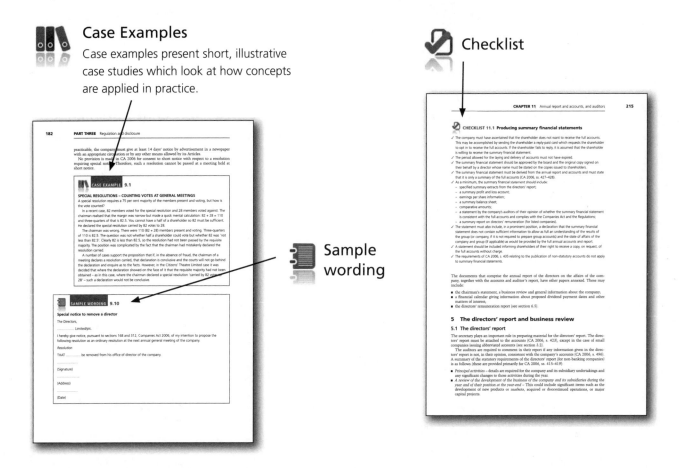

Case Law
Case law summaries provide overviews of significant legal cases.

Case Questions
Case questions relate to the part opening case study, encouraging you to apply the theory you're learning to a real-world business scenario.

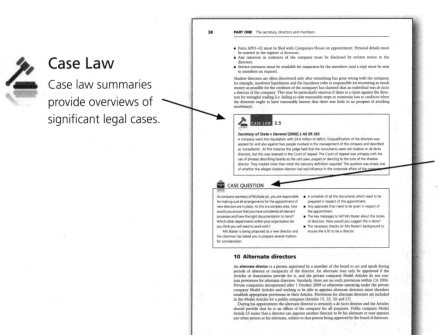

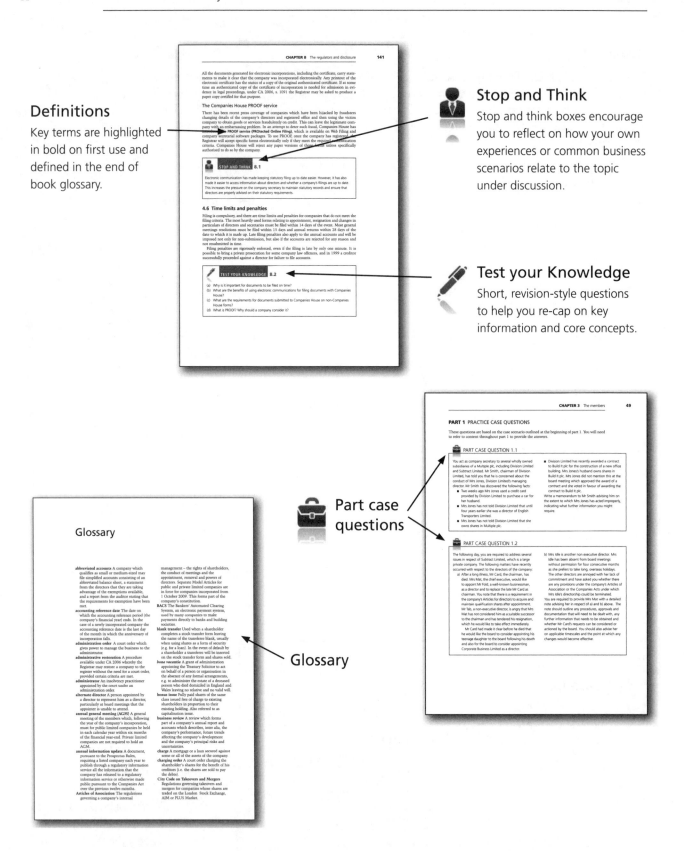

Definitions

Key terms are highlighted in bold on first use and defined in the end of book glossary.

Stop and Think

Stop and think boxes encourage you to reflect on how your own experiences or common business scenarios relate to the topic under discussion.

Test your Knowledge

Short, revision-style questions to help you re-cap on key information and core concepts.

Part case questions

Glossary

Reference material

The text ends with a range of additional guidance and reference material.

Most texts will include Appendices which comprise additional reference material specific to that module.

Other reference material includes a glossary of key terms, a directory of further reading and web resources and a comprehensive index.

Corporate Governance syllabus

Module outline and aims

The aim of the Corporate Governance module is to equip the Chartered Secretary with the knowledge and key skills necessary to act as adviser to governing authorities across the private, public and voluntary sectors. The advice of the Chartered Secretary will include all aspects of the governance obligations of organisations, covering not only legal duties, but also applicable and recommended standards of best practice.

The module will enable the development of a sound understanding of corporate governance law and practice in a national and international context. It will also enable you to support the development of good governance and stakeholder dialogue throughout the organisation, irrespective of sector, being aware of legal obligations and best practice.

Learning outcomes

On successful completion of this module, you will be able to:

- Appraise the frameworks underlying governance law and practice in a national and international context.
- Distinguish between and compare the legal obligations for governance and recommended best practice.
- Advise on governance issues across all sectors, ensuring that the pursuit of strategic objectives is in line with regulatory developments and developments in best practice.
- Analyse and evaluate situations in which governance problems arise and provide recommendations for solutions.
- Demonstrate how general concepts of governance apply in a given situation or given circumstances.
- From the perspective of a Chartered Secretary, provide authoritative and professional advice on matters of corporate governance.
- Assess the relationship between governance and performance within organisations.
- Apply the principles of risk management and appraise the significance of risk management for good governance.
- Compare the responsibilities of organisations to different stakeholder groups, and advise on issues of ethical conduct and the application of principles of corporate responsibility or corporate citizenship.

Syllabus content

Governance is a continually developing subject, and good candidates will be aware of any major developments that have occurred by the time they take their examination.

The detailed syllabus set out here has a strong UK emphasis, and it is expected that UK corporate governance will be the focus of study for most candidates. A good knowledge of the principles and provisions of the UK Corporate Governance Code will therefore be required, together with any supporting Guidance on the Code published from time to time by the Financial Reporting Council. However, a good knowledge and understanding of the code of corporate governance in another country will be acceptable in answers, provided that candidates indicate which code they are referring to in their answer.

The UK Corporate Governance Code ('the Code'; formerly 'the UK Combined Code') is subject to frequent review and amendment by the Financial Reporting Council. You are advised to check the student newsletter and student news area of the ICSA website to find out when revisions to the Code will first be examined.

General principles of corporate governance – weighting 20%

Candidates are expected to demonstrate an awareness of all areas of governance, and to be able to review common themes. They will be able to understand the scope of corporate governance, the various issues with which governance is concerned, and how these issues relate to each other. Meaning of corporate governance

- Difference between governance and management
- Purpose of good governance

Agency theory, transaction cost theory, stakeholder theory
Stakeholder value approach, enlightened stakeholder approach, stakeholder approach
Governance, risk and financial stability

- The balancing of conflicting objectives

Potential consequences of poor corporate governance

- Business failure and the contribution of poor governance

Governance and ethics, corporate ethics, corporate codes of ethics, professional ethics
Key issues in corporate governance

- Role and composition of the board, remuneration of directors and senior executives, accounting and audit, relations with shareholders and other stakeholders

Applying best practice in governance: voluntary and regulatory approaches, rules or principles, concept of 'comply or explain'
Governance problems for global companies and groups
Governance issues in the public sector

- Nolan Principles

Governance issues in the voluntary sector (charities)

Candidates may be required to be aware of the unique circumstances that may apply to governance for a non-corporate entity or a global company

Legal and regulatory aspects of governance

Candidates may study and apply the legal and regulatory measures on governance in their own country, but should also be aware of the following:
   Governance aspects of the UK Companies Act 2006, including duties of directors and reporting and disclosure requirements

- Statutory duties of directors, and the concepts of duty of care and skill and fiduciary duty on which these statutory duties are based
- Business review requirements are referred to elsewhere in the syllabus
- An awareness of the requirements for reporting on directors' remuneration is required, but not the detailed regulations

Corporate governance aspects of EU Directives (and subsequent legislation)

- An awareness is required of the EU as a potential source of new legislation on governance issues, with examples of changes introduced by the EU

Governance issues for financial organisations arising from the Financial Services and Markets Act 2000 and the Basel 'rules'

- The regulatory supervision of banks: its implications for governance

Law relating to insolvency and regulations relating to assessment of going concern status
Law on insider dealing and market abuse

- The nature of insider dealing: the law and inside dealing, its implications for governance

Governance aspects of UK Listing Rules, including the Model Code

- Comply or explain
- Model code and directors' dealings in shares

Governance aspects of Sarbanes-Oxley Act 2002

- Section 302: CEO/CFO certifications
- Section 404(a): internal control report

Codes of corporate governance practice and reports on governance

Candidates will be expected to demonstrate an awareness of the prominent codes or reports on governance and to be aware of current developments, such as when these codes or reports are being reviewed or re-drafted.

- UK Corporate Governance Code
- OECD Principles
- King Reports

Role of the company secretary

Role of the company secretary in the identification of governance issues, and the application of governance rules and principles in practice.

Comparison of the governance role of the company secretary and the role of the company lawyer.

The application of governance rules and principles – weighting 40%

Candidates will be required to discuss in detail statutory rules and the principles or provisions of governance codes, and apply them to specific situations or case studies. Candidates will also be expected to understand the role of the company secretary in providing support and advice regarding the application of best governance practice. Although the syllabus presents governance issues mainly from the perspective of companies, candidates may be required to apply similar principles to non-corporate entities, such as government organisations and organisations in the voluntary sector.

The broad areas that will be examined are as follows:

The board of directors or governing board

Role of the board and its governance responsibilities
Unitary and two-tier boards
Matters reserved for the board

- ICSA Guidelines

Roles of the chairman and chief executive officer
Size, structure and composition of the board: board balance, independence
Independent non-executive directors

- Functions of the independent NED

Good boardroom practice

- Responsibilities of the chairman and company secretary

Appointments to the board: nominations committee

- Contribution of the nominations committee to good governance
- Higgs Guidance on duties of the nomination committee
- Tyson Report

Information and professional development for board members

- Induction and ongoing training
- Role of the company secretary in the efficient provision of information
- Directors and external professional advice

Effectiveness of the board, its committees and individual board members. Performance evaluation of the board

- UK Corporate Governance Code
- Annual performance evaluation of the board, its committees and individual directors
- Higgs Guidance on performance evaluation

Re-election of board members

- Retirement by rotation

Boardroom ethics

- Link to statutory duties of directors

Dealings by directors in shares of their company

- Link to law on insider trading, stock market rules on dealings by directors

Liability of directors: directors' and officers' liability insurance

- The reasons for and nature of directors' liability

Personal interests of directors in transactions of their company
Independent and non-independent non-executive directors: their role and effectiveness

- Good practice suggestions from the Higgs Report
- Senior independent director: role
- Criticisms of the ineffectiveness of NEDs

Remuneration of directors and senior executives

Principles of remuneration structure: elements of remuneration
Remuneration policy

The design of performance-related remuneration

- Elements of a remuneration package
- Candidates will not be required to discuss performance targets in detail, but need to be aware of short-term incentives (e.g. cash bonuses) and longer term bonuses (share grants, share options). They also need to be able to discuss the difficulties in designing a suitable remuneration structure

Role of the remuneration committee

- Higgs Guidance on role of the remuneration committee

Deciding a remuneration package for individual directors and senior executives
Compensation for loss of office
Disclosures of directors' remuneration

- Candidates will be expected to show an awareness of issues relating to the disclosure of directors' remuneration in the annual report and accounts, but not the detail (e.g. not the detail of the directors' remuneration report)

Shareholder approval of incentive schemes and voting rights with regard to remuneration

- Candidates will be required to show an understanding that approval of remuneration schemes by shareholders may be required, but legislation on this topic will not be examinable

The recommendations or guidelines of institutional investor groups on matters relating to directors' remuneration, including the avoidance of 'reward for failure'

Reporting to shareholders and external audit

Financial reporting, going concern status (review of future solvency): responsibilities of the board, executive management and the external auditors

- The need for reliable financial reporting: true and fair view
- The nature of the going concern statement and its relevance for governance
- Directors' responsibility for the financial statements
- Responsibility of the external auditors
- Responsibility for the discovery of fraud

Role of the audit committee: the audit committee and the external auditors

- Composition of the committee and skills of committee members
- ICSA Guidance on terms of reference of audit committees
- FRC Guidance on Audit Committees

Independence of the external auditors

- The significance of auditor independence: threats to auditor independence
- Auditors and non-audit work

Principles of reporting requirements for good governance: accountability, transparency

- The meaning of transparency

Disclosures of governance arrangements
Reporting non-financial information: business review or operating and financial review

- The significance of narrative reporting for better governance

Relations with shareholders

The equitable treatment of shareholders

- The meaning of equitable treatment: examples of inequitable treatment

Rights and powers of shareholders
Dialogue and communications with institutional shareholders (companies) or major stakeholders
Role of institutional investor organisations (or major stakeholders)

- In the UK, the role of the ABI and NAPF and the relevance for corporate governance

Constructive use of the annual general meeting
Shareholder activism

- The recommendations or guidelines of institutional investor groups on matters relating to activism and considered use of votes

Other shareholders: short-term investors, small investors

- The rights of minority shareholders

Candidates will be required to have an awareness of the benefits of electronic communications between companies and their shareholders, but will not be required to know the detailed law and regulations on electronic communications.

Risk management and internal control – weighting 20%

Candidates will be able to discuss aspects of risk facing an organisation, and to comment and advise on the systems in place for the identification and assessment of risks, the management of risk and monitoring the effectiveness of risk management and internal control systems.
The nature of risks facing companies and other organisations: categories of risk

- The difference between 'business risk' and 'governance risk' (internal control risk)

Risk tolerance levels: risk and return, risk appetite
Responsibilities for risk management and internal control: board of directors, executive management, audit committee, internal and external auditors

- Risk management committees in companies

Risk management policies, systems and procedures
Risks in the business environment

- The implications of business risk and strategy selection for governance: a general understanding only is required

Internal control risks: financial, operational and compliance risks
Elements of an internal control system

- The Turnbull Guidance and subsequent reviews of this guidance

Function, scope and status of internal audit and internal auditors: independence of the internal auditors: the need for internal audit

- Role of internal audit within an internal control system

Identifying key risk areas: key performance indicators
Disaster recovery plans
Whistle-blowing policy and procedures

- ICSA best practice on whistle-blowing procedures

Reviewing and reporting on the effectiveness of the risk management system
Reviewing and reporting on the effectiveness of the internal control system

- UK Corporate Governance Code requirements and Turnbull guidelines

Corporate social responsibility and sustainability – weighting 20%

The nature of corporate responsibility and corporate citizenship
Corporate responsibility and stakeholders

- Internal and external stakeholders
- Responsibility to various stakeholder groups
- Interest and influence of various stakeholder groups

Elements of corporate social responsibility: employees, the environment, human rights, communities and social welfare, social investment, ethical conduct
Reputation risk: placing a value on reputation
Other risk issues

- Economic
- Political, legal, regulatory
- Social: demographic risk, educational issues
- Possible implications of these risks for the social and environmental policy of companies

Corporate social responsibility: financial performance, business ethics and public relations
Formulating and implementing a policy for corporate social responsibility
The nature of sustainability
Sustainability and long-term corporate performance
Reporting to stakeholders: CSR reporting
Sustainability reporting: triple bottom line reports

- The content of sustainability reports (also CSR reports, ESG reports, social and environmental reports)

Benchmarking with other organisations
Social responsibility in the public and voluntary sectors
The recommendations or guidelines of institutional investor groups on matters relating to social and environmental issues.

NOTE: Candidates will not be required to have a detailed knowledge of the 'history' of the development of corporate governance guidelines and rules. For example, knowledge of the detailed content of the Cadbury Report, Greenbury Report and Hampel Report in the UK will not be required.

Acronyms and abbreviations

ABI	Association of British Insurers
ACCA	Association of Chartered Certified Accountants
ACEVO	Association of Chief Executives of Voluntary Associations
AGM	annual general meeting
AIM	alternative investment market
APB	Audit Practices Board
AQF	Audit Quality Forum
ASB	Accounting Standards Board
ATOL	Association of Travel Operators
CA	Companies Act
CACG	Commonwealth Association of Corporate Governance
CDO	Collateralised debt obligations
CEO	chief executive officer
CFO	chief financial officer
CIMA	Chartered Institute of Management Accountants
CIPFA	Chartered Institute of Public Finance and Accountancy
COSO	Committee of Sponsoring Organizations of the Treadway Commission
CRO	Chief risk officer
CSR	corporate social responsibility
CTN	Charity Trustee Network
D&O	Directors and officers (as in, Directors' and officers' liability insurance)
DTI	Department of Trade and Industry
EBITDA	earnings before interest, taxation, depreciation and amortisation
EGM	extraordinary general meeting
ESB	Ethical Standards Board
ESG	environmental, social and governance
EU	European Union
FRC	Financial Reporting Council
FSA	Financial Services Authority
FSMA	Financial Services and Markets Act
GRI	Global Research Initiative
HAZOPS	hazard and operability studies
IBE	Institute of Business Ethics
ICAEW	Institute of Chartered Accountants in England and Wales
ICGN	International Corporate Governance Network
IDP	Investigation and Discipline Board
IFAC	International Federation of Accountants
IFRS	International Financial Reporting Standard
IMA	Investment Management Association
IoD	Institute of Directors
IOSCO	International Organisation of Securities Commissions
IPC	investor protection committee
IPPR	Institute for Public Policy Research
ISC	Institutional Shareholders Committee
ISS	Institutional Shareholder Services Inc
IT	Information technology
KPI	key performance indicators
LLA	liability limitation agreement
NAPF	National Association of Pension Funds
NCVO	National Council of Voluntary Organisations
NDPB	non-departmental public body
NED	non-executive director
NRSRO	nationally recognised statistical ratings organisation
NYSE	New York Stock Exchange
OECD	Organisation for Economic Co-operation and Development

OFR	Operating and Financial Review
OPM	Office for Public Management
PBIT	profit before interest and tax
PDMRs	Persons discharging managerial responsibilities
PIRC	Pensions and Investment Consultants Limited
QCA	Quoted Companies Alliance
RIS	Regulated Information Service
RREV	Research Recommendations and Electronic Voting
SEC	Securities and Exchange Commission
SEE	social, environmental and ethical
SID	senior independent director
SMEs	small and medium-sized enterprises
SOX	Sarbanes-Oxley Act 2002
SRI	socially responsible investment
TCE	transaction cost economics
Transpub	Transparency and Publicity Act
TSR	total shareholder return
UKSA	UK Shareholders Association
VaR	Value at Risk
VFM	value for money

Acknowledgements

The publishers would like to thank the following organisations:

Appendix 1 and Appendix 4

The UK Corporate Governance Code and The UK Stewardship Code are both ©FRC and adapted and reproduced with the kind permission of the Financial Reporting Council. All rights reserved. For further information see www.frc.org.uk or call +44 (0)20 7492 2300

Appendix 2

The OECD Principles of Corporate Governance 2004 (OECD Publishing), http://dx.doi.org/10.1787/9789264015999-en are ©OECD (2004) and reproduced with permission.

Appendix 3

The King Code on Corporate Governance for South Africa (The Institute of Directors in Southern Africa) September 2009 is © The Institute of Directors in Southern Africa and is reproduced with permission.

General principles of corporate governance

■ **LIST OF CHAPTERS**

1 Definitions and issues in corporate governance
2 Legal and regulatory aspects of governance
3 Voluntary codes of corporate governance: role of the company secretary

■ **OVERVIEW**

The first part of this study text introduces corporate governance, its significance for the contemporary business world and the role of the company secretary in corporate governance awareness and compliance.

The term 'corporate governance' is commonly used, but it is often hard to define exactly what it means and what its objectives should be. Chapter 1 begins by providing a definition and explaining the possible consequences of poor governance. Different theoretical frameworks for an approach to best practice in governance are explained, and the close connection between governance and business ethics is explored. The chapter also highlights some of the key issues in corporate governance, including the structure and balance of the board of directors, boardroom practice, the remuneration of senior executives, financial reporting and auditing, shareholder communications, risk management systems and internal control systems. To put these in context, Chapter 1 includes a brief history of the development of corporate governance both in the UK and globally, and compares a voluntary approach to the practice of corporate governance with a regulatory approach. The chapter ends with a discussion of the similarities and differences in governance issues between companies and organisations in the public sector (including government itself) and the voluntary sector.

Chapter 2 looks briefly at how certain requirements relating to corporate governance are included in laws and regulations.

Chapter 3 looks at the voluntary frameworks for best practice in corporate governance, with particular focus on the corporate governance code in the UK, corporate governance principles issued by the Organisation for Economic Co-operation and Development and the ground-breaking code of governance in the King Code in South Africa. The chapter also explains the role of institutional investors in the promotion of best practice in corporate governance, and concludes by considering the role of the company secretary in corporate governance.

■ LEARNING OUTCOMES

Part One should enable you to:

- appraise the frameworks underlying governance law and practice in a national and international context

- distinguish between and compare the legal obligations for governance and recommended best practice

- discuss the role of the Chartered Secretary in providing authoritative, credible and professional advice on governance.

Definitions and issues in corporate governance

■ CONTENTS

■ INTRODUCTION

This chapter explains the nature and scope of **corporate governance**, the theoretical frameworks for corporate governance, and the voluntary and regulatory approaches that are used to apply best practice (i.e. the generally accepted best way of doing something) in corporate governance. Corporate governance is compared with governance in the public and voluntary sectors of the economy, for which codes of best practice have also been developed.

1 Defining corporate governance

'Governance' refers to the way in which something is governed and to the function of governing. The governance of a country, for example, refers to the powers and actions of the legislative assembly, the executive government and the judiciary.

Corporate governance refers to the way in which companies are governed and to what purpose. It is concerned with practices and procedures for trying to ensure that a company is run in such a way that it achieves its objectives. This could be to maximise the wealth of its owners (the shareholders), subject to various guidelines and constraints and with regard to other groups or individuals with an interest in what the company does. Guidelines and constraints include behaving in an ethical way and in compliance with laws and regulations. From a shareholder's perspective, corporate governance can be defined as a process for monitoring and control to ensure that management runs the company in the interests of the shareholders.

Other groups with an interest in how the company acts include employees, customers, suppliers, the communities in which the company operates and the general public. Individuals, organisations or groups with an interest in how a company operates are called **stakeholders**. It can be argued that companies should be governed in the interests of all its major stakeholders, not just its owners. This argument is particularly relevant to large companies whose activities have a big impact on the economy and society.

Governance might not be an easy concept to understand. In the case of governing a country, it would be concerned with who has the power to rule and what the governors of the country should be trying to achieve. The government of a democratic country presumably sets itself the objective of protecting its people and acting in their best interests, whatever these might be. Powers are shared between the legislative, executive and judiciary, but it is a matter of debate how these powers should be shared and exercised. In the UK, for example, there is healthy political debate about the respective powers of Parliament, the Prime Minister and the Cabinet, the UK law courts, and the powers of the government bodies and courts of the European Union.

In a large company, similar issues of governance arise. Corporate governance is concerned with how powers are shared and exercised by different groups, to ensure that the objectives of the company are achieved. Aspects of corporate governance are the rights of shareholders and other interest groups such as the employees, how powers are shared and exercised by the directors, and how the holders of power in a company should be held accountable for what they do.

- A company is a legal entity or 'legal person'. As a person, it is able to enter into contracts and make business transactions. It can own assets and owe money to others, and it can sue and be sued in law. However, although it is a legal person, decisions about what the company should do are taken by individuals in the company's name.
- Just as a country has citizens, a company has members. The members of a company are its owners, the 'equity' shareholders. The membership of large companies changes constantly, as investors buy and sell the company's shares.
- The citizens of a country, even in a democracy, have relatively few powers. Power is in the hands of the legislative (Parliament) and the executive (the government). Similarly, shareholders have relatively few powers, and these are restricted mainly to certain voting rights. Power is in the hands of the board of directors, or perhaps just one or two individual directors on the board.

For large companies, the main issue with corporate governance is the relationship between the board of directors and the shareholders, and the way in which the board exercises its powers. The relationship between the shareholders and the board can be described as a 'principal-agent' relationship. In some companies other stakeholders may have significant influence.

Principles of corporate governance are based on the view that a company should be governed in the interests of the shareholders, and possibly also in the interests of other stakeholder groups. The board ought to use its powers in an appropriate and responsible way, and should be accountable in some ways to the shareholders (and other stakeholders, perhaps).

1.1 Why is corporate governance important?

A company should have objectives. Some of these, such as the reasons for its existence, may be set out in its written constitution. Other objectives may be implied or assumed, rather than clearly documented. A company should be governed in a way that moves it towards the achievement of its objectives.

However, although a company exists as a legal person, in reality it is the organised, collective effort of many different individuals. It is controlled by a board of directors in the interests of its owners, the shareholders. The interests of the board and the shareholders ought to coincide, but in practice they may be in conflict with each other. The challenge of good corporate governance is to find a way in which the interests of shareholders, directors and other interest groups can all be sufficiently satisfied.

1.2 Governance and management

It is important to recognise the difference between the governance of a company and its management.

Powers to manage the affairs of a company are given to the board of directors, but most of these powers are delegated to a chief executive officer or managing director, and are delegated further to **executive directors** and executive managers. The board of directors should retain some powers and responsibilities, and certain matters should be reserved for board decision-making rather than delegated to the management team (see Chapter 4).

The board of directors should also be responsible for monitoring the performance of the management team. However, the board of directors is not responsible for day-to-day management. It is responsible for governing the company. Responsibilities for governance go beyond management, and governance should not be confused with management. Even so, it is probably true to say that when a senior executive manager is 'promoted' to the board, he or she may consider the position of an executive director to be a recognition of his senior executive position. However, the promotion of an executive manager to the board creates new responsibilities for governance that are not related to management. The executive director ought to think as a member of the board, rather than as a senior executive, in performing his duties as a director.

TEST YOUR KNOWLEDGE 1.1

(a) Why is corporate governance more significant for large companies than for small private companies?
(b) What is the difference between governance and management?

2   Consequences of poor corporate governance

Corporate governance is a matter of much greater importance for large public companies, where the separation of ownership from management is much wider than for small private companies. Public companies raise capital on the stock markets, and **institutional investors** (see Chapter 3) hold vast portfolios of shares and other investments. Investors need to know that their money is reasonably safe. Should there be any doubts about the integrity or intentions of the individuals in charge of a company, the value of the company's shares will be affected and the company will have difficulty raising new capital should it wish to do so. If there is weak corporate governance in a country generally, the country will struggle to attract foreign investment.

Commenting on the numerous corporate scandals in the US in 2001 and 2002, Arthur Levitt, a former **chairman** of the Securities and Exchange Commission (SEC), said in a speech:

'If a country does not have a reputation for strong corporate governance practice, capital will flow elsewhere. If investors are not confident with the level of disclosure, capital will flow elsewhere. If a country opts for lax accounting and reporting standards, capital will flow elsewhere. All enterprises in that country, regardless of how steadfast a particular company's practices, may suffer the consequences. Markets exist by the grace of investors. And it is today's more empowered investors who will determine which companies and which markets stand the test of time ...'

It might seem self-evident that good (or adequate) corporate governance supports capital markets. However, the impetus for the development of codes of best practice and stricter regulatory regimes has come largely from scandals and setbacks, where evidence of bad corporate governance has emerged, and company share prices and the stock market generally have suffered as a consequence.

CASE EXAMPLE 1.1

Maxwell Corporation consisted mainly of Maxwell Communication Corporation and Mirror Group Newspapers. As its chairman and **chief executive officer** (CEO), Robert Maxwell had a position of dominant power on the board of directors. He was also a domineering personality, who bullied the people working with him; he was able to run his companies in whatever way he liked. He apparently made no clear distinction between his privately owned companies and the public Maxwell Corporation. In the early 1990s, his companies got into serious financial difficulties. Maxwell drowned falling off his yacht in 1991; after his death it emerged that his companies had accumulated debts of £4 billion, and an unauthorised 'hole' of more than £400 million existed in the pension fund of Mirror Group Newspapers. Maxwell's ability to accumulate unsustainable debts and to raid the pension fund was attributed to a combination of his domineering personality and position of power, a weak board of directors and questionable accounting practices. The Maxwell 'empire' collapsed.

Bad corporate governance is a problem for any country with large companies and capital markets. Events over the past few decades have shown that it often takes a scandal to focus the attention of the regulators. In recent years, a number of corporate scandals have raised questions about governance in companies in the UK (e.g. Mirror Group Newspapers and Polly Peck International in the early 1990s), in the USA (e.g. Enron and WorldCom in 2001/2002 and more recently – and for different reasons – Lehman Brothers in 2008) and in mainland Europe (e.g. Ahold in the Netherlands, Parmalat in Italy and Siemens in Germany). The problems and challenges of corporate governance are worldwide, and laws and regulations about corporate governance are now applied in many countries across the world.

The USA was much slower than the UK to recognise problems of bad corporate governance, but in 2001 and 2002 there were a number of major corporate collapses that could be attributable partly to governance issues and fraud. The most well-known case is probably Enron Corporation.

 CASE EXAMPLE 1.2

Enron was founded in 1985 with the merger of two US natural gas pipelines. In the 1990s it diversified into selling electricity and other activities; by 2000 it was one of the world's largest companies when measured by reported annual revenue. It appeared to have a highly competent board of directors and **audit committee** (see Chapter 7). However, although investors and regulators were not aware of it at the time, the rapid growth in the reported assets and profits of Enron was attributable largely to misleading accounting practices. It inflated the value of its reported assets (sometimes recording expenses as assets) and it kept liabilities off its balance sheet by means of establishing 'special purpose entities'. It also anticipated profits by becoming the first non-financial services company to adopt 'mark to market' accounting techniques. This enabled it to earn profits on long-term contracts 'up front' as soon as the contract started. In one case it claimed a large profit on a 20-year contract agreed with Blockbuster Video in 2000, and continued to claim the profit even after the project failed to work successfully and blockbuster pulled out of the deal.

Senior management were rewarded on the basis of annual earnings and were highly motivated to continue reporting large increases in profits, regardless of the longer-term consequences. Investors began to have doubts about the reliability of Enron's reported profits in 2001. A 'whistleblower' (see Chapter 10) reported her concerns to the chief executive officer, but her allegations of dubious accounting practices were ignored. However, in October 2001 Enron was eventually forced to announce that it would be re-stating its accounts for 1997–2000 to correct accounting violations. The SEC announced an investigation into the company, and the stock price collapsed. There were also doubts about whether Enron had sufficient liquidity (cash) to remain in business for long. Its debt was downgraded to junk bond status and in December 2001 the company filed for bankruptcy.

The company's auditors were Arthur Andersen, one of the 'big five' global accounting firms. The firm – in particular its Houston office – took extraordinary measures to protect its client. When the SEC investigation was announced in 2001, Andersen staff attempted to cover up evidence of negligence in its audit work by destroying several tons of documents, and many emails and computer files. The firm, especially the Houston office, was accused of losing its independence to Enron and over-reliance on income from the non-audit work that it did for the company. Arthur Andersen was charged with obstructing the course of justice by shredding the documents and destroying the files. Although a guilty verdict was subsequently overturned by the Supreme Court, this was too late to save the firm from the loss of its major clients, and collapse.

Several Enron employees were brought to trial for a number of financial crimes. Andrew Fastow, a former chief financial officer (CFO) of Enron, was found guilty of crimes including fraud, money laundering, insider trading and conspiracy. Two former chief executive officers, Kenneth Lay and Jeffrey Skilling, were charged with a range of financial crimes and brought to trial in 2006. Both were found guilty: Skilling was imprisoned and Lay died before sentence was passed.

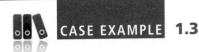 **CASE EXAMPLE** 1.3

Parmalat, which specialises in dairy and food manufacture and is one of the largest companies in Italy, was declared insolvent in December 2003. There was a fraud which the company's internal controls and the external auditors failed to identify. Forged documents indicated that there was a substantial amount of cash held by one of the company's subsidiaries, but this money did not exist. The scandal, as in the case of Enron, suggested a need for more effective external audits and for a whistleblowing system within companies. At Parmalat, several employees had suspected wrongdoing, but no one reported their suspicions.

Poor corporate governance by no means always has such an extreme outcome, but the case examples of Maxwell (1.1), Enron (1.2) and Parmalat (1.3) are useful studies of what could possibly go wrong.

 STOP AND THINK 1.1

In 2008 a number of major banks suffered enormous losses, partly through their involvement in markets for collateralised debt obligations (CDOs) linked to high-risk mortgages ('sub-prime mortgages'). The problems began in the USA, but quickly spread to Europe and parts of Asia. For various reasons, many banks were faced with a critical shortage of cash (liquidity) and capital (due to their huge losses). Banks were criticised for their poor corporate governance and failure to manage risks adequately. They had allowed their businesses to grow through high-risk operations and had failed to provide for the possibility that events might eventually turn out unfavourably.

2.1 What do we mean by bad corporate governance?

The issues involved in governance are described in more detail throughout this text. Briefly however, aspects of poor corporate governance include:

- a board of directors that fails to perform its duties properly, perhaps because it is dominated by one or more individuals, or because it fails to carry out the tasks that it is supposed to
- misleading financial reporting to shareholders and other investors, and perhaps inadequate auditing of the **financial statements**
- a poor relationship between the board and the main shareholders
- ineffective systems of risk management, and exposure to errors and fraud due to inadequate internal control systems
- inappropriate remuneration and reward systems for directors and senior executives
- unethical business practices.

A key issue in corporate governance is the relationship between the board of directors, the shareholders and other important stakeholders.

 TEST YOUR KNOWLEDGE 1.2

Give six examples of bad corporate governance practice.

3   Stakeholders

A stakeholder in a company is someone who has an interest or 'stake' in it, and is affected by what the company does. A stakeholder, in turn, has an influence on what companies do. Each stakeholder or stakeholder group may expect the company to behave or act in a particular way with regard to the stakeholders' interests. A stakeholder can also expect to have some say in some of the decisions a company makes and some of the actions it takes. The **balance of power** (see Chapter 4) between different stakeholder groups, and the way in which that power is exercised, are key issues in corporate governance.

A public company has a number of different stakeholder groups, which can be divided into:

- financial stakeholders, and
- other stakeholders.

3.1 Financial stakeholders

Financial stakeholders are stakeholders with a financial interest in the company. These consist mainly of shareholders and lenders. Lenders may be banks or investors in bonds.

- A company's members or equity shareholders are the owners. In a small company, the owners may also be directors. In a large public company, the directors may own some shares, but are not usually the largest shareholders. The interests of the shareholders are likely to be focused on the value of their shares and dividend payments. However, the powers of shareholders in large public companies are usually fairly restricted and shareholders have to rely on the board to act in their best interests.
- A different situation arises when there is a **majority shareholder** or a significant shareholder. A shareholder with a controlling interest is able to influence decisions of the company through an ability to control the composition of the board of directors.
- A distinction can also be made between long-term and short-term institutional investors. Short-term investors buy shares with the expectation of making a short-term profit from an increase in the price before selling the shares in the market. This includes, for example, hedge funds which buy shares in what they consider to be an undervalued and badly managed company with potential for a significant increase in value if the management problems can be resolved (or if the company becomes a takeover bid target). Long-term investors are more interested in the longer-term returns from a company than short-term profit.
- Lenders and bondholders provide debt capital to a company but are not owners. Even so, they have a financial interest in the company, and expect payment of interest and repayment of capital on schedule. Excessive borrowing by a company might put lenders as well as shareholders at risk financially; therefore, lenders have an interest in preventing the financial gearing or leverage of the company from getting too high. Loan covenants might set limits on borrowing by the company.

3.2 Other stakeholders

Other stakeholders in a company could also have significant influence. They include the board of directors, although some directors might also be large shareholders.

The board has the **responsibility** for giving direction to the company. It delegates most executive powers to the executive management, but reserves some decision-making powers to itself, such as decisions about raising finance, paying dividends and making major investments. Executive management is also held accountable to the board for the company's operational performance.

- A board of directors is made up of both executive directors and **non-executive directors** (NEDs). Executive directors are individuals who combine their role as director with their position within the executive management of the company. NEDs perform the functions of director only, without any executive responsibilities. Executive directors combine their stake in the company as a director with their stake as a fully paid employee, and their interests are therefore likely to differ from those of the non-executives.
- The board may take decisions collectively, but it is also a collection of individuals, each with his personal interests and ambitions. Some individuals are more likely to dominate

the decisions by a board and to exert strong influence over their colleagues. In particular, the most influential individuals are likely to be the chairman, who is usually a non-executive but may occasionally have executive powers and responsibilities, and the chief executive officer. The chairman is responsible for the functioning of the board. The chief executive officer is the senior executive director, and is accountable to the board for the executive management of the company. The term 'chief executive officer' (CEO) derives from the USA, but is now widely used in the UK (where the term 'managing director' is also used). The main interests of individual executive directors are likely to be power and authority, a high remuneration package and a wealthy lifestyle.

- Management is responsible for running the business operations and is accountable to the board of directors (and more particularly to the chief executive officer). Individual managers, like executive directors, may want power, status and a high remuneration. As employees, they may see their stake in the company in terms of the need for a career and an income.

- Employees have a stake in their company because it provides them with a job and an income. They too have expectations about what their company should offer them, e.g. security of employment, good pay and suitable working conditions. Some employee rights are protected by employment law, but the powers of employees are generally limited.

- Major suppliers have an indirect interest in a company, because they expect to be paid what they are owed. If they deal with the company regularly or over a long time, they will expect the company to do business with them in accordance with their contractual agreements. If the company becomes insolvent, unpaid creditors will take a more significant role in its governance, depending on the insolvency laws in the country, e.g. by taking legal action to take control of the business or its assets.

- A number of representative bodies act in the interests of members of the investment community and can influence public companies whose shares are traded on a stock market. Representative bodies include the Association of British Insurers (ABI) and the National Association of Pension Funds (NAPF) in the UK, and the **International Corporate Governance Network** (ICGN; see Chapter 3), an association of activist institutional investors around the world (insurance companies and pension funds are major investors in securities). These bodies may coordinate the activities of their members, e.g. by encouraging them to vote in a particular way on resolutions at the annual **general meetings** (AGMs) of companies in which they are shareholders. These bodies represent the opinions of the investment community generally.

- The general public are also stakeholders in large companies, often because they rely on the goods or services provided by a company to carry on their life. For example, households expect utility companies to provide an uninterrupted supply to their homes, or a reliable telephone connection. Commuters expect a rail company to be under an obligation to provide a convenient and reliable transport service to and from work, and at a reliable price. Pressure groups, such as environment protection groups, sometimes try to influence the decisions of companies in the interests of society in general.

 TEST YOUR KNOWLEDGE **1.3**

(a) List the major stakeholders in a school that is run by a non-profit-making charity organisation.
(b) Do you agree with the view that a board of directors should give more consideration to the interests of its longer-term shareholders than to those of short-term shareholders such as hedge funds? Give your reasons.

4   Theoretical frameworks

It is useful to consider the theoretical justification for a system of rules or guidelines on corporate governance. There are three different frameworks:

1   agency theory
2   transaction cost theory
3   stakeholder theory.

Agency theory and **transaction cost theory** can be used to justify a 'shareholder approach' to corporate governance. **Stakeholder theory** can be used to justify a 'stakeholder' approach. These alternative approaches are explained later.

4.1 Agency theory

Agency theory was developed by US economists Michael Jensen and William Meckling (1976). The theory is based on the separation of ownership and control in a company – the ownership of a company by its shareholders and control over the company's actions by its directors and senor executives. Jensen and Meckling defined the agency relationship as a form of contract between a company's owners and its managers, where the owners (as principal) appoint an agent (the managers) to manage the company on their behalf. As part of this arrangement, the owners must delegate decision-making authority to the management.

Jensen and Meckling suggested that the nature of governance in a company reflects the conflicts of interest between the company's owners and managers.

- The shareholders want to increase their income and wealth over the long term. The value of their shares depends on the long-term financial prospects for the company. Shareholders are therefore concerned not only about short-term profits and dividends; they are even more concerned about long-term profitability.
- The managers run the company on behalf of the shareholders. If they do not own shares in the company, managers have no direct interest in future returns for shareholders or in the value of the shares. They have an employment contract and earn a salary. Unless they own shares, or unless their remuneration is linked to profits or share values, their main interests are likely to be the size of their remuneration package and their status within the company.

Ideally, the 'agency contract' between the owners and the managers of as company should ensure that the managers always act in the best interests of the owners. However, it is impossible to arrange the 'perfect' contract because any decisions managers make affect their personal welfare as well as the interests of the owners.

Agency conflict

Agency conflicts are differences in the interests of owners and managers. They arise in several ways.

- Moral hazard. A manager has an interest in receiving benefits from his position in the company. These include all the benefits that come from status, such as a company car, use of a company plane, a company house or flat, attendance at sponsored sporting events, and so on. Jensen and Meckling suggested that a manager's incentive to obtain these benefits is higher when he has no shares, or only a few shares, in the company. For example, senior managers may pursue a strategy of growth through acquisitions, in order to gain more power and 'earn' higher remuneration, even though takeovers might not be in the best interests of the company and its shareholders.
- Level of effort. Managers may work less hard than they would if they were the owners of the company. The effect of this lack of effort could be smaller profits and a lower share price.
- Earnings retention. The remuneration of directors and senior managers is often related to the size of the company (measured by annual sales revenue and value of assets) rather than its profits. This gives managers an incentive to increase the size of the company, rather than to increase the returns to the company's shareholders. Management are more likely to want to reinvest profits in order to expand the company, rather than pay out the profits as dividends. When this happens, companies might invest in capital investment projects where the expected profitability is quite small, or propose high-priced takeover bids for other companies in order to build a bigger corporate empire.
- Time horizon. Shareholders are concerned about the long-term financial prospects of their company, because the value of their shares depends on expectations for the long-term future. In contrast, managers might only be interested in the short term. This is partly because they might receive annual bonuses based on short-term performance, and partly because they might not expect to be with the company for more than a few years.

Agency costs

Agency costs are the costs of having an agent make decisions on behalf of a principal. Applying this to corporate governance, agency costs are the costs that the shareholders incur by having managers to run the company on their behalf, instead of running the company themselves. Agency costs are potentially very high in large companies, where there are many different shareholders and a large professional management.

Agency costs consist of three elements.

1 Costs of monitoring. Shareholders need to establish systems for monitoring the actions and performance of management, to try to ensure that management is acting in their best interests. An example of monitoring is the requirement for the directors to present an annual report and accounts to the shareholders, setting out the financial performance and financial position of the company. These accounts are audited, and the auditors present a report to the shareholders. Preparing accounts and having them audited has a cost.
2 Bonding costs. Costs may be incurred in providing incentives to managers to act in the best interests of the shareholders. The remuneration packages for directors and senior managers are therefore an important element of agency costs, since they include both long- and short-term incentives.
3 Residual loss. Residual loss is the cost to the shareholder which occurs when the managers take decisions that are not in the best interests of the shareholders (but are in the interests of the managers themselves). Residual loss occurs, for example, when managers pay too much for a large acquisition. The managers would gain personally from the enhanced status of managing a larger group of companies. The cost to the shareholders comes from the fall in share price that results from paying too much for the acquisition.

The key elements of agency theory

Agency theory is based on the view that the system of corporate governance should be designed to minimise the agency problem and reduce agency costs. One approach to reducing the agency problem is to make the board of directors more effective at monitoring the decisions of the executive management. Another approach is to design schemes of remuneration for directors and senior managers that bring their interests more into line with those of the shareholders.

Agents should also be accountable to their principals for their decisions and actions. **Accountability** means reporting back to the principals and giving an account of what has been achieved, and the principal having power to reward or punish an agent for good or bad performance. Greater accountability should reduce the agency problem, because it provides management with a greater incentive (obtaining rewards/avoiding punishments) to achieve performance levels that are in the best interests of the shareholders.

Agency theory may therefore be summarised as follows.

- In large companies there is a separation of ownership from control. Professional managers are appointed to act as agents for the owners of the company.
- Individuals are driven by self-interest.
- Conflicts of self-interest arise between shareholders and managers.
- Managers, because they are driven by self-interest, cannot be relied on to act in the best interests of the shareholders. This creates problems in the agency relationship between shareholders and management.
- These agency problems create costs for the shareholders.
- The aim should be to minimise these costs, by improving the monitoring of management and/or providing management with incentives to bring their interests closer to those of the shareholders.

4.2 Transaction cost theory

Transaction cost theory provides a different basis for explaining the relationship between the owners of a company and its management. Although it is an economic theory, it also attempts to explain companies not just as economic units, but as an organisation consisting of people with differing views and objectives. The theory of transaction cost economics (**TCE**) is most closely associated with the work of Oliver Williamson in the 1970s.

The operations of a company can be performed either through market transactions or by doing the work in-house. For example, a company could obtain its raw materials from an external supplier or it could make the materials itself. Similarly, a company could hire self-employed contractors to do work or it could hire full-time employees. In economic terms, a firm's decision about whether to arrange transactions in the open market or whether to do the work in-house (itself) should depend on which is cheaper. When a firm does work in-house, it needs a management structure and a hierarchy of authority with senior management at the top. According to transaction cost theory, the structure of a firm and the relationship between the owners of a firm and its management depends on the extent to which transactions are performed in-house.

Total costs are defined as the sum of production costs and transaction costs.

- Production costs are the costs that would be incurred by the company in an ideal economic market. In an ideal economic market, production costs are minimised.
- Transaction costs are additional costs incurred whenever the perfect economic market is not achieved. For example, a company might buy goods from a supplier who is not the cheapest available, because it is not aware of the existence of the cheapest supplier. A company might sell goods on credit to a customer, not knowing that money owed will become a bad debt.

Transaction costs are sometimes higher when a transaction is arranged in the market, and they are sometimes higher when the transaction is done in-house. Carrying out activities in-house rather than arranging contracts externally is referred to as vertical integration. Total costs are minimised when transaction costs are minimised. This should determine the optimal size of the firm and the size of the management hierarchy in the firm. The way in which a company is organised, and the extent to which it is vertically integrated, also affect the control the company has over its transactions. As a general rule, it is in the interests of a company's management to carry out transactions internally, rather than in the external market. Performing transactions internally:

- removes the risks and uncertainties about prices of products and product quality, and
- removes all the risks and costs of dealing with external suppliers.

Traditional economic theory is based on the assumptions that all behaviour is rational and that profit maximisation is the rational objective of all businesses. Transaction cost economics changes these assumptions by trying to allow for human behaviour, and the fact that individuals do not always act rationally. Williamson based his theory on two assumptions about behaviour:

1 bounded rationality, and
2 opportunism.

Bounded rationality

Human beings act rationally, but only within certain limits of understanding. This means, for example, that the managers of a company will in theory act rationally in seeking to maximise the value of the company for its shareholders, but their bounded rationality might make them act differently. Business is very complex, and large businesses are much more complex than small businesses. However, in any business, there is a limit to the amount of information that individuals can remember, understand and deal with. No one is capable of assessing all the possible courses of action and no one can anticipate what will happen in the future. In a competitive market, no one can anticipate with certainty what competitors will do.

Playing chess has been used as an example of bounded rationality. The game is very complex and there are many different possible moves. The actions of the opponent in a game of chess cannot be predicted, so it is impossible to predict what the opponent will do in response to a particular move. The same problem applies to managing a company. It is impossible to predict with certainty what will happen, because there are too many factors and too many possibilities to consider.

Williamson was mainly concerned with what happens when individuals reach the boundaries of their understanding, because a situation is too complex or too uncertain. He wrote:

'Bounds on rationality are interesting...only to the extent that the limits of rationality are reached – which is to say under conditions of uncertainty and/or complexity.'

When uncertainty is high, or when a situation is very complex, there is a greater tendency to carry out transactions in-house and to have vertical integration.

Opportunism

Williamson also argued that individuals will act in a self-interested way and 'with guile'. They will not always be honest and truthful about their intentions. Williamson defined opportunism as 'an effort to realise individual gains through a lack of candour or honesty in transactions'. An individual might try to take advantage of an opportunity to gain a benefit at the expense of someone else. Managers are opportunistic by nature. Given the opportunity, they will take advantage of any way of improving their own benefits and privileges.

In terms of TCE, a problem with opportunism is that external parties (e.g. contractors and suppliers) cannot always be trusted to act honestly. As a result, there may be a tendency for a company to carry out transactions itself, rather than rely on external suppliers. However, there is also a risk that by taking control of transactions internally, managers will have opportunities to take decisions and actions that are in their personal interests. This self-interested behaviour needs to be controlled. In this respect, transaction cost theory has similarities with agency theory. Although they are based on different assumptions, both agency theory and transaction cost theory support the need for controls over corporate governance practices.

4.3 Stakeholder theory

Agency theory is based on the assumption that the main objective of a company should be to maximise shareholder wealth. Stakeholder theory takes a different view. The stakeholder view is that the purpose of corporate governance should be to satisfy, as far as possible, the objectives of all key stakeholders – employees, investors, major suppliers and creditors, customers, the government, local communities and the general public. A company's directors should therefore consider the interests of all the major stakeholders. However, some stakeholders are more important than others, so that management should give priority to their interests above the interests of other stakeholder groups. In the introduction to its principles of corporate governance, the Organisation for Economic Co-operation and Development (OECD) comments that an aim of government policy ('public policy') should be 'to provide firms with the incentives and discipline to minimise divergence between private and social returns and to protect the interest of stakeholders'.

The **OECD Principles of Corporate Governance** (see Chapter 3) recognise the role and rights of stakeholders; they state that the corporate governance framework should:

- recognise the rights of stakeholders that are recognised in law or through mutual agreements, and
- encourage active co-operation between companies and stakeholders in creating wealth, jobs and the **sustainability** (see Chapter 11) of financially sound enterprises.

Stakeholder theory states that a company's managers should make decisions that take into consideration the interests of all the stakeholders. This means trying to achieve a range of different objectives, not just the aim of maximising the value of the company for its shareholders. This is because different stakeholders each have their own (different) expectations of the company, which the company's management should attempt to satisfy.

Stakeholder theory also considers the role of companies in society, and the responsibility that they should have towards society as a whole. It could be argued that some companies are so large, and their influence on society so strong, that they should be accountable to the public for what they do. The general public are taxpayers and as such they provide the economic and social infrastructure within which companies are allowed to operate. In return companies should be expected to act as corporate citizens and act in ways that benefit society as a whole. This aspect of stakeholder theory is consistent with the arguments in favour of corporate social responsibility (CSR).

TEST YOUR KNOWLEDGE 1.4

(a) In agency theory, what are agency costs and what are the three main elements of agency cost?

(b) In agency theory, how is moral hazard an aspect of agency cost?

(c) How are agency costs minimised?

5   Approaches to corporate governance

There has been considerable debate about what the objectives of sound corporate governance should be. The different views can be divided into four broad approaches that can be related to the agency theory or the stakeholder theory of governance:

1   the shareholder value approach.
2   the **stakeholder approach**, also called the stakeholder inclusive approach or pluralist approach
3   the enlightened shareholder approach
4   an integrated approach, as recommended by the King Report (a report on recommended corporate governance practice for South Africa).

5.1   The shareholder value approach

The shareholder value approach is the well-established view, supported by company law in advanced economies, that the board of directors should govern their company in the best interests of its owners, the shareholders. This could mean that the main objective of a company should be to maximise the wealth of its shareholders, in the form of share price growth and dividend payments, subject to conforming to the rules of society as embodied in laws and customs. The directors should be accountable to their shareholders, who should have the power to remove them from office if their performance is inadequate. The shareholder view is closely linked to agency theory or transaction cost theory.

The OECD, in the introduction to its Principles of Corporate Governance, states that from a company's perspective, corporate governance is about 'maximising value subject to meeting the corporation's financial and other legal and contractual obligations. This inclusive definition stresses the need for boards of directors to balance the interests of shareholders with those of other stakeholders . . . in order to achieve long-term sustained value.'

The ICGN is an international body established to promote corporate governance practices worldwide. In 2005 it issued a revised statement on corporate governance principles. This includes the view that 'the overriding objective of the corporation should be to optimise over time the returns to its shareholders. Corporate governance practices should focus board attention on this objective.'

The strength of this approach to corporate governance is its general acceptance. Many people hold the view that public companies are in business to earn profits for the benefit of their shareholders. Successful companies are perceived as those paying dividends to shareholders and whose share price goes up. Within the broad objective of maximising shareholder values, the board of directors will also act fairly in the interests of employees, customers, suppliers and others with an interest in the company's affairs.

5.2   The stakeholder approach (pluralist approach)

An alternative approach to the requirements of good corporate governance is based on stakeholder theory. This argues that the aim of sound corporate governance is not just to meet the objectives of shareholders, but also to have regard for the interests of other individuals and groups with a stake in the company, including the public at large.

The OECD Principles of Corporate Governance state that:

'From a public policy perspective, corporate governance is about nurturing enterprise while ensuring accountability in the exercise of power and patronage by firms. The role of public policy is to provide firms with the incentives and discipline to minimise the divergence between private and social returns and to protect the interests of stakeholders.'

From a 'stakeholder view', corporate governance is concerned with achieving a balance between economic and social goals and between individual and communal goals. Sound corporate governance should recognise the economic imperatives companies face in competitive markets and should encourage the efficient use of resources through sound investment. It should also require accountability from the board of directors to the shareholders for the stewardship of those resources. Within this framework, the aim should be to recognise the interests of other individuals, companies and society at large in the decisions and activities of the company.

A problem with the stakeholder approach is that company law gives certain rights to shareholders, and there are some legal duties on the board of directors towards their company. However, the interests of other stakeholders are not reinforced to any great extent by company law.

A stakeholder or pluralist approach is that co-operative and productive relationships will be optimised only if the directors are permitted or required to balance shareholder interests with the interests of other stakeholders who are committed to the company. Changes in company law would be required to introduce such an approach in practice.

It is important to remember that although stakeholder interests are not well protected by company law, extensive protection is provided by other aspects of law such as employment law, health and safety legislation, and environmental law.

5.3 The enlightened shareholder approach

The **enlightened shareholder approach** to corporate governance is that the directors of a company should pursue the interests of their shareholders, but in an enlightened and inclusive way. It is a form of compromise between the agency view and the stakeholder view. The directors should look to the long term, not just the short term, and they should also have regard to the interests of other stakeholders in the company, not just the shareholders. Managers should be aware of the need to create and maintain productive relationships with a range of stakeholders having an interest in their company.

A UK Company Law Review Steering Group issued a consultative document in 1998, in which it commented that UK company law did not embrace the enlightened shareholder approach, and if this approach was desirable, suitable changes in the law would be needed. Enlightened change, it felt, would not come voluntarily, but (like a pluralist approach) would need the backing of the law.

A criticism of the enlightened shareholder view is that most shareholders do not fit the image of enlightened investors. Most shares in public companies are owned by institutional investors, who themselves may be relatively unaccountable to their beneficiaries. When companies become a target for a takeover bid, speculative investors such as hedge funds may acquire large but short-term shareholdings, with a view to making a quick profit from their investment. However, the role of institutional investors in corporate governance is likely to evolve in the future, with institutions expected to be more proactive in promoting the rights and interests of shareholders.

5.4 The King Report: a 'stakeholder inclusive' approach to corporate governance

The **King Code** or King Report (see Chapter 3), developed by the Institute of Directors in South Africa, was first introduced in 1994. A revised Code (King II) was published in 2004 and a further revision (King III) was published in 2009. King III (and King II before it) rejects an enlightened shareholder approach to governance in favour of a 'stakeholder inclusive' approach.

In the introduction to the King III Code, this approach is explained in some detail. The enlightened shareholder model and the stakeholder inclusive model both take the view that the board of directors should consider the interests and expectations of stakeholders other than shareholders; however, the two models differ significantly in their emphasis:

'In the "enlightened shareholder" approach the legitimate interests and expectations of stakeholders only have an instrumental value. Stakeholders are only considered in as far as it would be in the interests of shareholders to do so. In the case of the "stakeholder inclusive" approach, the board of directors considers the legitimate interests and expectations of stakeholders on the basis that this is in the best interests of the company, and not merely as an instrument to serve the interests of the shareholder.'

The King Code therefore states that a board of directors should consider what is best for the company and in doing so it should have regard to the legitimate interests and expectations of all stakeholders. It should then integrate these, or decide how they should be traded off against each other, on a case-by-case basis, with the aim of making decisions that are in the best interests of the company. The shareholder does not have any predetermined precedence over other stakeholders. The 'best interests of the company' are defined not in terms of maximising shareholder wealth, but 'within the parameters of the company as a sustainable enterprise and the company as a corporate citizen'.

TEST YOUR KNOWLEDGE **1.5**

(a) What are the limitations of the influence on corporate governance practice of national organisations (such as the ABI and NAPF) representing the interests of their institutional investor members?

(b) What are the main differences between the shareholder and pluralist approaches to corporate governance?

(c) According to King III, what is the main difference between an enlightened shareholder approach to corporate governance and a stakeholder inclusive approach?

6 Principles of good corporate governance

Several concepts apply to sound corporate governance in all countries where international investors invest their money. Many of these are ethical in nature and the King Code describes them as the 'overarching corporate governance principles':

- fairness
- accountability
- responsibility
- transparency.

6.1 Fairness

Fairness refers to the principle that all shareholders should receive equal consideration. **Minority shareholders**, for example (see Chapter 3), should be treated in the same way as majority shareholders. This concept might seem fairly straightforward in the UK, where the rights of minority shareholders are protected to a large extent by company law. In some countries, however, minority shareholder rights are often disregarded by the larger shareholders and the board of directors.

There should also be fairness in the treatment of stakeholders other than shareholders.

6.2 Accountability

Decision-makers who act on behalf of a company should be accountable for the decisions they make and the actions they take. In a company, the board of directors should be accountable to the shareholders, the company's owners. Shareholders should be able to assess the actions of their board of directors and the committees of the board, and have the opportunity to query them and challenge them.

A problem with accountability is deciding how the directors should be accountable, and in particular over what period of time. According to financial theory, if the objective of a company is to maximise the wealth of its shareholders, this will be achieved by maximising the financial returns to shareholders through increases in profits, dividends, prospects for profit growth and a rising share price. It might therefore follow that directors should be held accountable to shareholders on the basis of the returns on shareholder capital that the company has achieved.

However, there is no consensus about the period over which returns to shareholders and increases in share value should be measured. Performance can be measured over a short term of one year at a time, or over a long term of (say) five or ten years – or even longer. In practice, it is usual to measure returns over the short term and assess performance in terms of profitability over a 12-month period. In the short term, however, a company's share price may be affected by influences unrelated to the company's underlying performance, such as excessive optimism or pessimism in the stock markets generally. In the short term, it is also easier to soothe investors with promises for the future, even though current performance is not good. It is only when a company fails consistently to deliver on its promises that investor confidence ebbs away.

If company performance were to be judged by the return to shareholders over a 12-month period, the directors would focus on short-term results and short-term movements in the stock market price. Short-termism is easy to criticise, but difficult to disregard in practice if performance targets ignore the long term. They should really be looking after the underlying business of the company and its profitability over the longer term.

Writing in the *Financial Times* (29 January 2002), John Kay, reflecting on the reasons given by the former finance director of Marconi for the company's financial collapse in 2000, commented:

'[A director's] job is to run a business that adds value by means of the services it provides to customers. If he succeeds, it will generate returns to investors in the long term. And this is the only mechanism that can generate returns to investors. The problem is that the equivalence between value added in operations and stock market returns holds in the long run but not the short. Share prices may, for a time, become divorced from the fundamental value of a business. This has been true of most share prices in recent years.... In these conditions, attention to **total shareholder returns** (TSR; see Chapter 6) distracts executives from their real function of managing businesses.'

The problem of accountability remains, however. Even if it is accepted that company performance should not be judged by short-term financial results and share price movements, how can the board be made accountable for its contribution to longer-term success?

6.3 Responsibility

The board of directors is given authority to act on behalf of the company, and a further principle of corporate governance is that it should accept full responsibility for the powers that it is given and the authority that it exercises. A board of directors should understand what its responsibilities are, and should carry them out to the best of its abilities.

Accountability goes hand in hand with responsibility. The board of directors should be made accountable to the shareholders for the way in which it has carried out its responsibilities. Similarly, executive management should be responsible for the exercise of powers delegated to them by the board of directors, and should be made accountable to the board for their achievements and performance.

6.4 Transparency

Transparency means openness. In the context of corporate governance, this is a willingness by the company to provide clear information to shareholders and other stakeholders about what the company has done and hopes to achieve, without giving away commercially sensitive information. It might be useful to think of openness in terms of its opposite, which is to be a 'closed book' and refuse to divulge any information whatsoever.

Transparency should not be confused with 'understandability'. Information should be communicated in a way that is understandable, but transparency is concerned more with the content of the information that is communicated. A principle of good governance is that stakeholders should be informed about what a company is doing and plans to do in the future, and about the risks involved in its business strategies.

7 Ethics and corporate governance

Ethics are the rules or codes of behaviour that individuals and organisations apply in their decision-making and actions. Personal ethics and business ethics underlie the regulations and codification in corporate governance. The owners and leaders of companies should establish the standards of ethical behaviour that they expect all their employees to follow, and this behaviour (and the attitudes associated with them) should be consistent with the way in which the company is governed.

7.1 Personal ethics

Personal ethics are closely associated with morality and a view of what is right and what is wrong. Unethical behaviour by an individual is regarded as unacceptable. To some extent, the law can establish rules about what is 'wrong'. A breach of the criminal law is illegal. Other aspects of law, such as contract law and employment law, can also establish standards of behaviour that are required, and legal action can be taken against anyone in breach of the law.

However, standards of behaviour are determined by social attitudes of morality and good conduct, much more than by legal rules, even though the attitudes of individuals often differ about whether a particular action is 'wrong' and unethical. Ethical personal behaviour helps to build trust. In the context of corporate governance, ethical personal behaviour is commonly associated with integrity and transparency.

- Integrity is honesty and behaviour consistent with a clear set of moral rules. Ethical behaviour in this sense means telling the truth and carrying out promises.
- Transparency (as explained earlier) is openness, so that a person makes his views and intentions clear.

Unethical personal behaviour may be associated with selfishness, seeking personal satisfaction and the fulfilment of personal objectives. Company leaders are sometimes accused of this.

7.2 Corporate ethics

Corporate ethics are standards of behaviour in business. The way in which employees act can be influenced strongly by the way in which the employer expects them to act, and each company has its own ethical (or unethical) standards. This can affect the company's dealings with its employees, customers, suppliers and agents, as well as the government, local communities and society as a whole.

There is a connection between corporate ethics (or business ethics) and the different approaches to corporate governance. If a company has a shareholder approach to corporate governance, it puts the interests of shareholders ahead of the interests of anyone else. If it adopts a stakeholder approach to governance, it will act in a way that takes into consideration the needs and concerns of other stakeholders. The concerns of an ethical company that adopts a stakeholder approach are described briefly in the following section on corporate codes of ethics.

7.3 Professional ethics

The professions, such as medicine, law and accountancy, are governed by professional bodies that require all members to comply with standards of professional ethics. Members of the accountancy profession, for example, are required to act with integrity, to be independent in their opinion and judgement, to be objective (avoid bias), and to comply with all relevant laws and regulations. In addition, they are required in most circumstances to maintain client confidentiality. These broad principles apply to all accountants, including employees of companies as well as accountants acting as company auditors. In the UK several detailed ethical standards have been issued by the Institute of Chartered Accountants in England and Wales, which must be applied by company auditors.

In the context of corporate governance, it is essential that auditors should retain their independence, objectivity and integrity, because shareholders rely on the opinion they provide about the company's annual financial statements. Unfortunately, a number of corporate scandals in the past, notably the collapse of Enron (see Case example 1.2), have raised questions about the integrity of the information in financial statements and the independence and judgement of the company's auditors.

The measures that should be taken to protect auditor independence are described more fully in Chapter 7.

8   A corporate code of ethics

A large number of large companies have developed, adopted and disclosed a formal code of ethics that employees are required to apply. In the USA, one of the requirements for a listing on the New York Stock Exchange (NYSE) is that the company must adopt and disclose a code of business conduct and ethics for its directors and employees. Key features of a corporate code of ethics are that:

- it is a formal document
- it is adopted by the board of directors
- it is disclosed to employees and to the public, including other stakeholders who have direct dealings with the company
- it is made clear to employees that they should comply with the code
- its application in practice should be monitored, and breaches of ethical conduct should be dealt with according to established rules and procedures.

The effectiveness of a code of ethics depends on the leadership of the company – its directors and senior managers. These individuals must be seen to comply with the ethical code, otherwise employees will see no purpose in complying with the code themselves. The culture of a company drives its ethical behaviour, and a code of ethics provides useful guidance.

It has been suggested that there are three reasons why companies might develop a formal code of ethics. These are progressive, which means that companies might begin by having a code of ethics for the first reason, but then progress to the second and third reasons as they gain experience with implementing the code and appreciating its potential benefits.

- Compliance and customer service. The company wants to ensure that all its employees comply with relevant laws and regulations, and conduct themselves in a way that the public expects. Compliance with a code of ethics is necessary for both legal and commercial reasons. For example, companies providing a service to the general public need to ensure that their employees are courteous in their dealings with customers; otherwise it will lose customers.
- Managing stakeholder relations. A code of ethics can help to improve and develop the relations between the company and its shareholders, by improving the trust that shareholders have in the company. The code might therefore include the ethical stance of the company on the disclosure of information to shareholders and the investing public (openness and transparency) and respect for the rights of stakeholders.
- Creating a value-based organisation. It might be argued that an ethical company, like a well-governed company, is more likely to be successful in business in the long term. A company might therefore recognise the long-term benefits of creating an ethical culture, and encouraging employees to act and think in a way that is consistent with the values in its code of ethics.

8.1 Contents of a code of corporate ethics

There are no rules about what a code of corporate ethics should contain. The Institute of Business Ethics (IBE) identifies two styles of ethical code that could be developed: a stakeholder model code and an issues model code. The stakeholder model code focuses on ethical behaviour towards stakeholder groups. The issues model focuses on specific issues relating to ethical or unethical behaviour.

Preface or introduction

A code should explain its purpose and should describe the values that are important to senior management for the conduct of the business (e.g. integrity, responsibility and reputation). The code should also state the commitment of the directors to maintaining high standards both within the company and in its dealings with others. The introduction should also refer to the role of the company in the community and state the expectation that the standards set out in the code will be maintained by all the company's employees. There are also likely to be introductory statements about the ethical values of the company, such as:

- acting with integrity at all times
- protecting the environment
- the 'pursuit of excellence'
- respect for the individual
- maintaining the reputation of the company.

8.2 Stakeholder model of ethical code

If a code is structured according to the stakeholder model, there should be codes of behaviour for each specific stakeholder group.

- Employees. There should be a statement on how the business values its employees and its policies on working conditions, recruitment, development and training, rewards, health, safety and security, equal opportunities, retirement, redundancy, discrimination and harassment. There may also be guidelines on the use of company assets (such as motor vehicles) for private use by employees.
- Customer relations. The code should make a statement about the importance to the company of customer satisfaction and good faith in all agreements, quality, fair pricing and after-sales service.
- Shareholders and other providers of money. An ethical objective should be the protection of investment made in the company and proper 'return' on the money lent, and a commitment to accurate and timely disclosures on the company's business performance and prospects.
- Suppliers. The code might include statements about prompt settlement of invoices, co-operation with major suppliers, co-operation to achieve quality and efficiency, and a policy that no bribery or excess hospitality will be either accepted or given.
- Society/the wider community. A code of ethics should also include a statement about the company and its relationship with the communities in which it operates. The company might state its compliance with the spirit of laws as well as the letter of the law, its obligations to protect and preserve the environment, the involvement of the company and its staff in local affairs, and corporate policy on giving to education and charities.

8.3 Issues model of ethical code

An 'issues model' of ethical code may contain the following elements.

- Obeying laws and regulations. There may be a specific commitment to obeying the laws and regulations of all the countries in which the company operates.
- Prohibition of bribery. There may be prohibition of giving bribes and accepting bribes. Similarly, there may be restrictions on giving or receiving gifts, and giving or receiving corporate entertainment.
- Methods of competition. A company may undertake to compete fairly, and avoid practices such as industrial espionage and computer espionage.
- Avoiding conflicts of interest.
- Use of company assets by employees.
- Safeguarding important information, such as respect for the privacy of personal data held about customers.
- Rules on political donations and political involvement by senior employees.
- The application of human rights within the company and dealing with suppliers or customers who abuse human rights.
- Timely payment of suppliers.
- Environmental responsibilities.

8.4 Implementation of ethical codes

A code of ethics should include an explanation of the process by which the code is issued and used, and how employees can obtain advice on dealing with ethical problems. Senior management must be satisfied that the code of ethics is applied by everyone in the company, including the directors. The quality of a system to implement and manage ethical behaviour depends on factors such as:

- employee training in ethical conduct and procedures
- a system for monitoring compliance
- whistleblowing procedures
- reporting breaches of the code and enforcement of suitable disciplinary action
- regular review of the code to ensure that it is still suitable and applicable.

TEST YOUR KNOWLEDGE 1.6

(a) What is accountability? What is transparency in corporate governance, and why is it a feature of good governance practice?
(b) In what ways do personal ethics differ from corporate ethics?
(c) What are the typical contents of a code of corporate ethics?

9 Key issues in corporate governance

Good corporate governance should promote the best long-term interests of the company. It requires an effective board of directors, with an appropriate balance of skills and experience, and well-motivated individuals as directors. The composition of the board, its functions and responsibilities, and its effectiveness, are therefore core issues in corporate governance.

At the heart of the debate about corporate governance lie the conflicts of interest, or potential conflicts of interest, between shareholders, the board of directors as a whole and individual board members, and possibly also a number of other stakeholder groups. The directors may be tempted to take risks and make decisions aimed at boosting short-term performance. Many shareholders are more concerned about the longer term, the continuing survival of their company and the value of their investment. If a company gets into financial difficulties, professional managers can move on to another company to start again, whereas shareholders suffer a financial loss.

Issues in corporate governance where a conflict of interests might be apparent are:

- financial reporting and auditing
- directors' remuneration
- company–stakeholder relations
- risk-taking and the management of risk
- effective communication between the directors and shareholders
- ethical conduct and CSR.

These issues will be considered in more detail in the chapters that follow.

9.1 Financial reporting and auditing

The directors may try to disguise the true financial performance of their company by 'dressing up' the published accounts and giving less than honest statements. 'Window-dressed' accounts make it difficult for investors to reach a reasoned judgement about the financial position of the company. Concerns about misleading published accounts provided an early impetus in the 1980s and early 1990s to the movement for better corporate governance in the UK. Accounting irregularities in a number of companies led to a tightening of accounting standards, although the problems of window dressing are unlikely ever to disappear completely.

Concerns about financial reporting in the USA emerged with the collapse of Enron in 2001 (see Case example 1.2), which filed for bankruptcy after 'adjusting' its accounts. This was followed by similar problems at other US companies, such as telecommunications group WorldCom (which admitted to fraud in its accounting), Global Crossing and Rank Xerox. Problems then emerged in some European companies, most notably at the Italian group Parmalat at the end of 2003 (see Case example 1.3). It was also suggested that incomprehensible or misleading accounts contributed to the global banking crisis in 2007–2009, with banks such as Lehman Brothers (which collapsed in 2008) possibly using questionable accounting practices to disguise the true state of their financial position. A corporate governance issue is the question of the extent to which the directors were aware in each case of the impending collapse of their company, and if they knew the problems why shareholders were not informed much sooner. It is now widely accepted that the directors of a company should be responsible for giving an assurance to their shareholders that they consider their company to be a going concern that will not collapse within the next 12 months.

When the annual financial statements of a company prove to have been misleading, questions are inevitably raised about the effectiveness of the external auditors. There are two main issues relating to the external audit of a company:

- whether it should be the job of the auditors to discover financial fraud and material errors, and
- the problem of the relationship between a client company and its auditors, and the extent to which the auditors are independent and free from the influence of the company's management.

If auditors are subject to influence, they might be persuaded to agree with a controversial method of accounting for particular transactions, which shows the company's performance or financial position in a better light. Arthur Andersen, which collapsed in 2002, appears to have lacked independence from its major client Enron (see Case example 1.2).

9.2 Directors' remuneration

Directors may reward themselves with huge salaries and other rewards, such as bonuses, a generous pension scheme, **share options** (see Chapter 6) and other benefits. Institutional shareholders do not object to high remuneration for directors. However, they take the view that rewards should depend largely on the performance of the company and the benefits obtained for the shareholders. The main complaint about 'fat cat' directors' remuneration is that when the company does well, the directors are rewarded well, which is fair enough, but when the company does badly, the directors continue to be paid just as generously.

Interest in arguments about directors' pay has varied between different countries. In the UK, concerns led to the establishment of the Greenbury Committee in the 1990s and the production of the **Greenbury Report**. Directors' remuneration has remained a contentious issue ever since. In 2002 company law was changed by the Directors' Remuneration Report Regulations, requiring listed companies to produce a directors' remuneration report annually and to invite shareholders to vote on the report at the company's annual general meeting (AGM).

9.3 Company–stakeholder relations

Most decision-making powers in a company are held by the board of directors. The corporate governance debate has been about the extent to which professional managers, acting as board directors, exercise those powers in the interests of their shareholders and other stakeholders in the company, and whether the powers of directors should be restricted. This aspect of corporate governance is about:

- the structure of the board of directors and the role of independent non-executive directors (NEDs)
- the responsibilities of the board of directors
- the duties of directors
- the powers of shareholders under company law and whether these should be extended by corporate law reform, e.g. by giving shareholders the right to approve the company's remuneration policy or its remuneration packages for board members (see Chapter 6)
- whether shareholders actually make full use of the powers they already have, for example by voting not to re-elect directors.

9.4 Corporate governance and risk management

As a general rule, investors expect higher rewards to compensate them for taking higher **business risks** (see Chapter 9). If a company makes decisions that increase the scale of the risks it faces, profits and dividends should be expected to go up. Another issue in corporate governance is that the directors might take decisions intended to increase profits without giving due regard to the risks. In some cases, companies may continue to operate without regard to the changing risk profile of their existing businesses.

When investors buy shares in a company, they have an idea of the type of company they are buying into, the nature of its business, the probable returns it will provide for shareholders and the nature of its business and **financial risks** (see Chapter 10). To shareholders, investment risk is important, as well as high returns. Directors, on the other hand, are rewarded on the basis of the returns the company achieves, linked to profits or dividend growth, and their remuneration is not linked in any direct way to the risk aspects of their business. Risk management is now recognised as an ingredient of sound corporate governance.

Some companies are also guilty of poor procedures and systems, so that the risk of breakdowns, errors and fraud can be high. In addition to controlling 'business risk', companies should also have effective internal controls for managing **operational risks** (see Chapter 10).

9.5 Information and communication

Another issue in corporate governance is communication between the board of directors and the company's shareholders. Shareholders, particularly those with a large financial investment in the company, should be able to voice their concerns to the directors and expect to have their opinions heard. Small shareholders should at least be informed about the company, its financial position and its plans for the future, even if their opinions carry comparatively little weight.

The responsibility for improving communications rests with the companies themselves and their main institutional shareholders. Companies can make better use of the annual report and accounts to report to shareholders on a range of issues and the policies of the company for dealing with them. The annual report and accounts should not be simply a brief **directors' report** (see also Chapter 7) and a set of financial statements. The company should explain its operations and financial position in a business review and report on a range of governance issues, such as directors' remuneration, internal controls and risk management and policies on health, safety and the environment. Many companies now use their website to report on such matters. A company can also try to encourage greater shareholder attendance and participation at AGMs as a method of improving communications and dialogue. Electronic communications, including electronic voting, should also be considered. For their part, institutional investors should develop voting policies and apply these in general meetings. Where necessary, they can vote against the board to alert the directors to the strength of their views.

9.6 Ethical conduct and corporate social responsibility (CSR)

The relevance of ethical conduct to corporate governance has already been described. There is also a growing recognition that many companies need to consider social and environmental issues, for commercial reasons and governance reasons, as well as ethical reasons. Many shareholders (including institutional shareholders) and many customers expect companies to have regard to social issues and environmental issues; furthermore, the financial risks from government regulation to protect the environment continue to grow. Social and environmental issues can therefore affect reputation, sales, profits and the share price.

TEST YOUR KNOWLEDGE 1.7

List six key issues in corporate governance.

10 A brief history of corporate governance

10.1 Corporate governance in the UK

Concerns about corporate governance have grown over time. The main impetus for better practices in corporate governance began in the UK in the late 1980s and early 1990s. The Report of the Committee on the Financial Aspects of Corporate Governance (the 'Cadbury Report') was published in 1992, and was later described as 'a landmark in thinking on corporate governance'. The Report included a Code of Best Practice (the **Cadbury Code**), and UK listed companies came under pressure from City institutions to comply with the requirements of the Code.

In 1995, a working group was set up to look into the relationship between companies and institutional investors. It was chaired by Paul Myners, who was then chairman of Gartmore plc, and produced the **Myners Report**, which made a number of recommendations about how the relationship between institutional investors and company management should be conducted. The Report included suggestions for improving the communications between companies and institutional investors and for the conduct of AGMs. The significance of the Myners Report is that it urged institutional investors to reassess their role as shareholders, their responsibilities for ensuring good corporate governance and the success of the companies in which they invest. When a company is performing badly, institutional investors should try to do something to put matters right, instead of selling their shares and washing their hands of the company. Myners went on to argue that unless institutional investors voluntarily became more active in the governance of companies and exercised their rights more forcibly, they should be compelled to do so by legislation. Representative bodies of the institutional investor organisations, such as the ABI and the NAPF, responded by issuing guidelines for their members on corporate governance issues and principles of corporate governance.

On the recommendation of the Cadbury Committee, another committee was set up to review progress on corporate governance in UK listed companies. This committee issued the Greenbury Report in 1995, which focused mainly on directors' remuneration. At the time, the UK press was condemning 'fat cat' directors, particularly those in newly privatised companies. The Greenbury Report issued a Code of Best Practice on establishing remuneration committees, for disclosures of much more information about the remuneration of directors and remuneration policy, and for more control over notice periods in directors' service contracts and compensation payments in the event of early termination of contracts.

A Committee on Corporate Governance, chaired by Sir Ronald Hampel, was set up in 1995 to review the recommendations of the Cadbury and Greenbury Committees. The final report of the **Hampel Committee** was published in 1998. This covered a number of governance issues, such as the composition of the board and role of directors, directors' remuneration, the role of shareholders (particularly institutional shareholders), communications between the company and its shareholders, and financial reporting, auditing and internal controls. The Hampel Report also suggested that its recommendations should be combined with those of the Cadbury and Greenbury Committees into a single code of corporate governance. This suggestion led to the publication of the original 1998 **Combined Code** on Corporate Governance (Combined Code), which applied to all UK listed companies.

Corporate governance issues remained in the spotlight in the UK, and two influential reports were produced in January 2003. The **Higgs Report**, commissioned by the government, considered the role and effectiveness of NEDs. The Smith Report, commissioned by the Financial Reporting Council (FRC), provided guidance for audit committees. The responsibility for the Combined Code was transferred to the FRC and in 2003 a revised Combined Code was issued, incorporating many of the Higgs and Smith recommendations.

Although the Combined Code has been voluntary, the UK Listing Rules included an obligation on listed companies to disclose the extent of their compliance with it. Listed companies were required to state that they have complied in full with the provisions of the Code, or must explain any non-compliance. This **'comply or explain' rule** for listed companies applies to all provisions of the Code.

The UK Code and related guidelines are now the responsibility of the FRC. The FRC has reviewed and amended the Combined Code regularly, and in June 2010 issued a revised version of the Code, under the new name of the **UK Corporate Governance Code**.

The global financial markets and world economy were badly damaged by a banking crisis that emerged in 2007 and 2008. In the USA Lehman Brothers collapsed and other banks and brokerage firms were taken over to prevent their collapse. In the UK, Northern Rock bank collapsed in 2007 and in 2008 Royal Bank of Scotland was virtually nationalised and the government acquired a major stake in Lloyds TSB Bank after Lloyds had agreed to take over another ailing bank, HBOS. Recognition of governance problems in UK banks led to a review by Sir David Walker and the Walker Report (2009). Some recommendations of the Walker Report have been included by the FRC in the 2010 UK Corporate Governance Code.

Some aspects of corporate governance have been brought into UK law, with much of the initiative coming from the European Union (EU) and **EU Directives** (see Chapter 2). New regulations in 2002 were introduced for greater disclosures of directors' remuneration by listed companies, replacing similar regulations that had been included in the Listing Rules. (See Chapter 6 for more details.) The Companies Act 2006 introduced **statutory duties** of directors (similar to the duties that existed previously in common law and equity), and contains a requirement for quoted companies to be more accountable to shareholders by publishing a business review in narrative form each year. Amendments to the Fourth and Seventh EU Company Law Directives approved in 2006 included a requirement for quoted companies to include a corporate governance statement in their annual reports, and amendments to the Eighth Company Law Directive in 2008 requires 'public interest entities' (which include listed companies) to have an audit committee consisting of independent NEDs and to publish an annual corporate governance statement.

A largely separate, although interconnected, development has been a growing awareness on the part of large companies of the potential risks to their reputation and long-term success from failures to comply with laws and regulations or to act ethically. Many companies have also claimed to recognise the potential long-term benefits from acting in a socially responsible manner.

STOP AND THINK **1.2**

From what you have read or heard in news reports, identify a recent example of pressures for better corporate governance that is bringing about changes in a company's management, policies or practices.

10.2 Corporate governance in other countries

Although the UK is seen as a leading country in the development of a corporate governance framework, there have been similar developments in many other countries. For many countries, particularly developing countries, good corporate governance is seen as an essential basic requirement for attracting foreign investment capital. In South Africa, a code of corporate governance was developed by the King Committee. This was revised and strengthened in 2002 and again in 2009. On an international basis, recommended principles on corporate governance have been published by the OECD.

The USA appeared to show little concern for better corporate governance throughout the 1990s, although there were some activist institutional shareholders such as CalPERS. The situation changed dramatically with the collapse of Enron in 2001 and some other major companies. The major auditing and accountancy firm Arthur Andersen, caught up in the Enron scandal and prosecuted for obstructing the course of justice, collapsed and was broken up in 2002 (see Case example 1.2). Recommendations for change were proposed by the NYSE, and statutory provisions on corporate governance were introduced in 2002 with the Sarbanes-Oxley Act. However, the adequacy of corporate governance provisions in the US (and the UK) has been questioned following the banking crisis in 2007–2009.

Many other countries now have corporate governance codes and legislation covering aspects of corporate governance practice. The regulations and guidelines vary between countries. A summary of the laws and guidelines in each country can be found on the website of the European Corporate Governance Institute, at www.ecgi.org/codes/all_codes.php.

10.3 National variations in corporate governance

As stated earlier, the need for good corporate governance is a matter of international concern. However, it is important to be aware that although corporate governance has become a matter of some interest in many countries, the pace of change and the nature of corporate governance vary substantially between countries.

Much of the pressure for change has come from institutional investors, particularly in the USA, who have invested fairly heavily in companies in other countries. As shareholders in foreign companies, US investors expect to be allowed to exercise their right to vote and to be treated on an equal footing with other equity shareholders. In countries where minority shareholder rights are not always well respected, US investor influence has probably been influential in the corporate governance changes that have been introduced. The ICGN is a voluntary organisation established to promote good governance practice worldwide; this has issued a corporate governance code, based largely on the UK model.

In many developing countries, there have been substantial investments in recent years by multinational companies. It might be expected that US and UK multinationals would establish a system of corporate governance within their subsidiaries along similar lines to the parent company, e.g. with NEDs on the board representing interest groups in the local country. Many multinationals are aware of their reputation in overseas markets, and alert to the demands of pressure groups as well as governments in the countries where they have operating subsidiaries.

 CASE EXAMPLE 1.4

RiskMetrics is a US shareholder advisory group that advises shareholders holding up to 20 per cent of some leading German companies. It criticised the decision of Infineon (a German company that manufactures electronic chips) to appoint an individual as chairman-designate that it considered unsuitable, and advised its clients to support a rival candidate for the chairmanship at the company's AGM in 2010. Its view was supported by Hermes, the UK investment fund and a major German institutional investor.

In January 2010 as a result of the pressure, the chairman-designate promised to step down early, saying he would serve only one year instead of five if elected as chairman. The opposing shareholders were pleased with the offer, but insisted that an acceptable compromise had to include the appointment of their candidate to the supervisory board. (In Germany, shareholders can appoint board members, but the supervisory board members elect the chairman.)

 TEST YOUR KNOWLEDGE 1.8

What is the 'comply or explain rule' in corporate governance for listed companies?

11 Arguments for and against corporate governance regimes

There are differences of opinion about the benefits of corporate governance, and whether these justify the costs of compliance with corporate governance regulations. It is therefore useful to consider just what the benefits of good corporate governance might be for public companies, and what the arguments may be against having laws or codes of corporate governance practice.

The main arguments in favour of having a strong corporate governance regime for listed companies are as follows.

- Good governance will eliminate the risk of misleading or false financial reporting, and will prevent companies from being dominated by self-seeking chief executive officers or chairmen. By reducing the risks of corporate scandals, and promoting fairness, accountability, responsibility and transparency in companies, investors will be better protected. This should add generally to confidence in the capital markets, and help to sustain share prices.
- It has been argued that companies that comply with best practice in corporate governance are also more likely to achieve commercial success. Good governance and good leadership and management often go hand-in-hand. Badly governed companies may be very successful, and well-governed companies may fail; however, the probability is greater that badly governed companies will be less successful and more likely to fail than well-governed ones.

- Well-governed companies will often develop a strong reputation and so will be less exposed to **reputation risk** (see Chapter 9) than companies that are not so well governed. Reputation risk can have an adverse impact on investors and customers.
- Good governance encourages investors to hold shares in companies for the longer term, instead of treating shares as short-term investments to be sold for a quick profit. Companies benefit from having shareholders who have an interest in their longer-term prospects.

The main arguments against having a strong corporate governance regime for listed companies focus on costs, benefits and value are as follows.

- It is argued that, for many companies and institutional investors, compliance with a code of corporate governance is a box-ticking exercise (see Chapter 3). Companies adopt the required procedures and systems without considering what the potential benefits might be. The only requirement is to comply with the 'rules' and put a tick in a box when this is done. Corporate governance requirements therefore create a time-and-resource-consuming bureaucracy, with compliance officers, and divert the attention of the board of directors from more important matters.
- Good corporate governance is likely to reduce the risk of scandals and unexpected corporate failures. However, it could be argued that the current regulations or best practice guidelines are far too extensive and burdensome.
- When regulations and recommended practice become burdensome, there is an inevitable cost, in terms of both time and money, in achieving compliance. It could be argued that less regulation is better regulation. However there has not yet been an authoritative assessment of the costs of corporate governance compliance with the benefits of better corporate governance systems.
- Companies that are obliged to comply with corporate governance regulations or best practice are at a competitive disadvantage to rival companies from countries where corporate governance regulation is weaker. (As corporate governance regimes have extended to more countries, however, this argument is weaker than it used to be. There is no evidence, for example, that UK companies have lost competitiveness because of the relatively strong governance regime in the UK.)
- The connection between good corporate governance and good financial results (due to good leadership and management) has not been proved or demonstrated.

TEST YOUR KNOWLEDGE 1.9

(a) What are the arguments in favour and against the application of corporate governance codes of practice to large companies?
(b) What are the aims of the ICGN?

12 Corporate governance in the public sector

A key development for the corporate governance of the UK public sector was the Nolan Committee on Standards in Public Life. The Committee was set up in 1995 in response to concerns that the conduct of some politicians was unethical and, in particular, allegations of MPs taking cash for putting parliamentary questions. While the Committee focused on MPs, its terms of reference also covered government departments and non-departmental public bodies (**NDPBs**). The Principles, set out in the following text, were originally intended as guidelines for individuals who were involved in public affairs and public bodies, whether as paid employees or as non-paid members of governing bodies. They are now considered to have much wider relevance and have formed the basis in the UK for developing governance guidelines for both the public sector and the voluntary sector.

Nolan's seven principles of public life

1 Selflessness. Holders of public office should take decisions solely in terms of the public interest. They should not do so to gain financial or other material benefits for themselves, their family or their friends.

2 Integrity. Holders of public office should not place themselves under any financial or other obligation to outside individuals or organisations that might influence them in the performance of their duties.

3 Objectivity. In carrying out public business, including making public appointments, awarding contracts or recommending individuals for rewards and benefits, holders of public office should make choices on merit.

4 Accountability. Holders of public office are accountable for their decisions and actions to the public and must submit themselves to whatever scrutiny is appropriate to their office.

5 Openness. Holders of public office should be as open as possible about the decisions and actions that they take. They should give reasons for their decisions and restrict information only when the wider public interest clearly demands.

6 Honesty. Holders of public office have a duty to declare any private interests relating to their public duties and to take steps to resolve any conflicts arising in a way that protects the public interest.

7 Leadership. Holders of public office should promote and support these principles by leadership and example.

The public sector includes central government, state government (in some countries) and local government, state-run health and education services and many other regulatory and advisory bodies. Many of the principles of good corporate governance can be applied to the governing bodies of the public sector, but there are also significant differences. For example, public bodies are not profit-making and are not accountable to shareholders. Some governors of public sector bodies do their work for no remuneration. The influence of the public as stakeholders in public bodies is also much greater than with private companies.

The public sector has therefore adapted principles of good governance to its own specific circumstances, and to some extent the definition of 'governance' for the public sector differs in some ways from 'governance' of companies. In the UK, the Chartered Institute of Public Finance and Accountancy (CIPFA) and Solace (the Society of Local Authority Chief Executives and Senior Managers) published a governance framework aimed at local government bodies called 'Delivering Good Governance in Local Government: Framework' (2007). This sets out principles of governance that local government bodies are encouraged to adopt and apply to their own particular circumstances. This Framework defines governance as:

'[H]ow local government bodies ensure that they are doing the right things, in the right way, for the right people, in a timely, inclusive, open, honest and accountable manner. It comprises systems and processes, and cultures and values, by which local government bodies are directed and controlled and through which they account to, and engage with, and, where appropriate, lead their communities.'

12.1 'Good Governance Standard for Public Service'

The Independent Commission for Good Governance in Public Service was established by the Office for Public Management (OPM) and the CIPFA, in partnership with the Joseph Rowntree Foundation. The role of the Commission was to develop a common code and set of principles for good corporate governance across all public services in the UK.

In 2004 it published 'Good Governance Standard for Public Service'. This is a guide for everyone concerned with governance in the public services, and applies to all organisations that work for the public using public money. Its application therefore extends from public sector bodies to all private sector organisations that use public money to work for the public.

In justifying the need for the application of good governance principles and practice in the public service sector, the Commission has commented that:

- good governance encourages public trust and participation, whereas
- bad governance fosters low morale and adversarial relationships.

The Commission's Good Governance Standard, which builds on Nolan's Principles, consists of six main principles, each with supporting principles, together with guidelines on how these might be applied in practice. It is useful to look at these and compare them with the principles (to be described later in the text) that apply to good corporate governance in the commercial (profit-making) sector. There are many similarities between these principles and those that should apply in corporate governance to companies.

The six main principles and their supporting principles are as follows.

1 Focusing on the organisation's purpose and on its outcome for citizens and users of the organisation's services.
   - Being clear about the purpose of the organisation and its intended outcomes for citizens and service users. It is suggested that the concept of 'public value' may be useful in helping organisations to identify their purpose and intended outcomes.
   - Making sure that users receive a high-quality service.
   - Making sure that taxpayers get value for money (VFM).

2 Performing effectively in clearly defined functions and roles.
   - Being clear about the functions of the organisation's governing body. It is recommended that the governing body should describe in a published document its approach to achieving each of its stated functions. This document can then be used as a basis for measuring actual performance and achievements by the governing body. Functions could include, for example, 'scrutinising the activities and performance of the executive management' and 'making sure that the voice of the public is heard in discussions and decision-making'.
   - Being clear about the responsibilities of the non-executive and the executive governors; these will differ. Many governing bodies consist of both executives and non-executive members (who may be unpaid for their services). However, they should have equal status in discussions on policy and strategy. The Framework recommends that the roles of chief executive and chairman of the governing body should not be held by the same individual.
   - Making sure that these responsibilities are properly carried out.
   - Being clear about the relationship between the governors and the public, so that both sides in this relationship knows what to expect from the other.

3 Promoting values for the whole organisation and demonstrating good governance through behaviour.
   - Putting the values of the organisation into practice. The governing body should take the lead in doing this.
   - Individual governors behaving in ways that uphold and exemplify effective governance.

4 Taking informed and transparent decisions and managing risk.
   - Being rigorous and transparent about how decisions are taken by the governing body. There should be clearly defined levels of delegation within the organisation. The governing body should not be concerned with matters that are more properly delegated to management. It should also be clear about what the objectives of its own decisions are.
   - Using good quality information, advice and support.
   - Making sure that an effective risk management system is in operation.

5 Developing the capacity and capability of the governing body to be effective.
   - Making sure that the governors have the skills, knowledge and experience to perform well.
   - Developing the capabilities of individuals with governance responsibilities.
   - Striking a balance in the membership of the governing body between continuity and renewal.

   The creation and refreshing of a governing body is similar in many respects to similar guidelines in corporate governance, although in the public sector, some governors may be elected representatives.

6 Engaging stakeholders and making accountability real.
   - Understanding formal and informal accountability relationships.
   - Taking an active and planned approach to dialogue with and accountability to the public.
   - Taking an effective and planned approach to accountability to staff.
   - Engaging effectively with institutional stakeholders. Institutional stakeholders in the public sector are very different from institutional shareholders in the corporate world.

In local government, for example, institutional stakeholders include bodies representing local people. Engagement with stakeholders should help to improve the accountability of the public sector body to the public.

These are general principles, and individual public sector bodies can develop their own codes of governance that are consistent with and based on these principles.

An important aspect of governance for public sector bodies, as with corporate governance, is risk management. When referring to 'risk management' in the public sector, the focus is likely to be mainly on 'internal control'. Public sector organisations have a long history of wasteful spending, inefficiency, errors and fraud. In England, for example, local government bodies are required by law to publish a statement of internal control each year.

12.2 The state as shareholder

A company may be part-owned by the government. When this is the case, a question arises about what the interests of the state as shareholder are. A government might act like any other shareholder and simply look for maximum long-term returns from its investment. On the other hand, the government may recognise more openly the interest of other stakeholder groups, such as the company's employees or the public as a whole.

- Shareholders other than the government need to know what the government's interests are, and how these might affect decision-making by the board, in order to put a value to their own investment.
- The board of directors may also take decisions in the belief that should they make mistakes, and should the company get into financial difficulties, the government will be likely to provide further financial support, to prevent job losses.
- In some cases, a government that privatises a nationalised industry retains a 'golden share', giving it the right to veto decisions taken by the company if these appear to be against the national interest, for example, giving it the right of veto over any sale of the company to a foreign buyer.

12.3 State-owned industries in emerging countries

The Commonwealth Association for Corporate Governance (CACG) issued a set of guidelines in 1999, which makes particular reference to state-owned industries in the emerging countries of the Commonwealth. In emerging countries:

- most of the largest and economically significant industries are state-owned, and the private sector is often very small
- many directors are not independent, and are often political appointments
- there is a severe shortage of individuals with the necessary skills to act as directors.

The CAGC argued that although state-owned industries differ from public companies, the directors of these industries have a duty to taxpayers and the community:

'While the conventional fiduciary relationships between shareholders and the board (as found in the private sector) do not necessarily apply, directors of state enterprises nevertheless owe a fiduciary responsibility to account to a country's taxpayers and the communities which such enterprises serve for the efficient utilisation of state-owned assets.'

They owe a duty to taxpayers for the proper use of the money raised in taxes. They also owe a duty to the communities for the efficient delivery of services (electricity, water and so on).

CAGC also suggested that sound corporate governance in state-owned industries is extremely important in developing economies because they provide a role model for companies in the growing private sector. If state-owned industries govern themselves well, private companies can be persuaded to do the same. If state-owned industries are badly governed, it will be difficult to persuade the private sector to do anything better.

13 Corporate governance and the voluntary sector

The voluntary sector includes a wide range of organisations, including charities and mutual self-help groups. Many UK charities are established as a trust, which is governed by a board of trustees. Large charities employ full-time managers and employees, whereas others rely entirely on voluntary and unpaid help.

Governance in the voluntary sector has been defined as:

'[T]he way that trustees work with chief executives and staff (where appointed), volunteers, service users, members and other stakeholders to ensure their organisation is effectively and properly run, and meets the needs for which the organisation was set up ('Good Governance: a Code for the Voluntary and Community Sector', 2005).

The development of codes and rules for corporate governance in the commercial sector and governance in the government sector has also reached the voluntary sector. For example, the National Council of Voluntary Organisations (NCVO) adapted Nolan's seven principles of public life into a code of conduct for charity trustees; and the Charity Commission's Statement of Recommended Practice requires larger charities to include a statement on risks in their annual report.

Awareness of the need for good governance has also developed in the voluntary sector response to sector-specific issues, including:

- the increase in size and importance of the voluntary sector, particularly as a result of the contracting out of public service to voluntary organisations
- a perception of a decline in public confidence in charities; charities and other bodies have tried to improve their standards of governance as a way of retaining public confidence in what they are doing
- greater competition for funding; charities with better standards of governance may succeed better in attracting funds from government and the public
- a lack of clarity about the duties of voluntary board members, and in particular concerns about the liabilities of charity trustees; these concerns are similar to those in corporate governance, about the responsibilities of the board, the duties of directors and the potential liability of directors
- a growing demand for accountability to users and beneficiaries of the services provided by charities
- demands for greater transparency on how charities spend their donated income, and in particular the proportion spent ('wasted') on administration.

13.1 'Good Governance: a Code for the Voluntary and Community Sector'

In 2005, 'Good Governance: a Code for the Voluntary and Community Sector' was published in the UK. This governance code was developed and endorsed by the Charity Commission and the NCVO, the Association of Chief Executives of Voluntary Associations, the Charity Trustee Networks and the Institute of Chartered Secretaries and Administrators. The Code is not mandatory, but organisations that comply with it are invited to say so in their annual report and other relevant published material. Smaller charities are invited to focus on complying with the general principles of the Code rather than the detailed guides included in the Code on how to apply the principles into practice. The Code contains seven key principles.

1 Board leadership. Every organisation should be led and controlled by an effective board of trustees who collectively ensure the delivery of its objects, set its strategic direction and uphold its values.
2 The board in control. The trustees as a board should be collectively responsible and accountable for ensuring that the organisation performs well, is solvent and complies with all its obligations.
3 The high-performance board. The board should have clear responsibilities and functions, and should compose and organise itself to make sure that it discharges them effectively.
4 Board review and renewal. The board should periodically review its own effectiveness and the effectiveness of the organisation, and take any necessary steps to ensure that both continue to work well.
5 Board delegation. The board should set out the functions of sub-committees, officers, the chief executive officer and other staff and agents in clear, delegated authorities, and should monitor their performance.

6 Board and trustee integrity. The board and individual trustees should act according to high ethical standards and ensure that conflicts of interest are properly dealt with.
7 The open board. The board should be open, responsive and accountable to its users, beneficiaries, members, partners and others with an interest in its work.

Each key principle has two or more supporting principles, and for each supporting principle the Code suggests ways of applying it in practice.

TEST YOUR KNOWLEDGE 1.10

(a) How does governance in the public sector and not-for-profit sector differ from corporate governance?
(b) What are Nolan's seven principles of public life?
(c) What might be the consequences of bad governance practice in a police force?
(d) For what reasons have governance guidelines and codes of practice been developed for the not-for-profit sector?

CHAPTER SUMMARY

■ Corporate governance refers to the way in which a company is led, mainly by its directors. It is not concerned with executive management or business operations.
■ Experience has shown that when companies collapse, poor corporate governance has contributed to the collapse. It is also widely believed that best practice in corporate governance results in good company performance over the long term.
■ Companies (and all organisations) have stakeholders. These are individuals or groups with an interest in what the company does. Stakeholders in companies include financial stakeholders (such as shareholders and lenders) and non-financial stakeholders (such as senior management, other employees, suppliers, customers and the general public). Some stakeholders are more influential than others.
■ Agency theory examines the conflicts of interest between the owners of a company and their agents, the company directors. These conflicts give rise to costs, such as the costs of monitoring the activities of agents and costs of incentivising them. Ideally, the aim should be to minimise these agency costs.
■ Transaction cost theory is a theory of economic organisation that includes the view that managers are opportunistic and where possible will take opportunities to act in their own best interests.
■ There are different approaches to corporate governance, which vary according to the extent to which the interests of stakeholders other than the company shareholders are recognised. The differing approaches may be referred to as a shareholder approach, an enlightened shareholder or inclusive approach, and a stakeholder or pluralist approach. The approach taken by the directors of an organisation affects decision-making at a strategic level.
■ Principles of good governance are fairness, accountability, responsibility and transparency.
■ There is a close connection between best practice in governance and ethical behaviour. Individuals have personal ethics and professional bodies require professional ethical behaviour from their members. Corporate ethics refer to the way in which a company conducts its business: companies may have a corporate code of ethics that employees are expected to comply with.
■ The main issue in corporate governance is the effectiveness of the board of directors in promoting the long-term success of the company. Other key issues in corporate governance are financial reporting and auditing, the remuneration of senior executives, relationships between a company and its stakeholder groups, risk management and internal control, communication between a company and its shareholders, ethics and CSR.
■ The UK has a history of mainly voluntary corporate governance practice. Its first governance code was the Cadbury Code (1992). The Combined Code (1998–2010) was revised and renamed the UK

Corporate Governance Code in 2010. The UK Code and related guidelines are the responsibility of the Financial Reporting Council (FRC). Other countries have developed their own corporate governance regimes, mainly based on voluntary codes of practice for listed companies. The USA relies more on a regulatory system of corporate governance.

- Concepts of good governance practice have been extended from companies to the public sector and also the voluntary sector.
- In the UK, 'Good Governance Standard for Public Service' was published in 2004, building on Nolan's Seven Principles of Public Life (selflessness, integrity, objectivity, accountability, openness, honesty and leadership).
- Similar codes of governance may be issued for the voluntary sector. In the UK, 'Good Governance: a Code for the Voluntary and Community Sector' was published in 2005.
- Although there are some differences, concepts of good governance in non-commercial organisations are similar to concepts of best practice in corporate governance.

2 Legal and regulatory aspects of governance

■ INTRODUCTION

This brief chapter considers the extent to which best practice in corporate governance is imposed on companies by the law or other regulations. There are two different approaches to establishing a system of best practice in corporate governance. One approach is to establish voluntary principles and guidelines, and invite (or expect) companies to comply with them. A second approach is to establish laws and other regulations for corporate governance that companies must obey. In practice, many countries combine legal and regulatory requirements with voluntary principles and codes of conduct. After reading and understanding the contents of this chapter and working through the 'Test your knowledge' questions, you should be able to:

- identify aspects of corporate governance practice that may be regulated by law or regulations
- appreciate that laws and regulations on corporate governance vary in their scope between countries, so that some countries adopt a 'rules-based' approach to governance and other countries rely more on a 'principles-based' approach.

1 Governance and the law

Governance is concerned with the way in which companies are led. The directors of a company should be responsible for safeguarding the assets of the company and for protecting the rights and interests of the shareholders and other stakeholders, and they should also be accountable to the shareholders. It is inevitable that some aspects of governance practice should be regulated by law, and that companies should be required to comply with 'best practice'. Regulations on corporate governance may be found in:

- company law
- laws regulating financial markets and financial services
- insolvency law
- laws on money laundering and insider dealing.

1.1 UK company law and governance

In the UK, the main item of company legislation is the Companies Act 2006. This includes regulations relating to:

- the preparation and auditing of annual financial statements, for approval by the shareholders
- the powers and duties of directors

- other disclosures to shareholders, such as the requirement for companies to publish an annual business review
- the disclosure of information about directors' remuneration
- general meetings of companies, and shareholder rights to call a general meeting
- shareholder voting rights at general meetings, including the right to re-elect directors.

Similar regulations are included in the company legislation of other countries; however, this study text will concentrate mainly on UK company law. Each of the aspects of governance listed earlier will be described in the relevant chapters that follow.

There have been a number of EU Directives relating to company law. A proposal for a new or amended EU Directive is initiated by the **European Commission** in Brussels. Legislation is then agreed by the European Council and the European Parliament in a process known as the 'co-decision procedure'. When a Directive has been agreed, its contents must be implemented by all EU member states within a stated time frame, either in a law or other regulation, if suitable legislation does not already exist. EU Directives on company law have included a requirement for companies to publish an annual business review and, for companies whose shares are traded on a regulated exchange, there have been:

- a Shareholder Rights Directive
- requirements to publish an annual corporate governance statement
- requirements to have an audit committee
- requirements to introduce measures that provide for the independence and ethical conduct of their external auditors.

The EU has therefore been responsible for the extension of legislation for aspects of corporate governance, and in doing so it has been influenced by the rules-based approach adopted in the USA (see later in section 3, 'The USA and the Sarbanes-Oxley Act 2002').

1.2 Governance, the law and financial services

Countries with regulated stock markets and markets for other financial products and services need legislation to regulate the conduct of participants in the markets. Financial markets should be regulated in order to give investors confidence to invest. Customers are important stakeholders in banks, and some elements of financial services legislation are intended to provide consumer protection. In the UK, following the crisis in the banking industry in 2007–2009 the Financial Services Authority (FSA; the UK financial markets regulator) recognised serious weaknesses in corporate governance in banks, particularly inadequate risk management systems, and its responsibility for enforcing improvements.

1.3 Insolvency law and governance

Companies become insolvent for reasons unconnected with corporate governance. Occasionally, however, the directors of a company may allow it to continue in business when they are aware that it is insolvent and will be unable to pay its creditors or employees. In the UK, the Companies Act 2006 includes provisions that make fraudulent trading a criminal offence and the Insolvency Act 1986 makes wrongful trading a civil offence. Fraudulent trading and wrongful trading are explained in Chapter 5.

1.4 Criminal law and governance

Some aspects of 'bad' corporate governance practice are illegal.

- Directors and other individuals may possess price-sensitive 'inside' knowledge about a company to buy or sell shares in the company with the intention of making a profit (or avoiding a loss). **Insider dealing** is related to corporate governance because it is often carried out by a director or professional adviser of a company. It is also a criminal offence. (In the UK, insider dealing is a criminal offence under Part V of the Criminal Justice Act 1993.)
- **Money laundering** is the process of disguising the source of money that has been obtained from serious crime or terrorism, so that it appears to come from a legitimate source. Companies are often used for the purpose of money laundering, which is a criminal offence in most countries, and the owners or directors of the companies concerned are often involved in the money laundering activity themselves.

There is no Corporate Governance Law in any country: rather, some aspects of corporate governance are regulated by sections of different laws. Other aspects of governance are not regulated by law at all, or are regulated only partially. Even in the USA, where there is greater emphasis on regulation of corporate governance, many elements of 'best practice' in corporate governance are voluntary.

TEST YOUR KNOWLEDGE 2.1

(a) What aspects of corporate governance are regulated by company law (the Companies Act 2006) in the UK?
(b) What is the relevance of the law on insider dealing to corporate governance?
(c) What is the relevance of money laundering to good corporate governance practice?
(d) Give an example of a situation where insider dealing might occur.

2   The UK Listing Regime and corporate governance

In every country where there is a regulated stock market, companies whose shares are traded on the market are required to comply with certain rules of conduct. In the UK, these are contained in the United Kingdom Listing Authority Rules. These include the **UK Listing Rules** and also Disclosure Rules and Transparency Rules (DTR). These Rules are the responsibility of the Financial Services Authority, the UK financial services regulator. All companies that have a listing for their shares on the main UK stock market (the main market of the London Stock Exchange) must comply with the Rules.

A few of the UK Listing Rules are concerned with corporate governance. These will be explained in some detail in later chapters. Briefly, however, most listed companies in the UK – including non-UK companies with a **premium** (UK) **listing** – must comply with all aspects of the UK Corporate Governance Code or explain their non-compliance in their annual report and accounts. Another rule requires listed companies to provide a 'going concern statement' in their annual report and accounts.

A section of the **Disclosure and Transparency Rules** set out regulations relating to audit committees and corporate governance statements by listed companies.

TEST YOUR KNOWLEDGE 2.2

How are the UK Listing Rules enforceable?

3   The USA and the Sarbanes-Oxley Act 2002

A different approach to the regulation of corporate governance was taken in the USA, following a number of financial scandals and corporate collapses in 2001–2002 involving major corporations such as Enron, WorldCom and Tyco. Previously, corporate governance issues had not been considered a matter of any significance. As a result of Enron and the other corporate scandals, there was an immediate recognition of a need to protect investors, mainly by improving the accuracy and reliability of financial reporting and other disclosures by companies.

The USA took a regulatory approach to dealing with the problems that were recognised at the time, and a number of corporate governance measures were included in the **Sarbanes-Oxley Act 2002** (sometimes referred to as SOX). The law applied to all public companies in the USA and also to all non-US companies that had shares or debt securities registered with the Securities and Exchange Commission (SEC). Chief executive officers and chief financial officers were made personally liable for the accuracy of the financial statements of their company, and new rules on financial reporting were introduced including a requirement to publish an internal audit report with the annual financial statements. Several other corporate governance measures were included in the Act, such as a requirement for legal protection for whistleblowers (explained in Chapter 10).

With the enactment of SOX, the USA was considered to have adopted a rules-based approach to corporate governance, different from the 'principles-based' approach in most other countries (described in Chapter 3). However, SOX is not a comprehensive law on corporate governance, and many aspects of corporate governance are not covered by the Act. For example, SOX does not contain any rules about the composition of the board of directors, remuneration of senior executives or dialogue between companies and their shareholders.

TEST YOUR KNOWLEDGE 2.3

Identify two of the main requirements of the Sarbanes-Oxley Act 2002 in relation to corporate governance practice in corporations (companies) registered with the Securities and Exchange Commission in the USA.

4 Compulsory regulation and voluntary best practice

This chapter has identified aspects of corporate governance where laws or regulations might apply. In many countries there are voluntary codes of corporate governance, based mainly on principles of good governance rather than detailed and specific rules. Each of these approaches to governance – compulsory regulation and voluntary best practice – has limitations and advantages.

There are several advantages with compulsory regulation of corporate governance issues.

- There are areas of business where laws are essential to protect the interests of shareholders, employees and other stakeholders in companies. For example, employment laws are needed to give protection to employees against unfair treatment by employers. There should be a legal requirement for companies to prepare annual financial statements and have them audited, and the duties of directors should be subject to the law, in order to protect shareholders. There may be different views about the extent of regulation that is required; however, the need for some regulation seems unquestionable.

- Best practice in corporate governance has some connection with ethical business practice. Some aspects of corporate behaviour may be considered unethical but legal. Laws are needed to prevent or punish activities that are considered so unethical that they should be illegal. Bribery is an example of corporate behaviour that has been tolerated in the past but which is now accepted as illegal by most countries.

- Regulation may be needed to address public concerns and maintain public confidence in the capitalist system. This has probably been most evident in the USA. The Sarbanes-Oxley Act was a response to public outrage against the many corporate scandals that emerged after the collapse of Enron. Public fury against the banks following the financial crisis in 2007–2008 prompted demands for legislative action that would affect the governance of banks.

There are arguments in favour of voluntary corporate governance systems.

- It is difficult to devise a set of rules that should apply to all companies in all circumstances. Rules that are appropriate for one company might not be appropriate for another company whose circumstances are very different. Although a voluntary system of corporate governance (such as the system in the UK) places an expectation on listed companies to comply with the guidelines, it also allows them to breach the guidelines if it seems appropriate and sensible to do so.

- The biggest concerns about corporate governance practice apply to large stock market companies with large numbers of shareholders. Governance is less of a problem in small companies.

As a general rule, governance issues become greater as a company gets bigger. A voluntary code of best practice in governance can be targeted at the largest companies (listed companies), and smaller companies are able to choose whether they want to model their own governance systems on parts of the code for listed companies. Governance practices can therefore be adapted to the circumstances of the company.

■ There may be a risk that if different countries have their own corporate governance regulations, companies will migrate to those countries where the rules are less onerous. Governments may therefore compete to offer a corporate governance regime that is more attractive in their country than in other countries, in order to attract foreign companies.

■ Excessive regulations may deter companies from becoming a listed company, particularly if the rules for listed companies are stricter than the rules for private companies.

In practice, corporate governance is a combination of regulation and voluntary best practice. In some countries there is more emphasis on regulation and in others there is greater reliance on voluntary codes of practice for large companies. However, unless corporate governance is regulated by law, it is probable that standards of governance will vary substantially between companies, especially in small and medium-sized enterprises (SMEs).

Voluntary best practice is explained more fully in Chapter 3.

 TEST YOUR KNOWLEDGE 2.4

Explain the disadvantages of a rules-based approach to corporate governance, compared with a principles-based approach

CHAPTER SUMMARY

■ Corporate governance practices are guided partly by laws and regulations, and partly by voluntary adoption of codes of practice.

■ In many countries, including the UK, certain aspects of corporate governance are covered by the law. These include parts of companies' legislation and laws on corporate insolvency, insider dealing and money laundering.

■ The UK has a voluntary system of corporate governance, but this voluntary system is enforced on UK listed companies (including foreign companies with a premium listing in the UK) by regulations in the UK Listing Rules and the Disclosure and Transparency Rules.

■ The USA has a system of corporate governance based largely on regulation, originating with the Sarbanes-Oxley Act in 2002.

Voluntary codes of corporate governance: the role of the company secretary

3

■ CONTENTS

■ INTRODUCTION

This chapter describes the nature and purpose of voluntary codes of corporate governance, and compares a 'principles-based' approach to governance with a 'rules-based' approach. It describes the general principles of governance set out in some of the more well-known codes, and makes some comparisons between them. At the end of this chapter you should have an appreciation of the general principles of good corporate governance, but you should also be aware that differences in emphasis exist between the different codes. The chapter then goes on to explain the nature and purpose of guidelines issued by institutional investor organisations for their members: the focus is on the main UK organisations – the Association of British Insurers and the National Association of Pension Funds. The chapter concludes with an explanation of the role of the company secretary in applying best practice in corporate governance, including complying with governance principles and provisions.

1   Voluntary codes of best governance practice

1.1 The nature and purpose of a voluntary code

A voluntary code of (corporate) governance is issued by an authoritative national or international body and contains principles or best practice in corporate governance that major companies (listed companies) are encouraged to adopt and apply. The principles may consist of main principles with associated supporting principles, and for each principle, there may also be provisions or recommendations about how the principle should be applied in practice. Voluntary codes have been adopted in many countries, e.g. in all the countries of the Commonwealth and all the countries of the EU.

There is no statutory requirement for companies to apply the principles or provisions of a voluntary code. However, a well-established code should attract the support of major companies and investors, and this develops an expectation that companies should adopt the code unless their circumstances are such that non-compliance with some of the code's provisions is a more sensible option.

Although voluntary, companies whose shares are traded on a major stock market may be required by their Listing Rules to adopt the country's code of governance or to explain in their annual report and accounts their non-compliance with any aspect of the code and their reasons for non-compliance.

In the UK, the Listing Rules require listed companies that are incorporated in the UK to include in their annual report and accounts:

- a statement of how it has applied the main principles of the UK Corporate Governance Code, and
- a statement of whether it has complied throughout the period with all the relevant provisions of the Code; if it has not complied with any of the provisions, it must explain the nature of the non-compliance and the reasons for it.

This requirement, common in many countries, is known as 'comply or explain' (see Chapter 1). (Foreign companies with a primary listing in the UK are required to disclose in their annual report and accounts whether they comply with the corporate governance code of their country of incorporation, and the significant ways in which their corporate governance practices differ from those set out in the UK Corporate Governance Code.)

The purpose of a voluntary code is to raise standards of corporate governance in major companies (although other companies are also encouraged to comply with relevant provisions). It is principles-based, because there is a recognition that the same set of rules is not necessarily appropriate in every way for all companies, and that there will be situations where:

- non-compliance with provisions in the Code is desirable, given the circumstances that the company faces
- implementing a principle of best practice is not always best achieved by following the detailed provisions or recommendations in the Code, and some flexibility should be allowed.

It is also recognised that a Code cannot provide detailed guidelines for every situation and circumstance. In a preface to the UK Corporate Governance Code in 2010, the chairman of the Financial Reporting Council (FRC) commented:

'It seems that there is almost a belief that complying with the Code in itself constitutes good governance. The Code, however, is of necessity limited to being a guide only in general terms to principles, structure and processes. It cannot guarantee effective board behaviour because the range of situations in which it is applicable is much too great for it to attempt to mandate behaviour more specifically than it does.'

1.2 'Comply or explain' and 'apply or explain'

In the UK, the Listing Rules require listed companies to comply with the UK Corporate Governance Code or explain any non-compliance. In other countries there is a view that the word 'comply' will encourage companies to follow the provisions of a code in all its details, without giving proper consideration to the principles that underpin the code. This encourages a **box-ticking approach**, and a view that the detailed provisions must be followed without considering whether the provisions might actually be appropriate or a suitable way of applying the governance principles in the actual circumstances.

For this reason some countries have adopted what they call an **'apply or explain' rule** (or approach), not a 'comply or explain' approach. The King Code III (the governance code for South Africa) gives its reasons for doing this:

'The "comply or explain" approach could denote a mindless response to the King Code and its recommendations, whereas an "apply or explain" regime shows an appreciation for the fact that it is often not a case of whether to comply or not, but rather to consider how the principles and recommendations can be applied.'

The UK Corporate Governance Code recognises the dangers of a 'box-ticking' mentality with 'comply or explain' and stresses that it is not intended to be a set of rules:

'The Code is not a rigid set of rules ... It is recognised that [non-compliance with a provision] may be justified in particular circumstances if good governance can be achieved by other means.'

The Code then goes on to suggest that when a company is in breach of one of its provisions, the explanation for non-compliance should be clear. Shareholders may wish to discuss the situation with the company, particularly if their voting intentions at an AGM may be influenced by the non-compliance:

'Whilst shareholders have every right to challenge companies' explanations if they are unconvincing, they should not be evaluated in a mechanistic way and departures from the Code should not be automatically treated as breaches.'

TEST YOUR KNOWLEDGE 3.1

(a) What is the difference between principles and provisions in a code of corporate governance?
(b) In the UK, how does the 'comply or explain' rule apply to foreign companies with a premium listing?
(c) What is the difference between 'comply or explain' and 'apply or explain'?
(d) What is a box-ticking approach to compliance with corporate governance requirements and how might such an approach be harmful for companies?

2 Corporate governance codes and guidelines in the UK

2.1 The UK Corporate Governance Code

There has been a code of corporate governance for listed companies in the UK since the Cadbury Code in 1992. From 1998 it was the Combined Code and in 2010 a revised code was re-named the UK Corporate Governance Code. The Financial Reporting Council (FRC) has responsibility for the Code.

It is useful to look at the main sections of the Code, to see what the main areas of corporate governance are. The Code has five sections:

- Leadership. This contains principles and provisions relating to the responsibilities of the board as a whole, its chairman and its non-executive directors.
- Effectiveness. This section is concerned with the effectiveness of the board of directors. It deals with issues such as the composition of the board of directors, the appointment and re-election of directors, induction and training for directors, and annual performance reviews for the board, its committees and individual directors.
- Accountability. This section deals with the accountability of the board of directors, and also its responsibility for risk and risk management, including internal control risk (see also Chapter 10).
- Remuneration. The fourth section of the Code contains principles and provisions relating to the remuneration of directors and senior executives.
- Relations with shareholders. The final section of the Code sets out the responsibilities of the board for establishing a dialogue with shareholders, and using the AGM to communicate with shareholders and encourage their participation.

The Combined Code, which was replaced by the UK Corporate Governance Code in 2010, used to have a section that was addressed specifically to institutional shareholders, and dealt with the responsibilities of institutional investors for good corporate governance. This has now been replaced by a separate UK Stewardship Code, which is also the responsibility of the FRC.

2.2 Additional guidance

When the Combined Code was published in the UK in 2003, there was some uncertainty about how some aspects of the Code should be applied. This led to the development of three additional guidelines, which are all now the responsibility of the FRC.

- A report was produced on the role of the chairman and independent non-executive directors, known as the Higgs Report (or the Higgs Guidance). This was updated in 2010 following a review on behalf of the FRC by the ICSA, and amended guidance was issued with the title 'Improving Board Effectiveness'.
- Another report was published providing more detailed guidance on the role of the audit committee. It was originally called the Smith Report (after the name of the committee chairman) but is now called the FRC Guidance on Audit Committees.

- A third report, known as the Turnbull Report, was published giving additional guidance on the responsibilities of the board for the systems of risk management and internal control in the company. This is still called the Turnbull Guidance.

Relevant sections of the UK Code and the guidelines will be described in subsequent chapters.

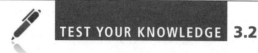

TEST YOUR KNOWLEDGE 3.2

(a)   Which body is responsible for the UK Code of Corporate Governance?

(b)   What are the five sections of the UK Corporate Governance Code?

3   OECD Principles of Corporate Governance

In 1999, the Organisation for Economic Co-operation and Development (OECD) issued some non-binding principles on corporate governance. These were reviewed and amended in 2004. They are intended to serve as a reference point for countries to use when evaluating their legal, institutional and regulatory provisions for corporate governance. They also offer guidance and suggestions for stock exchanges, investors, companies and other bodies involved in developing good corporate governance practices.

Unlike national codes of corporate governance, such as the UK Code, the OECD Principles do not contain any detailed provisions about how the principles should be applied in practice. They are simply a set of main principles and supporting principles, with some additional explanations or 'annotations'. The principles deal with six aspects of governance, as follows.

1   Ensuring the basics for an effective corporate governance framework.
2   The rights of shareholders and key ownership functions.
3   The equitable treatment of shareholders.
4   The role of stakeholders in corporate governance.
5   Disclosure and transparency.
6   The responsibilities of the board.

3.1 Ensuring the basics for an effective corporate governance framework

The OECD Principles begin with a statement that the corporate governance framework should:

- promote transparent and efficient markets
- be consistent with the rule of law, and
- clearly articulate the division of responsibilities among different supervisory, regulatory and enforcement authorities.

In the UK these basics are probably accepted as 'normal' for public companies, but it is a useful reminder that this is not necessarily the case at all times or in all countries.

3.2 The rights of shareholders and key ownership functions

The framework of principles provided by the OECD is notable because of the emphasis they give to shareholder rights. It should be remembered that the principles are intended to apply to all countries with public companies, not just to countries with advanced economies or only with an Anglo-Saxon corporate culture.

An initial principle is that equity shareholders have certain property rights that should be protected. These are the rights to:

- secure methods of ownership registration
- transfer shares, e.g. by selling them
- obtain relevant information about the company on a timely and regular basis

- participate and vote in general meetings of the company
- elect and remove directors
- share in the profits of the company.

These may seem basic rights, but they have not been respected at all times in all countries.

The principles also state that shareholders should have the right to be informed about matters that would fundamentally change the company and to participate in decisions about them. Examples of such matters are:

- amendments to the constitution of the company
- authorising the issue of additional shares
- extraordinary transactions, such as the transfer of all or most of the assets of the company (which would effectively mean the sale of the company, or substantially all of it).

Shareholders should in particular have rights to information about and to vote on matters that

To allow shareholders the opportunity to exercise their voting rights properly, the OECD Principles include guidelines for the conduct of general meetings. Shareholders should be given sufficient information about the matters to be raised at a forthcoming general meeting, including questions relating to the external audit, and should be given this information in good time. They should also be given full and timely notification of the date, time and location of general meetings. Shareholders should be given an opportunity at a general meeting to put questions to the board of directors, including questions relating to the external audit, and should be able to vote in person by attending the meeting or by proxy. The votes of shareholders not in attendance should carry equal weight to the votes of shareholders who do attend a general meeting. This guideline was aimed at preventing the board of directors from packing a general meeting with supporters and making it difficult for other shareholders to:

- find out when and where a general meeting will be held
- find out what issues will be discussed and voted on, or
- cast a vote if they are unable to attend.

The OECD guidelines also deal with companies that have a capital structure and shareholder voting rights that allow certain shareholders to obtain a degree of control disproportionate to their shareholding. For example, a company might have a special class of equity shares that gives the shareholders greater voting rights than the main class of equity shareholders. Alternatively, a company might restrict to a maximum amount the number of votes that any individual shareholder can cast, regardless of how many shares the person actually owns. The guidelines do not prohibit such arrangements, but simply state that such capital structures and arrangements 'should be disclosed'.

In many countries, including in Europe, the rules governing mergers and acquisitions do not provide properly for the adequate protection of all shareholders. The guidelines state that the markets for corporate control should be allowed to operate in an efficient and transparent manner. Shareholders should be informed of the details of a proposed takeover bid and their rights. During the course of a takeover attempt, transactions in the sale of the target company's shares should occur at transparent prices and under fair conditions that protect the rights of all the shareholders. For example, a higher price should not be offered for the shares of some of the shareholders when the same price is not offered or available to other shareholders.

In some countries, companies are able to use anti-takeover devices ('poison pills'). In stating that such devices should not be used to 'shield management from accountability' the OECD has commented:

'Both investors and stock exchanges have expressed concern over the possibility that widespread use of anti-takeover devices may be a serious impediment to the functioning of the market for corporate control. In some instances, takeover defences can simply be devices to shield the management from shareholder monitoring.'

The principles do not make any particular recommendations to institutional investors about actively using their votes, but state that institutional investors acting in a fiduciary capacity 'should disclose their overall corporate governance and voting policies with respect to their investments, including the procedures that they have in place for deciding on their voting rights'.

3.3 The equitable treatment of shareholders

The previous section on the OECD Principles is concerned with the rights of shareholders. The equitable treatment of shareholders is a different issue, and is concerned with ensuring that all shareholders in the same class receive equal treatment, and that some do not receive more favourable treatment than others. The OECD Principles state that:

- all shareholders in the same class should be treated equally
- insider trading and 'abusive self-dealing' should be prohibited, and
- directors and senior executives should be required to disclose to the board any material interest they may have in transactions with the company.

The OECD was concerned about unfair treatment of minority shareholders by major shareholders, and of foreign shareholders (often US institutional shareholders) by boards of directors and major shareholders, as the following examples show.

- In a takeover negotiation, major shareholders might be offered better terms by a bidder than small shareholders.
- Company meetings might be held at short notice and subject to voting procedures that make it difficult for foreign shareholders to vote.

Consequently, the OECD Principles state that:

- 'Minority shareholders should be protected from abusive actions by … controlling shareholders … and should have effective means of redress.'
- 'Impediments to cross-border voting should be eliminated.'
- 'Company procedures should not make it unduly difficult or expensive to cast votes.'

These principles are more easily stated than applied in practice, however, as notes to the OECD Principles acknowledge:

'Investors' confidence that the capital they provide will be protected from misuse or misappropriation by corporate managers, board members or controlling shareholders is an important factor in the capital markets. Corporate boards, managers and controlling shareholders may have the opportunity to engage in activities that may advance their own interests at the expense of non-controlling shareholders … One of the ways in which shareholders can enforce their rights is to be able to initiate legal and administrative proceedings against management and board members. Experience has shown that an important degree of the extent to which shareholder rights are protected is whether effective methods exist to obtain redress for grievances at a reasonable cost and without excessive delay.… There is some risk that a legal system, which enables any investor to challenge corporate activity in the courts, can become prone to excessive litigation.… In the end, a balance must be struck between allowing investors to seek remedies for infringement of ownership rights and avoiding excessive litigation.'

The rights of foreign shareholders are also a matter for some concern in corporate governance. The basic problem is that foreign shareholders may not be given the opportunity to exercise their rights in full. The notice of a general meeting might be sent out too late for the shareholders to organise representation at the meeting and difficulties may be placed in the way of voting by proxy, e.g. electronic voting may not be allowed.

The OECD Principles argue for the fair treatment of foreign shareholders. Given the growing investments of investment institutions (particularly from the USA) in companies in other countries, this is an issue that may become more significant. For example, many politicians and company managers in Germany were offended by the success of 'activist' UK and US shareholders in the Deutsche Börse (the German stock market) in 2005 in forcing their company to back down from its plans to take over the London Stock Exchange. They took the view that the powers of shareholders should not be allowed to restrict the company's management from pursuing policies that they considered to be in the best interests of the company.

Insider dealing and market abuse

Under the general heading of equitable treatment of shareholders, an OECD Principle is that 'insider trading and abusive self-dealing should be prohibited'. In its comments on the principles, the OECD added that insider dealing is prohibited by law or securities regulations in most

OECD countries, although it was not illegal in some jurisdictions and in others, enforcement of the laws was not rigorous.

Disregard for the rights and equitable treatment of minority shareholders is best understood by studying examples and case histories. A well-publicised case, which was eventually amicably resolved, was a dispute between the fashion company Gucci and LVMH.

 CASE EXAMPLE 3.1

Luxury goods company LVMH had a large shareholding in fashion company Gucci, a Dutch-registered company. However, in March 1999, the Pinault-Printemps-Redoute group (PPR) acquired a 42 per cent stake in the company. The PPR share purchase was arranged through a $3 billion increase in Gucci's capital, diluting LVMH's stake from 34 per cent to 20 per cent. LVMH applied to the Enterprise Chamber of the Amsterdam Court of Appeals, in an attempt to get the capital increase annulled.

Meanwhile, Gucci instigated criminal proceedings against LVMH for alleged defamation, backed by PPR.

In a counter-move, LVMH said it would ask the US Securities and Exchange Commission (SEC) to examine the disclosure of a stock option plan of Gucci. (Gucci shares were listed in New York as well as in Amsterdam.) LVMH believed it had discovered an unlawful move to cover up the true nature of the share options offered at the time of the PPR share acquisition in Gucci, and believed it had sufficient evidence to force PPR to make a full takeover bid. (Under Dutch company law, PPR did not have to make a full takeover bid for Gucci even though it had control of the company.)

In November 2000, LVMH had already asked the Dutch court to establish whether two employees in Gucci, the chief executive and the chief designer had received eight million undisclosed share options in return for their supporting the PPR bid in 1999. Gucci counter-argued that the share options were granted later, and only about six million (not eight million) were granted. The two managers disclosed that their stock options were equal to 5 per cent of Gucci's equity. The SEC was now being asked to examine whether Gucci had violated rules for stock options in terms of disclosure and audit under US accounting rules, rather than under the less rigorous Dutch laws.

The crux of the argument was still the validity of the capital increase, but the stock option argument had opened up a second route of investigation.

LVMH wanted to be bought out by PPR, but a sticking point was the share price. Gucci shares were trading below the price that LVMH wanted. The shareholders' meeting at which the stock option plan had been agreed in June 2000 was held just two days after PPR and LVMH announced that they had failed to find a settlement to their dispute, and LVMH abstained from the vote. LVMH said later that it did not vote against the stock options because it had been misled about who would benefit from them.

In January 2001, Gucci made a complaint to the European Commission, alleging that LMVH was abusing its dominant market position and that LMVH was using its 20 per cent stake in Gucci to frustrate Gucci's business plans. It called on the Commission to force LMVH to divest itself of the shareholding. Gucci was complaining that another lawsuit filed by LMVH in the Netherlands disputing Gucci's takeover of the fashion house Yves St Laurent was not in the interests of shareholders.

3.4 The role of stakeholders in corporate governance

The OECD Principles also recognise that companies should recognise the rights and role of stakeholders other than shareholders. The emphasis is mainly on the recognition of legal rights. The corporate governance framework should 'recognise the rights of stakeholders established either by law or mutual agreements, and should 'encourage active co-operation between corporations and stakeholders in creating wealth, jobs and the sustainability of financially sound enterprises'.

- Stakeholder rights established by law or by mutual agreements should be respected.
- Performance-enhancing mechanisms for employee participation should be allowed to develop.
- Employees and other stakeholders should be should be able to 'freely communicate their concerns about illegal or unethical practices to the board'.
- Corporate governance should be complemented by an efficient insolvency framework and the effective enforcement of creditors' rights.

3.5 Disclosure and transparency

Another aspect of the OECD Principles is a requirement for 'timely and accurate' disclosure of information by a company. (The importance of transparency for good corporate governance was explained earlier.) The information provided by companies should include material information about their financial and operating results, corporate objectives, major share ownership, details of members of the board and their remuneration, material risk factors, material issues affecting employees and other stakeholders, and governance structures and policies.

Channels for disseminating information should provide equal, timely and cost-efficient access to relevant information by users.

An annual audit should be conducted by an independent, competent and qualified auditor. External auditors should be accountable to shareholders and owe a duty of professional care to the company in the conduct of the audit. The audit provides external and objective assurance that the financial statements give a fair representation of the financial position and performance of the company.

In notes to the Principles, the OECD comments:

'A strong disclosure regime is a pivotal feature of market-based monitoring of companies and is central to shareholders' ability to exercise their voting rights. Experience in countries with large and active equity markets shows that disclosure can also be a powerful tool for influencing the behaviour of companies and for protecting investors. A strong disclosure regime can help to attract capital and maintain confidence in the capital markets.... Insufficient or unclear information may hamper the ability of the markets to function, may increase the cost of capital and result in a poor allocation of resources.'

In the case of multinational companies operating in other countries, disclosure also helps to improve the understanding of the local populations about the company, its activities and its policies, with respect to environmental and ethical standards and the relationships between the companies, and the communities in which they are operating.

3.6 The responsibilities of the board

The OECD Principles end with a section on the responsibilities of the board of directors:

'The corporate governance framework should ensure the strategic guidance of the company, the effective monitoring of management by the board and the board's accountability to the company and the shareholders.'

The board should fulfil certain key functions, including:

- reviewing and guiding corporate strategy, risk policy, annual budgets and business plans, major capital expenditures and acquisitions and divestments
- monitoring the effectiveness of corporate governance
- the recruitment and compensation of key executives
- the remuneration of key executives, which should be aligned with the long-term interests of the company and its shareholders
- the integrity of the company's accounting and financial reporting systems, including the external audit, and the effectiveness of systems of control and risk management
- overseeing the process of disclosure and communication.

TEST YOUR KNOWLEDGE 3.3

(a) What are the six aspects of corporate governance covered by the OECD Principles?

(b) List six rights of shareholders in the OECD Principles.

(c) Why might here be impediments to cross-border voting by foreign shareholders?

(d) Identify three ways in which the treatment of shareholders might be made more equitable, according to the OECD Principles.

(e) What do the OECD Principles state about the role of stakeholders in corporate governance?

(f) According to the OECD Principles, what are the benefits of a strong disclosure regime?

4 The King Code

Most codes of corporate governance are based on a 'shareholder' approach or 'enlightened shareholder' approach to corporate governance. The King III Code (2009), which is the corporate governance code for South Africa, is distinctive because:

■ it is a well-established governance code for a major developing economy, and

■ it adopts a 'stakeholder inclusive' approach to corporate governance.

In taking this approach, King III includes some aspects of governance that are not found in other voluntary codes such as the UK Code. The 'stakeholder inclusive' approach of the King Code is described in Chapter 1.

The introduction to King III states that the 'philosophy of the (Code) revolves around leadership, sustainability and corporate citizenship'.

■ Leadership. Companies should be given effective leadership, which should be characterised by the ethical governance values of fairness, accountability, responsibility and transparency.

■ Sustainability. This is the ability of a company to operate its business without compromising the needs of future generations, e.g. through excessive consumption of natural resources or irreversible environmental damage. King III refers to sustainability as a 'primary moral and economic imperative'.

■ Corporate citizenship. A company is a person and like other people it should be aware of its role in society and the need to act as a good citizen. Companies should therefore consider social and environmental (sustainability) issues in the decisions that they make.

Another feature of the King Code is its requirement for 'integrated reporting'. This is reporting that integrates financial aspects of performance with sustainability aspects. (It also recommends forward-looking elements to reporting as well as reporting of historical performance.)

The King II Code (2004) recommended that companies should produce annual sustainability reports, in addition to their financial statements. King III goes further by calling for an integrated report that combines financial and sustainability issues.

An additional unique feature of King III is that it states specifically that, unlike its predecessor King II, it applies to all entities regardless of the form of their establishment or incorporation. This means that the Code applies not only to companies, but also to public sector and not-for-profit organisations.

The Code itself has nine sections. (Relevant parts of these will be discussed in relevant chapters of this text.) Some of these deal with the same issues as the UK Code; others are different or possibly unique.

■ Ethical leadership and corporate citizenship. Compared with the UK Code, King III places more emphasis on ethical behaviour.

■ Boards and directors.

■ Audit committees.

■ The governance of risk.

- The governance of information technology (**IT**). This was not included in the earlier King II Code. However, it was considered that directors should be made aware of their responsibilities for IT governance, including the formulation of IT strategy (having due regard for IT risk) and the need for a robust framework for internal control of IT systems.
- Compliance with laws, rules, codes and standards. King III states specifically that **compliance risk** (see Chapter 10) should be an integral part of the risk management process.
- Internal audit. King III states that there should be an effective risk-based internal audit, and an internal audit function.
- Governing stakeholder relationships. By taking an 'inclusive stakeholder' approach to governance, the board of directors should manage the 'gap' between the expectations of stakeholders and company performance. Relations with stakeholder groups should be managed, and decisions should be taken by the board in the best interests of the company, which means taking into account the legitimate interests and expectations of stakeholders.
- Integrated reporting. As stated earlier, companies should provide integrated annual reports, combining financial and sustainability aspects of performance.

TEST YOUR KNOWLEDGE 3.4

What are the three broad concepts on which the King III Code is based?

5   Guidance from institutional investor groups

5.1 Institutional investors and their interest in corporate governance

Codes of corporate governance are directed primarily at companies and their leaders. However, it is also accepted that in order to achieve best practice in corporate governance, shareholders should be prepared to participate in the process. Most shareholders in major companies are now institutional investors, such as pension funds, life assurance companies and mutual funds. These investor organisations often delegate decisions about which investments to buy or sell to investment managers in specialist fund management companies, but they retain responsibility for the investments they hold and should be accountable to their beneficiaries (such as pension scheme members and life assurance policy holders).

The interests of institutional investors in good corporate governance can be explained as follows.

- Investors expect a return on their investment. Most evidence suggests that well-governed companies deliver reasonable returns over the long term, and shareholders in these companies are less exposed to downside risk than shareholders in companies that are not so well governed.
- Some decisions by companies can have important implications for profits, dividends and share values, in either the short term or the long term. For example, business risk strategies and risk management, and executive remuneration policies, have implications for profitability. Investment institutions, as shareholders in companies, should expect to have some influence on policies relating to risk management and executive remuneration, as well as on the appointment of company leaders, particularly company chairmen.
- Institutional investors also have legal responsibilities (fiduciary duties) to the individuals on whose behalf they invest. For pension funds, these individuals are the beneficiaries of the funds. In fulfilling their responsibilities, institutions should try to ensure that they make a decent return on investment, and promoting good corporate governance is one way of trying to do this.

5.2 Institutional investor groups and guidance on corporate governance to members

Most institutional investors are members of 'trade associations' that represent their interests on certain matters (such as discussions with government). In the UK, institutional investor organisations include the Association of British Insurers (ABI) and the National Association of Pension Funds (NAPF). The ABI and NAPF, together with the Investment Management Association and the Association of Investment Trust Companies, are represented on the Institutional Shareholders Committee (ISC), which is a representative body for the UK investment industry as a whole.

With the development of corporate governance in the UK, these institutional investor groups have provided guidance to their members on how they should deal with various aspects of corporate governance, particularly in matters that they may be able to influence decision-making by the companies in which they invest. In the UK, guidance from institutional investment groups to their members includes the following.

- A Joint ABI/NAPF Statement on Executive Contracts and Severance (reviewed 2008): this deals with matters such as trying to ensure that there are no 'rewards for failure' when senior executives are dismissed for poor performance.
- ABI Guidelines on executive remuneration (policies and practices), revised in 2009.
- NAPF Corporate Governance Policy – Voting Guidelines (2007), which provides guidance to members on how they should vote when a company is in breach of provisions in the corporate governance code.
- ISC Code on the Responsibilities of Institutional Investors, (revised in 2009) which was used as the basis for developing the UK Stewardship Code, published in 2010.

These guidelines are described in relevant chapters of this text.

5.3 ICGN Global Corporate Governance Principles

The International Corporate Governance Network (ICGN) was established in 1995 at the instigation of a group of major international institutional investors. It consists of investors, companies, financial intermediaries and academics; its aims are to promote international dialogue and best practice in corporate governance. A significant feature of ICGN policy pronouncements arises from the fact that ICGN is an organisation of global investment institutions, and its policy guidelines apply to the activities of its members in all countries in which they invest.

The ICGN has published its own Global Corporate Governance Principles (revised 2009), which its members are encouraged to promote in the countries in which they invest.

- The Principles are for general application worldwide.
- The Principles are based on a belief that effective dialogue between shareholders and companies is essential for improving corporate governance and maintaining standards of good governance.

The ICGN has commented:

'High standards of corporate governance will make boards properly accountable to shareholders for the companies they manage on their behalf. They will also help investee companies to make decisions and manage risks to deliver sustainable and growing value over time. Pursuit of high standards of governance is therefore an integral part of institutions' fiduciary obligations to generate value for beneficiaries.'

The ICGN Principles are similar to other codes of corporate governance, but with a strong emphasis on ethical behaviour in companies. They are based on an 'enlightened shareholder' approach.

'The objective of companies is to generate sustainable shareholder value over the long term ... Companies will only succeed in achieving this in the long run if their focus on economic returns and their long-term strategic planning include the effective management of their relationships with stakeholders, such as employees, suppliers, customers, local communities and the environment as a whole.'

TEST YOUR KNOWLEDGE **3.5**

Why should institutional investors want companies to comply with a code of corporate governance?

6 Role of the company secretary in corporate governance

6.1 General responsibilities

Company secretaries are in a unique position to fulfil an important role in corporate governance. They are not members of the board of directors, and so do not have direct responsibility for corporate governance and accountability to shareholders. Without being a director, they know about what is going on at board level in the company and can give advice and assistance, not only to the chairman but also to the board as a whole, board committees and individual directors.

Company secretaries have a range of different responsibilities, including company administration matters and providing support for board meetings. Many of these responsibilities are not related to corporate governance, or are only indirectly related to corporate governance. Some responsibilities, however, are specifically related to corporate governance matters.

The King III Code includes as one of its principles that the board should be assisted by a company secretary who is 'competent, suitably qualified and experienced'. As recommended practice, it specifies what the governance-related responsibilities of the company secretary should be.

The UK Code includes some specific references to the role of the company secretary in corporate governance.

- Under the direction of the chair[person], the company secretary should be responsible for ensuring good information flows:
  – within the board and its committees, and
  – between senior managers and non-executive directors.

Good corporate governance relies on communication and the exchange of information, and the company secretary is in a position to help ensure that this happens. By attending board meetings and committee meetings, he should ensure that relevant information is passed from board to committee or from one committee to the board or another committee. By acting as a point of communication and contact for non-executive directors (NEDs), the company secretary should also be able to contribute to the flows of information between NEDs and senior executive managers in the company.

- 'The company secretary should be responsible for advising the board through the chairman on all governance matters.' The company secretary should have a full understanding of corporate governance requirements, and should be able to identify governance issues that arise and advise the board accordingly.
- 'All directors should have access to the advice and services of the company secretary, who is responsible to the board for ensuring that board procedures are complied with.'

'Improving Board Effectiveness' (referred to previously) suggests that the company secretary should consider whether board procedures and other governance procedures are 'fit for purpose' and should advise the chairman of any improvements that could be made.

The specific responsibilities of a company secretary for corporate governance matters should be decided by the company. The 'ICSA Guidance on Corporate Governance Role of the Company Secretary' (2008) provides a list of responsibilities relating to corporate governance. These are divided into three main areas.

1 Specific responsibilities derived from the UK Code.
2 Responsibilities relating to statutory and regulatory compliance.
3 Corporate responsibility.

The responsibilities in the ICSA Guidance are listed below in section 6.2 (although the list is not comprehensive). They are detailed, and you may find it useful to return to this section when you have finished reading this text.

6.2 Specific responsibilities derived from the UK Code

Some responsibilities can be assumed from the provisions of the UK Code. The broad headings below are the same as those in the Guidelines.

Board composition and procedures

- The company secretary should establish a list of matters reserved for decision-making by the board as a whole. Having established a list, the company secretary should ensure that the board deals with all the matters on it, and should not delegate responsibility for decision-making for any matter on the list to executive management or a board committee.
- The UK Code requires companies to establish certain board committees. The company secretary should ensure that the constitution and membership of committees of the board comply with the requirements of the Code, and that their membership is refreshed regularly.
- The company secretary schedules meetings of the board and its committees, and helps the chairman to set agendas for meetings. Much of this work is administrative and not directly related to corporate governance, except that a properly functioning board is essential to good governance. The secretary should also ensure that information and papers for meetings are sent out to board members in advance.
- It should also be the responsibility of the company secretary to ensure that appropriate directors' and officers' liability insurance is available for the directors. The reason for this is explained in Chapter 5.
- A requirement of good governance is that there should be succession planning for major positions on the board, particularly for the positions of chairman and chief executive officer. Non-executive directors (NEDs) are usually appointed in the UK for periods of three years, after which time their contract is not renewed or they are invited to stand for re-election. The company secretary should provide assistance with succession planning by the board and should oversee the rotation of NEDs.

Board information, development and relationships

- The company secretary should contribute to the flow of information between the board and its committees, and between the board and executive management. Good governance also depends on fostering relationships.
- The secretary should therefore be responsible for facilitating information flows between board members and should help to develop good relationships between executive directors and NEDs.
- The company secretary should develop relationships with individual board directors, and act as a source of information and advice. The secretary should be the main point of contact for NEDs.
- The company secretary should arrange for directors to take independent professional advice at the company's expense, if they require it.
- The secretary should arrange for major shareholders to be offered the opportunity to meet with newly appointed NEDs, if they wish to do so.
- The company secretary should also have responsibility for the development of board directors, by:
  - building induction programmes for NEDs after being appointed to the board
  - assisting with performance evaluations of the board, its committees and board members. (Performance evaluation is required by the UK Code, for which the chairman has most of the responsibility. The company secretary should provide support and assistance to the chairman.)

Remuneration

The UK Code contains provisions on the remuneration. These include a requirement for companies to have a remuneration committee to decide the remuneration of executive directors and other senior executives.

- The company secretary should be responsible for ensuring that the remuneration committee is familiar with the guidelines on remuneration in the Code and that the company's remuneration policies for directors and senior executives comply with the Code.
- The secretary should also ensure that any new long-term incentive scheme is submitted to shareholders for approval.
- The chairman of the remuneration committee is required to make a report in the annual report and accounts. In addition there is a legal requirement in the UK for companies to include a directors' remuneration report in the annual report and accounts. The company secretary should help with the drafting of these reports.

Audit and internal control

- The UK Code contains provisions on the responsibility of the board for the review of internal control in the company. There is also a requirement for companies to have an audit committee. The company secretary should have a detailed knowledge of these requirements and should advise the board and audit committee on their application.
- The secretary should also ensure that the company's whistleblowing procedures are implemented, and should monitor their effectiveness.

Relationships with shareholders

The company secretary should ensure that the board keeps in touch with shareholders' opinions on a continuing basis and should manage relations with major institutional shareholders on corporate governance issues.

Disclosure and reporting

The UK Code requires that certain disclosures should be made on corporate governance matters, in the annual report and accounts or in circulars to shareholders or on the company's web site. The company secretary should be responsible for ensuring that these disclosures are made.

6.3 Responsibilities of the company secretary for statutory and regulatory compliance

Compliance with laws and regulations is a requirement of good governance.

- The company secretary should be responsible for ensuring compliance with all the statutory and regulatory requirements relating to corporate governance. In the UK, these include the requirements of the Companies Act 2006, and the Listing Rules, Prospectus Rules and Disclosure and Transparency Rules of the Financial Services Authority (FSA).
- The company secretary should also be responsible for ensuring proper disclosures of information to the stock market (the dissemination of regulatory news announcements to the stock market, such as trading statements and information about share dealings by directors).
- The Listing Rules require companies to comply with the **Model Code**, which sets out rules about when directors should not usually be permitted to buy or sell shares in the company. For example, directors should not deal in the company's shares during 'close periods' before an announcement of their financial results. The company secretary is responsible for making sure that directors understand the requirements of the Model Code and comply with them.
- The company secretary should also keep under review all legal and regulatory developments affecting the company's operations, and making sure that the directors are properly briefed about them.

6.4 The company secretary and corporate social responsibility

The ICSA Guidelines refer to guidelines on corporate social responsibility published by the ABI and NAPF on how to incorporate environmental, social and governance issues into investment decision-making. The ICSA Guidelines state that:

'[T]he company secretary should share responsibility with relevant specialist functions for ensuring that the board is aware of current guidelines in this area and that it identifies and takes account of the significance of corporate responsibility issues in its stewardship and oversight of the company.'

The company secretary should therefore try to ensure that the interests of all important stakeholders are borne in mind when important business decisions are made, particularly those affecting employees.

The role of the company secretary should be kept in mind as you read the following chapters on the various major issues in corporate governance.

The following case example (3.2) is an illustration of the involvement of the company secretary in corporate governance matters, in this case where concerns were raised about illicit or improper share dealings by a director, and poor communications between the company and its shareholders. Issues of corporate governance are rarely clear-cut, as this case suggests. As a useful exercise, you should consider the role of the company secretary in these events and what the company should have done, if anything, differently from what it actually did do.

CASE EXAMPLE 3.2

In March 2000, the Anglo-French IT services company Sema acquired LHS, an Atlanta-based software company that sold mobile phone billing software. It was bought for £3 billion in March 2000, at a 75 per cent premium to its current share price. Herr L, the founder of LHS and a major shareholder, became a non-executive director of Sema. The acquisition by Sema was seen as a strategic move by the company into the US market.

Investors started to become uneasy when Sema's interim results were announced in September 2000. These had very little to say about either the acquisition or Sema's expansion plans in the USA. Analysts were also annoyed by what they regarded as window dressing in the company's interim financial results. The company included in its profits a £14.3 million refund from its Swedish pension fund. Stripping out this one-off non-operational item would have left operating profits much lower. The share price fell by about 17 per cent in the week the interim results were announced.

Unbeknown to Sema's board, in the week leading up to its interim results, Herr L had started selling shares in large quantities. He sold 1.8 million Sema shares for £24 million in the run-up to the Sema interim results, making three separate sales through a German bank. Each of these sale transactions was in breach of the Model Code requirement for UK listed companies that directors should not deal in shares of their company in a 'closed period', i.e. in the two months before the announcement of the company's results. Her L sold a further 800,000 shares for £9 million on the day the results were announced. The average sale price for these transactions was about £12.70.

Sema's company secretary was reported as saying that he learned of the improper sales on 11 October, when he was contacted by an investment bank. It appears that when Sema purchased LHS, an arrangement in the transaction (intended to avoid German tax penalties) was that Herr L would hold on to his LHS shares after the acquisition, but with an option to exchange them for Sema shares from January 2002. From the investment bank, the Sema company secretary learned in October that Herr L had exercised his option over part of his stake, ahead of schedule and without notifying anyone at Sema.

The company secretary tried to obtain details of the share deals by Herr L, in order to make an announcement to the stock market. However, he needed the transaction dates, number of shares sold and price received for Sema in order to make a statement. He found Herr L obstructive and unhelpful and it took two weeks to get the information. Sema then informed the UK Financial Services Authority.

Herr L apparently stated that he made the share transactions in all honesty, misunderstanding the stock exchange rules. Investors, however, were sceptical, since LHS had been quoted on the **Nasdaq** stock market in the US, and so its directors would have been familiar with the restrictions in the US on director share dealings.

A further problem for Sema was the poor trading performance of LHS after the acquisition. Far from growing, as the market had been led to expect when the acquisition was made in March, sales slumped from £42 million in the first quarter to £36 million in the second quarter and £24 million in the third. Profits were consequently well below expectations, and the company issued a profits warning on 25 November. The market suspected that Sema had known about the problem long before it issued the warning. The share price fell 44 per cent on the day of the profits warning, and a further 10 per cent (to 329 pence) on the following Monday. This was a long way below the level at which Herr L had sold his shares in September.

On 28 November, the *Financial Times* carried a report that the company was going to ask him to resign 'after concluding that he was damaging the company's standing with investors'. On 29 November, Sema announced that Herr L had resigned. The story of the share dealings by Herr L was given in the financial press, and it was reported that Herr L had apparently not followed Sema's formal compliance procedures and that an investigation was started by the FSA. Investors were said to be angry about the delay in informing the FSA, with questions asked about the company's compliance procedures. How could the company have remained ignorant for so long about the share dealings by Herr L? With the profits warning as an additional problem, and the lack of adequate information from the company, the credibility of the company's senior management was at risk.

(Continued)

CASE EXAMPLE **3.2** (*Continued*)

The *Daily Telegraph* commented on 3 December 2000:

'A botched acquisition, a profits warning and a share dealing scandal have shredded management credibility. After years of growth, the shares ended last week at a sixth of their February peak, threatening Sema's place in the **FTSE** 100 index.'

A stockbroker was reported to have said:

'The issue for everyone, and the reason the shares have been so weak since the profits warning, is that the market believes it has been misled for most of this year.'

The financial press identified a major problem as poor communications with investors by Sema's chief executive and finance director, caused to some extent by language difficulties. The report ended with a comment that the board needed strengthening, with someone who will 'fight the corner' of British investors, given the dominance of French directors at the moment.

On 4 December, the Sema share price fell to 271p and the company subsequently dropped out of the FTSE 100. This followed a decision by the company to postpone until January a scheduled meeting with analysts on 6 December. The company stated the postponement was 'appropriate' and that it had set up a board committee to investigate why the company did not warn earlier of the problems at LHS, and to examine the share dealings of Herr L. The board committee would consist of the company's chief executive officer, the board chairman, one other non-executive director and the company secretary, and would be advised by solicitors Clifford Chance.

This immediately raised another corporate governance concern. One institutional investor, holding 2 per cent of Sema shares, was reported to have said that an independent committee would have been more appropriate.

'We would prefer the involvement of independent accountants other than their auditors. This would give added credibility to the outcome of the process, and seems particularly necessary given the constitution of the committee ... Clearly the co-operation of Sema's executives is important. But it would have been quite possible for the board to have set up a committee with the power to co-opt the views of the executives from time to time.'

The company's difficulties were not yet over. On 23 January 2001, it made another profits warning. The share price fell 47.5p. Its pre-tax profit forecast for the year was reduced to £90 million to £95 million, having been cut the previous November from £130 million to £100 million. Sema also announced that it had started the search for a new chief executive to replace 'in due course' the current CEO. The low level of Sema's share price was thought to make it vulnerable to a bid. France Telecom, the largest investor in Sema with a shareholding of 18 per cent, stated that it did not regard its holding in Sema as 'core'.

6.5 The company secretary as the conscience of the company

In the context of business ethics and corporate governance, the company secretary can be described as the 'conscience of the company'. There will often be situations where it is the best short-term interests of a company to ignore best governance practice or even act in an unethical way. For example, the board of directors may want to 'window dress' the financial statements and make the financial performance of the company appear better than it really is. Or a company may wish to bribe a government official in order to win a major contract. The company secretary should speak out against bad governance and unethical practice, and remind the board and senior executives of the appropriate course of conduct and the principles of good governance that they should apply.

In order to act in this way, as a 'conscience' for the directors and senior executives, the company secretary must be independent-minded, and should not be under the influence of any other individual, such as the company chairman or CEO.

6.6 Independence of the company secretary: appointment and removal

The role of the company secretary in corporate governance is such that it is essential to ensure his or her independence from undue influence and pressure from a senior board member. An ICSA Guidance Note on Reporting Lines for the Company Secretary has commented:

'Boards of directors have a right to expect the company secretary to give impartial advice and to act in the best interests of the company. However, it is incumbent on boards of directors to ensure that company secretaries are in a position to do so, for example by ensuring that they are not subject to undue influence of one or more of the board of directors. If the board fails to protect the integrity of the company secretary's position, one of the most effective in-built internal controls available to the company is likely to be seriously undermined. The establishment of appropriate reporting lines for the company secretary will normally be a crucial factor in establishing that protection.'

The Guidelines recommend that:

- in matters relating to his duties as an officer of the company, the company secretary should, through the chairman, be accountable to the board as a whole
- if the company secretary has additional executive responsibilities to his core role, he should report to the CEO or appropriate executive director on such matters
- the company secretary's remuneration should be set (or at least noted) by the board as a whole, or by the remuneration committee of the board on the recommendation of the chairman or CEO.

The UK Code also makes a specific provision about the appointment and removal of the company secretary. It states that: 'Both the appointment and removal of the company secretary should be a matter for the board as a whole.' In this way, the company secretary is not dependent on one individual, or a small group of board members, for his or her job.

Similar recommended practice is included in King III, which states that the board should appoint and remove the company secretary and empower the individual to enable him to fulfil his duties properly. It also recommends that the company secretary should have an 'arm's length relationship' with the board, emphasising the requirement for independence.

6.7 The company secretary and the in-house lawyer

Many of the corporate governance duties of a company secretary have a legal aspect or involve compliance with regulations or a voluntary code of governance practice. It could be argued that many of these tasks could be performed better by an in-house lawyer working for the company, since corporate lawyers are specialists in company law and regulations.

However, as stated previously, independence is a critical aspect of the corporate governance role of the company secretary. To perform the task effectively, the company secretary needs to be as independent as it is possible for a full-time employee to be.

In his legal work, an in-house lawyer must at times consider the specific interests of the company and individual directors, and may be required to advise them on the most appropriate way of dealing with legal issues that arise. In performing this role, the lawyer will often have to 'take sides' to represent a particular interest. This would be inconsistent with the requirement to be independent when advising on governance issues.

It would therefore be inappropriate for the company's in-house lawyers to take on the responsibilities for corporate governance that are usually given to the company secretary in a listed company. An individual who has trained and qualified as a professional lawyer could be a suitable candidate to act as company secretary or take on corporate governance responsibilities within the company, but only if two key conditions are applied:

- the qualified lawyer does no legal work for the company, and also
- the independence of the individual can be protected in the same way as for a company secretary, with the board as a whole responsible for appointing and dismissing him or her and deciding his remuneration.

TEST YOUR KNOWLEDGE 3.6

(a) List 15 corporate governance responsibilities that could be given to a company secretary.
(b) What is the meaning of 'conscience of the company'?
(c) Why is it important that a company secretary should be independent, and how can this independence be protected?
(d) Why is it inappropriate to give corporate governance responsibilities to an individual who acts as the company's in-house lawyer?

CHAPTER SUMMARY

■ A voluntary code of corporate governance is a code issued by a well-established body that sets out principles and provisions of best practice in corporate governance. Most codes are issued nationally, but some are issued internationally.

■ National codes of corporate governance are effectively 'enforced' on listed companies in practice, because of a 'comply or explain' or 'apply or explain' requirement in the rules for companies whose shares are traded on the main national stock market(s).

■ Voluntary codes of governance are principles-based, and consist of general principles supported by some practical provisions. They are not 'rules-based' (i.e. consisting of many detailed rules for application).

■ The code of corporate governance in the UK is the UK Corporate Governance Code (revised 2010). This is the responsibility of the Financial Reporting Council, which also has responsibility for other supporting guidance on the application of the Code in practice, including the Higgs Guidance, the FRC Guidance on Audit Committees and the Turnbull Guidance.

■ The OECD has issued general principles of good corporate governance, with the intention of encouraging countries to improve their standards of corporate governance.

■ The code of corporate governance for South Africa is the King III Code. This is notable for its advanced views on corporate governance, including an integrated approach to corporate governance and the view that companies should act as corporate citizens, with concerns for social and environmental issues as well as financial issues.

■ The application of best practices in corporate governance also required commitment from the major shareholders, who should try to exert influence over the companies in which they have invested. Institutional investors, such as the ABI and NAPF in the UK, issue guidelines for their members and encourage their application. In the UK a code of corporate governance for shareholders was issued by the Institutional Shareholders Committee (ISC) in 2009, and this has been adopted as a UK Stewardship Code by the FRC.

■ The company secretary should be in a position to ensure that best practice in corporate governance is implemented by the company, and that the board is kept aware of governance issues.

Governance in practice

■ **LIST OF CHAPTERS**

■ **OVERVIEW**

The second part of this study text looks at the practical application of principles and provisions of best practice in corporate governance.

Chapter 4 describes the governance responsibilities of a board of directors, which should be specified in a list of 'matters reserved for the board'. In most countries companies have unitary boards, but in some countries have a two-tier board structure. With a unitary board, directors have the same legal duties and fulfilling these duties is an aspect of good corporate governance. The chapter discusses the roles of the company chairman and chief executive officer, the size of a board and the composition of its members and the roles of non-executive directors and board committees in helping to apply best governance practice.

Chapter 5 considers several aspects of boardroom practice and behaviour, such as the appointment, election and re-election of directors, and performance appraisal of the board, its committees and individual directors. It then goes on to discuss boardroom ethics and the ethical conduct of directors. It concludes by explaining the potential personal liability of directors for their actions, and how directors' and officers' liability insurance provides some protection against this.

Chapter 6 explains why the remuneration of directors and senior executives has been a major corporate governance issue and the problems with the practical application of suitable principles of remuneration. Issues covered in this chapter include the elements of a remuneration package, the role of the remuneration committee of the board and the problems of 'rewards for failure' when individual directors are dismissed for poor performance.

Chapter 7 explains the importance of reporting as an element of corporate governance, because reports should provide both accountability and transparency. Companies report mainly to shareholders, but some reports are produced for other stakeholders. The main report from a company is the annual report and accounts, which includes the annual financial statements of the company and also a variety of mainly narrative reports. The annual report and accounts are required to give a 'true and fair view', and the external auditors are expected to give an independent professional opinion to shareholders about whether they do so. The chapter discusses the relationship between a company and its external auditors, the independence and competence of the auditors, and the role of the audit committee, and the relevance and importance of these for good governance.

Agency theory in corporate governance is based on a conflict of interests between shareholders and the directors. Chapter 8 explains how the interests of shareholders can be protected, and the objectives of the company promoted, through a constructive two-way relationship between institutional shareholders and the board ('shareholder engagement' and 'dialogue') and constructive use of the annual general meeting. Institutional shareholders should be prepared where necessary to use their influence and exercise their rights, and the chapter explains shareholder activism and also the responsible use of voting.

■ LEARNING OUTCOMES

Part Two should enable you to:

- advise on governance issues across all sectors, ensuring that the pursuit of strategic objectives is in line with regulatory developments and developments in best practice

- assess the relationship between governance and performance within organisations

- advise on the structure and composition of the board to maximise effectiveness and meet regulatory requirements

- understand, interpret and apply the principles of the UK Corporate Governance Code in relation to boardroom practice and behaviour

- understand the role and responsibilities of the key board committees

- understand, interpret and apply the principles of the UK Corporate Governance Code in relation to audit and disclosure

- understand the powers and rights of shareholders and the responsibility of both the board and institutional investors to develop constructive dialogue between each other with a view to improving corporate governance.

PART 2 CASE STUDY

Stenning Tull Limited was established 15 years ago by Don Stenning and Rebecca Tull. The company specialises in design consultancy and in recent years has grown rapidly through both organic growth and small acquisitions. It now employs about 200 people and is highly profitable. The board of directors consists of a chairman (Don Stenning), a chief executive officer (Rebecca Tull), a finance director, an artistic design operations director and a technical design operations director. There are no non-executive directors.

The board would like to grow the business and see opportunities for further acquisitions. The company's bank is reluctant to lend more to finance growth unless the company increases its equity capital, and Don Stenning and Rebecca Tull, who between them own 90 per cent of the company's shares, have been persuaded by take the company on to the stock market in order to raise equity capital.

An investment bank has agreed to sponsor the company's flotation as a listed company.

To prepare for a stock market flotation, the investment bank has asked for extensive and detailed information about the company. Among the information gathered are the following items.

1 Don Stenning and Rebecca Tull both have salaries of £750,000 per year and in addition receive dividends on their shares of about £500,000 each per year. They have contracts of employment with the company that entitle them to a notice period of three years.

2 The other directors earn between £125,000 and £175,000 each in salary, and are entitled to a notice period of one year. All three have some equity shares in the company. The company has no formal annual bonus scheme and no long-term incentive scheme for its executives.

3 The company has used the same firm of auditors, Penn Ledger, since its incorporation.

4 Because the company's main shareholders are also senior board members and executive managers in the company, board meetings have combined board business with senior executive management committee business.

5 The company produces an annual directors' report and financial statements in accordance with the minimum requirements of the Companies Act.

6 Company secretarial duties are performed by the senior accountant.

7 Stenning Tull has already become a public limited company (plc) in preparation for the stock market flotation.

The investment bank has advised Don Stenning and Rebecca Tull that major changes will be required in corporate governance arrangements before the company can become a listed company. In addition, they will both be expected to reduce their shareholding to 10% of the total equity in the company, and the flotation will therefore involve both an issue of new shares for cash and also the sale of some of their shares by both Don Stenning and Rebecca Tull.

4 The board of directors

■ CONTENTS

■ INTRODUCTION

An efficient and effective board of directors is a key requirement of good corporate governance. The board should have a clear idea of its responsibilities, and should fulfil these to the best of its abilities. There should be a suitable balance of skills and experience, and also power, on the board. This chapter considers the role and composition of a board and the duties and responsibilities of directors and committees. By the end of the chapter, you should have an understanding of what is needed to achieve an effective board, and how a weak board structure is a threat to good corporate governance.

This chapter (and the following chapter) will make a number of references to principles and provisions of the UK Corporate Governance Code, and in particular Sections A and B of the Code on Leadership and Effectiveness. There will also be references to both the Higgs Guidance and the ICSA's review of the Higgs Guidance on behalf of the Financial Reporting Council. The ICSA's review, 'Improving Board Effectiveness', contains guidance on a range of issues relating to the board of directors. The purpose of this guidance is to help board of directors with implementing Sections A and B of the Corporate Governance Code.

1 Governance responsibilities of the board

The board of directors is the key decision-making body in a company. A company should have an effective board of directors dedicated to ensuring that the company achieves its objectives. The UK Code states as one of its main principles:

'Every company should be headed by an effective board, which is collectively responsible for the long-term success of the company.'.

The 2010 Code introduced the phrase 'long term' into this principle. This recognises that the board should not focus on short-term achievements, if these are inconsistent with longer-term success.

The UK Code also states that the role of the board should be to:

- provide entrepreneurial leadership for the company within a framework of prudent and effective risk management
- set the company's strategic aims
- make sure that the necessary financial and human resources are in place for the company to meet its objectives
- review management performance
- set the company's values and standards
- make sure that the company's obligations to its shareholders are understood and met.

The guidance 'Improving Board Effectiveness', referred to at the beginning of this chapter, states that an effective board is one that:

- provides direction for management and creates a high-performance culture
- through its non-executive directors, provides control through checks and balances and holding management to account
- takes well-informed and high-quality decisions
- behaves ethically and promotes throughout the company behaviour that is consistent with the culture and values of a high-performing organisation
- creates the right framework for helping directors to meet their statutory duties. The statutory duties of directors in the UK are described later.

The guidance adds that a board which demonstrates that it has suitable governance policies and systems in place is much more likely to generate trust and support among its shareholders and other stakeholders.

Except for its monitoring role, the board should not get involved with operational matters, for which the responsibility is delegated to executive management. The Code also states that all directors must act in what they consider to be the best interests of the company, without specifying what those 'best interests' are or might be. King III identifies other responsibilities for the board, including responsibility for:

- ethical conduct and sustainability of the business
- compliance with laws, regulations and codes, and
- governing the relationships between the company and its stakeholders.

The ICGN Global Corporate Governance Principles link the governance responsibilities of the board much more closely to the main issues in corporate governance that were described in Chapter 1. These are summarised briefly in the table below.

TABLE 4.1 ICGN Principles: responsibilities of the board

Responsibility for achieving corporate objectives	Board effectiveness	Financial reporting and other disclosures	Risk management and internal control	Remuneration
Reviewing and approving corporate strategy, budgets and business plans; setting objectives and monitoring performance; oversight of major capital expenditures, acquisitions and divestments.	Ensuring a formal and transparent system for the nomination and election of directors, and the replacement of directors; responsibility for succession planning; reviewing its own performance.	Overseeing the integrity of the company's accounting and financial reporting systems; overseeing the integrity of the external audit process; overseeing the process of disclosure and communications, and being available for dialogue with shareholders.	Ensuring that an appropriate system of internal control is in place; responsibility for risk policy; overseeing a formal risk management process; monitoring and managing conflicts of interest, including misuse of corporate assets and related party transactions.	Responsibility for the alignment of remuneration of executive directors and other key executives with the long-term interests of the company and its shareholders.

1.1 Decision-making by the board

Decision-making is an important board activity. The board should have clear policies about what matters need a board decision or approval, and the processes required for each type of decision. Good decision-making can be improved by giving directors sufficient time to prepare for meetings, allowing sufficient time for issues to be discussed at board meetings, and making clear to executives what action they must take to implement board decisions.

'Improving Board Effectiveness', referred to in the introduction to this chapter, recognises that even with suitable policies and procedures for decision-making, the quality of decision-making by the board can be impaired by:

- the effect of a dominant personality on the board or a dominant group
- a reluctance by executive directors to involve the non-executive directors in certain matters
- a weak organisational culture, including inadequate information
- weak ethical standards
- lack of awareness of significant risks ('poor line of sight to all areas of significant risk').

The guidance suggests that boards may wish to consider extra measures to reduce the risk of flawed decisions, such as:

- commissioning an independent report on a matter
- seeking advice from an expert
- setting up a specific sub-committee to look at a matter in detail
- having additional meetings so that a matter can be discussed several times before a final decision is reached, giving the directors more time to consider the issues and discuss their concerns.

TEST YOUR KNOWLEDGE 4.1

(a) According to the UK Code of Corporate Governance, what are the governance responsibilities of a board of directors?

(b) What additional governance responsibilities of the board are identified in the King III Code?

(c) According to the guidance 'Improving Board Effectiveness', what are the characteristics of an effective board?

---

2 Unitary and two-tier boards

Companies in most countries have **unitary boards**, consisting of both executive and non-executive (NEDs) directors under the leadership of the company chairman. A unitary board makes collective decisions and is accountable to the shareholders. It is commonly accepted governance practice that the non-executive directors in a listed company should be independent, although this is not a legal requirement.

2.1 Two-tier boards

Some countries, including Germany and Austria, have **two-tier boards**. With a two-tier structure, there is a **supervisory board** and a **management board**.

- The management board is responsible for managing the company. It is led by the chairman of the managing board, who is the chief executive officer; its members are appointed by the supervisory board. It develops strategy for the company, in co-operation with the supervisory board, and is responsible for implementing the agreed strategy. It also has responsibility for risk management and for the preparation of the annual financial statements (which are examined by the auditors and the supervisory board; see also Chapter 7).
- The supervisory board is responsible for general oversight of the company and of the management board. Its members are elected by the shareholders, except that in public companies

with more than 500 employees, a minimum proportion of the supervisory board must consist of representatives of the employees. The supervisory board is led by the company chairman. It advises the management board and must be involved in decision-making on all fundamental matters affecting the company; these include 'decisions or measures which fundamentally change the asset, financial or earnings situations of the enterprise' (German Corporate Governance Code). The audit committee consists entirely of supervisory board members.

In a two-tier structure, there has to be a functional relationship between the management board and the supervisory board, and the chairman of the supervisory board plays a key role. He is responsible for making sure that the two boards work well together, and the most powerful individuals in the company are the chairman of the supervisory board and the chief executive officer who is in charge of the management board. The chief executive officer reports to the supervisory board chairman. If the relationship between these two works well, the chairman will effectively speak for the management at meetings of the supervisory board.

The management board consists entirely of executive directors. The supervisory board consists entirely of NEDs. In Germany, supervisory board members include:

- representatives of trade unions and/or the company's employees
- representatives of major shareholders
- former executives of the company.

The supervisory board NEDs are therefore not necessarily independent, particularly employee representatives. It can therefore be difficult to reconcile the differing views of employee representatives and representatives of major shareholders, without antagonising the executives on the management board. On the other hand, where there is a large number of former executives on the supervisory board, there is a risk that the supervisory board could take a lenient and easy-going view of what management are doing. In addition, some independent supervisory board directors might well be senior managers of other companies, where they are management board members. These individuals might therefore sympathise with the views of the management board.

The success of corporate governance depends on a good working relationship between the supervisory board and the management board, and in particular a good working relationship between the company chairman and the head of the management board. The German code states that 'the Management Board and Supervisory Board co-operate closely to the benefit of the enterprise' and the management board should discuss the implementation of strategy regularly with the supervisory board

2.2 Criticisms of the two-tier board structure

There have been some criticisms of a two-tier board structure. The main concerns are as follows.

- Supervisory boards are too big, having up to 20 members. German supervisory boards include a large number of employee representatives, and large numbers can result in inefficient meetings.
- It has been common to appoint retired former managers of the company to the supervisory board, and these individuals might be tempted to retain some influence over the actions and operational decisions of their successors. This is not the purpose of a supervisory board. On the other hand, if former managers are appointed to the supervisory board, the supervisory board will benefit from their knowledge and experience of the business. A new law introduced in Germany in 2009 now prohibits former managers from 'moving upstairs' to the supervisory board for at least two years, unless the move receives the support of at least 25 per cent of shareholders; the rationale for this law is that for the first two years after retiring, a former executive will not be sufficiently independent.
- Companies with more than 500 employees are required to have workers' representatives or trade union representatives on the supervisory board. (Companies with more than 2,000 employees are required to have an even greater percentage of employee representatives on the supervisory board.) This requirement is an enforcement of the principle of 'co-determination', embodied in German law, that the workers as well as the management and owners should determine the future of their companies. Unfortunately, workers' representatives often lack the competence to consider strategic issues or are not independent from the company. In some instances, worker members of a supervisory board opposing planned initiatives by

the company have been accused of leaking confidential information to the press. Concerns about information leaks can damage communications between supervisory and management boards.

The German Corporate Governance Code suggests that in practice, the unitary board system and two-tier board system are becoming much more similar 'because of the intensive interaction between the Management Board and the Supervisory Board'. The German Code also suggests that the two types of board structure are 'equally successful'.

Developments in some German companies in recent years also suggest that the supervisory boards of large German companies are becoming more responsive to the interests of their shareholders.

 CASE EXAMPLE 4.1

There was a bribery scandal at German engineering group Siemens in 2005, with allegations that senior managers had paid €1.3 billion in bribes worldwide to secure contracts. The supervisory board took legal action against the managers concerned, including the former chief executive officer and chairman of the company. Its members believed that they had no choice other than to take legal action to obtain compensation, since shareholders would otherwise sue them. In December 2009 it was announced that settlements had been reached with nine former Siemens executives, who each agreed to pay compensation to the company.

The **Walker Report** in the UK (2009) on corporate governance in banks considered whether unitary boards may have contributed to the scale of the financial crisis in 2007–2009, and whether a two-tier board structure might therefore be more suitable for large banks. Its conclusions were fairly critical of the two-tier structure:

'In practice, two-tier structures do not appear to assure members of the supervisory board of access to the quality and timeliness of management information flow that would generally be regarded as essential for non-executives on a unitary board. Moreover, since, in a two-tier structure, members of the supervisory and executive boards meet separately and do not share the same responsibilities, the two-tier model would not provide opportunity for the interactive exchange of views between executives and NEDs, drawing on and pooling their respective experience and capabilities in the way that takes place in a well-functioning unitary board. Directors and others whose experience is substantially that of the unitary model appear generally to conclude that such interaction is commonly value-adding in the context of decision-taking in the board. On this criterion, the two-tier model did not in general yield better outcomes than unitary boards in the period before the recent crisis phase and recent experience, in particular in Germany, Switzerland and the Benelux makes no persuasive case for departing from the UK unitary model.'

 TEST YOUR KNOWLEDGE 4.2

(a)   What are the respective roles of a management board and a supervisory board in a two-tier board structure in Germany?

(b)   What are the criticisms of a two-tier board structure?

---

3   The powers of directors

3.1 The general powers of directors

The powers of the board of directors are set out in a company's constitution. In the UK, this means the articles of association. UK company legislation provides a standard form of articles of association (known as **model articles of association**). For companies formed under the

Companies Act 1985 this means the 1985 Table A articles, which most companies have used as a model for their own articles. The Companies Act 2006 revised the model articles and introduced different model articles for public and private companies. (The Companies (Model Articles) Regulations 2008 apply to all new companies incorporated under the Companies Act 2006 on or after 1 October 2009.) The powers of directors are broadly comparable, however, in all the model articles.

Article 3 of the new model articles for public companies states: 'Subject to the articles, the directors are responsible for the management of the company's business, for which purpose they may exercise all the powers of the company.' The shareholders may instruct the directors what they should do (or should not do) but only by passing a special resolution in general meeting, and a special resolution of the shareholders cannot invalidate what the directors have already done.

Article 5 of the new model articles for public companies states that the directors may delegate any of the powers conferred on them under the articles to any person (e.g. the chief executive officer) or committee (e.g. to an audit committee), by such means (including by power of attorney), to such an extent, in relation to such matters or territories, and on such terms and conditions as they think fit. If the directors so specify, any such delegation may authorise further delegation of the directors' powers by any person to whom they are delegated. For example, the chief executive officer may delegate some of his powers to other executive managers.

Standard articles of association in the UK, therefore, provide for the board collectively to be the main power centre in the company, but with delegation of powers to **board committees** and executive directors.

A distinction should be made between the powers and duties of executive directors as members of the board, and their responsibilities as managers of the company. Under the articles of association, managers have neither powers nor duties. The relationship they have with the company (including their authority and responsibilities) is established by their contract of employment and by the law of agency.

3.2 Borrowing powers of directors

In the UK, there is no restriction in law on how much the directors can borrow on behalf of their company unless the constitution (articles of association) includes a specific restriction. As far as the law is concerned, the borrowing powers of companies are limited only by what lenders are prepared to make available to them. Conceivably, the directors could therefore put the investment of their shareholders at risk by borrowing more than the company can safely afford.

4 The duties of directors to their company

The directors act as agents of their company. They have certain duties, which are to the company itself, but not to its shareholders, its employees or any person external to the company, such as the general public. Although a company is a legal person in law, it is not human. Since the relationship between directors and the company is by its very nature impersonal, it might be wondered just what 'duty' means.

The concept of duty is not easy to understand, and it is helpful to make a comparison with the duties owed by other individuals or groups.

Examples of individuals owing a duty to something inanimate are not common, although personnel in the armed forces have a duty to their country. It is more usual to show loyalty to something inanimate than to have a duty. For example, individuals might be expected to show loyalty to their country, and they might voluntarily show loyalty to their sports team or group of friends or work colleagues. Arguably, solicitors have a duty to their profession to act ethically, although the solicitors' practice rules in the UK specify that solicitors owe a duty of care to their clients. Similarly, doctors have a duty to act ethically, but their duty is to their patients. Duty is normally owed to individuals or a group of people. It might therefore be supposed that directors should owe a duty to their shareholders and possibly to the company's employees, but this is not the case.

- Accountability and responsibility should not be confused with duty.
- Directors have a responsibility to use their powers in ways that seem best for the company and its shareholders.

- They should be accountable to the owners of the company, the shareholders, for the ways in which they have exercised their powers and/or the performance of the company.
- They have duties to the company.

If a person is guilty of a breach of duty, there should be a process for calling him to account. There might be an established disciplinary procedure, for example, in a court or before a judicial panel, with a recognised set of punishments for misbehaviour. With companies, however, disciplinary mechanisms are difficult to apply in practice, except perhaps in extreme cases of misbehaviour. Where measures are taken, they are likely to be initiated by shareholders seeking legal remedies on behalf of the company.

4.1 Common law duties and statutory duties of directors

Before the Companies Act 2006, the main legal duties of directors to their company were duties in common law – a **fiduciary duty** and **duty of skill and care** to the company. These are duties to the company, not its shareholders. The Companies Act 2006 has now written the common law duties of directors into statute law. It states that these general duties 'are based on certain common law rules and equitable principles as they apply to directors, and have effect in place of those rules and principles as regards the duties owed to a company by a director' (Companies Act 2006, section 170). The Act goes on to state that the statutory general duties should be interpreted in the same way as the common law rules and equitable principles.

It is therefore useful to begin by looking at the nature of the common law duties, and what they have meant.

4.2 Fiduciary duty of directors

'Fiduciary' means given in trust, and the concept of a trustee (as established in US and UK law) is applicable. The directors hold a position of trust because they make contracts on behalf of the company and also control the company's property. Since this is similar being a trustee of the company, a director has a fiduciary duty to the company (not its shareholders).

If a director were to act in breach of his fiduciary duty, legal action could be brought against him by the company. In such a situation, 'the company' might be represented by a majority of the board of directors, or a majority of the shareholders, or a single controlling shareholder.

A director would be in breach of his fiduciary duty in carrying out a particular transaction or series of transactions in any of the following circumstances.

1   The transaction is not in any way incidental to the business of the company. For example, the chief executive officer of a building construction company might decide to trade in diamonds and lose large amounts of money in these diamond trading transactions.
2   The transaction is not carried out *bona fide*, which means in good faith, with honesty and sincerity.
3   The transaction has not been made for the benefit of the company but for the personal benefit of the director or an associate. A director has a fiduciary duty to avoid a conflict of interest between him or herself personally and the company, and must not obtain any personal benefit or profit from a transaction without the consent of the company. In other words, it would be a breach of fiduciary duty for a director to make a **secret profit** from a transaction by the company in which he has a personal interest.

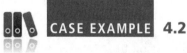 **CASE EXAMPLE** 4.2

A company wishes to buy some land and has identified a property for which it would be prepared to pay a large sum of money. The chief executive officer secretly sets up a private company of his own to buy the property, and then sells this on to the company of which he is chief executive officer, making a large profit in the process. The actions of the chief executive officer are breach of fiduciary duty, because his actions have not been *bona fide* and he has made a secret profit at the expense of the company. Under the Companies Act 2006 these actions of the chief executive officer would now be a breach of statutory duty.

4.3 A director's duty of skill and care

Directors are also subject to a duty of skill and care to the company. This was a common law duty that became a statutory duty with the Companies Act 2006. A director should not act negligently in carrying out his duties, and could be personally liable for losses suffered by the company as a consequence of such negligence.

The standard of skill and care expected of a director is the higher of the skill that he has or the skill that would objectively be expected of a director of the particular company. In the case Re D'Jan of London (1993; see Case law 4.2), the judge ruled that the common law duty of care was the equivalent to the statutory test applied by section 214 of the Insolvency Act 1986. This statutory test refers to what would be expected of: 'a reasonably diligent person having both:

- the general knowledge, skill and experience that may reasonably be expected of a person carrying out the same functions as are carried out by that director in relation to the company, and
- the general knowledge, skill and experience that that director has.'

A director is expected to show the technical skills that would reasonably be expected from someone of his experience and expertise. If the finance director of a scientific research company is a qualified accountant, he would not be expected to possess the technical skills of a scientist, but would be expected to possess some technical skill as an accountant.

The duty of skill and care does not extend to spending time in the company. A director should attend board meetings if possible, but at other times is not required to be concerned with the affairs of the company. This requirement is perhaps best understood with NEDs, who might visit the company only for board or committee meetings. The duties of a director are intermittent in nature and arise from time to time only, such as when the board meets. If a director holds an executive position in the company, a different situation arises, because he is an employee of the company with a contract of service. This contract might call for full-time attendance at the company or on its business. However, this requirement arises out of his job as a manager, not out of his position as a director.

It is also not a part of the duty of skill and care to watch closely over the activities of the company's management. Unless there are particular grounds for suspecting dishonesty or incompetence, a director is entitled to leave the routine conduct of the company's affairs to the management. If the management appears honest, the directors may rely on the information they provide. It is not part of their duty of skill and care to question whether the information is reliable, or whether important information is being withheld.

A board of directors might make a decision that appears ill-judged or careless. However, the courts in the UK are generally reluctant to condemn business decisions made by the board that appear, in hindsight, to show errors of judgement. Directors can exercise reasonable skill and care, but still make bad decisions.

For a legal action against a director to succeed a company would have to prove that serious negligence had occurred. It would not be enough to demonstrate that some loss could have been avoided if the director had been a bit more careful.

 **CASE LAW 4.1**

Dorchester Finance Co. Ltd v Stebbing [1989]

In the UK legal case Dorchester Finance Co. Ltd v Stebbing [1989], a company brought an action against its three directors for alleged negligence and misappropriation of the company's property. The company (Dorchester Finance) was in the money-lending business and it had three directors, S, H and P. Only S was involved full-time with the company; H and P were non-executives who made only rare appearances. There were no board meetings. S and P were qualified accountants and H, although not an accountant, had considerable accountancy experience. S arranged for the company to make some loans to persons with whom he appears to have had dealings. In the loan-making process he had persuaded P and H to sign blank cheques that were subsequently used to make the loans. The loans did not comply with the Moneylenders Acts and they were inadequately secured. When the loans turned out to be irrecoverable, the company brought its action against the directors.

It was held that all three directors were liable to damages. S, as an executive director, was held to be grossly negligent. P and H, as non-executives, were held to have failed to show the necessary level of skill and care in performing their duties as non-executives, even though it was accepted that they had acted in good faith at all times.

4.4 Wrongful trading and the standard of duty and care

The standard of duty and care required from a director has been partly defined in a number of UK legal cases relating to **wrongful trading**. Under the Insolvency Act 1986, directors may be liable for wrongful trading by the company, when they allowed the company to continue trading, but knew (or should have known) that it would be unable to avoid an insolvent liquidation. When such a situation arises and a company goes into liquidation, the liquidator can apply to the court for the director to be held personally liable for negligence. The duty of a director under the Insolvency Act was used in the case of Re D'Jan of London [1993] (see Case law 4.2) to illustrate a director's general duty of skill and care.

CASE LAW 4.2

Re D'Jan of London [1993]

An insurance broker completed a fire insurance proposal form with an incorrect answer, but a director of the company (Re D'Jan) applying for the insurance policy signed the form. The company premises burned down, and the insurance company, on discovering the mistake on the proposal form, repudiated all liability under the policy. The company went into insolvent liquidation. The liquidator brought an action against the director who had signed the proposal form, alleging a failure to exercise reasonable care to the company. The court found that although it would be unreasonable to expect a director to read every word of every document that he signed, in this case the form consisted of a few simple questions that the director was the best person to answer. The director was therefore guilty of a breach of duty of care, although, in this particular case, the director was exonerated on other grounds.

4.5 Duties of directors and delegation

Since directors owe a duty of skill and care to their company, it could be asked how much time and attention a director should give to the company's affairs, and to what extent a director can delegate responsibilities to another person without being in breach of his duty.

CASE EXAMPLE 4.3

Andrew Tuckey, former deputy chairman of Barings bank, was responsible for the supervision of Nick Leeson, the derivatives trader whose unauthorised speculative trading notoriously brought the bank to collapse in 1995. In a case concerning the disqualification of Tuckey as a director, it was alleged that he had failed to exercise his duty of care to the company. The situation was summarised as follows by the judge in the case, Mr Justice Parker.

- Directors, both individually and collectively, have a duty to acquire and maintain sufficient understanding of the company's business to enable them to discharge their duties properly.
- Subject to the articles of association, directors are allowed to delegate particular functions to individuals beneath them in the management chain. Within reason, they are also entitled to have trust in the competence and integrity of these individuals. However, delegation of authority does not remove from the director a duty to supervise the exercise of that delegated authority by the subordinate.
- There is no universal rule for establishing whether a director is in breach of his duty to supervise the discharge of delegated functions by subordinates. The extent of the duty, and whether it has been properly discharged, should be decided on the facts of each case.

When there is a question about the extent of the director's duties and responsibilities, a significant factor could be the level of reward that the director was entitled to receive from the company. Prima facie, the higher the rewards, the greater the responsibilities should be expected.

In the Barings case, Mr Justice Parker concluded that Tuckey had failed in his duties because he did not have a sufficient knowledge and understanding of the nature of the derivatives markets and the risks involved in derivatives dealing (which led to the collapse of Barings). He was therefore unable to consider properly matters referred to the committee of which he was chairman.

TEST YOUR KNOWLEDGE 4.3

What is a fiduciary duty of a director?

5 The statutory general duties of directors: Companies Act 2006

The duties of directors in common law and equity to their company were introduced into UK statute law by the Companies Act 2006 (sections 171–177). These consist of a duty to:

- act within powers
- promote the success of the company
- exercise independent judgement
- exercise reasonable care, skill and diligence
- avoid conflicts of interest
- not to accept benefits from third parties
- declare any interest in a proposed transaction or arrangement.

It is worth remembering that these duties (as in common law) apply to non-executive as well as to executive directors. The fiduciary duty and the statutory duties of directors are referred to in the UK Corporate Governance Code, which includes a supporting principle that: 'All directors are fiduciaries who must act objectively in the best interests of the company and in accordance with their statutory duties.'

The consequences for breach of these duties are most likely to be legal action taken in the name of the company (perhaps by shareholders). However, failure to declare an interest could result in a criminal prosecution of the director concerned.

5.1 Duty to act within powers

A director must act within his powers in accordance with the company's constitution, and should only exercise these powers for the purpose for which they were granted. (However, if a director acts outside his powers to make a contractual agreement with a third party, the company is still liable for any obligation to the third party, provided that the third party has acted in good faith.)

The ICSA's 'Guidance on Directors' General Duties' (2007) suggests that directors must ensure that they comply with the company's constitution. For example, when a group of directors meets, it must be clear whether the meeting is a full board meeting, a meeting of a board committee or an unofficial meeting of directors. Unless the meeting is a formal board meeting, the directors would be acting outside their powers if they took a decision on a matter that is reserved for decision-making by the board.

5.2 Duty to promote the success of the company

A director, in good faith, must act in the way he considers would be most likely to 'promote the success of the company for the benefit of its members as a whole'. The Act does not define 'success', but the term is likely to be interpreted as meaning 'increasing value for shareholders'. However, in doing so, a director must also have regard, among other matters, to the:

- likely long-term consequences of any decision
- interests of the company's employees
- need to foster the company's relationships with its customers, suppliers and others
- impact of the company's operations on the community and the environment
- desirability of the company maintaining its reputation for high standards of business conduct, and
- need to act fairly as between members of the company.

The Act does not create a duty of directors to any stakeholders other than the shareholders (members), but it requires directors to give consideration to interests of other stakeholders in reaching their decisions. The Act specifically mentions employees, customers, suppliers and the community. It therefore appears, in a small way perhaps, to promote a form of enlightened shareholder approach to corporate governance.

This aspect of directors' duties has given rise to some concerns that directors will need to create a 'paper trail' to provide evidence if required in a court of law to show that they have given due consideration to the interests of other stakeholders in their decision-making, although the government has denied that this is intended by the Act.

5.3 Duty to exercise independent judgement

A director must exercise independent judgement. However, this requirement does not prevent a director from acting in a way authorised by the company's constitution (e.g. accepting resolutions passed by the shareholders in general meeting) or from acting in accordance with an agreement already entered into by the company that prevents the director from using discretion. The requirement for independent judgement does not prevent a director from taking advice and acting on it.

The 'Guidance on Directors' General Duties' comments as follows on this duty.

- A director must not allow personal interests to affect his independent judgement. This means that if the board is considering a contract in which a director has a personal interest ideally he should leave the meeting whilst the matter is being discussed. (This is also relevant to the duty of directors to avoid any conflict of interest with the company.)
- An executive director should not attend a board meeting to 'promote a collective executive line'. He should attend the board meeting in his own right and give the board the benefit of his independent opinion.
- Similarly directors representing a particular interest should 'set any representative function aside and make final decisions on their own merits'. For example, a director who is a representative of a family interest in the company 'may consult his family but be clear that he will make the final decision'.

5.4 Duty to exercise reasonable care, skill and diligence

This is similar to the common law duty of care.

5.5 Duty to avoid conflicts of interest

A director has a duty to avoid conflicts of interest with the interests of the company. However, this duty is not breached if the director declares to the board his interest in a transaction and the interest is authorised/approved by the board.

In the commercial world, it is inevitable that many directors will have a potential conflict of interest, whether direct or indirect, with their company. For example, a company might be planning to trade with another company in which one of its directors is a shareholder. In such a situation, the director concerned is required to declare that interest in the proposed contract to the other directors and must not make a secret profit.

A director or a connected person might have a material interest in a transaction undertaken by the company. For example, the company might award a contract to a firm of building contractors to rebuild or develop a property owned by the company, and the director or his/her spouse might own the building company.

A director might also have a direct or indirect interest in a contract (or proposed contract) with the company. For example, the director might be a member of another organisation with which the company is planning to sign a business contract. Such a contract is not illegal, although the company can choose to rescind it should it wish to do so.

If a director has an interest in a contract with the company and has failed to disclose it, and has received a payment under the contract, he will be regarded as holding the money in the capacity of constructive trustee for the company (and so is bound to repay the money).

The 2006 Act recognises three situations in which an actual or potential conflict of interests may arise.

1　A conflict of interest may arise in a situation where the company is not a party to an arrangement or transaction, but where the director might be able to gain personally from 'the exploitation of any property, information or opportunity'. For example, a director might pursue an opportunity for his personal benefit that the company might have pursued itself.

2　A conflict of interest may arise in connection with a proposed transaction or arrangement to which the company will be a party. If a director has a direct or indirect personal interest in any such transaction or arrangement, he must disclose his interest to the board of directors before it is entered into by the company. An example would be a proposal to acquire a target company in which a director owns shares.

3　A third type of conflict of interest arises in relation to existing transactions or arrangements in which the company is already a party. It can be a criminal offence for a director not to make or update his declaration of interest in an arrangement or transaction to which the company is a party.

5.6　Duty not to accept benefits from third parties

A director must not accept benefits from a third party unless they have been authorised by the shareholders or cannot reasonably be regarded as giving rise to a potential conflict of interest. Clearly, accepting a bribe from a supplier in return for awarding a supply contract would be a breach of this duty. It would also be illegal to accept lunch or dinner from the same supplier or customer every week, accepting an all-expenses paid holiday or accepting frequent invitations to 'hospitality' events. On the other hand it should be within the law to accept an invitation to a day out to tennis at Wimbledon, or an invitation to dinner to celebrate the successful completion of a project.

In practice many listed companies already have strict internal policies on the acceptance of gifts and corporate hospitality, especially from other companies that are or might be about to tender for business with the company. An internal policy might include a requirement for a director to obtain clearance from another director before accepting any such benefits, and for all instances of gifts or hospitality to be recorded in a register.

5.7　Duty to declare interests in proposed transactions with the company

This duty is linked to the duty relating to conflicts of interest. A director must declare the nature and extent of his interest to the other directors, who may then authorise it.

A director may have a personal interest in a proposed transaction with the company. For example, a director may own a building that the company wants to buy or rent; or a director may be a major shareholder in another company that is hoping to become a supplier or customer. Proposed transactions do not necessarily create a conflict of interests, but they must nevertheless be declared, and subject to approval by the rest of the board. (If a conflict of interest would arise from the proposed transaction, the director must take measures to ensure that the conflict is avoided.)

5.8　Consequences of a breach of the statutory general duties: derivative actions by shareholders

A director owes his duties to the company, so if the director is in breach of these duties, only the company can bring a legal claim against that director. In practice, this has usually meant that the rest of the board might bring an action against a fellow director in the name of the company.

The 2006 Act states that the consequences of a breach of a director's general duties are the same as if the corresponding common law rule or equitable principle applied, but it does not set out in detail what these consequences should be.

In addition, the Act also introduces a procedure whereby individual members of the company can bring a legal action for a derivative claim against a director. A **derivative action** may be brought in respect of 'an actual or proposed act or mission involving negligence, default, breach of duty or breach of trust by a director of the company'. A shareholder would have to bring the action against a director in the name of the company. If the action is successful, the company and not the individual shareholder would benefit.

The procedures for bringing a derivative action are set out in sections 260–264 of the 2006 Act. They include safeguards designed to prevent individual shareholders from bringing actions that are not reasonable on the basis of the prima facie evidence. Even so, there is a possibility that in future legal actions against directors might be brought by shareholders under the derivatives claims procedure for breach of their general duties.

5.9 Directors' responsibilities to company outsiders

Although the duty of directors is to their company, a breach of that duty could also affect outsiders. When the directors make a contract with an outsider, the contract is binding on the company when it is in accordance with its constitution (articles of association). However, the directors might exceed their powers in making the contract, for example, because they should have obtained shareholder approval first, but failed to do so. Contracts entered into without proper authority are known as 'irregular contracts', and might seem to be void.

An outsider making a contract in good faith with the directors, when the contract is irregular, would be unable to enforce the contract if it is void. On the other hand, if an irregular contract is not void and is enforceable, a company has no protection against the consequences of unauthorised actions by its directors. So should irregular contracts be void or should they be enforceable by an outsider?

The main provision of UK company law is that an irregular contract is binding on a company when an outsider, acting in good faith, enters into the contract and the contract has been approved by the board of directors. The directors will be liable to the company for any loss suffered. This rule means that irregular contracts do not affect third parties (outsiders). Instead, when they occur, they would be a corporate governance problem.

5.10 Related party transactions and the UK Disclosure and Transparency Rules for listed companies

For listed companies, the requirements of UK law are reinforced by the UK Disclosure and Transparency Rules, which include a section on **related party transactions**. In broad terms, a related party means a substantial shareholder of the company, a director of the company, a member of a director's family or a company in which a director or family member holds 30 per cent or more of the shares. A related party transaction is a transaction between a company and a related party, other than in the normal course of business.

For most related party transactions above a minimum size, a listed company is required to:

- make an announcement to the stock market giving details of the transaction
- send a circular to shareholders giving more details, and
- obtain the prior approval of the shareholders for the transaction.

The effect of the Rules should be to prevent directors or major shareholders of UK listed companies from obtaining a personal benefit from any non-business transaction with their company, unless the shareholders have given their approval.

TEST YOUR KNOWLEDGE 4.4

(a) What are the seven statutory duties of directors under the provisions of the UK Companies Act 2006?

(b) In what circumstances is it acceptable for a director to have an interest in a third party transaction with the company?

(c) What is a derivative action for breach of a statutory duty by a director of a UK company?

(d) What are the provisions of the UK Disclosure and Transparency Rules for listed companies with regard to related party transactions with the company?

6　Matters reserved for the board

The main decision-making powers belong to the board of directors. Although the board delegates many of the operational decision-making responsibilities to executive management, it should:

- retain the most significant decisions to itself, and
- monitor the performance of the executive management.

An aspect of corporate governance is therefore the nature of the decisions the board reserves to itself (rather than delegating them to executive management). The UK Corporate Governance Code does not specify which matters should be reserved by the board for its own decision-making, but states simply in a provision that: 'There should be formal schedule of matters reserved for its decision.'

It then goes on to state that the annual report should include a statement of how the board operates and a high-level statement of the types of decision that it reserves for its own decisions and the types of decision that it delegates to executive management.

The ICSA has produced a Guidance Note on the matters that should be reserved for the board's own decision-making, which is consistent with the provisions of the UK Code. The list of items in the Guidance Note is quite long, and includes decisions relating to matters such as:

- approval of strategy
- approval of annual operating and capital expenditure budgets
- oversight of operations (including accounting, planning and internal control systems)
- compliance with legal and regulatory requirements
- performance review
- changes in corporate or capital structure
- approving the annual report and accounts
- declaring an interim dividend and recommending a final dividend
- approval of formal communications with shareholders
- approval of major contracts and investments, and
- approval of policies on matters such as health and safety, corporate social responsibility and the environment.

The company secretary may be given the task of preparing and maintaining the list of matters to be reserved for the board (for board approval), and reminding the board whenever necessary that certain decisions should not be delegated.

TEST YOUR KNOWLEDGE 4.5

List ten matters that should be reserved for decision-making by the board of directors.

7　The roles of chairman and chief executive officer

7.1　The chief executive officer

The chief executive officer (CEO) leads the executive team and is responsible for the executive management of the company's operations. As the title suggests, he is the senior executive in charge of the management team and to whom all other executive managers report. Other executive managers might also be directors of the company, but the CEO is answerable to the board for the way the business is run and its performance.

The CEO and the executive team also have certain corporate governance responsibilities. They have the primary responsibility for:

- communicating to employees the expectations of the board with regard to the company's culture and values, and
- ensuring that appropriate standards of governance are applied at all levels within the organisation.

7.2 The chairman

Whereas the CEO is responsible for the executive management, the chairman's responsibilities relate primarily to managing the board of directors, and ensuring that the board functions effectively. To do this, he needs to ensure that the board discusses relevant issues in sufficient depth, with all the information needed to reach a decision, and with all the directors contributing to the discussions and decision-making. Key roles of a chairman are therefore to:

- set an appropriate agenda for board meetings
- ensure that relevant information is provided to the directors, in advance of the meeting
- encourage open discussions to board meetings, with constructive debate and discussion
- encourage all directors to contribute to discussions and decision-making.

The ICGN Corporate Governance Principles state that the chairman should 'work to create and maintain the culture of openness and constructive challenge which allows a diversity of views to be expressed'. In addition, the chairman represents the company in discussions and dealings with shareholders.

The UK Corporate Governance Code includes similar principles relating to the company chairman, as shown below.

- 'The chairman is responsible for leadership of the board and ensuring its effectiveness on all aspects of its role.'
- 'The chairman is responsible for setting the board's agenda and ensuring that adequate time is available for discussion of all agenda items, in particular strategic issues.'
- 'The chairman should also promote a culture of openness and debate by facilitating the contribution of non-executives in particular and ensuring constructive relations between executive and non-executive directors.'
- 'The chairman should ensure that communications with shareholders are "effective".'

These principles emphasise the role of the chairman in trying to ensure that all directors, and in particular non-executive directors, contribute effectively to board discussions. There is always a risk that individuals who do not work full time for the company may have difficulty in challenging the views of full-time executive directors. The chairman should make sure that this does not happen.

'Improving Board Effectiveness' (2010) states that the role of the chairman is 'pivotal' in creating conditions for an effective board and individual director effectiveness. It provides a list of matters for which the chairman is responsible for:

- setting the board agenda, which should focus mainly on strategy, accountability, competitive performance and value creation
- ensuring that decisions relating to relevant issues are reserved for the board, including decisions about the significant risks that the board is willing to accept in the implementation of its strategy
- making sure that an effective decision-making process operates at board level, and that the board's committees are properly structured with appropriate terms of reference
- encouraging active engagement of all board members in board and committee meetings
- building effective relationships both within and outside the boardroom, built on mutual respect and open communication, between the non-executive directors and the executive management team
- developing a constructive working relationship with the CEO
- consulting the senior independent director when appropriate
- ensuring, in consultation with the nomination committee, that there are effective processes for succession planning and ensuring that composition of the board provides sufficient diversity
- taking the lead on matters relating to director development and acting on the results of formal reviews of board and director performance (discussed in the next chapter)
- ensuring effective communication with shareholders and other stakeholders, and ensuring that all directors are made aware of the views of major investors.

An effective chairman is therefore a team-builder. He should develop a board whose members communicate effectively and enjoy good relationships with each other. He should develop a close relationship of trust with the CEO, giving support and advice whilst still respecting the chief executive officer's responsibilities for executive matters. He should also ensure the effective implementation of board decisions, provide coherent leadership for the company and understand the views of the shareholders.

7.3 Independence of the chairman

As a general rule, the chairman of a listed company should be independent when he is first appointed. This is a provision of the UK Code.

In addition, the CEO of a company should not subsequently become the chairman. This is consistent with the view that the chairman should be independent when he is first appointed: a former CEO will not be independent. (The King III Code, however, states that a former CEO should not become chairman for at least three years after ceasing to be CEO, taking the view that this is sufficient time in which to become independent.) If, exceptionally, it is proposed that the current CEO should become the company chairman when the existing chairman retires, investors should be first consulted. The UK Code also states that the reasons for appointing a former CEO as chairman should be explained to shareholders both at the time of the appointment and in the next annual report and accounts.

- A governance problem with 'promoting' the CEO to become the company chairman is that the incoming CEO may find it difficult to run the company as he wishes because the former CEO is still on the board, monitoring what he/she is doing.
- Even so, there have been several cases where a CEO has gone on to become chairman without any serious protest from shareholders or investor groups. For example, in 2006 the CEO of international bank HSBC, Stephen Green, was appointed as the new chairman of the company.

NAPF's Corporate Governance Policy and Voting Guidelines also recommend that if the chairman is not independent on appointment, the company should consult its investors and explain why it considers the appointment desirable. The shareholders should then consider the case on its merits.

7.4 Separating the roles of chairman and chief executive officer

As leader of the management team and leader of the board of directors, the CEO and chairman are the most powerful positions on the board of directors.

It is important for the proper functioning of the company that the chairman and CEO should be able to work well together. Acting in alliance, the chairman and CEO can dominate the board and its decision-making, particularly if the chairman also has executive responsibilities in the company's management.

When the same person holds the position of both chairman and CEO, there is a possibility that he could become a dominant influence in decision-making in the company. As leader of the executive management team, a chairman-cum-CEO may be reluctant to encourage challenges from NEDs about the company's performance or to question management proposals about future business strategy.

In some countries (including the USA), it is common to find company leaders who are both chairman and CEO, although separation of the roles has become more common there. The UK Code states as a principle that the roles should be separated:

'There should be a clear division of responsibilities at the head of the company between the running of the board and the executive responsibility for the running of the company's business. No one individual should have unfettered powers of decision.'

The UK Code therefore states that the roles of chairman and CEO should not be performed by the same individual. In addition, the division of responsibilities between the chairman and CEO should be set out clearly in writing, to prevent one of them from encroaching on the area of responsibility of the other.

When an individual holds the positions of chairman and CEO, he could exercise dominant power on the board, unless there are strong individuals on the board, such as a deputy chairman or a **senior independent director**, to act as a counterweight. If the individual also has a domineering or bullying personality, the situation will be even worse, because a chairman-cum-CEO who acts in a bullying manner will not listen to advice from any board colleagues, and the board would not function as an effective body.

There is even a risk that the individual will run the company for his own personal benefit rather than in the interests of the shareholders and other stakeholders. The only way to prevent a chairman-cum-CEO from dominating a company is to have an influential group of directors capable of making their opinions heard. However, it is important to distinguish between:

- the position of 'unfettered power' that is created when the roles of chairman and CEO are combined and given to one individual, and
- acting in a dominant or tyrannical way, possibly out of self-interest.

Combining the two roles increases the risk that the company and its board will be dominated by a tyrannical individual, but this does not happen every time.

However, there might occasionally be situations where it is appropriate for the same person to be both chairman and CEO. When a company gets into business or financial difficulties, for example, there is an argument in favour of appointing a single, all-powerful individual to run the company until its fortune has been reversed. The combination of the roles of chairman and CEO might have been necessary in the short term to give a company strong leadership to get it through its difficulties.

 CASE EXAMPLE 4.4

In the UK, Mr Luc Vandevelde was appointed as chairman and CEO of Marks & Spencer some years ago, at a time when its business operations were in difficulty and the share price was falling sharply. This appointment attracted some criticism but appears to have been a successful short-term measure. By 2002, the company's fortunes had improved to the point where he relinquished the position CEO announced his intention to become part-time chairman. However, in 2008 Marks & Spencer's CEO, Sir Stuart Rose, was also appointed as company chairman for a limited period until a successor to the role of CEO could be identified and appointed. This appointment, given the previous appointment of Vandevelde, attracted strong criticism from institutional investors. Institutional investor Legal & General publicly criticised the decision by Marks & Spencer to appoint Sir Stuart Rose as executive chairman, saying it was an arrangement that made it difficult to appoint a successor to Sir Stuart as CEO. However, shareholders could not prevent the appointment of the new chairman because this was a decision of the board. Shareholders were able, however, to vote on the re-election of Sir Stuart Rose as director at the AGM in 2008, and 22 per cent of shareholders either opposed his re-election or abstained in the vote.

 CASE EXAMPLE 4.5

In 2007 the Association of British Insurers stated that it would issue an 'amber top' warning to its members over plans by pharmaceuticals company Shire to appoint its CEO as non-executive chairman. The company also proposed to replace the CEO with the company's long-standing finance director. The director of investment affairs at the ABI was reported to have said: 'The chairman is supposed to oversee strategy and makes sure the board tests it and decision-making is robust (sic). If the chairman was the chief executive who developed the strategy, he is supervising himself. There are risks in that.'

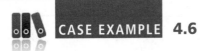 **CASE EXAMPLE** 4.6

The potential risk of a company and board being subjected to a dominant personality can be illustrated by the case of the UK company Polly Peck International. Polly Peck, a FTSE 100 company during the 1980s, was effectively run by a single individual, Asil Nadir, who was both CEO and board chairman. The company collapsed without warning in October 1990. During the administration process, the system of internal controls at the company's London head office was found to be virtually non-existent. As a result, Nadir had been able to transfer large amounts of money from the company's UK bank accounts to personal accounts with a bank in Northern Cyprus, without any questions being asked. After the company collapsed, Nadir fled to Northern Cyprus, where he lives in exile outside the reach of the UK law enforcers.

It has also been suggested that poor corporate governance contributed to the collapse of investment bank Lehman Brothers in 2008. Richard Fuld, chairman and CEO of the company, was a dominant figure and was reported to have personally rejected several deals that might have enabled the company to survive.

7.5 Holding more than one chairmanship of a major company: the chairman's other commitments

A problem with non-executive chairmen – as with non-executive directors generally – is that the individual may not have enough time to devote to the role of chairman because of a large number of other commitments. For example, the chairman of a large company may also be the chairman of other companies, not-for-profit entities and government-sponsored bodies, so that he does not have enough time to fulfil all these roles adequately.

Originally, the UK Code stated that an individual should not be the chairman of more than one FTSE 100 company. However, possibly because of a recognised shortage of individuals capable of acting as chairman of a major company, this provision in the Code was abolished in 2008.

Even so, chairmen need to be able to demonstrate that they have sufficient time to perform their role to the standards expected. NAPF's Corporate Governance Policy and Voting Guidelines state that where a chairman has 'multiple appointments', investors will require a 'compelling explanation' of how the chairman will be able to handle all the various appointments without any detriment to the company. The Walker Report on corporate governance in banks (2009) following the financial crisis of 2007–2009 suggested that the chairmen of large banks would need to spend about two-thirds of their time with the company.

The UK Corporate Governance Code is less specific on the amount of time that a chairman should commit to the company. However, a provision of the Code is that when a chairman is appointed, the **nomination committee** (see also Chapter 5) should prepare a job description, which should:

- include an assessment of the amount of time commitment that should be expected, and
- recognise the need for the chairman to make himself available in a time of crisis.

The chairman's other commitments should be disclosed to the board before his appointment and included in the next annual report and accounts. If there are changes to the time commitment required from or provided by the chairman, these should be disclosed to the board and reported in the next annual report and accounts.

 TEST YOUR KNOWLEDGE 4.6

(a) What is the role of a company chairman? Why should this role not be combined with the role of CEO?

(b) What are the requirements of the UK Code of Corporate Governance with regard to the independence of the company chairman?

(c) In what circumstances is it acceptable for an individual to be the chairman of more than one FTSE 100 companies at the same time?

CASE QUESTION

Refer back to Stenning Tull, the company featured in the case study at the beginning of Part Two. In your view, should a new chairman be appointed externally, or should the current chairman be allowed to remain in place as head of the board of directors? Give your reasons.

8 Size and composition of the board

The effectiveness of a board of directors depends on its size and composition.

8.1 The size of the board

The typical size of a board of directors varies with the size of the company and possibly also the industry or business sector in which it operates. In addition, the average size of boards in listed companies varies between different countries.

- A board should not be larger than it needs to be. Large boards are more difficult to manage, because there are more individuals involved, and board meetings can be very long and waste time.
- On the other hand, boards should be sufficiently large so that its members collectively have the knowledge, skills and experience to make effective decisions.

The UK Code also suggests that the board should be sufficiently large to avoid a situation in which it becomes over-reliant on one or two individuals, for example as chairmen of board committees (nominations, remuneration, audit and risk committees). It states:

'The board should be of sufficient size that the requirements of the business can be met and that changes to the board's composition and that of its committees can be managed without disruption, and should not be so large as to be unwieldy.'

 STOP AND THINK 4.1

Select any listed company that you know. Given the size and complexity of its business, make an estimate of how large its board of directors might be. Next, find the company's website and check the size and composition of its board. (If you have difficulty in finding this information, it should be contained in the directors' report in its report and accounts.) See how close your estimate was to being correct.

8.2 The composition of the board

The composition of a board of directors depends partly on its size. In the UK, the board of a large public company commonly consists of a:

- chairman
- possibly a deputy chairman
- CEO
- senior independent director (who may also be the deputy chairman)
- executive directors
- non-executive directors (NEDs).

Collectively, the members of the board should have sufficient skills and experience to provide effective leadership for the company. This suggests that they should have a variety of different backgrounds and expertise.

There should also be a suitable balance of power on the board, so that one individual or a small group of individuals is unable to dominate the board and its decision-making. In countries such as the UK, it is therefore considered appropriate to appoint independent non-executive directors to a board, because:

■ they act as a counter-balance to executive directors, who may give priority to their own interests above those of the shareholders (and other stakeholders), and
■ they have skills and experience that executive directors do not have, because they come from a different background and so are able to contribute different ideas and views to board discussions and decision-making.

Because they do not have a strong personal financial interest in the company, NEDs are more easily able to represent the interests of shareholders and to act (where required) as a restraint on executive management.

These principles relating to board composition are set out in the UK Code as follows

■ 'The board and its committees should have the appropriate balance of skills, experience, independence and knowledge of the company to enable them to discharge their respective duties and responsibilities effectively.'
■ 'The board should include an appropriate combination of executive and non-executive directors (and in particular independent non-executive directors) such that no individual or small group of individuals can dominate the board's decision-taking.'

In the UK, a key principle of good corporate governance is that there should be a sufficient number of independent NEDs on the board of directors to create a suitable balance of power and prevent the dominance of the board by one individual or by a small number of individuals. The UK Code sets out different requirements for large listed companies and for smaller companies. (Smaller companies are defined as companies outside the FTSE 350 for the whole of the year immediately prior to the reporting year.)

■ Except for smaller companies, at least one half of the board, excluding the chairman, should be independent NEDs.
■ For smaller companies, there should be at least two independent NEDs.

Guidelines about the composition of a unitary board differ between countries. The King III Code, for example, recommends that the majority of directors should be NEDs and the majority of NEDs should be independent, but also adds that there should be at least two executive directors on the board – the CEO and chief finance officer (finance director).

 TEST YOUR KNOWLEDGE 4.7

(a) What would be the disadvantages of a large listed company in the UK restricting the total size of its board to six members?
(b) What are the provisions in the UK Code for the size and composition of the board of directors of a listed company in the FTSE350?

9 Non-executive directors

A non-executive director (NED) is a member of the board of directors without executive responsibilities in the company. NEDs should be able to bring judgement and experience to the deliberations of the board that the executive directors on their own would lack.

To be effective, an NED has to understand the company's business, but there appears to be general consensus that the experience and qualities required of an NED can be obtained from working in other industries or in other aspects of commercial and public life. NEDs may therefore include individuals who:

■ are executive directors in other public companies
■ hold NED positions and chairmanship positions in other public companies
■ have professional qualifications (e.g. partners in firms of solicitors)
■ have experience in government, as politicians or former senior civil servants.

However, research has been carried out into identifying and recruiting suitable individuals as NEDs from a wider variety of sources and backgrounds (see below).

NEDs are expected not only to bring a wide range of skills and experience to the deliberations of the board, particularly in the area of strategy and business development, but also to ensure that there is a suitable balance of power on the board. A powerful chairman or CEO might be able to dominate other executive directors, but in theory at least, independent NEDs should be able to bring different views and independent thinking to board deliberations. Decisions taken by the board should therefore be better and more in keeping with the aims of good corporate governance.

9.1 Higgs Guidance on the role of the non-executive director

The Higgs Report, published in January 2003 and reviewed in 2006, looked at the role and effectiveness of NEDs, and many of the Higgs recommendations were included in the UK's governance code. The Higgs Suggestions for Good Practice were added as an appendix to the code, providing guidance on the role of NEDs. This guidance stated that the role of an NED has four key elements, which non-executives are perhaps in a better position to provide than executives. These were as follows.

- Strategy. NEDs should constructively challenge and help to develop proposals on strategy.
- Performance. NEDs should scrutinise the performance of executive management in achieving agreed goals and objectives, and monitor the reporting of performance.
- Risk. NEDs should satisfy themselves about the integrity of financial information and that the systems of internal controls and risk management are robust.
- People. NEDs are responsible for deciding the level of remuneration for executive directors, and should have a prime role in appointing directors (and removing them where necessary) and in **succession planning** (see also Chapter 5).

These roles explain the requirements for audit, remuneration and nomination committees consisting entirely or mainly of independent NEDs.

9.2 The UK Corporate Governance Code on non-executive directors

The UK Code contains similar views about the role of NEDs.

- A principle of the Code is that as part of their role, NEDs should 'constructively challenge and help develop proposals on strategy'.
- NEDs should also scrutinise the performance of management in meeting agreed goals or targets of performance, and they should monitor the reporting of performance (to ensure that this is honest and not misleading).
- NEDs should satisfy themselves about the integrity of the financial information produced by the company, and that the financial controls and systems of risk management are 'robust and defensible'.
- They should be responsible for deciding the remuneration of executive directors.
- They should have a significant role in the appointment (and where necessary removal) of executive directors and in succession planning for the major positions on the board.

The UK Code recognises there are matters that the NEDs should discuss without executive directors being present, and a provision of the UK Code is that:

- the chairman should hold meetings with the NEDs without executive directors being present, and
- without the chairman and led by the senior independent director (see section 10 'Senior independent directors'), the NEDs should meet at least once a year to discuss the performance of the chairman. They should also meet on other occasions if this is considered necessary or appropriate.

9.3 'Improving Board Effectiveness' on the role of non-executive directors

The review of the Higgs Guidance, 'Improving Board Effectiveness', made the following recommendations.

- In order to become effective contributors to the board, NEDs need to build up a recognition of their contribution among the executive directors. To do this, they should both support the executive directors in their management of the business, but also monitor their conduct within an atmosphere of 'mutual respect'. (This is perhaps more easily stated that achieved in practice!)
- NEDs should make sufficient time available so that they can develop a good understanding of the company and its business. A new NED should insist on receiving comprehensive, formal and tailored induction. Subsequently NEDs should also seek constantly to develop and refresh their knowledge and skills.
- Their letter of appointment should specify the amount of time that the NED will be expected to spend on the company's business, and should indicate the possibility that additional time will be required at times of particular board activity, such as when a takeover is planned or when the company is facing a major problem in its operations.
- Because of the importance of decision-making as a board responsibility, NEDs should insist on receiving accurate, clear and comprehensive information sufficiently in advance of board meetings, so that they have time to read and study all the material. (Although the chairman, assisted by the company secretary, is responsible for providing timely, clear and comprehensive information, NEDs should make sure that they get it.)
- NEDs should seek to learn the views of shareholders and other stakeholders, either directly or indirectly (conveyed to them by the chairman or CEO or – in special circumstances – the senior independent director).

9.4 The Walker Report on the role of non-executive directors in banks

The Walker Report, referred to earlier in this chapter, suggested that the role of NEDs is crucial to the effectiveness of a board in formulating and implementing business strategy. The report included the following comments.

- Value of NEDs. Shareholders have a right to expect that in a unitary board there should be a material input from the NEDs to decisions on strategy and oversight of strategy implementation. It should also be expected that when there is such shared decision-taking between executive and non-executive directors, the company should perform better in general and over time than if strategy were determined exclusively by the executive management. This expectation appeared to have been justified by the banking crisis in the USA and Europe. 'And certainly in the light of recent experience on both sides of the Atlantic, several banks whose strategies appear to have been determined by long-entrenched executives with little external input to their decision-taking appear to have fared materially worse than those where there was opportunity for effective challenge within the boardroom.'
- Role of NEDs to challenge executives. NEDs should provide a 'disciplined but rigorous challenge on substantive issues'. This should be seen as the norm, not an exception, and if any NED has insufficient strength of character to participate in providing a challenge, his continued suitability to remain as a board member should be thrown into question. 'This does not, of course, mean open season for challenge to the executive team. Appropriate balance will only be achieved where the executive expects to be challenged, but where the board debate surrounding such challenge is conducted in a way that leaves the executive team with a sense of having drawn benefit from it.'

9.5 Independence of non-executive directors

The UK Code does not suggest that all NEDs should be independent. Non-independent NEDs are permissible, although the majority of the total board should consist of independent NEDs. However, if there are NEDs on the board who are not considered to be independent, this could create problems with the size and composition of the board. It may be considered necessary to appoint independent NEDs to act as a counter-balance to the NEDs who are not independent.

Executive directors cannot be independent. Not only are they involved in the running of the company's operations and report (and are accountable to) to the CEO for this aspect of their work, they also rely on the company for most (if not all) of their remuneration.

NEDs are either independent or non-independent. An NED is not independent if his opinions are likely to be influenced, in particular by the senior executive management of the company or by a major shareholder.

Independent NEDs are supposed to bring an independent view to the deliberations of the board. However, they are in a difficult position as they are legally liable in the same way as executive directors. For example, they have the same fiduciary duties to the company, and the duty of skill and care. As fellow directors, they might also be reluctant to blow the whistle on their executive colleagues. If they have been selected and appointed by the chairman or the CEO, they will be less likely to ask tough questions about the way the company is being run. This is sometimes known as the 'St Thomas à Becket' problem. (The twelfth-century Archbishop of Canterbury Becket was appointed to by Henry II, but then took a stand against him on issues concerning the roles of the King and the Church in the governance of the country.)

So what is meant by 'independent'? It is easier to answer this question by specifying what is 'not independent'. An NED is **not** independent if his opinions are likely to be influenced by someone else, in particular by the senior executive management or by a major shareholder.

If an NED is likely, for whatever reason, to side with the CEO, he is unlikely to bring the much-needed balance of power to the board. The independence of an NED could be challenged, for example, if the individual concerned:

- has a family connection with the CEO – a problem in some family controlled public companies
- until recently used to be an executive director in the company
- until recently used to work for the company in a professional capacity (e.g. as its auditor or corporate lawyer)
- receives payments from the company in addition to their fees as an NED.

A person cannot be independent if he personally stands to gain or otherwise benefit substantially from:

- income from the company, in addition to his fee as an NED
- the company's reported profitability and movements in the company's share price.

An NED cannot be properly independent, for example, if he accepts a fee from the company for consultancy work. Consultancy involves the individual in the operational aspects of the company, and by implication puts him on the side of the executives. Nor can an individual be independent if he has been awarded a large number of share options by the company. Holding share options gives the individual a direct interest in the share price of the company around the time the options can be exercised. He might therefore favour decisions that improve the reported profitability of the company at this time, because good financial results are likely to be good for the share price.

A committee of the board of directors of the New York Stock Exchange (NYSE), reporting in June 2002 on corporate governance in NYSE-listed companies, commented:

'No director qualifies as "independent" unless the board of directors affirmatively determines that the director has no material relationship with the listed company (either directly, as a partner, shareholder or officer of an organisation that has a relationship with the company). Companies must disclose these determinations.'

The report added:

'We do not view ownership ... of a less than controlling amount of stock as a per se bar to an independence finding.'

A former executive director might be appointed as an NED on his retirement. When this happens, his attitudes and judgements are likely to remain on the side of the executive management, and he is unlikely to make criticisms of the executive management that might indirectly reflect adversely on his own performance as an executive manager prior to retirement.

Occasionally, NEDs are appointed to represent the opinions of a major shareholder. In such cases, the individual can be expected to voice the wishes of the shareholder, and so could not be regarded as independent.

To ensure that NEDs should not rely for their tenure in office on one or two individuals, the UK Code recommends that they should be selected through a formal process.

9.6 Criteria for judging independence

The UK Corporate Governance Code requires the board to identify in the annual report each NED it considers to be independent. Although this is a matter for the board's judgement, the Code sets out circumstances in which independence would usually be questionable. The board would need to explain why it considers an NED to be independent in any of these circumstances:

■ The director has been an employee of the company within the last five years.
■ The director has a material business relationship with the company (or has had such a relationship within the last three years). This relationship might be as a partner, shareholder, director or employee in another organisation that has a material business relationship with the company.
■ The director receives (or has received) additional remuneration from the company other than a director's fee, or is a member of the company's pension scheme, or participates in the company's share option scheme or a performance-related pay scheme.
■ The director has close family ties with any of the company's advisers, directors or senior employees.
■ The director has cross-directorships or has significant links with other directors through involvement in other companies or organisations. A cross-directorship exists when an individual is an NED on the board of Company X and an executive director on the board of Company Y, when another individual is an executive director of Company X and an NED on the board of Company Y.
■ The director represents a significant shareholder.
■ The director has served on the board for more than nine years since the date of his first election.

These criteria of independence should be applied to the chairman (on appointment) as well as other non-executive directors. Circumstances may change, and the independence of NEDs should be kept under review.

9.7 The nine-year rule on independence

The provision in the UK Code (also in the King III Code) that an NED should not be considered independent after serving on the board for over nine years arises from the general view that the independence of an NED is likely to diminish over time, as the NED becomes more familiar with the company and executive colleagues. The risk is that the NED will take more of the views of executive colleagues on trust and will be less rigorous in his questioning.

The Higgs Report commented:

'There will be occasions where value will be added by a non-executive director serving for longer, but I would expect this to be the exception and the reasons explained to shareholders.'

On the other hand, the Quoted Companies Alliance (QCA) commented (in a submission to the Financial Reporting Council in 2005) that if an NED ceases to be considered independent after nine years, this should not be a reason to end his appointment if he is still making a valuable contribution to the board. The QCA added that this is particularly important for smaller quoted companies, because effective NEDs are often difficult to find and (unlike a larger quoted company), when a director ceases to be independent, there is no change in the number of independent NEDs required on the board – the requirement remains for just two.

Even larger quoted companies appear reluctant to lose NEDs after nine years of service, due largely to a perceived lack of potential candidates with the suitable qualifications to be an effective NED. It is therefore worth remembering that the UK Code is pragmatic in its approach to the nine-year rule. If the board considers that a director is still independent even after nine years' service, he may still be considered 'independent' for the purposes of the corporate governance provisions.

9.8 Protecting the independence and effectiveness of board committees

As a way of protecting the independence and improving the effectiveness of board committees, the UK Corporate Governance Code includes the following supporting principles.

■ When deciding the chairmanship and membership of board committees, consideration should be given to the benefits of ensuring that committee membership is refreshed (i.e. membership rotation) and that undue reliance is not placed on particular individuals.

■ The only individuals who are entitled to attend meetings of the nomination, remuneration and audit committees are the chairman and members of the committee, although other individuals may attend at the invitation of the committee.

9.9 Comparison of executive and non-executive directors

Unlike NEDs, executive directors are full-time employees of the company, with executive management responsibilities in addition to their responsibilities as directors. For the executive directors, there is a tension between:

■ their role as members of the board, 'one step down from the shareholders', and

■ their role as senior operational directors, 'one step up from management'.

Executive directors, led by their CEO, may often want to present a united front to the rest of the board, to justify what the management team has done and achieved, or what it would like to do. However, if the executive directors come together with a united opinion, this will question their ability to fulfil the role of all directors to provide effective challenge in discussions on strategy. In comparison, independent NEDs do not have this problem, which is why they should be more effective in providing effective challenge in board discussions, encouraged by the chairman.

The problems for executive directors are therefore that:

■ they may be inclined to support the views of the CEO on all matters, including strategy

■ they may mistrust the NEDs as 'outsiders' who do not know much about the company and its business.

In recognition of this problem, the guidance 'Improving Board Effectiveness' suggests that executive directors should see themselves as representatives of the shareholders rather than as executive managers who are responsible and accountable to the CEO. The chairman should encourage this attitude among the executive directors, partly through ensuring that they receive appropriate induction and training for their role as company director.

Executive directors should have a very detailed knowledge of the company and its business, and should apply this knowledge when making judgements about company strategy. However they should also recognise that constructive challenge from NEDs is an essential part of good corporate governance, and they should welcome and encourage such challenges. For an effective board, the executive directors and NEDs must work constructively together.

TEST YOUR KNOWLEDGE 4.8

(a) What are the intended functions of independent NEDs?

(b) According to Higgs, what are the four broad roles of NEDs?

(c) According to the UK Code of Corporate Governance, what are the roles of NEDs?

(d) List six circumstances in which an NED would not normally be considered independent.

(e) To comply with UK corporate governance requirements, what measures should be taken if a company appoints an NED who is not considered independent?

---

10 Senior independent directors

There could be occasions when institutional shareholders are in disagreement with the board of directors, but are unable to make their opinions heard due to the negative attitudes of the chairman and CEO. For this reason, a provision was included in the UK governance code that the board of directors of large companies should nominate an independent NED as the senior independent director, whom shareholders could approach to discuss problems and issues when the normal communication route through the chairman has broken down.

In addition, if the chairman fails to pass on the views of the institutional shareholders to the NEDs, there should be another channel of communication that could be used instead.

The UK Corporate Governance Code states that the board should appoint one of the independent NEDs to be the senior independent director (SID).

- The SID should provide a sounding board for the chairman, and as such may act as an intermediary through whom the other NEDs can express their views, for example their concerns to the chairman.
- The SID should also 'be available to shareholders if they have concerns which contact through the normal channels of chairman, chief executive or other executive directors has failed to resolve, or for which such contact is inappropriate'. The SID is therefore a channel of communication between the company and its shareholders when normal channels don't work – perhaps when the principles of good corporate governance are not being applied.

'Improving Board Effectiveness' makes a distinction between the role of the SID in 'normal times' and when the board is undergoing 'a period of stress'.

At normal times, the role of the SID is to:

- provide support for the chairman
- ensure that the views of other directors, particularly the other NEDs, are conveyed to the chairman
- ensure that the views of the shareholders, particularly matters that concern them, are conveyed to the rest of the board
- ensure that the chairman is giving sufficient attention to succession planning
- carry out the annual review of the performance of the chairman, in conjunction with the other NEDs (see Chapter 5).

At times of stress for the board, the role of the SID should be to take the initiative to resolve the problem, working with the other directors and shareholders and/or the chairman, as appropriate. Examples of problems where intervention by the SID may be appropriate include situations where:

- there is a dispute between the chairman and the CEO
- shareholders or the NEDs have expressed serious concerns that are not being addressed by the chairman or CEO
- the strategy pursued by the chairman or CEO is not supported by the rest of the board
- there is a very close relationship between the chairman and the CEO, and decisions are being taken without the approval of the board
- succession planning is being ignored.

Issues where intervention may be required should be considered when defining the responsibilities of the SID and should be set out in writing.

The role of the SID is therefore likely to be more important at times when the board is under stress, such as when there are disagreements between the chairman and major shareholders, or between the NEDs and executive directors. Critics of the SID concept argue that the chairman should be able to resolve difficulties between a company and its shareholders, and the position of SID should therefore be superfluous. Opening up the possibility of an additional channel of communication for shareholders is perhaps more likely to undermine company–shareholder relationships than improve them.

However, the ICGN Global Corporate Governance Principles put forward reasons why a 'lead independent director' or independent deputy chairman is necessary.

- If the chairman is the CEO or former CEO, or was for another reason not independent when first appointed, the SID should provide independent leadership for the board, and should have a key role in setting the agenda for board meetings and acting as spokesman for the independent members of the board.
- Even when the chairman was independent when first appointed, his role inevitably brings him closer than the NEDs over time to the views of the CEO and executive management.

The SID should provide leadership to the independent members of the board when this situation creates a problem.

■ The ICGN Principles also recognise the role of the lead independent director as an alternative conduit for communication with the shareholders.

11 Board committees and non-executive directors

An aspect of best practice in corporate governance is that for some issues that the board should decide, the executive directors should be excluded from the decision-making or monitoring responsibilities. This is achieved by delegating certain responsibilities to committees of the board. A board committee might consist entirely or mostly of NEDs, and have the responsibility for dealing with particular issues and making recommendations to the full board. The full board is then usually be expected to accept and endorse the recommendations of the relevant board committee.

In the UK, three committees are recommended by the UK Corporate Governance Code:

1 a nomination committee
2 an audit committee
3 a remuneration committee.

In the UK there is no statutory requirement for a nomination committee or a remuneration committee, but, following the implementation of the EU Statutory Audit Directive in 2008, quoted companies are required to have an audit committee. The roles of these committees are explained in subsequent chapters.

Some boards might establish other committees. For example, a company might have an environment committee if its business activities are likely to have important consequences for the environment, involving government regulation, the law and public opinion. However, there is no requirement for these committees to consist wholly or mainly of NEDs.

Table 4.2 summarises the UK Code's recommendations about membership of board committees.

TABLE 4.2 Summary of the UK Code's recommendations regarding membership of board committees

Nominations committee	Audit committee	Remuneration committee
Chairman should be the chairman of the board or an independent NED.	Composition: all independent NEDs – in large companies, at least three, in smaller companies two.	Composition: all independent NEDs – in large companies, at least three, in smaller companies two.
Composition: majority of members should be independent NEDs.	In smaller companies, the chairman of the board may also be a member of the audit committee (but not chairman of the committee), in addition to the independent NEDs – but only if he was independent on appointment to the chairmanship.	The chairman of the board may also be a member of the audit committee (but not chairman of the committee), but only if he was independent on appointment to the chairmanship.
If the board chairman is the company chairman, he should not act as chair when the committee is considering a successor for the chairmanship.	At least one member of the committee should have 'recent and relevant financial experience'.	

12 Effectiveness of non-executive directors

There are differing views about the effectiveness of NEDs. The accepted view is that NEDs bring experience and judgement to the deliberations of the board that the executive directors on their own would lack. An alternative view is that the effectiveness of NEDs can be undermined by:

- lack of knowledge about the business operations of the company
- insufficient time spent with the company
- the weight of opinion of the executive directors on the board
- delays in decision-making.

12.1 Insufficient knowledge

The quality of decision-making depends largely on the quality of information available to the decision-maker. The UK Code states that the board as a whole should be 'supplied in a timely manner with information in a form and of a quality appropriate to enable it to discharge its duties'. However, the senior executives in a company control the information systems, and so control the flow of information to the board. It is quite conceivable, for example, that the CEO and other executive directors might have access to management information that is withheld from the board as a whole, or that is presented to the board in a distorted manner. Lacking the 'insider knowledge' of executive managers about the business operations, and having to rely on the integrity of the information supplied to them by management and executive directors, restricts the scope for NEDs to make a meaningful contribution to board decisions.

12.2 Insufficient time

NEDs often have executive positions in other companies and organisations, where most of their working time is spent. As a general rule, NEDs do not have an office at the company headquarters and may spend at most one or two days a month on the company's business. A further criticism of NEDs is that some individuals hold too many NED positions, with the result that they cannot possibly give sufficient time to any of the companies concerned. It could be argued, for example, that an individual cannot be an effective NED of a company if he is also the CEO of another public company and holds four or five other NED positions in other companies.

The UK Code states that all directors should be able to allocate sufficient time to the company to discharge their responsibilities effectively. Although this principle of the Code applies to all directors, the main concern is with NEDs (since executive directors are usually full-time employees) and in particular the chairman. The UK Code requires that when a chairman is appointed, the nomination committee should prepare a job specification that includes an assessment of the expected time commitment and recognising the need for the chairman to be available to the company in times of crisis.

Similarly, when an NED is appointed (other than a chairman), the letter of appointment should set out the expected time commitment.

12.3 Overriding influence of executive directors

Yet another criticism of NEDs is that if a difference of opinion arises during a meeting of the board, the opinions of the executive directors are likely to carry greater weight, because they know more about the company. NEDs may be put under pressure to accept the views of their executive director colleagues. This potential problem provides an argument for the role of a strong senior independent director, to ensure that the opinions of the independent NEDs are properly considered.

12.4 Delays in decision-making

It may be argued that NEDs delay decision-making within a company. Major decisions should be reserved for the board; therefore, to implement an important new strategy initiative it may be necessary to call a board meeting. The time required to hold the meeting, giving the NEDs sufficient time to reach a well-informed opinion about the matter, may delay the implementation of the proposed strategy. It has also been argued that NEDs may be conservative in outlook, whereas the board of directors needs to be 'entrepreneurial'.

One counter-argument is that when a major new strategy or initiative is proposed, it should be given full and careful consideration before a decision is made. NEDs, with their range of skills and experience, can contribute positively to this decision-making process.

12.5 Myners Report and criticisms of non-executive directors

Weaknesses in the system of appointing NEDs has been recognised for many years and criticisms made in 2002 are probably still valid today. In February 2002 Paul Myners (subsequently appointed as a government minister) issued a UK government-backed report into pension fund investment. He accused boards of directors of public companies of being a 'self-perpetuating oligarchy', which failed to stand up for shareholders' rights against over-powerful executives. He condemned NEDs as the 'missing link' in the chain of good corporate governance. In particular, he criticised the way NED appointments were made and the number of NED positions that some individuals held.

- Some individuals held too many NED positions in large public companies, more than they could possibly serve effectively.
- Non-executive directorships were frequently given to the executive directors of other listed companies, giving rise to the concerns about a 'you scratch my back and I'll scratch yours' mentality. An NED might tacitly undertake not to ask awkward questions or take a stand against executives on the board, provided that the NEDs of his own company act in the same way.
- NEDs should help to make the board more accountable to the shareholders. However, shareholders have opportunities to discuss the company's affairs with the NEDs in a formal setting, at general meetings of the company only. Any other discussions between shareholders and NEDs must be informal, if they take place at all.
- The law makes no distinction between executive and non-executive directors. In principle, the NEDs could be equally liable with the executive directors for negligence and failure of duty. Arguably, this threat of criminal or civil liability could make NEDs more likely to support their executive colleagues.
- Faith in NEDs to bring sound corporate governance practice to public companies could therefore be misplaced – a view that has been expressed. Lord Young, outgoing president of the UK Institute of Directors (IoD), for example, argued in a speech to the IoD annual convention in the same year as the Myners report (2002) that NEDs cannot hope to govern their company better than the executive directors, because they cannot know as much about the company as full-time executives: 'The biggest and most dangerous nonsense is the role we now expect non-executive directors to perform. Even if they spend one day a week in the company, can the non-execs ever know the business as well as the execs? No, they can't. So why bother with non-execs at all?'

TEST YOUR KNOWLEDGE 4.9

What are the main criticisms that have been made about NEDs?

 CASE QUESTION

1 What changes should be made to the size and structure of the board of directors of Stenning Tull, and to decision-making processes in the company, to bring the company into compliance with the UK Corporate Governance Code?

2 What other appointments could the company make to strengthen its future development and governance?

CHAPTER SUMMARY

- Every company should be headed by an effective board, which has the collective responsibility for the long-term success of the company. Various corporate governance codes have identified the responsibilities of the board.

- In most countries, there is a unitary board structure. In a few countries, notably Germany, there is a two-tier board structure with a supervisory board of non-executive directors led by the company chairman and a management board of executives led by the CEO. The two boards need to interact closely and constructively, even though one has a supervisory role over the other.

- Directors, and not shareholders, may exercise all the powers of the company. These powers are defined in the company's constitution (articles of association) but are subject to some restraints in provisions of company law.

- In UK common law, directors have a fiduciary duty and a duty of skill and care to the company. This duty is owed to the company, not the shareholders. The common law duties of directors have now effectively been included in UK statute law, with the inclusion of a number of statutory general duties of directors in the Companies Act 2006. These statutory duties are the duties to act within their powers, promote the success of the company, exercise independent judgement, exercise responsible care skill and diligence, avoid conflicts of interest, not accept benefits from third parties and declare any interest in a proposed transaction.

- If a director is in breach of a duty, shareholders may bring a derivative claim against him for breach of duty, in the name of the company.

- In the UK, listed companies are required by the Disclosure and Transparency Rules to announce to the stock market any proposed related party transaction above a certain size, and to obtain shareholder approval for the transaction.

- There should be a schedule of matters reserved to the board for its own decision-making. The ICSA has issued a Guidance Note indicating what these matters should be.

- The chairman is the leader of the board and the CEO is the leader of the executive management team.

- The UK Code states that the chairman should be independent on first appointment. It is therefore inappropriate to appoint a former CEO as chairman.

- The UK Code also states that the roles of chairman and CEO should not be combined and given to one individual, because this would create a position of 'unfettered power' on the board and would disturb the balance of the board and the ability of NEDs to challenge the executive management.

- A board should not be so large that it is unwieldy nor too small so that it lacks sufficient skills and experience. The UK Code recommends that at least 50 per cent of the board (excluding the chairman) should be independent NEDs, except for smaller companies (listed companies outside the FTSE350) where there should be at least two independent NEDs.

- NEDs fulfil various roles: they contribute to discussions and decision-making by the board on strategy, they review the performance of executive management, they have a responsibility to ensure the integrity of financial information issued by the company and the effectiveness of risk management and internal control, and they are involved in the appointment of new directors and the remuneration of executive directors and other senior executives.

- 'Independence' of an NED is defined by the UK Code in terms of circumstances where an NED would normally be considered 'not independent'.

- The UK Code recommends that one of the independent NEDs should be nominated as the senior independent director.

- The UK Code (and other national corporate governance codes) calls for the establishment of board committees with governance responsibilities. The remuneration committee and the audit committee should consist entirely of independent NEDs and the nominations committee should have a majority of independent NEDs.

- There have been criticisms of NEDs. These include the argument that they are ineffective because they devote insufficient time to the company or have insufficient knowledge of the company's business.

5 Governance and boardroom practice

■ INTRODUCTION

This chapter deals with a variety of governance issues relating to the board of directors. In 2009 the ICSA issued a paper on boardroom behaviours, suggesting that the effectiveness of a board is often damaged by poor boardroom behaviours, and recommending that guidelines on boardroom behaviours should be produced. There are also important governance issues relating to the identification and appointment of new directors, and the **induction** and continuing professional development of board directors. Finally, the chapter considers boardroom ethics, the potential personal liability of directors and the need for directors to check that sufficient directors' and officers' liability cover is provided by the company to give adequate protection.

1 Good boardroom practice and board behaviours

1.1 Boardroom practice

Boardroom practice describes the way in which a board conducts its procedures and reaches its decisions. The ICSA has argued that it is not sufficient to rely on unwritten boardroom procedures and practices, and it has issued a Code for Directors and Company Secretaries on Good Boardroom Practice, which includes the following provisions.

- There should be written procedures for the conduct of board business. Compliance should be monitored, preferably by an audit committee (see also Chapter 7).
- Each director, on first appointment, should be given sufficient information to enable him to carry out the duties of a director properly. This should include details of procedures for obtaining information about the company and requisitioning a board meeting.
- Two fundamental concepts in the conduct of board business are that (1) all directors should be given the same information, and (2) they should be given sufficient time to consider it.
- The board should identify those matters that require its prior approval. As a basic principle, all material contracts should be referred to the board for approval before the company is legally committed to them.

- Decisions about the agenda for a board meeting should be taken by the company chairman, in consultation with the company secretary.
- The company secretary should be responsible to the chairman for the proper administration of board meetings, the meetings of board committees and general meetings of the company. To carry out these responsibilities, the company secretary should be entitled to be present at and prepare the minutes for all such meetings. The minutes of meetings should record all decisions that were taken, and procedures should be established for the approval and circulation of minutes.
- The board should give its prior approval for the membership, terms of reference and powers of any committee of the board that is established. Minutes of board committees should be circulated to all board directors prior to the next board meeting, to give them an opportunity to raise questions at that meeting.

The Code is supplemented by the ICSA Guidance Note on Matters Reserved for the Board, which details decisions which should be taken by the board as a whole and not delegated. These were described in Chapter 4.

1.2 Character

In a report on its review of the UK Code, the FRC commented (2009) that the quality of corporate governance depends ultimately on the behaviour of individuals, not on procedures and rules. Consequently, there is a limit to the ability of procedures and regulation to provide good corporate governance.

The Walker Report argued that both character and culture of the board members are important for an effective board. It commented that:

'Board conformity with laid-down procedures ... will not alone provide better corporate governance overall if the chairman is weak, if the composition and dynamic of the board is inadequate and if there is unsatisfactory ... engagement with its owners.'

The Report went on to argue that the main weaknesses in the boards of banks had been caused by behavioural factors and a failure to challenge.

'The sequence in board discussion on major issues should be: presentation by the executive, a disciplined process of challenge, decision on the policy or strategy to be adopted and then full empowerment of the executive to implement. The essential "challenge" step in the sequence appears to have been missed in many board situations and needs to be ... clearly recognised and embedded for the future.'

1.3 Frequency of board meetings

A basic requirement of an effective board is that there should be regular board meetings. The UK Corporate Governance Code states simply that the board should meet sufficiently regularly to discharge its duties effectively, and there should be a formal schedule of matters reserved for the board.

1.4 The agenda

The agenda for board meetings is a corporate governance issue in the sense that the chairman decides what the board will discuss when he sets the agenda. Although directors can raise matters as 'any other business', most of the time at board meetings is spent in discussion of the items listed by the chairman on the agenda.

It is therefore important that the agenda should include all matters reserved for board decision, whenever they arise. The company secretary can assist the chairman by providing advice and reminders.

1.5 Information

To enable them to contribute effectively to board discussions, directors must be provided with relevant information. They should receive relevant documents in advance of a board meeting, so that they have time to read them and think about the issues they deal with. The UK Code states that:

'The board should be supplied in a timely manner with information in a form and of a quality sufficient to enable it to discharge its duties.'

The chairman has the responsibility for ensuring that directors receive the information that they need in sufficient time. The Code states that management has an obligation to provide the required information, but that the directors should ask for clarification or additional information if required.

Information flows should be both formal and informal. Information is provided formally in documents or files, but this is supplemented by informal communication by e-mail, telephone or face-to-face conversation. Whether providing information formally or informally, the company secretary should ensure that there are good information flows between the board and its committees, between committees, and between executive managers and NEDs.

1.6 Support

In addition to receiving relevant and timely information, directors should be given access to independent professional advice, at the company's expense, when they consider this necessary in order to fulfil their duties as director (UK Code). For example, a director might ask to consult a lawyer for advice on a matter where the legal position is not clear.

NEDs and possibly also executive directors may also need administrative support or advice on routine matters, and the UK Code includes provisions that:

- board committees should be provided with sufficient resources to carry out their duties, and
- all directors should have access to the advice and assistance of the company secretary.

1.7 ICSA report: Boardroom Behaviours

In 2009, the ICSA submitted a report to Sir David Walker, who was conducting an investigation into the corporate governance issues that may have contributed to the 2007–2009 banking crisis in the UK. The ICSA report suggested that the corporate governance problem was partly attributable to inappropriate 'boardroom behaviours'.

Behavioural problems were only a part of the problem of ineffective governance, the report suggested, but insufficient attention had been given to the problem, and there should be better guidance to directors on how to improve board behaviours.

The report suggested that best practice in boardroom behaviour is characterised by:

- a clear understanding of the role of the board
- the appropriate deployment of knowledge, skills, experience and judgement
- independent thinking
- the questioning of assumptions and established orthodoxy
- challenge which is constructive, confident, principled and proportionate
- rigorous debate
- a supportive decision-making environment
- a common vision, and
- the achievement of closure on individual items of board business.

The report commented that:

'Despite the importance of these … considerations, it is remarkable that there is practically no guidance in the Code on the main drivers of, and factors affecting, boardroom behaviours.… To improve on existing standards of behaviour in the boardroom, directors need to develop a greater awareness of, and commitment to, "fit for purpose" governance as the means by which the board can collectively agree the business objectives of the company and a strategy for their implementation by executive management.'

- Directors need to see best practice in corporate governance as a 'business facilitator' and not a 'business killer'. The pursuit of best practice in governance should be seen as a way of achieving competitive advantage, because it strengthens the process and quality of decision-making by the board.
- Directors also need to be aware that failure to perform at a satisfactory level can have negative consequences, and directors need to be aware of their duties and potential liabilities.

Directors need to consider a wider range of factors other than short-term profit to deliver a sustainable business.

Failure to provide best practice in corporate governance, and failure to perform at a satisfactory level, creates a risk to the reputation of boards of directors and individual directors.

1.8 Guidance on boardroom behaviours

The ICSA report provided an outline of the guidance that might be useful to directors about boardroom behaviours.

- All directors, including executive directors, need to improve their performance in these important areas of boardroom behaviours. The process of achieving this for non-executive directors (NEDs) can be made more effective by giving them greater exposure to the company's operations.
- A knowledgeable board is a function of board balance, and there may be insufficient balance if the board is shrunk to just two executive directors (chief executive officer (CEO) and finance director) in order to achieve a majority of NEDs without making the board too big. Limiting the number of executive directors 'has, unintentionally, led to a situation of information flow through two or sometimes three executive directors who, with the best will in the world, will be unable to master the whole corpus of the company's objectives and operations'.
- Diversity of board membership is necessary to provide sufficient independent challenge. 'It is evident that boards do not currently contain a sufficiently wide range of skill sets, experience and background.'
- High standards of performance evaluation are needed to increase the effectiveness of a board.
- At the moment the remuneration of executive directors appears to focus on maximising short-term 'value' rather than pursuing the goal of a sustainable business. Remuneration arrangements should give more emphasis to the behaviours of directors in the boardroom, working in the long-term interests of the company.
- In terms of developing a wider perspective of the business, directors should look 'forward and out, as well as backwards and in'.
- The board should lead by example, 'evidenced by high levels of visibility and integrity, strong communications, and demanding expectations.'
- Practical issues, such as the timely circulation of board papers, 'can have a disproportionate effect on the quality of decision-making'.

TEST YOUR KNOWLEDGE **5.1**

(a) List five provisions in the ICSA's Code on good boardroom practice.
(b) According to the UK Code of Corporate Governance, how often should a board of directors meet?
(c) How does the agenda for board meetings contribute to good corporate governance?
(d) What should be the requirements relating to the provision of information to directors for board meetings?
(e) What are the characteristics of best practice in boardroom behaviour, as identified by the ICSA (2009)?
(f) Explain the meaning of the statement that directors should look on best practice in corporate governance as a 'business facilitator', not a 'business killer'.

2　Appointments to the board: nomination committee

2.1 Board appointments

The membership of a board of directors changes regularly, as some individuals resign or retire and new appointments are made. There are no regulations on the overall size of the board (unless a provision about the composition of the board is included in the company's constitution), so that:

- there are no restrictions on making new appointments; and
- with the exceptions of the positions of chairman and CEO, there is no requirement to replace individuals stepping down from the board.

It is an accepted principle of good corporate governance that the power over board appointments should rest with the whole board. In the UK, new appointments are made to the board at any time during the year, but each newly appointed director must offer himself for re-election at the next AGM. (The chairman of the company and the chairmen of the board committees are appointed by the board, and chairmanship appointments are not subject to shareholder approval at the next AGM.)

Recommendations about new appointments should not belong exclusively to the chairman and/or the CEO. Appointments should be made on merit and against objective criteria; however, in practice, criticism has been expressed about the way in which most appointments are made, particularly appointments of NEDs. This criticism centres on the fact that most NED appointments come from a fairly small circle of successful businessmen, many of whom know each other, whereas the net should be cast much wider and individuals from more diverse backgrounds should be chosen.

The UK Corporate Governance Code states that there should be 'a formal, rigorous and transparent procedure for the appointment of new directors to the board'.

- A formal procedure involves the nomination committee (see section 2.2 Nomination committee).
- The procedure of identifying candidates for a directorship should be rigorous, and candidates should be investigated thoroughly before the directorship is offered. The UK Code states that appointments should be made on 'merit' and 'against objective criteria'. However, it does not specify what these 'objective criteria' should be.
- Perhaps somewhat controversially, the Code also states that appointments to the board should be made 'with due regard to the benefits of diversity on the board, including gender'. This reflect the widely expressed concern that the boards of major UK companies are dominated by middle-aged to older white males with a commercial or financial background, and that there are not enough directors with different attributes, talents and experience to provide boards with an appropriate balance. The relative shortage of female board directors has been well-publicised.
- The procedure should be transparent so that shareholders and other stakeholders are able to see what is happening (what type of person the company is looking for and why a particular individual has been appointed).

2.2 Nomination committee

The detailed corporate governance guidelines on the role of the nomination committee vary between countries, but in many countries they are similar. In the UK, the recommended framework for making appointments is that:

- the search for new directors should be carried out by a nomination committee of the board, to which the full board delegates the responsibility
- the nomination committee should make recommendations to the board
- the board should consider the recommendations of the committee, and in normal circumstances should be expected to accept the recommendation.

It is important to note that a nomination committee does not have the authority to make new appointments; it simply carries out the search and makes the recommendation. Appointing new directors is a matter for the board, and decisions should therefore be made by the whole board.

It is also important to note that the need for a new board appointment, or a replacement for an existing board member (succession planning), is not necessarily decided by the nomination committee. The chairman has responsibility for ensuring that the composition of the board is appropriate, and may discuss his ideas with the chairman of the nomination committee. The need for a new NED may also emerge from the annual review of board performance, if an existing NED has not been performing as well as expected, or if a gap is identified in the range of skills and experience that the board needs.

The chairman is also responsible for ensuring that there is succession planning for board positions, and may therefore ask the nomination committee to identify potential successors.

The UK Corporate Governance Code recommends that a nomination committee should be established by the board, and this committee should 'lead the process for board appointments and make recommendations to the board'.

- The majority of members should be independent NEDs.
- The committee chairman should be either the board chairman or an independent NED. If the board chairman is the chairman of the nomination committee, he should not chair the committee when it is dealing with the succession to the chairmanship.

The existence of a majority of NEDs should ensure that the appointments process is not dominated by the chairman and CEO. The committee should consider new appointments to the board and make recommendations to the full board. The full board should then reach a decision about offering a position to the individual concerned so that final responsibility for board appointments remains with the board as a whole.

2.3 The main duties of the nomination committee

The principal duties of the nomination committee were summarised in the Higgs Suggestions for Good Practice. These are that the nomination committee should:

- be responsible for identifying candidates to fill vacancies on the board, as and when they arise, and nominate them for approval by the board
- (before making an appointment) evaluate the balance of skills, knowledge and experience on the board, and on the basis of this evaluation, prepare a description of the role and capabilities required for the particular appointment
- (each year) review the time required from an NED (the annual performance evaluation of an NED should include an assessment of whether the NED is spending enough time on his/her duties)
- consider candidates for appointment from a wide range of backgrounds, and look beyond the 'usual suspects'
- give full consideration to succession planning (see section 4 of this chapter)
- regularly review the structure, size and composition of the board, and make recommendations for any changes to the board
- keep under review the leadership needs of the company, both executive and non-executive, with a view to ensuring that the company remains competitive
- make available its terms of reference, explaining clearly its role and the authority delegated to it by the board
- ensure that on appointment to the board, NEDs receive a formal letter of appointment, setting out what is expected of them, including time commitment and membership of board committees.

Recommendations by the nomination to the board should include:

- plans for the succession of NEDs and executive directors
- recommendations about the reappointment of NEDs at the end of their term of office
- recommendations about the submission of any director for re-election by the shareholders under the retirement by rotation rules in the company's constitution (articles of association)
- matters concerning the continuation in office of any director at any time.

It is also the responsibility of the chairman of the nomination committee to ensure that the UK Corporate Governance Code provisions relating to the composition of the board are complied with.

The UK Code requires that a separate section of the annual report should describe the work of the nomination committee, including the process it used in relation to appointments that were made during the year. An explanation should be given if neither the services of an external search consultancy ('headhunters') nor advertising were used in making the appointment of chairman or non-executive director. (If advertising the vacancy or the services headhunter was not used, this would suggest that the appointment was made of a person that the nomination committee already knew or who was recommended privately: this would be contrary to the requirement for a formal, rigorous and transparent appointment procedure.) Executive directors may be appointed from within the company, so the requirement applies only to the appointment of a chairman or NED.

2.4 UK Corporate Governance Code provisions on board nominations

The UK Code includes several provisions about appointments to the board.

- The committee 'should evaluate the balance of skills, experience, independence and knowledge and experience of the board, and, in the light of this evaluation, prepare a description of the role and capabilities required for the particular appointment'.
- On initial appointment, the chairman should meet the criteria for independence.
- For the appointment of a chairman, the nomination committee should prepare a job specification, including an assessment of the time required and recognising the need for the chairman's availability in times of crisis.
- The departing chairman should not chair the nomination committee when it is meeting to consider the appointment of the successor to the chairmanship.
- A proposed new chairman's other significant commitments should be disclosed to the board before an appointment is made, and included in the annual report. (Subsequent changes should also be disclosed and reported.)

Provisions relating to succession planning and the time commitment of NEDs are also included in the Code, and are explained later in this chapter.

2.5 Practical aspects of board appointments: time commitment

In practice, a nomination committee is likely to carry out its responsibilities by:

- using a firm of headhunters to find individuals outside the firm who might be suitable for appointment (as NED, CEO, finance director, and so on)
- vetting the candidates put forward by the headhunters, and
- making a selection and recommendation to the full board.

When an individual is appointed to the board, the appointment may be for a fixed term. This is usually the case with NEDs; in the UK, NEDs are typically appointed on a fixed three-year contract, which may then be renewed at the end of each three-year term. Executive directors are commonly appointed for an indeterminate length of time, subject to a minimum notice period (typically one year or even less).

'All directors must be able to allocate sufficient time to the company to discharge their responsibilities effectively' (UK Code). Executive directors are full-time appointments, so the problem of time commitment is not usually significant for them (unless the executive is also appointed as NED for another company). The main problem is ensuring that the chairman and NEDs give sufficient time to the company. More time will probably be required from the chairman than from an NED, and some NEDs (e.g. the chairman of the audit committee) will be expected to commit more time than other NEDs.

When the nomination committee prepares a job description for the position, this should include an estimate of the time commitment expected. An NED should undertake that he will have sufficient time to meet what is expected of them. This undertaking could be written into the NED's contract.

If an individual who is proposed to the board as chairman or NED has significant time commitments outside the company, this should be disclosed to the board before the appointment is made.

A company should also protect itself against the risk that an executive director is unable to commit sufficient time to the company because of NED appointments with other companies. The UK Code states that the board should not allow one of its own executive directors to take on:

- more than one NED post in a FTSE 100 company, or
- the chairmanship of a FTSE 100 company.

2.6 The talent pool for new directors: Tyson Report

There could be a tendency for directors, and NEDs in particular, to be recruited from a narrow circle of potential candidates. The Higgs Report (January 2003) found that only 7 per cent of NEDs on UK public limited company boards were non-British nationals, only 6 per cent were women and only 1 per cent were from ethnic minorities. The majority of NEDs were white, middle-aged males, many with previous experience as a plc board director.

Following publication of the Higgs Report, the government set up a taskforce under the chairmanship of Laura Tyson, Dean of the London Business School, to look into the recruitment and development of NEDs. The Tyson Report on the Recruitment and Development of Non-Executive Directors was published in June 2003. The report argued that a range of different experiences and backgrounds amongst board members could enhance the effectiveness of the board, and suggested how a broader range of NEDs could be identified and recruited.

The Report criticised the practice (current at that time) of appointing individuals without a formal interview. This method of recruitment tended to overlook a number of potentially rich sources of NEDs, such as those listed below.

- The 'marzipan layer' of corporate management, just below board level. The chief executive officer of a company might be willing to allow managers to act as NEDs of companies that are not competitors, although they might be less willing if the demands on the individual's time increase. Another advantage of this source of NEDs is that the 'marzipan layer' includes a large number of women.
- Individuals in private sector companies.
- Individuals in the public sector/non-commercial sector.
- Individuals working for business consultancies or professional firms (lawyers, accountants) and retired professional accountants.

Some 'search' firms specialise in looking for suitable individuals in private sector companies or the non-commercial sector, and companies could use their services. Although there has been some increase in the 'talent pool' for selecting NEDs, change has been slow.

As stated earlier, the UK Code states that appointments to the board should be made on merit and against objective criteria 'and with due regard for the benefits of diversity on the board, including gender'.

TEST YOUR KNOWLEDGE 5.2

(a) In the UK, what are the responsibilities or rights regarding new appointments to the board of the nominations committee, the board of directors and the company's shareholders?

(b) What are the responsibilities of a nomination committee?

(c) According to the UK Code, what should be the composition of a nominations committee in a FTSE 350 company and who may be its chairman?

(d) How much time should NEDs be required to commit to the company, and should this be a contractual commitment?

(e) What were the recommendations of the 2003 Tyson Report?

(f) What are the provisions in the UK Corporate Governance Code relating to nominations and appointments to the board?

3 Accepting an offer of appointment as a non-executive director

The formal procedures for appointing a new NED are the same for the appointment of an executive director. However, an NED will be less familiar with the company than a senior executive manager and he should not accept an appointment unless he is satisfied that there are no matters of concern. An individual should not be willing to accept an appointment as NED if:

- the company uses unethical business practices or has a bad reputation
- the company is a going concern and is not in financial difficulties

- he can commit to the role the time that the company expects
- the individual believes that he can contribute positively to the effectiveness of the board
- there is no risk that the directors of the company could be held liable for any breach of duty, or that there is sufficient directors' and officers' liability insurance as protection against this risk
- the fee that the company has offered is adequate.

The Higgs Guidance therefore recommended that before accepting an appointment, a prospective NED should carry out a 'due diligence' check or examination of the company. The ICSA has commented:

'By making the right enquiries, asking the right questions and taking care to understand the replies, a prospective director can reduce the risk of nasty surprises and dramatically increase the likelihood of success.'

Questions that the prospective NED should ask should cover the following.

- Those about the business, e.g. its nature and size, and the company's market share, financial performance and financial position.
- Those about governance and investor relations – who the major shareholders are, and about the structure of the board of directors and its committees.
- Those about the role that the NED would be expected to perform, including membership of board committees. The prospective NED should be satisfied that he has the necessary qualities or experience to make an effective contribution to work of the company's board.
- Those about the company's risk management systems and controls.
- Those about ethical issues, and whether there are any ethical matters that might give cause for concern.

Answers to many of these questions can be obtained from published documents that are available, in paper form or on a website, to the general public. These include the annual report and accounts of the company, the company's articles of association, any **sustainability report** (see also Chapters 11 and 12) or social and environmental report that the company publishes, and press reports about the company.

3.1 Terms of engagement

If a prospective NED decides to accept the offer of the appointment, terms of engagement should be agreed with the company (either the board as a whole or its nomination committee). The terms that must be agreed are as follows.

- The initial period of tenure in office (normally three years).
- Time commitment. The company must indicate how much time the NED is expected to commit to the company, and the NED should make this commitment. This should be included in the formal letter of appointment. Typically, NEDs are expected to commit between 15 and 30 days each year, and possibly more for a committee chairman.
- Remuneration. The annual remuneration of the NED should be agreed. This is usually a fixed annual fee. It is generally considered inappropriate for NEDs, including the chairman, to be remunerated on the basis of incentive schemes linked to company performance, because this would undermine their independence.

The terms of engagement should be set out in a formal letter of appointment. As well as including details of the role that the NED will be required to perform (including initial membership of board committees), the expected time commitment, the tenure and the remuneration, the letter of engagement should also:

- specify that the NED should treat all information received as a director as confidential to the company
- indicate the arrangements for induction
- give details of directors' and officers' liability insurance that will be available
- indicate the need for an annual performance review process for directors
- state what company resources will be made available to the NED (e.g. desk, computer terminal and telephone).

What issues should an individual consider before accepting the offer of an appointment as independent NED of a listed company?

4 Succession planning

The key positions on the board of directors are the chairman of the board and the CEO. The individuals holding these positions will retire or resign at some time, e.g. because the individual has reached retirement age or has come to the end of a fixed-term contract.

The board of directors should try to ensure a smooth succession, with a replacement lined up to take the place of the departing individual. In the case of a departing CEO, the successor might be an existing executive manager who has been groomed for the role. In the case of a departing non-executive chairman, the successor might be an external appointment. A smooth succession is desirable to avoid disruptions to the company's decision-making processes or changes in policy or direction. The succession can also be planned well in advance, so that the newly appointed individuals will have an opportunity to learn about their new role before the actual succession occurs.

A supporting principle in the UK Corporate Governance Code states that:

'The board should satisfy itself that plans are in place for orderly succession for appointment to the board and to senior management, so as to maintain an appropriate balance of skills and experience within the company and on the board, and to ensure progressive refreshing of the board.'

Succession planning should be delegated to the nomination committee. If the board intends to breach the governance code by appointing the current CEO as the next chairman, it would be advisable for a suitable representative of the board (e.g. the chairman of the nomination committee or the senior independent director) to discuss the reasons for their choice with major shareholders and representative bodies of the institutional shareholders. These discussions should take place well in advance of any final decision about the appointment.

There should also be succession planning for NEDs. As stated above, NEDs are typically appointed in the UK for a fixed period of three years, but the contract may be extended at the end of that time for another three years and so on. Over time, an NED may lose some of his independence. It was explained in the previous chapter that an NED is generally considered 'not independent' if he has been with the company for nine years or more. The UK Code also includes a provision any term beyond six years for an NED should be subject to particularly rigorous review. The board should be continually refreshed, and this is achieved by appointing a new NED when the three-year term of an existing NED reaches its end. The nominations committee may recommend the re-appointment of an NED at the end of his first year term, but should be more inclined to terminate the appointment after six years, when the second three-year term ends.

The UK Code states that there should be 'progressive refreshing of the board'. Refreshing the board calls for succession planning, and the nomination committee should be aware when a vacancy is expected to arise and should plan in advance to appoint the type of person it considers would improve the balance of skills and experience on the board.

5 Re-election of directors: refreshing the board membership

5.1 Re-election of directors

The re-election of directors by the shareholders at annual general meetings (AGM) is primarily a matter for the company's constitution (articles of association). However, it is widely accepted that directors should be subject to re-election by the shareholders at regular intervals. The UK Code states as a main principle that:

'All directors should be submitted for re-election at regular intervals, subject to continued satisfactory performance.'

In the UK, the governance code until 2010 recommended that each director should be subject to election by the shareholders at the AGM following his appointment, and then subject to re-election every three years (until the director resigns, chooses not to stand for re-election or is removed from office).

The financial crisis in banking in 2007–2009 led to a re-assessment of this provision, when it was argued that some or all of the board should be subject to annual re-election.

- Annual re-election increases the accountability of the directors to the shareholders.
- It also gives more power to the shareholders, who are able to threaten to vote against a director at the next AGM (instead of possibly having to wait up to three years before having the opportunity).

After extensive consultation by the FRC, the provisions included in the 2010 UK Code are:

- annual re-election of directors of FTSE 350 companies
- annual re-election of all NEDs who have served longer than nine years on the board
- the same recommendations as before for directors of other companies subject to the UK Code: all other directors to be subject to re-election at the first AGM following their appointment and re-election subsequently at intervals of no more than three years.

The UK Code also requires that when the board proposes an NED for election at an AGM, they should present reasons why the directors believe that the individual should be appointed. When a director is proposed for re-election, the chairman should confirm to the shareholders that following a formal performance evaluation of the individual, he has concluded that the individual's performance continues to be effective and the individual remains committed to the role.

5.2 Refreshing the board membership

The requirement for the board to ensure planned and progressive refreshing means that re-election of current directors, particularly NEDs, should not be an automatic process. As indicated earlier, plans to refresh the board with new NEDs should be a part of succession planning.

 TEST YOUR KNOWLEDGE 5.4

(a) Why is it desirable to plan for **board succession**?

(b) What are the requirements in the UK Corporate Governance Code regarding the re-election of directors?

---

6 Induction and training of directors

6.1 Induction of new directors

The induction of directors is a process by which new directors familiarise themselves with the business, its products or services and how it operates. New directors need induction in order to become effective contributors to the board decision-making process. The need for induction is more important for NEDs than for internally appointed executive directors, who should be familiar with much of the business before their appointment to the board. However, newly appointed executive directors may not be familiar with all the responsibilities and duties of being a director, and may need induction to make them more aware of what will be expected of them in their new role.

The UK Code of Corporate Governance states that **all** directors should receive induction on joining the board and that 'to function effectively all directors need appropriate knowledge of the company and access to its operations and staff'.

The chairman is responsible for ensuring that new directors receive 'full, formal and tailored' induction. Although there is no specific reference to the company secretary, the chairman will probably ask the company secretary to arrange for each director to receive a personalised induction programme. The aim should be to make the director an effective member of the board as quickly as possible, and an induction programme may therefore focus initially on providing essential information and familiarity with the company. Over time, further induction may then be provided.

A programme of induction may include:

■ providing copies of minutes of previous board meetings and copies of any current strategy documents that the board has approved
■ visits to key company sites
■ product presentations
■ meetings with senior management and staff
■ meetings with external advisers of the company, such as the auditors or company's solicitors
■ meetings with major shareholders (should any such shareholders want one). The UK Code states that as part of the induction process, directors should be offered the opportunity to meet with the company's major shareholders.

Reading is an effective way for an individual to absorb new information quickly, and the company secretary might therefore wish to give a new director a selection of documents as an induction pack. The ICSA's Guidance Note on Induction of Directors (2003) comments:

'The objective of induction is to inform the director such that he can become as effective as possible in their new role as soon as possible. The provision of reams of paper in one go is, obviously, not conducive to this process.'

The ICSA's recommendation is therefore that information should be provided to new directors in an induction pack in stages:

■ essential information to be provided immediately, including information about the duties of directors
■ material to be provided over the first few weeks following the appointment, at the most appropriate time.

'Improving Board Effectiveness' provides useful guidance on induction. 'The chair, the new director and the company secretary should work closely together to devise an effective induction programme which is suited to the needs of the individual. The induction programme may extend over a period of time, and may involve a combination of presentations, seminars, face-to-face meetings including with shareholders and other major stakeholders, and other activities. Consideration should be given to visiting important business locations and meeting senior and middle management to develop a meaningful 'line of sight' into the business, and particularly those areas that carry significant risk.'

6.2 Induction of an executive manager as an executive director

The induction process described above is much more relevant to an individual joining as a director from outside the company. For an individual who is already an executive manager of the company and now appointed as executive director, the induction process needs a different focus. A senior executive of the company should already be familiar with many aspects of the company's operations (although his induction might include visits to parts of the company he has not worked with before).

An executive manager 'promoted' to the board is much more likely to lack knowledge and experience about being a director and corporate governance. (However, some large companies try to give their senior executives experience as a director, by allowing them to take a position as an NED in another company.)

An induction programme for such an individual may therefore need to focus on matters such as:

■ the role of the board, including matters reserved for the board and oversight of management
■ the powers and duties of directors, and the rights of shareholders (the new director should be given a copy of the company's constitution (articles of association))

- the role of board committees
- the role of the board in monitoring risk and **internal control** (see also Chapter 10)
- membership of the board and its committees, how the board operates and the role of the company secretary
- frequency of board meetings
- what the new director will be expected to contribute
- who the major shareholders are and their relationship with the company
- compliance with corporate governance requirements
- the law relating to fair dealing by directors (the law on insider dealing) and in the UK the Model Code on share dealing by directors
- the potential liabilities of directors
- directors' liability insurance;
- company policy on corporate social responsibility
- arrangements for monitoring the performance of board members.

This list is not exhaustive. However, in some cases it might be considered too long. The main point is that an executive manager appointed as a director needs to learn about the differences in the roles of manager and director, and that he has not been appointed as a director simply to be a 'high level' executive of the company.

6.3 Training and professional development

Directors should keep their knowledge and skills up to date, so that they can continue to perform effectively, and the company should ensure that this is provided. The appropriate training and personal development for each individual director will depend on the director's personal situation.

- All directors may need training or updating when there is a change in an important aspect of the law or when new regulations are introduced that affect the company's operations or its governance.
- Members of board committees may need to be updated or may need to acquire greater in-depth knowledge of matters affecting the work of their committee.
- Directors may need to be informed about an important new product or an important new acquisition for the company.

The UK Code states that:

'The chairman should ensure that the directors continually update their skills and the knowledge and familiarity with the company required to fulfil their role both on the board and on board committees. The company should provide the necessary resources for developing and updating its directors' knowledge and capabilities.'

The Higgs Report (2003) made the point that personal development is not simply a matter of receiving formal 'classroom training', although formal training will be suitable in many cases. The Report commented:

'On appointment, non-executive directors will already have relevant skills, knowledge, experience and abilities. Nevertheless, a non-executive director's credibility and effectiveness in the boardroom will depend not just on their existing capability but on their ability to extend and refresh their knowledge and skills. . . . The word "training" in this context is not altogether helpful as it carries rather limited connotations of formal instruction in a classroom setting. . . . By contrast, what I envisage is continued professional development tailored to the individual.'

The particular training and development needs for each individual director should be assessed by the chairman, but each director should be able to make suggestions about the type of training or development that might be suitable for him personally. The UK Code includes a provision that the chairman should agree a personalised approach to training and development with each director. This should be reviewed regularly. The obvious time to do this is during the annual performance review of the director. Performance reviews are described throughout section 7 below.

TEST YOUR KNOWLEDGE **5.5**

What should the induction of a new director consist of?

7 Performance evaluation of the board

7.1 Requirement for annual evaluation

A possibly contentious issue in corporate governance is the extent to which the performance of directors should be monitored and assessed, and what form such assessments should take. In the UK, a requirement for directors to undergo formal performance appraisals each year was introduced into the corporate governance code in 2003.

The UK Code states as a main principle that the board should undertake a 'formal and rigorous annual evaluation of its own performance and that of its committees and individual directors'.

Evaluation of individual directors should aim to show whether each director:

- continues to contribute effectively, and
- continues to demonstrate commitment to the role (e.g. in terms of time spent in carrying out the director's duties, attendance at board and committee meetings, and on other duties).

The evaluation of performance is probably particularly important for NEDs. Executive directors commit all or most of their time to the company and should be fully familiar with the business and the company's operations. In contrast, NEDs spend only a part of their time with the company, even though they make up the membership of key board committees – the audit and **remuneration committees** in particular (see also Chapter 6). There is a possibility that NEDs will lose some of their enthusiasm for the company, and may get into a habit of missing meetings and not spending as much time with the company as expected. In some cases, a director may fail to keep up to date with an important area of his supposed expertise.

The requirement for regular performance evaluation of directors varies between countries, but is not restricted to the UK. For example, it is included as a recommendation in the King III Code.

Originally, the UK governance code did not recommend how the performance evaluation of the board, its committees and individual directors should be carried out, or who should do it. It became established practice, however, that except for the performance review of the chairman himself, the chairman should organise the performance review process and should be closely involved in it.

One approach is for the chairman to carry out the reviews personally, possibly with advice and assistance from the company secretary. Alternatively, the chairman may be responsible for deciding on the process that should be used for the performance review, and should act on the findings of the review, but may hand the responsibility for conducting the review to the senior independent director. Companies may also use the services of specialist external consultants.

The UK Code requires that the board should state in the company's annual report how the performance evaluation of the board, its committees and individual directors has been carried out.

7.2 Evaluation of the board

In the UK, the potential value of external consultants has been recognised, and the UK Code now states that for the evaluation of the board as a whole:

- the evaluation of the board of FTSE companies should be 'externally facilitated' at least every three years; in other words, the company should use specialist external consultants at least once every three years, and
- where the company uses external consultants, the company should make a statement of whether the consultants have any other connection with the company. (Independent consultants are more likely to provide better advice.)

A FTSE 350 company might therefore use external consultants in one year, and then the chairman might use the lessons obtained from the consultants to carry out an internal performance evaluation for the next two years. In year four, external consultants might be used again as a way of learning new lessons or checking the quality of the internal evaluation process.

The possible reasons for an ineffective board may be any of the following.

- Insufficient information provided to the directors to enable them to make properly considered decisions.
- Directors not given sufficient time before a board meeting to read relevant papers, and so arrive at the meeting not properly briefed.
- Directors not bothering to take time before a board meeting to read relevant papers, and so arrive at the meeting not properly briefed.
- Individual directors failing to attend meetings of the board or meetings of board committees.
- Individual directors not being given enough opportunity to contribute to discussions in board meetings (this would arguably be a failing of the chairman rather than an indication of an ineffective board).
- The board failing to carry out its responsibilities in full.
- The board failing to take its annual performance evaluation seriously enough.
- The board making ill-considered (bad) strategic decisions.

To assess the performance of the board, a comparison should be made between what the board should be expected to achieve, and what it has actually achieved. One way of doing this may be to provide answers to a set of questions about performance, possibly through discussions at a special board meeting. Questions that may provide a useful basis for assessment of board performance are set out below.

- Does the board have any specific performance objectives, e.g. in terms of business performance or dividend payments? How well has the board performed against any such targets?
- What has the board contributed to the development of strategy and what has the board done to oversee the implementation of strategy and achievement of strategy targets?
- What has the board contributed to ensuring that the company has a robust and effective risk management system?
- Is the board concerning itself with the appropriate issues? Is the list of matters reserved for the board suitable or should it be amended?
- Is the board an appropriate size and is the mix of members suitable (in terms of spread of experience, knowledge, skills and/or background)? Are changes needed?
- How well does the board communicate with management, employees, shareholders and other stakeholders?

Questions may also be asked about the effectiveness of boardroom practice.

- Do board members receive relevant and clear information in good time for board meetings and decision-making? Is the amount and quality of this information adequate?
- Have there been sufficient board meetings in the past year?
- Are the board meetings too short to be effective or too long?

'Improving Board Effectiveness' suggests that companies will need to tailor the questions about board effectiveness to suit their particular circumstances, but that issues to consider will include a review of:

- the overall composition of the board, to confirm that it has a suitable mix of skills and experience and is suitably diverse
- the contribution and effectiveness of the chairman, committee chairmen, other individual directors and the board committees
- how the board works together (for example the relationship between the chairman and the CEO) and the effectiveness of the company secretary
- how decision processes work, including a review of strategy discussions and oversight by the board of the management of risk and internal control the effectiveness of the NEDs as a group, and whether the board is dominated by an individual or a small group
- how the board communicates with shareholders and other stakeholders and responds to their concerns.

7.3 Evaluation of board committees

Board committees should be evaluated in a similar way to the board as a whole. For each committee, there should be a comparison between what the committee is responsible for doing and what it has actually done.

- Has the nomination committee been successful in identifying suitable individuals for board appointments?
- Have any individuals been appointed to the board who, in retrospect, were not as good as originally thought?
- Has the nomination committee done any succession planning and if so, how good have its plans been?
- Has the committee made clear recommendations to the board, and has the board acted on its recommendations?
- Is the committee an appropriate size and is the mix of members suitable? Are changes needed?
- Have there been enough committee meetings during the past year?

Similar questions can be asked about the remuneration committee and audit committee, whose work is described in later chapters.

7.4 Evaluation of individual board members

The performance of individual executive directors as executive managers is not dealt with by a corporate governance code, because individual executive performance is not a governance issue. For governance purposes, the evaluation of performance relates to performance as a director.

For an independent NED, key questions for evaluation include the following.

- How many board meetings has the director attended, and how many times has he been absent?
- How well prepared has the individual been for meetings, e.g. has he read the relevant papers in advance?
- What has been the quality of contributions of the individual to board meetings, e.g. on strategic development and risk management?
- Has the individual shown independence of character, or has he tended to go along with the opinions of certain other board members?
- How many board committee meetings has the director attended and how many has he missed?
- What has the individual contributed to committee meetings?
- Has the time commitment of the director been sufficient? Has the time commitment been as much as expected, or as much as stated in the director terms of appointment?
- Does the NED continue to show interest in and enthusiasm for the company?
- Are there reasons why the director may no longer be considered independent?
- Does the director communicate well with the other directors and with senior executives of the company?

The UK Code states that: 'Individual evaluation should aim to show whether each director continues to contribute effectively and to demonstrate commitment to the role (including commitment of time for board and committee meetings and any other duties).'

7.5 Evaluation of the chairman

The UK Code states that the NEDs, led by the senior independent director, should be responsible for the performance evaluation of the chairman, 'taking into account the views of executive directors'. However, the actual performance review of the chairman may be conducted for the NEDs by external consultants.

The chairman's performance should be assessed by comparing his responsibilities with his achievements, and asking whether he has been successful in providing the board leadership that should be expected of him.

7.6 Using the results of a performance review

To obtain practical value from an annual evaluation of the board, its committees and its individual directors, the board should be prepared to act on its findings whenever performance is not considered to be as good as it should be. The chairman has the responsibility for acting to deal with poor performance.

The UK Corporate Governance Code makes the following provisions for how the performance review should be used:

'The chairman should act on the results of the performance evaluation by recognising both the strengths and weaknesses of the board and, where appropriate, proposing new members to be appointed to the board or seeking the resignation of directors.'

In the preface to the 2010 UK Code, the chairman of the Financial Reporting Council (FRC) has stated: 'Chairmen are encouraged to report personally in their annual statements how the principles relating to the role and effectiveness of the board have been applied.' The recommendation is that the chairman of a company should recognise his personal responsibility for performance and effectiveness of the board, and a company should not simply disclose its procedures for assessing performance in a 'boiler plate' fashion.

The chairman may also consider the need for changes to the composition of board committees and may ask for the resignation of a committee chairman. Some improvements may be achieved by changing board procedures (e.g. holding meetings more frequently, or changing the dates of meetings to give management more time to prepare the information required).

Although the chairman has the primary responsibility for acting on the results of the annual performance review, the guidance 'Improving Board Effectiveness' states that: 'The results of a board evaluation should be shared with the board as a whole and fed back, as appropriate, into the board's work on composition, the design of induction and development, and other relevant areas.'

7.7 Problems with performance reviews

The performance evaluation of the board and its directors is recognised in the UK as a valuable tool for the assessment of the effectiveness of the board, and institutional investors have shown an interest in obtaining information about the evaluation process.

- They want to know that an evaluation has taken place, but they also need assurance that the evaluation process is of a suitable quality standard and rigour. This is a reason why the UK Code introduced a requirement for external consultants to be used at least every three years.
- Investors would also like to know more about the action that has been taken following an annual performance review, because they want assurance that the review is being used to improve the effectiveness of the board. However, it may be difficult to provide as much information about the performance review, especially the review of individual directors, without compromising the confidentiality of the exercise.

TEST YOUR KNOWLEDGE 5.6

(a) What are the requirements in the UK Code for the performance evaluation of the board, its committees and its individual directors?

(b) What is the purpose of an annual performance evaluation of the board and its directors?

(c) What factors should be considered when reviewing the performance of an NED?

(d) How might a chairman arrange for the evaluation of the performance of the board and its directors?

8   Boardroom ethics

It was explained in Chapter 1 that ethical business practice is an important aspect of good corporate governance. Ethics are discussed in more detail in Chapters 1 and 11. The ethical culture of a company and its employees is established by the board of directors and senior executives. The following paragraphs deal with ways in which some unethical practices by directors are regulated, and how directors may be liable for failure to perform their duties adequately, e.g. their duty of skill and care – even if their failure of duty is unintentional.

8.1 Disqualification of directors

In UK law, the Company Directors Disqualification Act 1986 identifies certain categories of misconduct that could lead to the disqualification of a person from acting as a company director of any company for a number of years. Often, the misconduct is an offence in connection with the formation or insolvency of a company.

8.2 Dealings by directors in shares of their company

Restrictions on dealings in shares by directors

Directors usually own some shares in their company. Even if an executive director is not a long-term holder of the company's shares, he is likely to acquire shares at some time or another, through the grant of shares or exercising share options that have been awarded as part of his remuneration package.

A governance issue that arises with share dealing by directors is that the directors of a public company are likely to know more about the financial position of the company than other investors. They are also likely to hear about any takeover bid involving the company before it is announced to the stock market. It is therefore conceivable that some directors might take advantage of their inside knowledge to buy or sell shares in the company before information affecting the share price is released to the stock market. For example, a director might buy shares in the company if he knows that financial results shortly to be announced to the market will be very good, and likely to give a boost to the share price. Similarly, the directors might sell shares when they know the company is in trouble, and before the bad news is announced, in order to sell at a higher price than they would otherwise be able to obtain.

Insider dealing

In the UK, Part V of the Criminal Justice Act 1993 makes it a criminal offence for anyone to make use of 'inside information' to buy or sell shares in a company in a regulated stock market. (Other countries have similar legislation.) Inside information has the following characteristics.

- It has not yet been made public and released to the stock market.
- It is specific or precise. For example, it may be information that the company will announce an increase in annual profits of about 50 per cent or that the company is about to become the target for a takeover bid by Company X. Information that a company has had a good year financially and will be announcing higher profits is not specific enough to be 'inside information'.
- The information must also be price-sensitive. This means that if the information were to be made public, it would have a significant effect on the price of the company's shares.

An 'insider' is someone in possession of inside information. In UK law it is illegal for any insider to make use of **price-sensitive information** to deal in shares of a company or to encourage anyone else to deal in shares of the company. Directors are insiders and are subject to these prohibitions against insider dealing. This is hardly surprising. If a director made a personal profit from dealing in the company's shares by making use of inside information, the profit would be obtained at the expense of other investors – shareholders or former shareholders in the company. However, insiders may be other employees of a company or advisers to a company, such as accountants or investment bankers giving advice on a proposed takeover bid that has not yet been announced to the stock market. If an insider passes on price-sensitive information to someone else, the recipient of the information also becomes an insider, and must not deal in shares of the company until the information becomes public knowledge.

Insider dealing is a criminal offence, with offenders liable to a fine, imprisonment or both. However, in practice there have been relatively few successful prosecutions of individuals for insider dealing in the UK, because the guilt of an alleged insider dealer has been difficult to prove in specific cases.

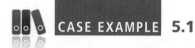 **CASE EXAMPLE 5.1**

Company X is a listed company in the UK. In July the company was at an advanced stage of negotiations for the friendly takeover of another listed company, Company Y. Documents relating to the proposed takeover bid were distributed to the directors of Company X, in advance of a board meeting at the end of July when the decision to approve the bid and announce it to the stock market would be made. The takeover went ahead in August and the cash purchase price for Company Y was 30 per cent above its market value just before the takeover was announced.

It was subsequently reported that the wife of one of the NEDs of Company X had purchased a large quantity of shares in Company Y at the end of July and had sold them at a profit in August. The NED was asked if he had told his wife about the takeover or shown her the relevant documents; he said no, that the documents had been in his close possession at all times except for one day when he had left them in the garden of his house when he went in for lunch for about an hour. When challenged, the wife of the NED denied all knowledge of the documents and confirmed that she had not spoken to her husband about the takeover.

The other directors of Company X did not believe the assurances of the NED, but had no evidence to prove insider dealing. They had to accept that the NED had not acted unethically.

The chairman of the board subsequently discussed with the chairman of the nomination committee the need to refresh the board, although the NED in question was not due to retire for another 18 months.

Market abuse

In the UK, activity that could be classified as insider dealing would also be classified as **market abuse** under the provisions of the Financial Services and Markets Act 2000. This Act gives the financial markets regulator the power to fine any individuals for market abuse, which is easier to prove than insider dealing under the Criminal Justice Act.

 **CASE EXAMPLE 5.2**

In 2010, the Financial Services Authority (the FSA UK financial markets regulator) imposed a fine of nearly £1 million on the chief executive of Genel Enerji, a Turkish exploration company. This individual had dealt in the shares of Heritage Oil, a UK listed company and partner of Genel Enerji in a business venture, on the basis of inside information. Two other executives in the company were also fined for a similar offence. The inside information related to the results of tests by Heritage at the Miran oil field: the individuals concerned bought shares in Heritage on the basis of the test results before these were disclosed to the stock market. When the test results were announced publicly, the shares in Heritage Oil rose in price by 25 per cent. In his defence, the CEO of Genel Enerji said that he was unaware of UK law prohibiting dealing in shares under these circumstances.

The Model Code and directors' dealings

The law on dealing in shares by directors might be supplemented, in the case of stock market companies, by stock market regulations. In the UK, the Listing Rules (which are a part of the FSA Handbook) require listed companies to have rules for share dealings by their directors that are no less stringent than the rules in the Model Code contained within the Listing Rules. The purpose of the restrictions is to try to ensure that directors 'do not abuse, and do not place themselves under suspicion of abusing, inside information that they may have or be thought to have, especially in periods leading up to an announcement of the company's results'.

The rules in the UK are more stringent than in some other countries, where dealing in shares of their company whilst in possession of price-sensitive information may be acceptable behaviour. Certainly, when a company gets into financial difficulties, suspicion is certain to fall on any directors selling shares in the period before the company's problems become public knowledge.

The Listing Rules include a Model Code for share dealing by directors and 'relevant employees'. Compliance with the Code should ensure that directors (and other individuals with access to key unpublished financial information about the company) do not breach the rules against insider dealing (a criminal offence) and do not give investors any grounds for suspecting insider dealing or unethical dealing in the company's shares.

The main provisions of the Model Code are as follows.

- Directors must not deal in shares of their company during the two months before the announcement of the company's interim and final results, or between the end of the financial year and the announcement of the annual results. These are known as **close periods**. (If the company produces quarterly results, the non-trading period is just one month before publication, in the case of the three interim quarterly results, but the same rules apply to the final results.)
- A director must not deal at any time that he is privy to price-sensitive information. Information is price-sensitive if its publication could have a significant effect on the share price.
- A director must seek clearance from the chairman (or another designated director) prior to dealing in the company's shares. Clearance must not be given during a 'prohibited period'. A prohibited period is a close period and any period during which there is unpublished price-sensitive information that is reasonably likely to result in an announcement being made. (The chairman must seek clearance to deal from the CEO, and the CEO must seek clearance from the chairman.)
- In exceptional circumstances, clearance to deal can be given during a prohibited period where the director has a pressing financial commitment or would suffer financial hardship if unable to deal.
- A director must ensure that none of his connected persons deals without clearance. Connected persons include spouse and infant children, and companies in which the director controls over 20 per cent of the equity.

Notification to the stock market of dealings in shares by directors

For stock market companies in the UK, there are requirements for disclosure of dealings by directors in shares in their company.

The regulations for listed companies are imposed by the Disclosure and Transparency Rules of the FSA. 'Persons discharging managerial responsibilities (PDMRs)' in listed companies must notify details of dealings by themselves and 'connected persons' in shares of the company, including details of the quantity of shares dealt and price. The company is then required to disseminate this information to the stock market through a Regulated Information Service (RIS).

TEST YOUR KNOWLEDGE 5.7

What are the requirements of the Model Code in the UK?

8.3 Material personal interest in a transaction with the company

Directors are required by UK law to avoid conflicts of interest with their company. However, a situation may arise in which a director has a material (significant) personal interest in a transaction with the company and will stand to gain if the transaction goes ahead. If the transaction is considered to be in the interests of the company, there would be no conflict of interest for the director.

The Companies Act 2006 makes it a duty of the director in these circumstances to disclose his interest in the transaction to the board of directors. If the rest of the board give their consent, the director is permitted to retain his interest in the transaction at the board meeting where the transaction is considered by the board, and he will not be required to account to the company for any profit or benefit that he makes from the transaction.

Failure by a director to disclose an interest in a contract with the company makes the contract voidable. This means that the company can choose to declare the contract void, but it is not automatically void. The company can also seek to hold the individual director to account for any profit that he has made on the contract.

9 Liability of directors

9.1 Potential personal liability of directors

There is some personal financial risk in becoming a company director or acting in an official capacity on behalf of a company. (See also Chapter 10.) If an individual commits a 'wrongful act' as a director, he could become liable (personally or together with other directors) and could become the target of a civil legal action. A director who is sued individually is exposed to certain costs, such as:

■ the costs of legal advice and paying for defence against the legal action, and
■ a compensation payment in the event that the legal action is decided in favour of the claimant and against the director.

'Wrongful acts' have been explained as 'actual or alleged breach of duty, breach of trust, misstatement, misrepresentation, omission or breach of warranty of authority, libel or slander'. For example, a director may be sued for an alleged misstatement in a document issued to shareholders by the board. There may be a legal action against a director for an alleged breach of duty, and even if the allegation is found to be unjustified, the director may find that he has incurred some costs that cannot be recovered from the person who made the allegation.

9.2 Directors' and officers' liability insurance

Directors should expect their company to provide insurance against some of these liabilities. The insurance that a company may pay for, to provide protection for its directors (and other officers) is called directors' and officers' (D&O) liability insurance.

D&O liability insurance is relevant to corporate governance because without it, directors could be dangerously exposed to the risk of legal action for 'wrongful acts'. If this risk is seen to be excessive, individuals should refuse to accept the offer of an appointment as director (or company secretary), and it could be extremely difficult for companies to appoint anyone to their boards.

D&O liability insurance contracts vary in some important ways.

■ They may differ in the nature of the 'wrongful acts' that are covered by the policy; some policies provide wider protection than others.
■ They may differ in the financial amount or value of protection that they provide.

A company cannot insure a director against personal liability for illegal or fraudulent acts by a director. However, directors can be insured against legal costs incurred in defending an action (civil or criminal) for alleged negligence, default, breach of duty or breach of trust in relation to the company. If a director is found guilty of a criminal action, there is no insurance cover for any fine or penalty that the court decides to impose. However, insurance cover can be provided for the costs of a settlement in a civil action.

A provision of the UK Corporate Governance Code is that the company has a responsibility for providing D&O liability insurance: 'The company should arrange appropriate insurance cover in respect of legal action against its directors.'

Before accepting an appointment as director, an individual should look carefully into the nature of the D&O liability insurance cover that will be provided. If necessary he should take legal advice to decide whether or not the cover is adequate.

9.3 Personal risk review

NEDs might be well advised to keep their potential liabilities under continual review, possibly by carrying out a personal risk review regularly throughout the term of their office. It might be useful to go through a 'tick' list of items for review, as below.

- Has the NED spent enough time on his duties? If not, is it likely that the NED has been negligent in some way?
- Has he kept his skills and knowledge refreshed?
- Have there been any concerns with financial reporting, narrative reporting or any other information issued by the company?
- Is the NED satisfied that the company remains a going concern?
- Does the company appear to have sound systems in place for monitoring and controlling risks?
- Are there any regulatory issues involving the company that might expose the NED to legal liability?
- Is the NED satisfied that the company has complied with the provisions of the UK Corporate Governance Code, or that reasons for any non-compliance are justified?

TEST YOUR KNOWLEDGE 5.8

What is directors' and officers' liability insurance?

CASE QUESTION

1 What do the original owners of Stenning Tull (Don Stenning and Rebecca Tull) need to be aware of when working with a new team of directors as board of a new listed company?

2 What recommendations would you make to ensure that the new and existing directors work effectively, both individually and together as a team?

CHAPTER SUMMARY

- There are certain fundamental requirements for an effective and efficient board. These include: having directors of appropriate character, sufficiently frequent board meetings, and appropriate agendas for board meetings; providing timely and sufficient information to all directors (but particularly NEDs); providing administrative support and advice to directors; and, when required, access to professional advice for directors. The provision of administrative support and advice to NEDs is usually the responsibility of the company secretary.
- The ICSA has issued a report on boardroom behaviours, identifying the characteristics of best practice in boardroom behaviour and suggesting guidelines for best practice.
- The board of directors may delegate to a nomination committee the task of recommending new appointees to the board. In the UK, the UK Corporate Governance Code recommends that a majority of the nominations committee should be independent NEDs and that its chairman should be either the chairman of the board or an independent director.
- The nomination committee should also be responsible for making recommendations for board succession and changes in the size and composition of the board. The committee should also consider the need to refresh the board with new NEDs, and should therefore also make recommendations

about the re-appointment of NEDs who are reaching the end of their contract. In 2003 the Tyson Report in the UK recommended that companies should search more widely for candidates to act as independent NEDs.

■ Appointments to the board are made by the board as a whole, on the recommendation of the nomination committee, but directors who have been appointed must (in the UK) stand for election by the shareholders at the following annual general meeting.

■ Before accepting the offer of appointment as NED, an individual should consider a range of issues. An NED is typically appointed with a three-year contract and is paid a fixed annual fee. Contracts may be renewed at the end of each three-year period, although the independence of an NED may be brought into question if he has held the position for nine years or more.

■ In the past it has been usual practice in the UK for directors to stand for re-election every three years, at the annual general meeting. A new requirement was introduced by the UK Corporate Governance Code in 2010. All directors of FTSE 350 companies and NEDs who have been board members for more than nine years should stand for re-election annually.

■ There should also be suitable induction for new directors. This is the responsibility of the chairman, who may delegate the task to the company secretary.

■ Directors should also receive further training throughout their term in office. The chairman is responsible for ensuring that appropriate training is provided.

■ The UK Code states that there should be an annual performance review of the entire board, its committees and individual directors. This is the responsibility of the chairman, but at least every three years the performance evaluation process should be 'externally facilitated' by specialist consultants.

■ The NEDs, led by the senior independent director, should carry out the performance review of the chairman.

■ The performance review of the board should assess its effectiveness. Guidelines have been issued about how the performance of the board, its committees and its individual directors (particularly the NEDs) may be assessed.

■ Directors should act ethically and provide ethical leadership. There are legal provisions for the disqualification of individuals who have been in serious breach of their duties as a director. A disqualified individual cannot hold any company directorship for the period of disqualification.

■ Insider dealing, by directors and others, is a criminal offence. In addition, directors of listed companies in the UK are required to comply with the rules of their company about the periods of time during which they cannot deal in shares in their company ('close periods'). These rules must be no less stringent than those set out in a Model Code.

■ Directors may be taken to court for alleged breaches of duty and could be personally liable for expenses resulting from this. Companies should provide directors' and officers' liability insurance as cover for this risk. An individual should not accept an appointment as director without being satisfied that the D&O liability insurance is sufficient.

Remuneration of directors and senior executives

6

■ CONTENTS

■ INTRODUCTION

The remuneration of executive directors and other senior executives has been a contentious issue, partly because of the amounts paid to top executives in some companies and partly because remuneration for senior executives has risen by a much bigger percentage than increases in pay for other employees. Remuneration packages should be sufficient to attract and retain executives of a suitable calibre, but should not be excessive. Remuneration packages should also reward executives for successful performance, in both the short term and the longer term, because pay incentives are expected to encourage executives to perform better. Contracts of employment for senior executives should also try to minimise the risk of paying large 'rewards for failure' when a senior director fails to perform to a satisfactory standard and is dismissed. This chapter looks at the role of the remuneration committee, the problems with negotiating a satisfactory remuneration package for senior executives, and what the elements of that package should be. Shareholders cannot decide the remuneration of directors and cannot vote to reject contracts of employment that have already been agreed. However, in the UK they have a legal right to be given information about directors' remuneration and to approve any new long-term incentive scheme for executives.

1   Remuneration as a corporate governance issue

Until the 1990s in the UK and early 2000s in the USA, the remuneration of executive directors and senior executives was not seen as a major problem of corporate governance. A sense that something might be wrong began when:

■ the general public, alerted by the media, criticised some top executives for being paid far more money than they were worth, and
■ investment institutions criticised directors for receiving ever-increasing rewards even when their company performed badly.

In the UK, the problem was further aggravated by the fact that in many listed companies during the 1980s and early 1990s, the chief executive officers (CEOs) and executive chairmen of many companies were involved in deciding their own remuneration package. Concern about remuneration has grown in other countries, particularly with regard to the banking crisis in 2007–2009 and the high rewards earned by senior bankers in spite of the large amounts of public funds provided to prevent banks from financial collapse.

In the UK, the remuneration of top executives has risen rapidly regardless of company performance throughout the 2000s and even through the global recession (and at a faster annual rate than the remuneration of other company employees), whereas a principle of good corporate governance is that remuneration should be linked to some extent to company performance, so that a director will earn more if the company does well, but less if it does badly.

1.1 Public attitudes

A general belief that directors pay themselves far too much can have a damaging effect on the stock market. Private investors may be reluctant to invest in companies that reward their leaders far more than they deserve. It can be particularly damaging to the capital markets when public anger is stirred against directors who continue to pay themselves more when their companies are performing badly.

The problem emerged in the UK during the 1990s, largely as a result of the privatisation of state-owned industries such as water and electricity supply companies. The same individuals who had run the former state-owned enterprises were appointed as directors of newly established listed companies, with a much improved remuneration package. The popular press led a campaign against 'fat cat' directors, such as the leaders of British Gas and United Utilities.

Similar concerns were expressed in the USA in the early 2000s, following a number of corporate scandals. Alan Greenspan (at the time chairman of the US Federal Reserve) commenting in 2002 on the collapse in the stock markets, accused senior executives of 'infectious greed' during the period of the stock market boom in the late 1990s, when the size of reported corporate profits and rapidly increasing value of shares provided an 'outsized increase in opportunities for avarice'.

In 2002 the President of the Federal Reserve, Bill McDonough, attacked the high levels of remuneration for CEOs as 'morally dubious'. He commented that the average CEO now earned more than 400 times the average employee's income, compared with 42 times more than the national average 20 years before, but their performance was not ten times better.

Public anger was also aroused by revelations in the divorce court that the pension perks of the former chairman of General Electric included the use of the company's Boeing 737, an apartment in Central Park, free wine, food, toiletries, flowers, limousine service, tickets to Wimbledon tennis and baseball games and country club memberships, all in addition to his $9 million a year pension. In response to the public outcry, he gave up most of his perks, acknowledging that if he did not, he would appear as 'someone who's out of touch in today's post-Enron world'.

In the UK, during 2002–2003, there was institutional investor concern, supported by widespread media coverage, about large remuneration packages for senior directors where the size of the reward did not seem sufficiently linked to performance, and large **severance payments** (payments on dismissal) to outgoing senior executives who had been ousted from their job following poor company performance. High severance payments to unsuccessful directors were seen as 'rewards for failure'.

Following the global banking crisis of 2007–2009, there was also widespread criticism of remuneration in banks, whereby top executives and traders received large bonuses even though their bank may have been close to collapse or in need of government financial support to remain in business.

The problem of inappropriate remuneration policies for senior executives is now well recognised, but a satisfactory solution has not necessarily been found. However, a distinction should be made between:

- the unethical 'corporate greed' of some senior executives, and
- a reasonable desire by senior executives to be well remunerated for what they do.

Similarly, it important to make the distinction between:

- high rewards that are justified by performance, and
- high rewards that are earned in spite of poor performance.

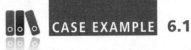 **CASE EXAMPLE** 6.1

In May 2009, shareholders of Royal Dutch Shell (part of the Shell group of energy and petrochemical companies) voted against an executive pay plan, voting down the remuneration report with a majority of 59 per cent. They were objecting to a discretionary pay award to directors for performance in 2006–2008, even though performance targets were not met. This was the second biggest vote against directors' pay in the UK in 2009, second only to an 80 per cent vote against Royal Bank of Scotland (RBS). The vote against the remuneration report is not binding, but the chairman said he would be talking to major shareholders. The only member of the remuneration committee up for re-election was re-elected with a large majority (only 5 per cent against), but following continuing investor pressure the chairman of the remuneration committee resigned later in the year. In February 2010 the company sent a letter to shareholders announcing changes to executive remuneration arrangements, which won investor support.

Agencies that advise institutional investors how to vote are influential. The ABI voting service issues red, amber, blue and green 'tops' to alert members about governance issues in company reports. RiskMetrics is another influential service, especially for cross-border voting. In the Shell case in 2009, the ABI issued an 'amber top', which indicates potentially serious issue of which shareholders should be aware before they vote.

In December 2009, shareholders of Punch Taverns (a UK pub-leasing and managing company) voted against the remuneration report with a 55 per cent majority. Shareholders were angered by the large pay awards given to executives in a year when the group suspended dividend payments after its annual loss quintupled to over £400 million. The ABI had issued a **red top alert**.

 STOP AND THINK 6.1

From your general reading or awareness of the business news, can you name any other example of public anger or concern about remuneration for 'greedy' corporate leaders? Are you aware of any opposition by institutional investors to a director's remuneration package, and what their reasons for opposing it were?

1.2 Why is remuneration a corporate governance issue?

Remuneration of senior executives is a corporate governance issue for several reasons.

- As indicated earlier, excessive remuneration for senior executives that is not clearly linked to good performance can undermine confidence in the stock markets. Executives should not be rewarded for failure.
- Large companies need to attract and retain talented professional businessmen to provide them with effective leadership. Top executives are attracted and retained by the remuneration packages they are offered.
- Companies need effective boards and senior executive management. Remuneration incentives can be used to motivate executives to perform better and to achieve better results for the company.
- However, remuneration incentives should be designed carefully to align the interests of the shareholders and executives as much as possible, in both the short term and the longer term.
- The remuneration of senior executives may antagonise employees (and employee representatives), when it appears that senior executives are paid excessive amounts in comparison with their own pay. A sense that benefits or rewards are unfairly distributed could lead to industrial unrest within the company.

- Institutional investors have demanded greater transparency about senior executive remuneration, and several countries (including the UK) now have laws that require disclosure of directors' remuneration in the annual report and accounts.
- Some concern has been expressed, particularly in the US and UK following the banking crisis, that the incentive elements of remuneration packages do not take risk into consideration, so that executives are encouraged to take excessive risks in order to boost profit performance and earn bigger rewards. The UK Walker Report into corporate governance in banks (2009) commented: 'It is of vital importance that [performance objectives] are risk-adjusted to take account of the incremental capital, liquidity, franchise or other risk that would be entailed in vigorous pursuit of … market share or revenue … Risk adjustment in remuneration structures is essential to counterbalance any executive disposition to increase risk as the means of increasing short-term returns.'

Remuneration as a governance issue applies to senior executives below board level, as well as to directors. This is because in most companies the board includes only a small number of executive directors, and the use of remuneration packages as an incentive to management applies to other powerful individuals who are not on the board.

STOP AND THINK 6.2

What are the potential problems for good corporate governance when the annual remuneration of senior executives rises at a very much higher percentage rate than the salaries of other employees over a period of several years?

TEST YOUR KNOWLEDGE 6.1

For what reasons are the remuneration of senior executives considered a corporate governance issues in some countries?

2 Principles of senior executive remuneration

Principles of remuneration are now included in the corporate governance codes of many countries. In a system of good corporate governance, the remuneration of directors and key senior executives should be sufficient to attract and retain individuals of a suitable calibre. At the same time, the structure of an individual's remuneration package should motivate the individual towards the achievement of performance that is in the best interests of the company and its shareholders, as well as those of the individual.

The UK Corporate Governance Code states as a principle that:

'Levels of remuneration should be sufficient to attract, retain and motivate directors of the quality required to run the company successfully, but a company should avoid paying more than is necessary for this purpose. A significant proportion of executive directors' remuneration should be structured so as to link rewards to corporate and individual performance.'

It is widely accepted that senior executives should be able to earn a high level of remuneration in return for the work they do and the responsibilities they carry. If a company does not offer an attractive package, it will not attract individuals of the required calibre. It is also generally accepted that the level of remuneration should be linked in some way to satisfactory performance. If an executive performs well, he should receive more rewards than if he performs only reasonably well.

The central issue for corporate governance is concerned with the link between pay and performance.

- The remuneration package should include a performance-related element. If the director successfully achieves predetermined levels of performance, he should be rewarded accordingly. There could be some debate as to how much remuneration should be performance related, but there is a view that a substantial part of a director's total potential remuneration should be linked to performance.
- The purpose of performance-related remuneration is to give a director an incentive to achieve the performance targets. This is why potential performance-related pay should be substantial.
- It is clearly in the interest of good corporate governance that directors should be motivated to perform, but it is equally important that the performance targets set for each individual director are: (1) sufficiently challenging; and (2) related to objectives that are in the interests of the company and its shareholders. Performance targets should therefore be challenging, and large rewards should not be paid for average performance.

Linking remuneration, wholly or in part, to performance is not an easy task, however, as the following shows.

- Unsuitable measures of performance may be selected, so that although the individual executive succeeds in achieving targets that earn high rewards, the company itself and its shareholders do not obtain a comparable benefit.
- Many performance measures are based on the short term, possibly linked to annual results. This may not be in the interests of the company's longer-term development and performance.
- Remuneration systems are normally designed to provide the reward after the performance has been made. This time delay means that if the company has poor results in the current year after having done well in the previous year, an executive may be paid high remuneration (for the previous year) at a time the company is doing badly.

The best remuneration packages align the interests of the individual directors with those of the company and its shareholders. However, some shareholders may focus on short-term performance with the intention of selling their shares if the share price rises. Other shareholders may intend to invest for the longer term, but could be persuaded to sell by a large rise in the share price. The interests of shareholders are therefore both short term and longer term.

A supporting principle states that the performance-related elements of a remuneration package for a senior executive should be 'stretching' and should also be designed in a way that:

- aligns the interests of the executive with the interests of the shareholders, and
- promotes the long-term success of the company.

The view of the UK Code is therefore that the interests of shareholders in the longer term should not be subordinated to short-term considerations.

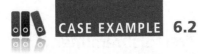 **CASE EXAMPLE 6.2**

Problems with setting suitable remuneration packages for executives are well illustrated by the 2002 case of Vodafone and its CEO Sir Christopher Gent. The company consulted widely with institutional investors about a new remuneration package for the CEO, and obtained their approval for the principles of the package. However, when the company eventually applied the principles to devise a detailed package, many shareholders were dissatisfied. Three particular controversies were reported in the run-up to the company's 2002 AGM.

- Sir Christopher was awarded a special payment of £10 million for his role in the acquisition of the German company Mannesmann. The problem with payments based on successful takeovers is that there is often no way of knowing for some time whether a takeover has

(Continued)

CASE EXAMPLE **6.2** (*Continued*)

been a success or not. In the case of Vodafone and Mannesmann, the takeover occurred at a time when the telecommunications industry appeared to be growing rapidly and share prices in telecommunications companies were rocketing. Two years or so later, after the worldwide share price collapse in 2001, the wisdom of the Mannesmann deal was called into question.

- A second problem was that Sir Christopher received large bonus payments for the year to 31 March 2002, when the company reported a loss of £13.5 billion, the largest in UK corporate history. Here, the problem is one of trying to ensure, as far as possible, that bonus payments are linked to the achievement of satisfactory performance targets, although these could include longer-term targets and non-financial targets.

- A third problem was the announcement of a new remuneration policy, in response to investor criticisms of the old policy. The company consulted with City institutions when formulating the new policy, with the intention of winning their approval. However, investment institutions might be willing to support the principle of a remuneration policy, yet still be angered by the details. Regardless of the general aims of a remuneration policy, the problem is in getting the details right. In particular, there could be general approval of which performance measures should be used, but disagreement about how challenging should the performance targets be, and what limits, if any, should be placed on the size of bonus payments. When the shareholders voted on the remuneration package at the company's annual general meeting in July 2002, the package was approved, but there was a fairly large vote against.

STOP AND THINK **6.3**

In response to the threat of measures by the UK government to levy a higher rate of tax on bonuses for bank executives, a UK bank was reported in 2009 to have increased the basic salaries of many of its executives by about 25 per cent to 30 per cent. Is this an example of poor government policy, bad corporate governance by the bank, or both?

3   Elements of remuneration for executive directors and other senior executives

3.1 The component elements of executive directors' remuneration

The remuneration package for a senior executive is likely to consist of a combination of:

- a basic salary
- a payment by the company into a pension scheme arrangement for the individual
- an annual bonus, tied perhaps to the annual financial performance of the company
- long-term incentives, usually in the form of share option awards or the granting of fully paid company shares (sometimes called 'restricted stock awards').

In addition, executives might enjoy a number of other perks such as free private medical insurance, a company car and the use of a company aeroplane or apartment. Remuneration can be divided into two elements, a **fixed pay** element and a **variable pay** element.

■ The fixed element is the remuneration received by the director regardless of performance, such as fixed salary and salary-related pension.
■ The variable element consists of the **performance-related incentives** (cash bonuses, awards of share options or shares depending on performance, etc.). The size of the remuneration depends on the performance achieved.

A problem in negotiating a remuneration package with an executive is to decide on the balance between the fixed and the variable elements, and to agree on measures of performance as the basis for deciding on how much the performance-related payments should be. The variable element can also be divided into:

■ short-term incentives, often in the form of cash bonuses or possibly bonuses in the form of grants of company shares
■ long-term incentives, in the form of share options or share grants.

Short-term incentives are based on annual performance targets. Long-term incentives may be awarded each year, but are linked to performance over a longer period of time, typically three years (or longer). Another problem in deciding a remuneration package is to find a suitable balance between short-term and longer-term incentives.

3.2 Short-term performance-based incentives

Performance-based incentives reward executives, usually with one or more cash bonus payments, if actual performance during a review period reaches or exceeds certain predetermined targets.

A performance target may be for an annual period, with the executive rewarded according to the financial performance of the company in a financial year. However, there are different ways of measuring financial performance. Here are just a few possible measures:

■ annual profit after taxation
■ annual profit before interest and taxation (PBIT)
■ annual earnings before interest, taxation, depreciation and amortisation (EBITDA)
■ the annual increase in profit, PBIT or EBITDA, compared with the previous year.

There are several problems with using profit measures as a basis for a reward system.

■ Annual profitability can often be manipulated within the accounting rules, so that executives seeking a high current annual bonus might be able to make the profit more than the profit that would be reported if more conservative accounting policies and judgements were applied.
■ Achieving profit targets does not necessarily mean that the shareholders benefit. Higher annual profits do not guarantee higher dividends and higher share prices. However, an ideal bonus system is one that links rewards to executives with the benefits accruing to shareholders, so that the interests of directors and shareholders are in alignment.

Other types of remuneration scheme are to reward executives on the basis of achieving:

■ a number of different performance targets, some of them non-financial, or
■ longer-term strategic objectives.

A CEO might have two or more annual cash bonus schemes, with one bonus payment linked to short-term financial results and another linked to longer-term strategic achievements. A problem with rewarding executives for long-term performance, however, is that an incoming CEO inherits the long-term results of the efforts of his predecessor. The CEO might also move on to another position before the full impact of his own efforts is fully appreciated.

It is important to recognise that there are different ways of arranging a bonus payments scheme for executives, but none are perfect because it is difficult to devise a scheme for individuals that ties bonus payments in a satisfactory way to performance that benefits shareholders in the long term.

In September 2002, the finance director of Anite plc (a UK IT software and services company), resigned in the face of strong criticism from investors who were angry at the company's remuneration policy and acquisition strategy.

- The individual concerned was one of the highest paid finance directors among UK technology companies, and his remuneration for the year to 30 April 2002 had risen 10 per cent, despite a collapse in the company's performance compared with the previous year.
- Bonuses for the CEO and the finance director were based on the profits before tax, exceptional items and goodwill, rather than earnings (profits after exceptional items, writing off goodwill and tax).
- The company had a policy of growth through acquisitions, and had made 17 acquisitions since April 2000. These resulted in large amounts of purchased goodwill, and writing off this goodwill reduced earnings, but not profits before goodwill.
- The acquisitions were made with an open-ended purchase price. The final purchase price depended on the performance of the purchased assets, with an 'earn-out' for the sellers of the acquired companies. All the purchases were paid for with new Anite shares.
- The Anite share price fell by about 80 per cent in the year to 30 April 2002, which meant that more shares had to be issued to pay for new acquisitions. The result was a big dilution in earnings per share.
- The dilution in earnings per share had no effect, however, on the bonuses of the CEO and finance director. On the contrary, the new acquisitions added to profits before tax, exceptional items and goodwill, even though profits after exceptional items and goodwill fell.
- The finance director, who was closely associated with the funding of the acquisitions, was therefore put under pressure to resign by shareholders. However, questions remained about the responsibility of the whole board for both the directors' remuneration policy and the acquisition funding policy.

Although the finance director was not removed from office by a vote of the shareholders at an annual general meeting, the threat that shareholders would exercise this right was sufficient in this case to achieve the desired result.

3.3 Long-term incentives: share options

Long-term incentive plans usually take the form of an award of either share options or fully paid shares in the company. The award of share options or the grant of shares should be conditional on the director or senior executive meeting certain performance targets.

Share options may be given to an executive director or manager. Each option gives its holder the right to buy new shares in the company at a fixed price, on or after a specified date in the future (typically three years after the options are issued) provided that the individual still works for the company at that time.

The fixed purchase price for the new shares (the exercise price of the options) may be the current market price of the shares when the options are issued. In the UK, the exercise price for options must not be less than the current market price for the company's shares on the date that the options are granted. This means that if the market price of the company's shares goes up in the period between the issue of the options and the date they can be exercised, the option holder will be able to make an immediate profit by exercising the options and selling the shares that he receives.

When options can be exercised, usually three years after they have been granted, they do not have to be exercised immediately. The executive can hold on to the share options and exercise them later, when the share price may have risen even further. (However, options must be exercised within a maximum period after they have been granted, typically nine years, after which they lapse.)

3.4 Long-term incentives: grants of shares

An alternative to a share option scheme is a share grant scheme. Directors or senior executives are rewarded by the grant of existing shares in the company (which the company has bought back from other shareholders) provided that he is still in his job after a specified period of time, typically three years. The granting of shares may also be conditional on the achievement of certain financial targets by the company during that time. For example, a scheme might award shares to a director provided that the company achieves targets for total shareholder return (TSR) over a three-year period relative to comparator companies. The individual might receive 30 per cent of the available shares, say, if the company matches the TSR of comparator companies and 100 per cent of the available shares if the company's TSR is comparable with the top quartile (25 per cent) of comparator companies.

With share options, the executive gets no benefit if the share price remains below their exercise price (and the options are 'under water').With share grant schemes, however, the executive benefits even if the share price falls, because the shares (unlike under water options at the exercise date) have a value.

A company might also offer a **deferred annual bonus scheme** whereby participating executive directors and other senior managers are entitled to use some or all their annual cash bonus to buy shares in the company. These shares might then be held in trust for three years, after which the individual is entitled to the award of additional free matching shares from the company, subject to a requirement that the company should have met a target growth objective for the three-year period.

3.5 The overall size of the remuneration package

The remuneration package offered to a senior executive has to be sufficient to attract him to accept the position. There is a perception that there are not enough individuals available to meet the demand with sufficient skills and talent to fill a senior executive post successfully. If this perception is correct, it is a sellers' market and talented executives can command ever-increasing remuneration packages, which companies are forced to pay to get the person they want.

One of the arguments in favour of high remuneration for top executives of international companies has been that high pay is necessary to stop executives being poached by other global companies. In the UK, for example, this argument has been used to justify comparisons of UK executives' salaries with those of top US businessmen. However, a report in 2002 by the International Corporate Governance Network (ICGN) argued that there is no international market for top executives, and so there is no point in structuring remuneration packages to prevent top executives from being lured to companies in other countries, the USA in particular.

The ICGN report admitted that some multinational companies face global competition for top executives, so have to offer packages that match those paid to top US executives. However, the ICGN argued that the number of multinationals in this position was much smaller than the number of companies using the international competition argument to boost top executives' pay. Measures should, therefore, be taken to prevent a senior executive remuneration spiral from getting even further out of hand.

Even so, as suggested earlier, remuneration packages should be designed to provide a suitable combination of fixed and variable remuneration, and a suitable balance between short-term and longer-term incentives.

3.6 Use of remuneration consultants

Companies often use remuneration consultants, who give advice to the remuneration committee on remuneration packages, including basic salary levels for senior executives. Consultants should not be given responsibility for deciding remuneration; this responsibility should remain with the remuneration committee of the boards.

Consultants may use competitive pay data to recommend a basic package for senior executives. Competitive pay data is simply information about the rewards that are being paid to senior executives in other top companies. At first sight, this might seem a sensible way of setting a total value for a remuneration package. Unfortunately, over-reliance on competitive pay data is likely to result in a sharp upward spiral in executive remuneration. Suppose, for example, that one of the top 100 companies in the stock market is looking for a new CEO; in order to decide on the remuneration package it should offer, it hires a firm of remuneration consultants. The remuneration consultants are likely to suggest that since the company is one of the top 100 companies in the country, it should be looking for a top-quality individual, and to get the man or woman it needs, the company should be prepared to pay above-average remuneration. Even a company that is at the bottom of the 100 companies might be encouraged to offer above-average remuneration. If every top company believes it must do the same, remuneration packages will inevitably rise rapidly.

A supporting principle in the UK Corporate Governance Code is that the remuneration committee should judge where to position the company relative to other companies, but it should exercise caution in making this judgement 'in view of the risk of an upward ratchet of remuneration levels with no corresponding improvement in performance'.

The UK Code also states that the remuneration committee should consider pay and employment conditions elsewhere within the group, especially when deciding the annual salary increases for the executive directors. However, remuneration consultants may not offer advice on this matter.

If a UK listed company does use the services of remuneration consultants, it should make available a statement of whether they have any other connection with the company. This statement may help to indicate whether the consultants are independent and provide objective advice.

3.7 UK Voluntary Code of Conduct for remuneration consultants

Remuneration consultants who provide advice on the remuneration of directors and other senior executives are usually hired by the remuneration committee, and the committee is their client. However, there has been criticism of their role and doubts have been expressed about the objectivity of the advice they give.

■ There can be a conflict of interests between the remuneration committee, representing the interests of the company and its shareholders, and the self-interest of the company's executive directors and other senior executives. In carrying out their work, it will usually be necessary for consultants to discuss aspects of remuneration with executives of the company. There is a possible risk that consultants will 'take the side of' executives, and will not necessarily provide advice that is in the best interests of the company.

■ Consultants may be inclined to recommend complex remuneration schemes, because this will make it more difficult for the remuneration committee to dispense with their services in future years.

■ Consultants may try to persuade a remuneration committee to take their advice, when the responsibility for remuneration decisions should remain with the remuneration committee, not its advisers. Advice therefore needs to be objective, and the basis for the advice that has been given should be clear ('transparent') to the remuneration committee and the executives concerned.

In the UK, the Remuneration Consultants Group was established in 2009, as a representative body for most firms of remuneration consultants. Its purpose was to publish a voluntary code of practice for firms and individual consultants in the industry. The first version of this Code was published in 2009, entitled 'Voluntary Code of Conduct in Relation to Executive Remuneration Consulting in the United Kingdom'.

The Code consists of a number of fundamental principles that consultants should apply in their work, particularly in giving advice to FTSE 350 companies. These principles are transparency, integrity, objectivity, competence, due care and confidentiality. An Appendix to the Code provides some guidelines on how the fundamental principles should be applied in practice.

3.8 Problems with linking rewards to performance

The purpose of incentive schemes is to provide an incentive to an executive director or senior manager to improve the company's performance by linking rewards to performance.

However, experience has shown that there are a number of severe practical problems in devising a satisfactory scheme.

- There may be disagreement about what the performance targets should be, and at what level they should be set. For example, should short-term incentives be based exclusively on one or more financial targets, or should there be rewards for the achievement of non-financial targets?
- Executives are usually rewarded with a cash bonus for achieving a short-term (annual) financial target, such as a target for growth in earnings per share. Short-term profit-based incentives are often set without any consideration being given to the potential long-term consequences for the company.
- Executives might develop an expectation that they should receive annual rewards regardless of the actual performance of the company.
- Newly appointed executives might benefit from a 'legacy effect' from their predecessor in the job. The bonuses paid to a new director, for example, might arise because of the effort and work of his predecessor in the job.
- Occasionally, rewards are paid to incentivise directors for doing something that should be a part of their normal responsibilities, such as rewarding a CEO for helping the nominations committee to find a successor to replace him when he retires.

3.9 Drawbacks to rewarding executives with options

There are several drawbacks to using share options and restricted stock awards. Rewarding executives with share options or shares is intended to align the interests of shareholders and directors (and other senior executives rewarded with options). However, an excessive use of options can result in a serious misalignment of interests.

- They reward the option holder for increases in the share price. Although shareholders also benefit from a rising share price, many might prefer higher dividends. For example, given the choice between a 10 per cent increase in dividends and no increase in dividends but a 1 per cent increase in the share price, many shareholders might prefer the higher dividends. Option holders do not benefit from dividend payouts, and executive directors holding share options may have a personal interest in a low dividend pay-out policy, in order to reinvest the company's profits to achieve further growth.
- Share price movements are unpredictable over the short to medium term. When the stock markets have a bull run, as they did for much of the 1990s, share prices tend to rise regardless of the underlying long-term strength of the company's business. In these circumstances, option holders can make profits on their options without having to do much to earn them. On the other hand, when the stock markets go into decline (a **bear phase**) options lose value, and might even become worthless. In 2001 and 2002, when the major stock markets went from a bull phase to a bear phase, many senior executives were able to cash in their profits on share options whilst share prices were still high, and then see the value of the company's shares tumble. For example, in the US, it was reported that the CEO of the conglomerate Tyco, Dennis Kozlowski, made $200 million of personal profits from selling shares in his company in the three years before he resigned at a time when the company had fallen into serious difficulties. Investors were angered by the ability of senior executives to make profits when their shareholders were suffering heavy losses.
- Share options lose all their value when their exercise price falls below the current market price of the shares. Options that are **out-of-the-money** or **under water** lose their ability to act as incentives to executives. When this happens, the remuneration committee of a company's board might decide to re-price the options, or to re-issue new options at a lower exercise price. The problem with re-pricing options, or issuing new options at a lower exercise price, is that executives are protected from the **downside risk** (see also Chapter 9) of a falling share price, whereas their shareholders have no such protection. The option scheme therefore fails to align the interests of executives and shareholders.

International Financial Reporting Standard 2 (IFRS) requires companies to recognise the award of share options as an expense, chargeable against the company's profits, from the time that the share options are granted. The potential effect of share option awards on reported profits may have discouraged some companies from using options as an incentive.

TEST YOUR KNOWLEDGE 6.2

(a) What are the main component elements of the remuneration package of a senior executive director?

(b) What does the UK Corporate Governance Code state about the general level of senior executive remuneration?

(c) What company performance targets might be used as a basis for fixing annual bonus payments to a CEO?

(d) What are the problems with linking rewards to performance for senior executives?

(e) What are the advantages and problems with the remuneration committee using the services of remuneration consultants?

(f) What company performance targets might be used as a basis for deciding how many shares should be granted to a senior executive as a long-term incentive arrangement?

(g) What are the drawbacks to using share options for long-term incentive schemes?

4 The design of performance-related remuneration

The UK Corporate Governance Code requires that the responsibility for setting the remuneration of executive directors (and possibly other senior executives) should be delegated by the board to a remuneration committee. The remuneration committee is explained in more detail later; however, an Appendix to the UK sets out provisions for the design of the performance-related elements of a remuneration package that the remuneration committee should apply. Some of these provisions offer a useful insight into how incentive schemes may be structured and approved.

4.1 The UK Code and general provisions for the design of remuneration packages

The Appendix to the UK Code includes some general provisions about performance-related remuneration.

- Payouts or grants under all incentive schemes should be subject to challenging performance criteria.
- These performance criteria should reflect the company's objectives, including non-financial objectives.
- Remuneration incentives should be compatible with the risk policies of the company and criteria for paying bonuses should be risk-adjusted.

The need for risk adjustments was recognised during the global banking crisis in 2007–2009. Many bank executives had exposed their bank to very large financial risks because they were rewarded with bonuses based on profit, without consideration for the risks that might be taken to increase profitability. They had no incentive to manage the risk. The UK Code therefore states the need for risk adjustment of bonuses, but does not give any details about how bonuses may be risk adjusted. This is something for companies to decide for themselves.

The Code provisions also state that only the basic salary of the director (a fixed element of remuneration) should be pensionable. A director may be entitled to a pension after retirement which is based partly on the number of years he has been with the company, and partly on his remuneration in the final year (or final few years) before retirement. Alternatively, a director may receive an annual payment into a personal pension scheme, with the amount of the annual contribution to the pension fund set at a fixed percentage of remuneration during the year.

- The Code states that variable elements of remuneration (bonuses and the value of share grants or options) should be excluded from 'pay' when pension entitlements are decided.
- The remuneration committee should also consider the consequences for pension costs of deciding to increase the basic salary of a director, especially for directors close to retirement.

Experience has shown that companies may be committed to very large pension payments to former directors for many years after they have retired, and remuneration committees should try to prevent these costs from becoming even more excessive.

4.2 The UK Code and short-term incentives

The Appendix to the UK Code states that the remuneration committee should consider whether the directors should be eligible for annual bonuses. If so, performance criteria should be 'relevant, stretching and designed to enhance shareholder value and to promote the long-term success of the company'.

- There should be upper limits to annual bonuses, and these limits should be disclosed.
- There may be a case for an annual bonus to be part-paid in shares, which the director is required to hold for a 'significant period'.

Concern has been expressed that executives may deliberately provide misleading information about the performance of their company in order to increase their entitlement to bonuses. For example, the CEO and finance director may be tempted to 'window dress' the accounts of the company in order to boost profits (see also Chapter 7), or to 'hide losses' so that reported profits are higher than they should be. The true situation may become apparent later, but the executives by that time may have received their bonuses. The Appendix to the UK Code therefore includes a further provision that consideration should be given by the remuneration committee to the use of provisions in the remuneration agreement for a director 'that permit the company to reclaim variable components in exceptional circumstances of misstatement and misconduct'.

4.3 The UK Code and longer-term incentives

The Appendix to the UK Code states that the remuneration committee should consider whether the directors should be eligible for benefits under long-term incentive schemes.

- Traditional share option schemes should be weighed against other types of long-term incentive scheme.
- Executive share options should not be offered at a discount to the current market price of the shares (except in certain cases permitted by the UK Listing Rules).
- Any proposed new long-term incentive scheme should be approved by the shareholders.
- The total rewards available in any long-term incentive scheme 'should not be excessive'.

In normal circumstances the benefits under share options schemes and share grant schemes should not be receivable in less than three years.

- Share options should not be exercisable within three years.
- Shares granted to an executive should not 'vest' (be receivable) in less than three years.

Directors should be encouraged to hold their shares for a further period after they have been granted or after the share options have been exercised (subject to the need to finance any costs of purchase or any associated tax liabilities). For example, suppose that a director is able to exercise options on 10,000 shares at an exercise price of £3 per share, when the share price is £5. The director would need £30,000 to buy the shares. Ignoring the tax that may be payable on the profit that the director has made, the provision in the Code suggests that the director should be encouraged to hold up to 4,000 shares for a period after exercising the options. (The director could pay for the 10,000 shares he has bought at £3 by selling 6,000 of the shares at £5, leaving him with 4,000 shares.)

The provisions in the Code also suggest that awards of share options and grants of shares should normally be phased over time rather than granted in a single large block. This is to avoid a situation in which the size of the rewards for a director relies excessively on the share price at a particular date. For example, suppose that a director receives a grant of 30,000 shares that 'vest' after three years on 1 January Year 4, and that he has no other long-term incentives from the company. Contrast this with a situation where a director is granted 10,000 shares each year, for three years, that 'vest' on 1 January in Year 4, Year 5 and Year 6. The director whose shares all vest on 1 January Year 4 will have an incentive to maximise the value of the company's shares at 1 January Year 4, whereas the director who receives shares each year will have a much longer-term interest in the share price.

TEST YOUR KNOWLEDGE 6.3

(a)   What are the general provisions in the UK Corporate Governance Code on the design of remuneration packages?
(b)   What are the provisions in the UK Corporate Governance Code on short-term and long-term incentive schemes?
(c)   Why, in the interests of good corporate governance, should NEDs be paid a basic annual fee and no incentive?

5   The remuneration committee

It is a well-established principle of 'best practice' in corporate governance that:

- there should be a formal procedure for deciding on remuneration for directors and senior executives, and
- no individual should be involved in setting his own remuneration.

This means that executive directors should not be involved in setting their remuneration packages (although they can negotiate with the individuals who make the decision) and NEDs should not decide their fees.

In the past, it has been quite common for the top executives in a company, notably the CEO and the executive chairman, to be involved in setting his own remuneration. Such a system, however, is open to abuse. Without controls and restraints, there is a risk that executives will pay themselves excessively.

The Enron affair (see also Chapter 1) provided revealing examples of poor governance by board directors with respect to remuneration. A Senate sub-committee, reporting in 2002, established the following.

- In one financial year, the company paid out cash bonuses of almost $750 million to senior executives when the reported total net income of the group was only $975 million.
- Executives were permitted to run off-balance sheet partnerships in association with the company, which earned hundreds of millions of dollars for the individuals concerned at Enron's expense.
- NEDs had financial ties with the company, including payments for consultancy services in some cases, and so were not independent.

The remuneration of executive directors was recognised as an important governance issue in the UK in the 1990s with the work of the Greenbury Committee, whose recommendations were subsequently incorporated into the UK governance code in 1998. The Greenbury Committee reached the following conclusions.

- The formulation of remuneration packages for senior executive directors was a fundamental issue for good corporate governance.
- However, the system was open to abuse if executives could decide their own remuneration levels.
- Shareholders are not in a position to decide directors' remuneration, although they had a right to extensive information about it.
- Remuneration for executive directors should therefore be decided by a remuneration committee of the board consisting entirely of independent NEDs.

5.1 UK Corporate Governance Code requirements for a remuneration committee

The UK Corporate Governance Code states that:
   'There should be a formal and transparent procedure for developing policy on executive remuneration and for fixing the remuneration packages of individual directors. No director should be involved in deciding his own remuneration.'

It goes on to make a provision that:

'[T]he board should establish a remuneration committee ... [which] should make available its terms of reference, explaining its role and the authority delegated to it by the board.'

The remuneration committee is responsible for both developing remuneration policy and for negotiating the remuneration of individual directors. Although these two matters are related, they are different.

- The remuneration committee should consist entirely of independent NEDs. In larger companies, the committee should consist of at least three members, and in smaller companies (i.e. companies below the FTSE 350) at least two members. The company chairman may be a member of the committee, but not its chairman, provided that he was considered to be independent on appointment as company chairman.
- The remuneration committee should have delegated responsibility for setting the remuneration for all executive directors and the chairman (including pension rights and any compensation payments or severance payments).
- The remuneration committee should also recommend and monitor the level and structure of remuneration for senior management. The definition of 'senior management' is a matter for the board to decide, but it will normally include the first level of management below board level.
- However, shareholders should be invited specifically to approve all new long-term incentive schemes (and changes to existing schemes) that are recommended by the remuneration committee and the board.

5.2 Consultation with the chairman or chief executive officer about executive remuneration

The UK Code states as a supporting principle that the remuneration committee should consult with the chairman and/or the chief executive officer about their proposals for the remuneration of the other executive directors. This is to ensure that the remuneration committee receives advice about the performance of executive directors from individuals who know about their contributions to the management team and to the work of the board.

The remuneration committee may ask for advice from other sources, including other senior executives.

- The remuneration committee is responsible for deciding whether to appoint remuneration consultants to advise it.
- If executives or senior managers are involved in giving advice to the remuneration committee, the committee should take care to recognise and avoid any conflicts of interest.

The remuneration committee should keep the chairman well informed about its decisions on remuneration policy and the remuneration of individual directors, because the chairman should be the point of contact for shareholders who want to ask questions about remuneration or make their opinions known to the company.

5.3 The principal duties of the remuneration committee

The Higgs Suggestions for Good Practice, which were annexed to the 2003 Combined Code, provided a list of duties of the remuneration committee. Higgs suggested the following main duties.

- The committee should determine and agree with the main board the remuneration policy for the CEO, the board chairman, and any other designated executive managers. This policy should provide for executive managers to be given appropriate incentives for enhanced performance.
- To maintain and assure his/her independence, the committee should also decide the remuneration of the company secretary.
- The committee should decide the targets for performance for any performance-related pay schemes operated by the company.
- It should decide the policy for and scope of pension arrangements for each executive director.

- It should ensure that the contractual terms for severance payments on termination of office are fair to both the individual and the company, that failure is not rewarded and that the director's duty to mitigate losses is fully recognised.
- Within the framework of the agreed remuneration policy, it should determine the remuneration package of each individual executive director, including bonuses, incentive payments and share options.
- It should be aware of and advise on any major changes in employee benefit structures throughout the company and group.
- It should agree the policy for authorising expense claims from the chairman and CEO.
- It should ensure compliance by the company with the requirements for disclosure of directors' remuneration in the annual report and accounts.
- It should be responsible for appointing any remuneration consultants to advise the committee.
- In the company's annual report, it should report the frequency of committee meetings and the attendance by members.
- It should make available to the public its terms of reference, setting out the committee's delegated responsibilities. Where necessary these should be reviewed and updated each year.

The company secretary (or someone from the company secretary's department) should act as secretary to the remuneration committee, because it is the company secretary's responsibility to ensure that the board and its committees are properly constituted and advised. The company secretary can also play a role as intermediary and co-ordinator between the committee and the main board.

TEST YOUR KNOWLEDGE 6.4

(a) What are the principal responsibilities of a remuneration committee?
(b) According to the UK Code, what should be the composition of a remuneration committee for a company in the FTSE 350 and who may be its chairman?
(c) Is it appropriate for a remuneration committee to consult the company chairman or chief executive officer on remuneration packages for individual executive directors?

6 The remuneration of non-executive directors

Non-executive directors are not company employees. They receive a fee for their services, not a salary. In the UK, it is usual for an NED to receive a fixed annual fee, typically in the region of £20,000 to £60,000 (or possibly more), for attending board meetings, some committee meetings and general meetings of the company.

The principle that individuals should not decide their own remuneration applies to NEDs as well as to executive directors. This means that a remuneration committee should not decide the fees of the NEDs. Deciding the remuneration of the NEDs should be the responsibility of the board (or the shareholders if required by the articles of association). Where permitted by the articles the board may delegate this responsibility to a committee which might include the CEO.

A provision in the UK Corporate Governance Code is that the level of remuneration for NEDs should reflect the time commitment and responsibilities of the role. A company may permit an executive director to serve as NED on the board of another company. When this happens in the UK, the company must disclose in its annual remuneration report (a part of the annual report and accounts) a statement about:

- whether or not the individual is allowed to retain his earnings as NED, instead of handing them to the company, and
- if the director does retain his earnings as NED for the other company, the amount of the earnings must be disclosed.

6.1 Additional fees

NEDs may receive other forms of remuneration or reward from the company, in addition to a basic fee, but this could raise questions about their independence. After Enron collapsed in the USA in 2001, it was revealed that a number of NEDs had obtained benefits from the company in addition to their basic fee as NED, and their lack of independence may have contributed to the company's difficulties.

For example, an NED might be paid additionally as a 'consultant' to the company. No matter how genuine and useful these consultancy services are, they put his independence at risk because the size of a consultancy fee is decided by executive management. Management also has the decision about extending or renewing a consultancy agreement.

- If an NED creates trouble for executive management in board meetings or at board committee meetings, there is always the chance that the consultancy agreement will be axed. If he is supportive, the fee may be raised.
- A consultancy agreement could also bring an NED and the executive management into a close working relationship, such that the independence of the NED is compromised, possibly through friendship or learning to look at problems from a management perspective.

6.2 The UK Code on performance-related rewards for non-executive directors

The UK Corporate Governance Code makes specific provisions about performance related rewards for NEDs, including the award of share options to NEDs.

- As a general rule the remuneration of NEDs should not include share options or any other performance-related reward.
- In exceptional cases, share options may be granted. However, the approval of the shareholders should be obtained in advance, and if the NED subsequently exercises options to acquire shares in the company, these shares should be held until at least one year after the NED leaves the board.
- Holding share options could affect the determination of whether or not the NED is independent.

 CASE EXAMPLE 6.4

In 2006, Coca-Cola in the US attracted considerable attention for a remuneration initiative for its NEDs. In April, Coca-Cola announced major changes in the remuneration structure for its NEDs. Previously, NEDs had been paid a fixed annual fee of $125,000 ($50,000 in cash, and the rest in Coca-Cola stock) and with extra fees for chairing board committees and attending board meetings and committee meetings. Under the new 'all-or-nothing' arrangement, directors would receive no remuneration unless earnings per share grew by at least 8 per cent compound over three years, and there would be no payments to the NEDs during that time. The aim was to achieve greater alignment of the interests of the NEDs with those of the shareholders.

Critics of the new scheme argued that linking NED pay to company performance could threaten the independence of the directors from executive management, rather than align the interests of NEDs and shareholders. In addition, it was argued that by delaying payment of non-executive remuneration for three years, it would be more difficult for the company to recruit directors from less affluent socio-economic backgrounds (on the assumption that this is a desirable objective).

 STOP AND THINK 6.4

Some NEDs, particularly company chairmen, have substantial shareholdings in their company. Would you consider that paying NEDs in shares rather than cash would be likely to compromise their independence?

7   Compensation for loss of office

7.1 Dismissal of directors and severance payments

Most executive directors have employment contracts with their company that provide for an annual review of their remuneration and a minimum period of notice in the event of dismissal. When a company decides to dismiss a director, it is bound by the terms of the employment contract.

There are various reasons why an individual might leave the company.

- He might be regarded as having failed to do a good job, and someone else should do the job instead. A high severance payment would be seen as 'rewarding failure'.
- There could be a disagreement or falling out between directors, resulting in one or more directors being asked to leave.

The service contract of a director might provide for the payment of compensation for loss of office. Alternatively, a company might be required to give the individual a minimum period of notice, typically one year or six months in the UK. If an individual is asked to leave, he might be paid for the notice period, without having to work out the notice. In addition the individual may be entitled to further bonus payments under the terms of his remuneration package – in spite of being considered a failure in the job.

Shareholder concerns with compensation for loss of office arise in cases where an individual is dismissed for having performed badly. In the past, severance payments have been high for executives who are seen to have failed, having led their company to setbacks in business strategy or even financial catastrophe. A large compensation payment can seem annoying, because it seems that the individual is being rewarded for failure. Large severance payments reduce company profits and returns to shareholders, and they have prompted institutional investor organisations to:

- issue guidelines on the subject, and
- put pressure on companies to make sure that severance payments ('rewards for failure') are restricted.

When a director is first appointed, it may seem inappropriate to negotiate terms in the contract that deal with dismissal; however, a failure to negotiate satisfactory terms could expose the company to very large payments if and when a decision is taken at a later date to get rid of the individual for poor performance. Measures that restrict severance payments must be taken when the individual is appointed and the employment contract is agreed.

7.2 UK Corporate Governance Code and severance payments

The UK Code contains two provisions about service contracts and compensation for termination of office.

- When negotiating the terms of appointment of a new director, the remuneration committee should consider what compensation commitments the company would have in the event of early termination of office. More specifically, the aim should be to avoid rewarding poor performance. The committee should 'take a robust line' on reducing the amount of compensation to reflect a departing director's obligation to mitigate losses.
- Notice periods in the employment contract of an executive director should be set at one year or less. If it is necessary to offer a longer notice period to a director coming into the company from outside, the notice period should subsequently be reduced to one year or less 'after the initial period'.

The reference to taking a robust line on a director's duty to mitigate losses is a suggestion that a director's contract should provide for a payment of compensation in stages, and which would be halted in the event of the director finding employment elsewhere.

7.3 Joint ABI/NAPF statement on severance pay

In the UK the ABI and NAPF have produced a joint statement (reviewed February 2008) on severance pay. The statement is aimed at the boards and remuneration committees of companies, and is intended to assist them in negotiating contracts with senior executives, and to make them aware that shareholders (institutional investors) want companies to avoid situations in which departing executives are rewarded for failure.

The joint statement sets out certain principles on executive contracts and severance pay, including the following.

- Employment contracts for senior executives should not provide for additional financial protection for any director in the event that the company performs badly. The level of remuneration that senior executives receive provides adequate compensation for the risk associated with their role.
- Severance payments arising from poor corporate performance should not extend beyond basic salary.
- Companies should provide full disclosure in their remuneration report of the constituent elements in a severance payment, and should justify the total amount and each of the elements paid.

The joint statement goes on to specify certain guidelines about severance payments.

- Remuneration committees must understand clearly their responsibility to negotiate suitable contracts and must be able to justify severance payments to shareholders.
- The board of directors must establish a policy that non-contractual payments should be linked to performance. No director should be entitled to a discretionary payment from the company in the event of termination of their contract for poor corporate performance.
- Remuneration committees should consider whether the company should retain an entitlement to reclaim bonuses if performance achievements are subsequently found to have been materially mis-stated.
- Contracts of employment should not provide for compensation payments to senior executives in the event of a change of control over the company (a takeover).
- Remuneration committees should ensure that the benefits of mitigation are obtained when an individual is dismissed. This should include a contractual obligation of the dismissed individual to mitigate the loss incurred through severance by looking for other employment. The contract should provide for the severance payment to be reduced in circumstances where the individual finds alternative employment.
- Phased payments are more appropriate than a severance payment as a single lump sum.
- Pension arrangements that guarantee pensions, with limited or no abatement in the event of dismissal or early retirement 'are no longer regarded as acceptable' (unless they are available to all employees, which is unlikely).

If companies choose to ignore the ABI/NAPF guidelines on severance pay, they face the risk that these organisations will advise their members to vote at the next company AGM against the company's remuneration report and against any remuneration committee member who is standing for re-election.

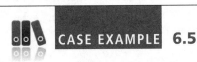 **CASE EXAMPLE 6.5**

In August 2006, the ABI sent a letter to the FTSE 350 companies, asking them to review their pension arrangements for senior executives, warning that some major shareholders would be concerned about the pensions aspect of excessive severance packages. The specific matter of concern was that executives might have employment contracts that entitle them to a large increase in their pension fund, as part of any severance package. The letter asked the remuneration committees to look at the pension arrangements in executives' contracts, to make sure that they were in line with best practice.

(Continued)

CASE EXAMPLE 6.5 (*Continued*)

The reason for the letter was a payout to four former directors of Scottish Power, who had all retired with large increases in their pension funds. The former CEO had benefited from a doubling of his pension fund arrangements. The company admitted that the cost of the retirement of the four directors had been £11 million, but justified the its action by stating that it was contractually obliged to make the pension increases, but was now reviewing its pension arrangements for senior executives.

The ABI expressed its concern that other companies might have similar arrangements that the shareholders were unaware of. Although the ABI has expressed its strong disapproval of any such arrangements that might exist, it would not necessarily be easy for companies (even if they wanted to do so) to persuade executives to agree to changes in the pension arrangements in their contracts.

TEST YOUR KNOWLEDGE 6.5

(a) What are the principles or provisions of the UK Code with regard to severance payments for senior executives?

(b) What principles on severance pay were recommended in the joint ABI/NAPF statement?

8 Disclosure of directors' remuneration details

The main arguments about directors' remuneration can be summarised as follows. Top executives have to be paid well in order to attract and retain them. A remuneration package for a senior executive should offer incentives for achieving performance targets, and incentive-based payments should be a substantial element in the total package. However, it is very difficult to devise an incentive-based system that properly aligns the interests of top executives with those of the shareholders. Top executives should not be allowed to decide their own remuneration packages. The responsibility for executive remuneration decisions can be given to a remuneration committee of NEDs. This committee should try to find the elusive balance between rewarding their top executives sufficiently, while structuring the reward package so as to bring the interests of shareholders and executives into alignment.

It is noticeable that within these arguments, the interests of shareholders are mentioned, but there is no suggestion that shareholders should get involved in making remuneration decisions themselves. Shareholder involvement, however, is desirable, and there are two ways in which this might happen: (1) disclosure; and (2) shareholder voting on remuneration.

8.1 Directors' remuneration report

In the UK, quoted companies are required by the Companies Act 2006 to include a directors' remuneration report for each financial year. This report must be approved by the board and signed on its behalf. A copy must be circulated to shareholders in the same way as the annual report and accounts, and it is normal for the remuneration report to be included in the same document.

Shareholders must vote at the AGM on a resolution (ordinary resolution) to approve the report. This is an advisory vote only. The shareholders cannot, for example, vote against the remuneration package awarded to any individual director. However, a vote against the remuneration report is a way for shareholders to express their strong disapproval of the company's remuneration policies and practices.

The report must contain extensive disclosures about directors' remuneration. A distinction is made between:

- items that are not subject to audit, and
- items that are subject to audit by the external auditors.

The auditors, in their **audit report** (see also Chapter 7), must state whether in their opinion the part of the report to be audited has been prepared properly in accordance with the Act. A signed copy of the report must also be filed with the Registrar of Companies, in the same way as the annual accounts, directors' report and auditors' report.

Information not subject to audit

Items to be included in the directors' remuneration report that are not subject to audit are as follows.

- The names of the directors who were members of the remuneration committee, and details about any remuneration consultants that were used (name, nature of services provided).
- A statement of the company's policy on directors' remuneration for the next financial years and the years after that (i.e. a forward-looking policy statement).
- A performance graph. This is a line graph showing the total shareholder return (TSR) on the company's shares over a five-year period, and the TSR on a holding of a portfolio of shares over the same period representing a named broad equity market index. The graph can therefore be used to compare shareholder returns on the company's shares with those of a market index. The Act specifies how TSR should be calculated.
- Information about the service contract for each director: the date of the contract, its unexpired term and details of any notice periods; any compensation payable for early termination of the contract and any other provisions in the contract affecting the liability of the company in the event of early termination (i.e. severance terms).

The forward-looking statement on the company's policy on directors' remuneration must include, for each director, the following.

- Details of the performance conditions that apply to decide the director's entitlement to share options or an award under a long-term incentive scheme, and an explanation of why these performance conditions were chosen.
- A summary of the methods used to decide whether these performance conditions have been met, and an explanation of why these methods were chosen.
- A description of any proposed significant amendment to the terms and conditions affecting the director's entitlement to share options or awards under a long-term incentive scheme (and an explanation of the reasons for the proposed change).
- Where the director's entitlement to share options or award under a long-term incentive scheme are not subject to meeting certain performance conditions, an explanation of why this is the case.
- The relative importance of those elements of the director's remuneration that are related to performance and those which are not.

The policy statement should also summarise and explain the company's policy on the duration of contracts with directors and the notice periods and termination payments under these contracts.

Information subject to audit

The remuneration report must contain the following items, which are subject to audit.

- For each director, the total remuneration for the year, broken down into salary and fees, bonuses, expenses received, compensation for loss of office and other severance payments, and non-cash benefits.
- For each director, details of interests in share options, both beneficial and non-beneficial. (Beneficial options are options held in the name of the director or a connected person, such as

the director's spouse or child under 18.) The information disclosed should include details of options awarded or exercised during the year, options that expired unexercised during the year, and any variations to the terms and conditions relating to the award or exercise of options. For options exercised during the year, the disclosures should show the market price of the shares when the options were exercised. For options not yet expired, the disclosures should give details of the price paid for their award (if any), the exercise price, the date from which the options may be exercised and the date they expire. The market price of the shares at the end of the year, and the highest and lowest market prices reached during the year should also be avoided.

- For each director, details of any long-term incentive schemes (other than share options). These should show the director's interest in each scheme at the start of the year and the end of the year, any changes during the year, and details of when the awards/entitlements can be taken.
- For each director, details of pension contributions or entitlements. The nature of the disclosures will vary according to whether the pension scheme is a defined benefit scheme or a defined contribution scheme.
- For each director, details of any excess pension benefits received or receivable in the year (i.e. benefits in excess of the director's contractual entitlement).
- Significant payments made during the year to former directors of the company.
- The total amount of any payments made to third parties for the services of any director.
- An explanation and justification of any element of directors' remuneration, other than basic salary, which is pensionable.

Value and significance of the directors' remuneration report

The ICSA's Guidance on the Directors' Remuneration Report (2008) commented on the value and significance of the report as follows:

'The requirement to produce a remuneration report as part of the annual report and accounts should not be seen simply in compliance terms. It is an opportunity for the company to demonstrate that remuneration policies and structures have a clear rationale which supports the business strategy and enhances shareholder value. There is significant reputational risk associated with the failure to manage and disclose executive remuneration and the remuneration report is a prominent opportunity to explain the company's position.'

8.2 Shareholder approval of directors' remuneration

Giving shareholders the right to vote on directors' remuneration is more contentious that providing shareholders with more information about remuneration. A distinction should be made, however, between two different types of shareholder vote on executive remuneration.

- Shareholders might be invited to vote on the company's remuneration policy for the directors. This vote could be binding on the company, so that if the shareholders voted against a remuneration policy, the remuneration committee (or whoever is responsible for remuneration policy in the company) would have to devise a new policy. Alternatively, a shareholder vote might not have the power to bind the company, but simply be treated as a form of advice. For example, the UK Corporate Governance Code requires listed companies to submit all new (or revised) long-term incentive schemes for senior executives to be submitted to the shareholders for approval. In the UK, listed companies are required to invite shareholders to vote on the remuneration policy (set out in the remuneration report), although the vote is not binding on the company.
- Shareholders may occasionally be invited to vote on the remuneration package of individual directors, in cases where the package has been negotiated subject to shareholder approval. A shareholder 'no' vote would force the company to renegotiate with the individual (who might choose to leave the company, having failed to win the support of the shareholders). Once a remuneration package has been agreed between a company and a director, this is a binding contract, and shareholders cannot then be allowed the right to alter the contract details, since this would put the company in breach of contract.

CASE EXAMPLE 6.6

In October 2002, the remuneration committee of Marconi, the troubled telecommunications equipment manufacturer, awarded bonuses of up to 1.5 times annual salary to the three executive directors who had led the company to an agreement on restructuring with its creditors. The board informed the shareholders at the AGM that the bonuses were payable in four tranches, and were designed to tie in the three individuals to the restructuring process.

Shareholders entitled to attend the AGM were due to see their total stake in the company reduced to about 0.5 per cent as a result of the restructuring, which involved a large debt-for-equity swap with creditors. It was reported that the bonuses were likely to 'further anger' the shareholders, but the company would disregard their concerns. There was little that the shareholders could do, given their limited rights and the precarious position of the company.

 CASE EXAMPLE 6.7

In 2006 US corporation Home Depot was heavily criticised by its shareholders and attracted considerable press attention, for the remuneration of its CEO Bob Nardelli. The company was expected to come in for intense shareholder questioning at its general meeting. However, no directors turned up to the meeting, except for Mr Nardelli himself, who then restricted the length of the meeting and discouraged shareholder questioning. Proposals seeking to allow shareholders more say in the CEO's remuneration and to restrict retirement pay for senior executives were both defeated. Even so, the level of criticism directed at the company provided evidence of the growing concern in the US about excessive executive pay.

 TEST YOUR KNOWLEDGE 6.6

(a) What are the rules on the UK for the disclosure of details of directors' remuneration by listed companies?
(b) Why might it be appropriate for shareholders to be allowed to vote on remuneration policy for directors, but not on the remuneration package of individual directors?

9 Institutional shareholder views on directors' remuneration

In the UK, the associations of institutional investors have developed strong views on directors' remuneration. The ABI and the NAPF have issued guidelines on executive remuneration, and regularly issue 'red top' notices (see also 1.1. earlier in this chapter) to their members recommending that they vote against the boards of companies on resolutions relating to pay.

9.1 ABI guidelines on executive remuneration

The ABI has issued guidelines on policies and practices for executive remuneration (updated in 2009). These are directed mainly at listed companies, which are encouraged to comply with them. The effect of the ABI guidelines is to notify listed companies about the concerns and expectations of institutional shareholders with regard to pay.

- Boards are responsible for adopting remuneration policies and practices that promote the success of the company by creating value in the longer term. Remuneration policies and practices should be clearly aligned with corporate objectives and business strategy, taking risks into account, and they should be reviewed regularly. Like the UK Corporate Governance Code, the ABI now recognises that the scale of incentives for executives should take into consideration the risks to which the company could be exposed by executives in their pursuit of target levels of performance.
- It is important that companies should maintain a 'constructive and timely dialogue' with the company's shareholders on matters relating to senior executive remuneration (such as changes in remuneration policy and share incentive schemes).
- Executive remuneration should be set at levels that retain and motivate. However, benchmarks used for setting targets and rewards should be used with caution, because of the risk that remuneration levels might 'ratchet' upwards without any corresponding improvement in company performance.
- Executive remuneration should be linked to individual and corporate performance through graduated targets that align the interests of the executives with those of shareholders.
- Shareholders will not support arrangement that entitle executives to rewards that are not justified by performance. Remuneration committees should ensure that service contracts contain provisions that are consistent with this principle.

9.2 Remuneration committees and their responsibilities

The main aspects of ABI guidance on remuneration committees are as follows.

- The remuneration committee is responsible for 'ensuring that the mix of incentives reflects the company's needs, establishes an appropriate balance between fixed and variable remuneration, and is based on targets that are 'stretching, verifiable and relevant and which take account of risk'.
- The committee should establish procedures for disclosure and communication of strategic objectives, so that shareholders can take an 'informed and considered view' of remuneration policy.
- The remuneration committee should ensure that remuneration levels for executives properly reflect the contributions of executives, and they should be rigorous in selecting a comparator group of companies.
- When designing share-based incentives, the remuneration committee should guard against the possibility of 'unjustified windfall gains'.
- The committee should consider legal redress where performance achievements are subsequently found to have been over-stated significantly, so that bonuses and other incentives that were paid should not in fact have been paid.
- The committee should pay particular attention to the remuneration of key executives who are not directors but who have significant influence over the company's ability to meet its strategic objectives. In this context, the ABI guidelines state that the remuneration committee should 'have oversight' of all the associated risks arising throughout the company as a consequence of executive remuneration (and performance-based incentives).

9.3 Base pay, bonuses, pensions and contracts and severance

The ABI's guidelines on remuneration policies and practices go into some detail on specific aspects of remuneration packages. Many of them are consistent with the UK Corporate Governance Code guidelines. They include the following.

Base pay and bonuses

On base pay, the ABI guidelines state simply that base pay should reflect the contribution of the executive concerned, and policy on base pay should be fully communicated to the shareholders. The remuneration committee should be 'robust' in setting and monitoring targets for bonuses, and bonus payments should reflect actual achievements against these targets. The other main provisions relating to bonuses are as follows.

- Any material ex gratia payments to an executive must be fully explained and justified, and should be subject to shareholder approval before they are paid.
- Shareholders are not supportive of 'transaction bonuses' that reward directors or other executives for effecting transactions irrespective of the future financial consequences of those transactions. For example a CEO should not receive a bonus for achieving the take-over of another company, or winning a major contract to supply a customer.

Additional guidance on bonuses is provided, including the following.

- Annual bonuses should be 'demonstrably related to performance'. Following the payment of a bonus, shareholders expect to see a full analysis in the remuneration report of the extent to which targets were actually met.
- Maximum participation levels in bonus schemes for each individual should be disclosed, and any increase in the maximum participation level from one year to the next should be disclosed.
- Annual bonuses should not be treated as pensionable pay.
- The remuneration committee should retain the right to reduce or reclaim a bonus if it is subsequently discovered that performance achievements were 'significantly misstated'.

Pensions

The remuneration committee should recognise the impact that pension arrangements can have on the mix between fixed pay (base salary) and variable pay (bonuses). The committee should recognise that pension costs can be very expensive and pension payments to a former executive are not directly linked to performance.

Contracts and severance

The ABI guidelines on severance pay are similar to those in the joint ABI/NAPF statement.

 **CASE EXAMPLE 6.8**

In May 2005, 76 per cent of shareholders of UK media group United Business Media voted against the directors' remuneration report at the AGM and another 11 per cent abstained. This was the first high-profile rejection of a directors' remuneration report by shareholders in the UK since the vote by 51 per cent of the shareholders in GlaxoSmithKline in May 2003.

Shareholders were objecting to an ex gratia payment of a £250,000 bonus to Lord Hollick, the departing CEO. There was some uncertainty about whether the payment was for helping to ensure a successful handover to the incoming CEO, or for the role Lord Hollick had played in the sale of NOP World, a polling subsidiary.

Following the vote, Lord Hollick agreed to waive the bonus. UBM announced that it would not make similar ex gratia payments to directors in the future.

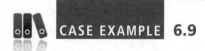

CASE EXAMPLE 6.9

Advisers to institutional investors do not always agree about whether remuneration packages for executive directors are acceptable. In May 2010, shareholders voted against the remuneration report of UK listed company SIG by a margin of 67 per cent to 33 per cent following a decision by the company to increase the basic salary of its CEO by about 15 per cent. Although the ABI had issued a 'red top' notice to its members, advising them to vote against the remuneration report, the shareholder activist group Pirc had considered the remuneration proposals of the company to be demanding and acceptable. On the same day, Cookson Group had its remuneration report accepted by a majority of only 51 per cent (with 32 per cent voting against): Pirc opposed pay proposals for the company's CEO whereas the ABI had given an 'amber top' notice to its members – advising them to use their considered judgement when voting on the remuneration report.

9.4 ABI guidelines for share-based incentive schemes

The main provisions of the ABI guidelines on share-based incentives are as follows.

- The ABI supports share incentive schemes that link remuneration to performance and align the interests of senior executives with those of the company's shareholders. The vesting of share awards or share options should therefore be based on performance conditions measured over a period of time that is appropriate to the strategic objective of the company. This should not be less than three years.
- All new share-based incentive schemes and any substantial changes to existing schemes should be subject to prior approval by the shareholders. Their operation, rationale and cost should be fully explained so that the shareholders can make an informed judgement.
- The operation of share incentive schemes should not lead to a dilution in the equity holding of the other shareholders in excess of acceptable limits.
- Share options should not be granted at an exercise price below the prevailing market price for the shares.
- It is desirable to align the interests of the chairman and independent NEDs with those of the shareholders, for example through payment in company shares bought at market prices. However, shareholders consider it inappropriate for the chairman or independent NEDs to receive incentive awards geared to the share price or corporate performance, since this would impair their ability to provide impartial oversight and advice.
- Shareholders encourage companies to require their executive directors and senior executives to build up 'meaningful' shareholdings in the company.

9.5 NAPF policy on directors' remuneration

The NAPF supports the ABI guidelines. It has also issued guidelines to its members about situations where poor remuneration practices by a listed company could trigger a vote against the company's remuneration report at the AGM. Practices that could result in a voting sanction include the following.

- Regularly increasing the base pay (fixed pay) of executives by a larger percentage amount than the rate of inflation.
- Guaranteed annual bonuses, discretionary annual bonuses, pensionable annual bonuses or transaction-related bonuses.
- Using inappropriate benchmarks to set base pay.
- The absence of individual limits for annual bonuses or long-term incentive schemes.
- Long-term incentive schemes featuring a performance period of less than three years.
- Ex gratia payments or other non-contractual payments.
- Issuing shares so that guidelines for the dilution of earnings for existing shareholders are breached.
- Unwarranted use of discretion by the remuneration committee in awarding bonuses and benefits.

9.6 EU recommendations on executive remuneration

Some recommendations on senior executive remuneration in EU-listed companies were issued by the European Commission in 2009. The recommendations are not compulsory, but member states are encouraged to introduce them into their national codes of corporate governance. Many of the recommendations are consistent with current UK practice, but the following suggestions may at some future time find their way into the UK Code.

- Variable pay should be subject to limits and predetermined performance criteria that promote the long-term sustainability of the company. The payment of a major part of the variable components of pay not be paid immediately but should be deferred, and the company should be entitled to reclaim any payments that have been made on the basis of information that has been 'manifestly mis-stated'.
- When remuneration committees use benchmarking to decide executive remuneration, they should make comparisons not only with peer group companies, but also with the levels of pay of other employees in the company.
- After executives have acquired shares by exercising share options, they should be required to hold them until the end of their employment with the company.

Further developments in guidelines for the remuneration of directors and senior executives should therefore be expected.

 CASE QUESTION

1 Referring to the case study at the beginning of Part Two, what changes if any would be appropriate in the remuneration packages and employments of Don Stenning and Rebecca Tull?

2 What measures should be taken by the remuneration committee and the board to introduce incentive schemes for senior executives?

CHAPTER SUMMARY

- Public hostility to excessive remuneration for directors can affect investor confidence in companies and the stock markets. Senior executives should be well rewarded, but not excessively so.
- An attractive basic salary should be offered to directors to attract and keep capable and talented individuals. A large part of an executive's remuneration package, however, should be in the form of incentives.
- A remuneration package consists of fixed pay elements (salary, pension contributions) and variable pay elements (annual bonuses, long-term incentives).
- Incentives could be bonus payments linked to short-term performance (e.g. growth in earnings per share) or possibly long-term performance. Unless appropriate incentives are selected, executives could earn a high bonus even when the company performance is disappointing.
- The UK Corporate Governance Code includes provisions and guidelines on remuneration.
- A major concern with corporate governance is that incentive schemes do not achieve their intended purpose, which is to attract and retain talented executives, and then to motivate them to achieve performance targets that are in the best interests of the company's shareholders.
- A problem is to find a suitable balance between fixed base pay (and pension entitlements) and variable rewards, and also to find a suitable balance between short-term cash bonuses and longer-term share-based incentives.
- NEDs should be paid a flat fee and in normal circumstances should not be given incentive-linked rewards.
- Individuals should not be allowed to fix their own remuneration. Remuneration for executive directors and other senior executives should be decided by a remuneration committee consisting entirely of independent NEDs, although this committee may consult the chairman and CEO.

The requirement for a remuneration committee is included in the UK Corporate Governance Code. Shareholders should have the right to approve all new and amended long-term incentive schemes.

- The UK Code includes provisions relating to severance payments when a director or senior executive leaves the company. The aim should be, as much as possible, to avoid rewarding departing executives for 'failure'. A joint statement on this subject has been issued by the ABI and NAPF.

- In the UK, the Companies Act requires listed companies to provide extensive information about directors' remuneration in the annual report and accounts. This report, which should also contain a statement of remuneration policy, should be submitted to the shareholders for approval at the AGM. The shareholders vote is an indicative vote, and has no power to bind the company.

- In the UK, institutional shareholders have indicated their concerns about the details of directors' remuneration packages, and the ABI and NAPF have issued guidelines on the subject. The ABI guidelines are quite extensive.

Reporting to shareholders and external audit

7

■ CONTENTS

■ INTRODUCTION

This chapter considers the relevance of financial reporting to good corporate governance and how financial reports could become misleading. It then goes on to look at the role and responsibilities of the external auditors, the issue of auditor independence and the responsibilities of the directors for financial reporting. Although the financial statements are an important source of information for shareholders and other stakeholders, listed companies also provide extensive information of a non-financial nature, much of it in narrative form. This chapter discusses some of this narrative reporting, although disclosures about directors' remuneration was explained in Chapter 6, and social and environmental reporting and sustainability reporting are described in Chapter 12.

'Improving Board Effectiveness' states that the annual report and accounts should be seen as the single most important communication between a company and its shareholders. Although much of the content of the report and accounts is determined by law and regulation, there is considerable scope for companies to communicate in some detail its governance arrangements, including board oversight of strategy and the key risks associated with strategy implementation.

1   Financial reporting and corporate governance

The annual report and accounts of a company (and the interim financial statements of a listed company) are the principal way in which the directors make themselves accountable to the shareholders. The financial statements present a report on the financial performance of the company over the previous financial year and the financial position of the company as at the end of that year. The directors' report (see also Chapter 1) and other statements published in the same document provide supporting information, much of it in narrative than in numerical form. For larger companies, the annual financial statements and elements of the annual report are audited by a firm of independent external auditors. Shareholders and other investors use the information in the annual report and accounts to assess the stewardship of the directors and the financial health of the company.

The annual report and accounts is an important document for corporate governance because it is a means by which the directors are made accountable to the shareholders, and provides a channel of communication from directors to shareholders. The report and accounts enable the shareholders to assess how well the company has been governed and managed. It should therefore be:

- clear and understandable to a reader with reasonable financial awareness, and
- reliable and 'believable'.

The reliability of the annual report and accounts depends on several factors, including those that follow.

- The honesty of the company in preparing them: if allowed to do so by accounting regulations, companies might indulge in **window dressing** their financial performance or financial position through the use of accounting policies (methods) that hide the true position of the company.
- The care used by directors to satisfy themselves that the financial statements do give a 'true and fair view' and that everything of relevance has been properly reported.
- The opinion of the external auditors, which the shareholders should be able to rely on as an objective and professional opinion.

If financial statements are produced in a way that is intended deliberately to mislead shareholders, the persons responsible would be guilty of fraud, which is a crime. Misleading financial statements, however, could only be issued if the:

- audit committee is satisfied with their preparation
- external auditors provide a 'clean' audit report, and
- board of directors approves the financial statements.

In most companies, this would require deception by a small group of executives, such as the CEO and finance director.

Although fraudulent financial reporting is a crime, so-called **aggressive accounting** policies may be permissible within existing accountancy regulations and standards, and accepted by the company's external auditors. The effect of aggressive accounting may be to make the financial performance and position of the company seem better than they really are, and to have the effect of hiding information from shareholders, at least in the short term. The financial performance of a company for the current financial year might be flattered by using certain accounting policies, but in the longer term (say, in one or two years' time) the 'bad news' will eventually emerge.

Significantly, many corporate governance 'scandals' resulting in the collapse or near-collapse of a company have involved fraudulent or aggressive financial reporting.

Trustworthy financial reporting and auditing is probably the most significant issue for corporate governance. Good corporate governance should ensure that financial reporting is reliable and honest, and that the opinion of the external auditors is objective and unbiased.

1.1 Financial reporting and investor confidence

In the UK, the Cadbury Code on corporate governance in 1992 happened as a direct consequence of concerns about the quality of financial reporting in the UK and the ability of the auditing profession to provide sufficient assurances to the investment community about the reliability of company financial statements. Similar concerns were expressed in the USA during the stock market depression of 2002. If investors have doubts about the honesty or transparency of financial reporting, they will hold back from investing, and share values will suffer as a result.

The problem extends to the corporate bond markets. Many companies have borrowed heavily by issuing bonds to investors. Bond investors rely on **bond credit ratings** in making their investment decisions. Investors are unlikely to purchase a company's bonds unless they have been rated for creditworthiness by at least one, and more usually two, top ratings agencies. In the USA, the top three agencies are Moody's, Standard & Poor's and Fitch, which have the status of nationally recognised statistical ratings organisations (NRSROs).

The US crisis of investor confidence about financial reporting in mid-2002 brought the role of the credit rating agencies into question. The agencies defended themselves publicly against allegations that they failed to identify the financial problems in companies such as Enron (see Chapter 1), when they should have been much more alert and in a position to forewarn investors about companies that were getting into financial difficulties. The reliability of credit ratings was also brought into question by the financial crisis in banking in 2007–2008, when many highly rated 'collateralised debt obligations' were found to be more or less worthless even though they were valued at substantial amounts in the accounts of the banks that owned them.

When a company proposes to issue new bonds, a ratings agency carries out an investigation and then gives a rating to the bonds. The interest rate the company has to offer on the bonds will depend on the rating awarded. After the bonds have been issued, the ratings agencies review the rating continually and adjust it if the financial condition of the company improves or worsens.

Bond investors therefore use the ratings agencies as 'gatekeepers to the financial markets'. Their decisions whether or not to invest in bonds, and the rate of interest they require for doing so, depend on the judgement of the agencies.

As mentioned earlier, the collapse of Enron is described in Chapter 1; however, it is useful to consider some of the financial reporting and auditing features of the Enron scandal.

 CASE EXAMPLE 7.1

Enron used accounting and financial transactions to increase reported income and asset values, and to take liabilities off its balance sheet. One technique was to record up to $200 million costs of projects as assets, even though the projects had been cancelled. This was justified on the grounds that the projects had not been officially cancelled. Capitalising expenses meant that the costs were not charged against reported profits. Another technique was to set up special purpose entities in order to take liabilities and losses off the balance sheet. In 2001 a whistleblower reported her concerns about the company's accounting practices to the chairman/CEO, but her allegations were rejected. Soon afterwards, the company was obliged to re-state its financial statements for the previous four years, which resulted in a reduction in the company's equity by over 10 per cent ($1.2 billion). Investors complained that the Enron accounts lacked transparency, and were so complex they were impossible to understand.

Enron's auditors were the Houston office of Arthur Andersen, one of the five largest audit firms in the world. However, the Houston office relied on Enron for much of its income for both audit and **non-audit work**. In 2000, the firm earned $25 million from the audit and $27 million from non-audit work for Enron – more than 25 per cent of the total annual income of the Houston office. It appears that Arthur Andersen, and the Houston office in particular, may have gone along with the financial reporting practices of Enron in order to retain the work, and their independence was compromised. When the Securities and Exchange Commission announced an investigation into Enron after its collapse in late 2001, Andersen tried to cover up evidence of inadequate audit work by shredding several tons of documents and deleting about 30,000 e-mails and computer files.

The Enron story is an excellent example of the importance for good corporate governance of transparent and honest financial reporting and independent **external audits**.

 STOP AND THINK 7.1

A report was published in the USA in March 2010 into the collapse of the bank Lehman Brothers in September 2008, the biggest bankruptcy in US history. The report stated that in late 2007 and 2008, Lehman Brothers had used sale and repurchase transactions at the end of each financial quarter in order to reduce the leverage (gearing) in its reported balance sheet. Normally, sale and repurchase transactions, or repos, are accounted for as short-term loans and the liability to repay the loan is included in debts in the balance sheet. The special transactions used by Lehman, known to the bank as repo 105 transactions, were treated as sales of securities. The cash received from

(Continued)

STOP AND THINK **7.1** *(Continued)*

these 'sales' (rather than 'loans') was used to pay off other debts. The result was that Lehman's reported balance sheet showed fewer assets and fewer liabilities than was the actual case in reality. Soon after the end of the financial quarter, Lehman had to borrow more money to pay back the cash received from the repo transactions, with interest. The bank did not disclose its use of these transactions, or its method of accounting for them, in its published accounts.

Critics of Lehman Brothers argued that the bank had deliberately manipulated its financial statements to mislead investors about its actual financial condition. In response, lawyers for former Lehman executives argued that the financial reporting was within the rules. The bank's accounts had been audited by Ernst & Young, who saw no problem with what the bank was showing in its accounts, and who stated that the bank's accounting methods were consistent with generally accepted accounting principles. The bank had also obtained a letter from UK law firm Linklaters stating that its scheme was 'legal' under British law.

Critics were therefore arguing that the accounting practices of the bank were intended to deceive investors and that the directors of the bank and the bank's auditors were culpable. The counter-argument was that everything the bank did was within the rules, and no one should be made liable for losses suffered by investors.

1.2 Misleading financial statements

There are several ways in which published financial statements could be misleading.

- There could be a fraudulent misrepresentation of the affairs of the company, where the company's management deliberately presents a false picture of the financial position and performance.
- The company might use accounting policies whereby it presents its reported position and profits more favourably than would be the case if more conservative accounting policies were used.
- The financial statements could be complex and difficult for investors to understand. It is a relatively easy matter for accountants, particularly in companies whose business is itself quite complex, to present financial statements in a way that readers will find difficult to comprehend properly.

Occasionally, some companies may want to report strong growth in revenues and profits, or even to improve the look of the balance sheet (statement of financial position) by 'hiding' debts or other liabilities. The company could probably succeed in presenting an excessively favourable picture of its performance for a number of years, particularly when the economy is strong and business is growing. Eventually, however, it becomes impossible to 'massage' the figures any further. Unless the business can sustain a strong 'real' growth in its operations, it cannot achieve strong profits growth indefinitely. Eventually, a company that uses 'creative accounting' methods will have to report declining profits or re-state the accounts for previous financial years and disclose hitherto hidden losses.

Improving the reported financial position, at least in the short term, shows the board of directors in a favourable light and helps to boost the share price. Individual directors could therefore stand to benefit from higher annual bonuses and more valuable share options.

1.3 Ways of window dressing financial reports

There are several ways in which a company might improve its reported financial position or reported performance and so window dress its financial statements. The methods used may sometimes be deliberately incorrect. More often, a company may use accounting policies that are acceptable to the auditors, but succeed in giving a flattering picture of the company's position.

- A company may claim to earn revenue and profits earlier than it probably should. For example, a company that enters into a three-year contract that will earn £12 million in total might try to claim all the revenue of £12 million in the first year instead of spreading the revenue over the three-year life of the contract.

■ A company may try to take debts off its balance sheet. This can sometimes be achieved by setting up separate companies known as 'special purpose vehicles'.

■ A company may try to disguise money from loans as operating income, to increase its reported cash flow from operating activities.

■ A company may over-value assets that it owns, either to increase its reported balance sheet reserves or avoid writing off a fall in value as a loss in its income statement.

The following examples of investor concerns about financial statements and company announcements are from the period of stock market turmoil in the USA during mid-2002. In each of these examples, concerns about the accuracy of financial reporting helped to undermine investor confidence in companies, because the financial report and accounts remain the principal method of communication between a public company and the investment community. If the report and accounts can't be trusted, what can?

 CASE EXAMPLE 7.2

In July 2002, a group of US investors filed a securities fraud lawsuit against Vivendi Universal (a media conglomerate) and its former chairman, Jean-Marie Messier, alleging that the company inflated the value of its shares by concealing a financial crisis. Between mid-January 2002 and early July 2002, when Messier was ousted from his position in the company, the share price fell from $48 to less than $14. Having issued press releases stating that the company did not face a cash crisis, it was revealed in July that a debt of $1.8 billion had to be repaid by the end of the month, and the company barely had that amount in cash and unused credit lines.

 CASE EXAMPLE 7.3

In June 2002, US telecommunications group Qwest Communications ousted its CEO, partly over concerns about the reliability of the company's financial statements. In July, the company disclosed that it had incorrectly accounted for large amounts of revenue over the past three years. Apparently, the company had recorded millions of dollars of income at the end of each quarter that should properly have been attributed to the next quarter. In this way, the company reported revenue and profits before they properly occurred. It was suspected that the company manipulated the accounts because it was under pressure from the investment community to reach certain revenue and profit targets for each quarter. In addition, the company's new auditors were investigating the company's accounting policies for over $1 billion of 'swap transactions', in which the company bought and re-sold network capacity to the same companies, thereby boosting reported revenues. It was questionable whether these swap transactions were genuine business transactions, or simply a ruse for increasing reported revenues.

 CASE EXAMPLE 7.4

In June 2002, US telecommunications company WorldCom announced a huge $3.8 billion accounting fraud. The Justice Department launched a criminal investigation. The nature of the fraud was apparently quite simple. WorldCom had incurred running costs of $3.8 billion that had been

(Continued)

CASE EXAMPLE **7.4** *(Continued)*

accounted for as capital expenditure. Instead of charging the expenses against profits, the cost had therefore been capitalised and reported as assets in the balance sheet, even though no assets existed. Another consequence of this fraud was that the company's reported cash flows looked much better than they actually were. Investment analysts judged the strength of the cash flows of telecommunications companies according to the cash generated by their business operations, and disregarded cash spent on capital expenditure, which was seen as necessary for growing capital-intensive businesses such as WorldCom. By reporting running costs as capital expenditure, the company therefore improved the look of its cash flows by $3.8 billion.

When WorldCom announced its accounting fraud, its auditors Arthur Andersen tried to lay the blame on the company's chief financial officer who, Andersen claimed, had withheld important information from them, preventing them from carrying out their audit properly. The fraud had been discovered by an internal auditor of the company in a routine audit check, and not by a member of the external audit team. Questions were raised, however, about the quality of the external audit: for a transaction of such a large size, it should be expected that the auditors would want to know what it was for and satisfy themselves that it had been accounted for properly.

1.4 Accountability and transparency

Producing the annual report and accounts is the main way in which a company's directors are held accountable to shareholders and other stakeholders. The information in the report and accounts is used to assess the success of the company and the effectiveness of its board.

It is therefore essential that the report and accounts should give a clear presentation of the position and performance of the company. In other words, there should be 'transparency' in reporting by companies, so that the recipients of the reports can see what the company has achieved and assess what is likely to happen in the future.

The UK Corporate Governance Code states as a main principle that: 'The board should present a balanced and understandable assessment of the company's position and prospects' in its report and accounts and in its interim reports and other public statements. This principle applies to narrative reporting in the annual report as well as to the financial statements.

In the past it has not always been clear, from reading a company's report and accounts, what the company's operations are or how it earns its revenue and profits. The UK Code includes a provision that the annual report should contain an explanation of:

- the basis on which the company generates revenue and makes a profit from its operations (its 'business model'), and
- its overall financial strategy.

This information will probably be included in the same part of the annual report as the business review, which is described later.

TEST YOUR KNOWLEDGE **7.1**

In what ways might financial statements be misleading to shareholders and other investors?

2   Financial reporting: directors' duties and responsibilities

The company's directors are responsible for the preparation and content of the financial statements. The UK Corporate Governance Code states that the directors should explain in the annual report their responsibility for preparing the annual report and financial statements. There should also be a supporting statement by the auditors (in their report) about their reporting responsibilities.

The UK Code also requires that the directors should include in their annual report an explanation of the:

- basis on which the company generates or preserves value over the longer term (its 'business model'), and
- strategy for delivering the objectives of the company.

2.1 Legal duties of directors for financial reporting: UK law

The directors of a company have certain legal duties with regard to financial reporting. The duties set out below relate to UK law.

- They have a duty to prepare annual company accounts and, in the case of a parent company, consolidated accounts for the group (Companies Act 2006). The accounts must be approved by the board and signed on behalf of the board by a director.
- They have a duty to prepare a directors' report, which must also be approved by the board and signed on its behalf by a director or the company secretary. Unless the company is subject to the small companies' regime, the directors' report must contain a business review. The business review is described in more detail later in this chapter.
- The directors of a quoted company have a duty to prepare a directors' remuneration report, which must be approved by the board and signed on its behalf by a director or the company secretary. This report is explained in Chapter 6.
- These accounts and reports of a public company must be laid before the shareholders in general meeting and the shareholders of a quoted company must be invited to approve the directors' remuneration report (in an advisory vote).
- In respect of each financial year the directors must file with the Registrar of Companies a copy of the annual accounts, the directors' report, the auditors' report and, in the case of quoted companies, the directors' remuneration report.

2.2 Responsibilities of the directors for financial reporting

There is sometimes confusion and misunderstanding about responsibilities for financial reporting, and a mistaken belief that the external auditors are responsible for the 'true and fair view' in the financial statements. If misleading and incorrect financial statements are produced, it may therefore be supposed that the auditors have been negligent and must be to blame. This view is incorrect. The directors are responsible for the financial statements: they prepare the financial statements and have the primary responsibility for the reliability of the information they provide.

- Management and the directors are therefore responsible for identifying and correcting any errors or misrepresentations in the financial statements.
- The responsibility of the external auditors is to obtain reasonable assurance, in their professional opinion, that the financial statements are free from material error or mis-statement. They present a professional opinion to the shareholders, not to the directors of the company, and the directors should not rely on the opinion of the external auditors in reaching their own view.

In UK law the directors are also potentially liable for any errors or misleading information in the annual report and accounts. Any person (for example, an investor) suffering a loss as a consequence of an error or misstatement in a company's report and accounts may sue the company, and the company may then take legal action against the directors to recover any losses it has occurred from the legal action.

2.3 Going concern statement

A key accounting concept is the 'going concern' concept. This is the view that the company will remain continue to trade for the foreseeable future (at least the next 12 months). The financial statements are therefore prepared on this basis, and assets are valued differently from what there value might be on a break-up basis (in a fire sale, if the company went into liquidation).

There are several rules or guidelines that require the directors to make a **going concern statement** in the annual report. This is a statement that in their opinion the company is a going concern and will continue to be so for at least the next year.

- The UK Corporate Governance Code includes a provision that the directors should report in the company's annual and half-yearly financial statements that the company is a going concern, 'with supporting assumptions and qualifications as necessary'. The statement should therefore give reasons why the directors have reached their view, and also indicate any doubts there might be.

- Similarly, the UK Listing Rules (refer back to Chapter 2) require the directors to make a statement in the report and accounts that the company is a going concern, together with supporting assumptions and qualifications as necessary.

- For other companies, there are requirements in both international and UK accounting standards that the directors should satisfy themselves that it is reasonable for them to conclude that the company is a going concern, so that the financial statements can be prepared in a going concern basis.

A typical going concern statement within a corporate report might be as follows:

'The directors, on the basis of current financial projections and facilities available, have a reasonable expectation that the company and group have adequate resources to continue in operational existence for the foreseeable future. The directors accordingly continue to adopt the going concern basis in the preparation of the group's financial statements.'

In the UK disclosures about the assumptions or qualifications with regard to going concern status are becoming more extensive. The directors may be personally liable if they make a statement that the company is a going concern without giving the matter careful consideration. Liability could arise if the company subsequently goes into liquidation within the next 12 months and shareholders claim that they relied on the going concern statement when making their investment decisions.

2.4 Directors' responsibilities for financial reporting: US law

In US law, the CEO and Chief Financial Officer (CFO) have personal responsibility for the accuracy of their company's financial statements, under the provisions of section 302 of the Sarbanes-Oxley Act. The Act requires that all companies with a listing in the USA must provide in annual or quarterly reports of the company a signed certificate to the Securities and Exchange Commission (SEC) vouching for:

- the accuracy of the information in the report, and
- the fairness of the financial information.

The CEO and CFO are therefore required to take direct personal responsibility for the accuracy of their company's financial statements. This requirement applies not only to US companies but also to foreign companies with a US listing. The authorities have rights of investigation, which means that US regulators have given themselves the powers to investigate the accounts of foreign companies, if they are required to file accounts in the USA.

TEST YOUR KNOWLEDGE 7.2

What is a going concern statement?

3   The role of the external auditors: the audit report

Investors, creditors and other stakeholders in a company rely on the information contained in the annual report and accounts, which are audited each year by a firm of independent auditors.

The purpose of an independent audit is to make sure, as far as reasonably possible, that the financial statements are objective and can be relied on.

After completing their annual audit, the auditors are required to prepare a report to the shareholders of the company, which is included in the published report and accounts of public companies. The audit report has two main purposes:

- to give an expert and independent opinion on whether the financial statements give a true and fair view of the financial position of the company as at the end of the financial year covered by the report, and of its financial performance during the year
- to give an expert and independent opinion on whether the financial statements comply with the relevant laws.

In the UK, auditors of listed companies are also required to review the company's compliance with the UK Corporate Governance Code, and to obtain evidence to support the company's **compliance statement** (in the annual report and accounts) of its compliance with the Code.

3.1 The purpose of the external audit

The audit report is contained in the company's annual report and accounts, and is addressed by the auditors to the shareholders of the company. The main purpose of the audit report is to give the users of a company's financial statements (and in particular the shareholders) some reassurance that the information in the statements is believable and that the financial statements present a 'true and fair view' of the company's financial position and performance. The opinion of the auditors should be the opinion of independent professional experts, based on an investigation of the company's control systems, accounting systems and financial/business transactions.

3.2 Responsibility for detecting errors and fraud

Shareholders would probably like to assume that if the auditors provide a favourable audit report, the financial statements must be 'correct', and there has not been any fraud or error that has resulted in:

- incorrect use of accounting policies
- omissions of fact
- misinterpretation of fact.

('Fraud' is intentional; 'error' is unintentional: both lead to incorrect figures in the financial statements, if they have not been discovered.)

This view is based on the belief that if professional accountants have checked the figures, they must be correct – unless the accountants have been negligent and have failed to do their job properly. However, it is a popular misconception that the auditor is responsible for detecting fraud or error in a company's financial statements. This is not the case.

- The board of directors is responsible for preventing fraud in their company, or detecting fraud if it occurs. The company's system of internal control, described in Chapter 10, should be designed to limit the risk of fraud and error, and the board is responsible for monitoring the effectiveness of the internal control system. The responsibility of the board (with delegated responsibility of management) for the prevention and detection of fraud and error is a core principle of corporate governance. The directors are fully accountable to the shareholders and so are fully responsible for the information presented in the annual report and accounts.
- It is not the primary responsibility of the external auditors to detect fraud. The auditors will assess the risk or possibility that fraud or error might have caused the financial statements to be materially misleading. The auditors should therefore design audit procedures that will provide reasonable reassurance that material fraud or error has not occurred, and that the financial statements give a true and fair view of the company's financial position and performance. The external audit might also act as a deterrent to fraud, because the auditors will carry out checks of control procedures, documents and transactions in the course of their audit work. They might discover fraud during the course of their audit work, in which case it would be their responsibility to report the matter to the directors (unless the fraud is carried out by the directors themselves).

No matter how well an audit is planned and carried out, there will always be some risk that fraud or error has occurred but not been detected. Given the nature of auditing, for which there is only a limited amount of time and resources, and which is carried out through a process of sampling and testing, it would be impossible to ensure that all errors are detected. Accounting systems and internal control procedures are also vulnerable to fraud and error, arising for example from:

- criminal collusion between employees
- decisions by management to override the system of controls.

An area for dispute, however, is whether the auditors ought to be able to identify fraud or a significant error during the course of their audit work, whenever a fraud or error occurs. Although they are not responsible for the financial statements, it can be argued that a failure by the auditors to discover a major fraud or material error might be the result of professional negligence. If they are negligent, they should be held liable to the company and its shareholders. (Uncertainty about the extent to which auditors might be held liable for professional negligence has led to new rules in the UK Companies Act 2006 that enable companies to limit auditor liability.)

3.3 The liability of auditors for negligence: liability limitation agreements (LLAs)

Auditors are potentially liable to shareholders and others who suffer loss as a result of negligence in carrying out an audit. Negligence would arise from failure to comply properly with professional audit guidelines and from a failure to carry out the audit with due skill, care, diligence and expedition.

Auditors are not liable to shareholders and lenders to a company if the company suffers a financial collapse and becomes insolvent, unless negligence can be shown. However, audit firms have argued that they are unfairly targeted by shareholders of collapsed companies because they are seen as having pockets that are deep enough to pay large sums of money in compensation. For example, Equitable Life, the life assurance organisation, brought an action against auditors Ernst and Young, claiming compensation for negligent audit work. The action failed in 2005, but Ernst and Young had faced the threat of a potentially huge liability if the case had gone against them.

In the UK, the Companies Act 2006 introduced new rules on auditors' liability for negligence, breach of duty or breach of trust in connection with the conduct of the audit. Shareholders of both public and private companies can vote by ordinary resolution to limit the potential liability of the external auditors, by means of a liability limitation agreement (LLA).

- Shareholder approval for the LLA may be obtained either before or after the company has entered into the agreement with the auditors.
- An LLA with the auditors must be disclosed in the annual report and accounts.
- An LLA is only valid if it applies to acts or omissions by the auditors in the course of one audit for one financial year.
- An LLA cannot limit the liability of the auditors to an amount that is less than what is fair and reasonable in the circumstances, having regard to the circumstances and the professional standards expected from the auditors.
- The limit on the auditors' liability might be expressed as a sum of money, a formula or a proportion of any loss suffered by the company, having regard to the auditors' liability for such loss.

The audit profession expressed its concern that when a legal action is brought against a collapsed company, the court might decide that it is reasonable for the auditors to compensate for the entire loss suffered by the company, on the grounds that only the auditors had enough money to cover the cost of the losses incurred. The Act therefore states that in considering what is fair and reasonable in the circumstances, the court should have no regard to the possibility or otherwise of recovering compensation from other persons who are jointly or partly responsible for the loss that has been incurred.

3.4 Criminal liability of auditors for recklessness

Although the Companies Act 2006 provides the possibility of some protection for auditors against liability for negligence or breach of duty with LLAs, it also introduced two new criminal offences for auditors in connection with the auditors' report. It is a criminal offence, punishable by a fine, to:

- knowingly or recklessly cause an audit report to 'include any matter that is misleading, false or deceptive in any material particular', or
- knowingly or recklessly cause an audit report to omit a statement that is required by certain specified sections of the Act.

 SAMPLE WORDING 7.1

Unmodified audit report

Here is a simplified example of a typical unmodified audit report.

Report on the financial statements

We have audited the accompanying financial statements of XYZ Company, which comprise the statement of financial position as at 31 December 20XX, and the statement of comprehensive income, statement of changes in equity, and cash flows for the year then ended, and a summary of significant accounting policies and other explanatory notes.

Management's responsibility for the financial statements

Management is responsible for the preparation and fair presentation of these financial statements in accordance with International Financial Reporting Standards. This responsibility includes: designing, implementing and maintaining internal control relevant to the preparation and fair presentation of financial statements that are free from material misstatement, whether due to fraud or error; selecting and applying appropriate accounting policies; and making accounting estimates that are reasonable in the circumstances.

Auditor's responsibility

Our responsibility is to express an opinion on these financial statements based on our audit. We conducted our audit in accordance with International Standards on Auditing. Those standards require that we comply with ethical requirements and plan and perform the audit to obtain reasonable assurance whether the financial statements are free from material misstatement.

An audit involves performing procedures to obtain audit evidence about the amounts and disclosures in the financial statements. The procedures selected depend on the auditor's judgement, including the assessment of the risks of material misstatement of the financial statements, whether due to fraud or error. In making those risk assessments, the auditor considers internal control relevant to the entity's preparation and fair presentation of the financial statements in order to design audit procedures that are appropriate in the circumstances, but not for the purpose of expressing an opinion on the effectiveness of the entity's internal control. An audit also includes evaluating the appropriateness of accounting policies used and the reasonableness of accounting estimates made by management, as well as evaluating the overall presentation of the financial statements.

We believe that the audit evidence that we have obtained is sufficient and appropriate to provide a basis for our audit opinion.

Opinion

In our opinion, the financial statements give a true and fair view (or present fairly, in all material respects,) of the financial position of XYZ Company as of December 31 20XX, and of its financial performance and its cash flows for the year then ended in accordance with International Financial Reporting Standards.

Report on other legal and regulatory requirements

(Form and content of this section of the report will vary depending on the nature of the auditor's other reporting responsibilities.)

Signed: (Auditor)

3.5 The significance of a modified audit report

The audit report itself provides only limited information to shareholders, even though shareholders often assume that an unqualified audit report means that the financial statements of the company are accurate and reliable.

An unmodified audit report (sometimes called an 'unqualified opinion') is given when the auditor believes that the accounts give a true and fair view of the company's financial position and performance. The wording of an unmodified audit report is usually fairly standard, although reports are longer for public companies (where the auditors might also report on some corporate governance statements) and differ between countries.

An unmodified audit report may include an 'emphasis of matter' paragraph. Although the audit report is not modified, and the auditors consider that the financial statements present a true and fair view, there is an item that the auditor wants to bring to the attention of users because it is of some importance for an understanding of the statements.

An audit report may be modified. It is unusual for auditors to present a modified report. When this happens, there is a potentially serious problem with the financial statements and, by implication, the financial condition of the company. It also means that the auditors have been unable to agree with the directors of the company about what information the financial statements should contain. Because the directors and the auditors cannot agree, the auditors have considered it necessary to give a statement to shareholders to this effect. There are three types of modified audit opinion:

- a qualified opinion
- an adverse opinion, and
- a disclaimer of opinion.

A qualified audit opinion is sometimes called an 'except for' opinion. It is given when, in the opinion of the auditor, the financial statements would give a true and fair view except for a particular matter, which the auditor explains.

An adverse opinion is given when the auditor considers that there are material mis-statements in the accounts and that these are 'pervasive'. In effect, the auditor is stating that the figures in the accounts are seriously wrong.

A disclaimer of opinion is given in cases where the auditor has been unable to obtain the information that he needs to give an audit opinion. The lack of information means that the auditor is unable to state that the financial statements give a true and fair view, and that there may possibly be serious mis-statements that the auditor has been unable to check.

In the rare circumstances that the auditors give a **modified audit report** to the shareholders, a situation has arisen where professional accountants have given an opinion that the shareholders cannot trust the information that has been given to them by the directors. If the shareholders cannot trust the directors, the quality of corporate governance could hardly be lower.

3.6 Auditors' liability to third parties (other stakeholders)

The auditors have a legal duty of care to the company and its shareholders. There is some doubt as to whether they might also have a duty of care to other parties. In the UK, the extent of auditor liability to external parties has been tested in two legal cases. In response to the outcome of the Bannerman case (see Case law 7.1), PricewaterhouseCoopers decided to include a disclaimer of liability to third parties using its audit reports. In January 2003, the Institute of Chartered Accountants in England and Wales recommended the inclusion of a disclaimer in audit reports.

A disclaimer within the audit report might be worded as follows:

'This report, including the opinion, has been prepared for and only for the company's members as a body in accordance with ... the Companies Act 2006 and for no other purpose. We do not, in giving this opinion, accept or assume responsibility for any other purpose or to any other person to whom this report is shown or into whose hands it may come save where expressly agreed by our prior consent in writing.'

CASE LAW 7.1

Caparo Industries plc v Dickman (1990)

In the UK legal case Caparo Industries plc v Dickman and others (1990), it was held by the House of Lords that auditors did not owe a duty of care in audit reports to third parties that they did not know at the time. The auditors of a company had negligently audited its accounts, and as a result the company reported a profit of £1.2 million instead of a loss of £400,000. Replying on these accounts, the respondents in the case made a successful takeover bid for the company. They subsequently brought an action against the auditors for breach of duty of care and skill. In ruling in the auditors' favour, the House of Lords held that there was no liability, since the auditors did not owe a duty of care to a member of the public. Their duty was simply to the company and its shareholders.

As a result of the Caparo case, it was considered that the auditors of a company did not hold a duty of care to any third party, until the subject came up for consideration again in the Royal Bank of Scotland v Bannerman Johnstone Maclay (2002). This was a case in the Scottish courts, and so was not binding on English courts, but it drew from leading English court cases and so is considered to have significant legal implications for England and Wales as well as Scotland.

In this case, Bannerman were the auditors of a company that arranged an overdraft facility with the bank. The overdraft facility letter between the bank and the company contained a requirement for the company to send the bank a copy of its audited annual accounts at the end of each year. In 1998, the company went into receivership owing over £13 million to the bank, which claimed that due to fraud, the accounts for the previous year were materially incorrect and the auditors were negligent. The bank also claimed that it had relied on the auditors' unqualified opinion to continue providing the overdraft facility to the company. In its defence, the audit firm claimed that it had no duty of care to the bank. The judge ruled that although there had been no direct contact between the audit firm and the bank, the auditors would have known about the facility letter. The knowledge they would have gained during the course of their audit work was therefore sufficient, in the absence of any disclaimer, to create a duty of care to the bank. In the judge's view, the absence of a disclaimer was a crucial feature of the case.

TEST YOUR KNOWLEDGE 7.3

(a) What is the purpose of the external audit?

(b) Who is responsible for detecting fraud or errors in financial statements?

(c) Who is responsible for detecting fraudulent activity within the company, by some of its employees or others?

(d) What are the responsibilities of the external auditors with regard to the financial statements of a company?

(e) What types of audit opinion might be given in an audit report? What is the significance of a modified audit opinion?

4 Independence of the external auditors

The external auditor should be independent of the client company, so that the audit opinion will not be influenced by the relationship between the auditor and the company. The auditors are expected to give an unbiased and honest professional opinion to the shareholders about the financial statements. An unmodified audit report is often seen by investors as a 'clean bill of health' for the company. However, doubts are sometimes expressed about the independence of the external auditors. It could be argued that unless suitable corporate governance measures are in place, a firm of auditors may reach audit opinions and judgements that are heavily influenced by their wish to maintain good relations with the management of a client company. If this happens, the auditors are no longer independent and the shareholders cannot rely on their opinion. For example, an official 2010 report on the collapse of Lehman Brothers (in the USA in 2008) criticised the external auditors Ernst & Young for allowing the company to account for certain transactions (repo 105 transactions) in a way that misleadingly improved the look of the end-of-quarter balance sheets during 2007 and 2008, in the months before the bank eventually collapsed.

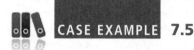

CASE EXAMPLE 7.5

The energy corporation Enron, which had been one of the largest corporations in the world by stock market value, collapsed towards the end of 2001. In January 2002, the company's auditor, Andersen, announced that its employees had shredded documents relating to Enron after it had received a subpoena from the Securities and Exchange Commission in November 2001. This announcement was part of a chain of events that led to Andersen being prosecuted for its role in the Enron affair.

In June 2002, Andersen was found guilty by a US court of obstructing justice during investigations into the collapse of Enron. The Enron scandal and the alleged role of Andersen prompted moves in both the USA and the UK to review accounting and auditing standards. Andersen subsequently lost major clients quickly and the firm collapsed. It was subsequently alleged that the Houston office of the firm, which conducted the annual audit of Enron, was not independent of its client and relied on Enron for a large proportion of its annual fee income.

4.1 Ethics and the accounting profession

Like other professionals, qualified accountants are expected by their professional body to act with integrity and honesty, and to follow a code of ethics in the work they do. However, there can be pressures on accountants to ignore ethical considerations and to allow their judgement to be affected by other considerations. These pressures might apply to both accountants in industry as well as those in the profession acting as auditors.

4.2 Threats to auditor independence

Perhaps the most significant threat to auditor independence is that the audit firm relies on the company's management to secure its appointment and re-appointment as the company's auditor. Although companies may give their audit committee responsibility for recommending the appointment of the auditors, the opinions of senior management are often decisive in the matter of auditor selection. The auditor is therefore reliant for future audit work from the company on the views of the management whose financial statements it is their job to audit. In addition, the audit firm has to rely extensively on management for the information and explanations needed to enable them to carry out their audit work. A UK Ethical Standards Board has commented on this situation that: 'Any reasonable and informed third party – for example, a shareholder – is likely to regard this as a significant threat to the auditor's objectivity.'

Professional guidelines are given to auditors by national and international accountancy bodies, notably the International Federation of Accountants (IFAC). The IFAC Code of Ethics for Professional Accountants identifies certain ways in which the integrity, objectivity and independence of the auditors might be put at risk.

- An audit firm should not have to rely on a single company for a large proportion of its total fee income, because undue dependence on a single audit client could impair objectivity. IFAC does not specify what amounts to 'undue dependence' on a single client. However, in the UK, the rules of the Association of Chartered Certified Accountants (ACCA) state that the fee income from a single audit client should not exceed 15 per cent of the gross annual income of the audit practice.

- A risk to objectivity and independence arises when the audit firm or anyone closely associated with it (such as an audit partner) has a mutual business interest with the company or any of its officers. Similarly, objectivity could be threatened when there is a close personal relationship between a member of the audit firm and an employee of the company.
- The audit firm should not have a client company in which a partner holds a significant number of shares.
- The IFAC Code does not have any objection in principle to an audit firm providing non-audit services (such as consultancy services) to a client, although the auditor should not perform any management functions in a company nor take any management decisions.

The audit profession has identified five categories of potential threats to auditor independence.

- Self-interest threats, e.g. if the audit firm earns a large proportion of its revenue from a client company, it may be unwilling to annoy that client by challenging the figures and assumptions used by management to prepare the company's financial statements.
- Self-review threat. This can arise when the audit firm does non-audit work for the company, and the annual audit involves checking the work done by the firm's own employees. The auditors may not be as critical of the work, or prepared to challenge it, because this would raise questions about the professional competence of the audit firm.
- Advocacy threat. This can arise if the audit form is asked to give its formal support to the company by providing public statements on particular issues or supporting the company in a legal case. Acting as advocate for a company means taking sides, and this implies a loss of independence.
- Familiarity threat. A threat to independence occurs when an auditor is familiar with a company or one of its directors or senior managers, or becomes familiar with them through a working association over time. Familiarity leads to trust and a willingness to believe what the other person says. The auditor will also be unwilling to think that the other person is capable of making a serious error or committing fraud. A familiarity threat arises through personal association (for example, family connections) and through long association with the company and its management.
- Intimidation threat. An auditor may feel threatened by the directors or senior management of a company. Both real and imagined threats can affect the auditor's independence. Intimidation may result from a domineering and bullying personality on the company's board of directors (for example the CEO). A company may also threaten to take away the audit or stop giving the firm non-audit work unless the auditor accepts the opinions of management.

Threats to auditor independence must be identified, and measures should be taken to limit the threat to an acceptable level of risk. Two areas of debate about how to ensure auditor independence have been:

- whether auditors should be prevented from carrying out non-audit work for clients, or whether the amount of non-audit work they do should be restricted, and
- whether there should be a regular rotation of either the audit firm or the audit partner and other senior members of the audit team.

4.3 Non-audit work for a client by an audit firm

The codes of conduct of national professional accountancy bodies are similar to the IFAC Code and lack any clear restrictions on the performance of non-audit work for an audit client. Suggestions for regulatory measures to ensure auditor independence have included proposals to restrict the amount of non-audit work, or the type of non-audit work, that the firm of auditors is permitted to carry out for a client company. Non-audit work might include:

- consultancy on taxation issues, for example helping a group of companies to minimise tax liabilities by setting up subsidiaries in countries with a low-tax regime
- investigating targets for a potential takeover bid
- helping a company to construct a bid for a major government contract
- providing advice and expert assistance on IT systems
- internal audit services

- valuation and actuarial services
- services relating to litigation
- services relating to recruitment and remuneration.

The main problem with auditors doing non-audit work is that when the firm audits transactions recommended by its consultancy arm, it is unlikely to take an independent view.

The risk to auditor objectivity and independence from carrying out non-audit work became apparent in the wake of the Enron collapse, which has been described previously. Arthur Andersen were the auditors of Enron, and in the financial year prior to the company's collapse in 2001, Andersen earned more fee income from Enron for non-audit work than from audit work. The audit firm was suspected of failing to carry out a proper audit of the company, with two main reasons being suggested.

1 It was claimed that the audit firm would have been reluctant to question the accounts of Enron because it would risk losing not just the audit work but also the substantial non-audit fee income.

2 In addition, it was suggested that since the information in the company's financial statements reflected the non-audit consultancy advice given by the audit firm, the firm's auditors would be unlikely to challenge the fairness and accuracy of the statements. In other words, Andersen's auditors would not challenge the opinions of Andersen's consultants.

Audit firms have denied that fees from non-audit work will affect their independence, arguing that the individuals who work as consultants for a client company (e.g. on IT projects) are not the same individuals who work on the company audit. Even so, activist shareholder groups continue to challenge this assertion. In the UK, a well-reported attempt was made several years ago (2002) by some institutional shareholders to vote against the re-appointment of Deloitte as auditors to Vodafone at the annual general meeting of the company. The 'dissidents' argued their case on the grounds that the audit firm did too much non-audit work for the company and so could not be considered sufficiently independent.

4.4 Approaches to the regulation of non-audit work

There are three broad approaches to the regulation of non-audit work by audit firms.

1 There should be no restrictions at all on non-audit work by the audit firm.
2 There should be a total prohibition on non-audit work for a corporate client by the audit firm.
3 There should be a partial prohibition on non-audit work for a corporate client by the audit firm. This could take either of two forms. There could be a prohibition on audit firms from taking on certain types of consultancy work where their independence as auditors could be put at risk, for example tax planning advice work. However, audit firms would be free to carry out other types of non-audit work. The second approach to restricting non-audit work would be to set a limit on the amount of fees an audit firm could earn from non-audit work, expressed perhaps as a proportion of the fees it earns from the audit. For example, a limit might be imposed restricting non-audit fees to, say, 50 per cent of the fees from the audit work.

The difficulty with a partial restriction on non-audit work is that rules have to be devised and agreed as to what permissible and non-permissible non-audit work should be, or what the maximum amount of non-audit fee income should be.

In the UK, the audit profession is governed by ethical principles rather than rules and regulations about non-audit work for audit clients. The Institute of Chartered Accountants in England and Wales (ICAEW) has made the following statements about non-audit work.

- 'The most effective way to ensure the reality of independence is to provide guidance centred around a framework of principles rather than a detailed set of rules that can be complied with to the letter but circumvented in substance.'
- 'A blanket prohibition on the provision of non-audit services to audit clients can be inefficient for the client and is neither necessary to ensure independence, nor helpful in contributing to the knowledge necessary to ensure the quality of the audit.'

The need for auditor independence when the audit form does non-audit work is recognised in the UK Corporate Governance Code. The Code includes a provision that:

'The annual report should explain to shareholders how, if the auditor provides non-audit services, auditor objectivity and independence is safeguarded.'

The King III Code states more specifically that:

'The audit committee ... must define a policy for non-audit services provided by the external auditor and must approve the contracts or non-audit services.'

In the USA, the Sarbanes-Oxley Act 2002 introduced restrictions on the types of non-audit work that can be carried out by the audit firm for a client company (sections 201 and 202). Prohibited services include book-keeping services and other services related to the accounting records or financial statements of the company, the design and implementation of financial information systems, actuarial services, valuation services, internal auditing services (out-sourced to external accountants), legal services, management functions, and broker/dealer or investment advice services. Tax services are specifically permitted by the Act, unless they come within a prohibited category of non-audit services.

4.5 Rotation of audit firm or audit partner

Another suggestion for protecting auditor independence is that there should be 'rotation' of auditors. There is an important distinction, however, between the following.

- Rotation of an audit firm, whereby a firm is required to give up the audit for a company after a maximum number of years, and the company must appoint different auditors, and
- Rotation of audit personnel, whereby the audit engagement partner and other key individuals involved in the annual audit should be removed from the audit after a certain number of years, and new individuals assigned to the work.

Rotation of audit firm

Rotation of the audit firm would enhance auditor independence because a firm of auditors would have little to gain by going along with the wishes of the client company, and carrying out a less than rigorous audit, if it knows that it will soon lose the audit work anyway. The work of outgoing auditors would also be subject to review – and criticism – by the firm of auditors taking their place.

The case for regular rotation of external auditors was strengthened by the accounting fraud at WorldCom in 2002. Its external auditors (Andersen) had been auditors of the firm since 1989, and in the year before fraud was uncovered, the firm was reportedly earning three times as much from WorldCom in consultancy fees as it was earning in audit fees ($12.4 million, compared with $4.4 million).

A disadvantage of **audit firm rotation** is that the incoming firm of auditors might need one or two years to get to know the business of the client company, and might be unable to conduct an audit to the same standard as their predecessor.

If the argument in favour of auditor rotation is accepted, however, there is still scope for disagreement about how frequently audit firm rotation should occur. Regular rotation might involve a company changing the audit firm every five years or so. An alternative argument is that audit firm rotation should be much more occasional, say every ten or fifteen years.

Audit partner rotation

An argument put forward by the major accountancy firms is that the requirement for rotation should apply, not to the firm of auditors, but to the individual partner of a firm in charge of the audit. For example, it might be acceptable for ABC Corporation to retain the services of Ernst &Young indefinitely, provided that the partner in charge of the company audit is replaced every, say, five or seven years. Supporters of this argument claim that the independence of the audit is threatened by the personal relationship an audit partner builds up with the client company, not the length of association of the audit firm with the company.

In the case of large companies, there is also an argument for a regular rotation of other senior audit managers, as well as the lead partner.

Peter Wyman, former president of the ICAEW, stressed the distinction between audit partner and audit firm rotation. Writing in the *Financial Times* (25 July 2002) he commented that:

'Improvements could be made in the area of audit partner and audit firm rotation, although it is vital not to confuse the two. Audit firm rotation achieves the appearance of greater auditor independence but research shows it is likely to produce a reduction in audit quality, particularly in the first two years after the new firm is appointed. Because people rather than organisations are likely to get "cosy" with one another, greater audit independence could be achieved by rotating the audit partner. This approach avoids quality loss, which arises when the entire cumulative knowledge of the audit firm is cast aside when a new firm is appointed.'

A counter-argument, however, is that **audit partner rotation** would not have prevented the problem that arose between Andersen and its clients Enron and WorldCom. Although Andersen as a whole was not over-dependent on Enron, the company was a vital client for the firm's Houston office, which carried out the audit. Similarly, the Andersen office in Jackson, Mississippi was heavily dependent on the work that it did for WorldCom. To prevent loss of audit independence, audit partner rotation would almost certainly have been ineffective, whereas audit firm rotation might have been much more effective.

Currently, regulations in most countries favour audit partner rotation rather than audit form rotation. In the UK for example the ICAEW's ethical standards require the rotation of various members of an audit team, including the rotation of the audit engagement partner at least every five years.

4.6 Directorships for former auditors

Yet another potential threat to auditor independence is the practice whereby public companies appoint a former auditor to their board as CFO/finance director. It could be reasoned that if an auditor sees the possibility of a lucrative promotion to the board of a major public company, he will do nothing to threaten the relationship built up with the management of the company.

A suggestion for countering this risk is that public companies should not be allowed to appoint a former auditor of the company to the board for at least a minimum period of, say, two years after the individual concerned has left the audit firm.

The UK Corporate Governance Code suggests that if a former audit partner is appointed to the board of a company, the individual is unlikely to be considered independent. (Independence must be called into question where the director within the previous three years has been a partner or senior employee in any entity that has (or has had) a material business relationship with the company. This includes the company's auditors.)

TEST YOUR KNOWLEDGE **7.4**

(a) Give examples of non-audit work for a company by a firm of auditors.
(b) What are the five categories of threats to auditor independence?
(c) What is the difference between audit firm rotation and audit partner rotation?

---

5 The audit committee

The UK Corporate Governance Code requires that a board of directors should establish formal and transparent arrangements for:

- considering how they should apply the corporate reporting and risk management and internal control principles, and
- maintaining an appropriate relationship with the company's auditors.

These arrangements should be met by establishing an audit committee, which should be given certain responsibilities by the board. The role of the audit committee in applying the principles of risk management and **internal audit** is described in Chapters 9 and 10; this chapter concentrates on the role of the audit committee is applying corporate reporting principles and maintaining an appropriate relationship with the external auditors.

5.1 Role and responsibilities of the audit committee

The UK Code lists the role and responsibilities of an audit committee. Excluding those concerned with risk management and internal control, they are as follows.

- To monitor the integrity of the company's financial statements and any formal announcements relating to the company's financial performance. In doing so, it should review 'significant financial judgements' that these statements and announcements contain.
- To make recommendations to the board in relation to the appointment, re-appointment or removal of the company's external auditors, for putting to the shareholders for approval in general meeting of the company.
- To approve the remuneration and terms of engagement of the external auditors (after they have been negotiated with the auditors by management).
- To review and monitor the independence and objectivity of the external auditors, and also the effectiveness of the audit process, taking into account relevant UK professional and regulatory requirements.
- To develop and implement the company's policy on using the external auditors to provide non-audit services. This should take into account any relevant external ethical guidance on the subject. The committee should report to the board, identifying actions or improvements that are needed and recommending the steps to be taken.

The terms of reference of the audit committee, including its role and the authority delegated to it by the board, should be 'made available' and a separate section of the annual report should describe the work of the committee.

5.2 Composition of the audit committee

The UK Code states that an audit committee should consist of at least three members (or at least two members in the case of smaller companies, outside the FTSE 350). All its members should be independent non-executive directors.

- In FTSE 350 companies, the company chairman should not be a member of the committee.
- In companies outside the FTSE 350, the chairman may be a member of the audit committee (but not chairman of the committee) provided that he was considered independent on appointment as chairman.

The FRC has published Guidance on Audit Committees (revised 2008), which suggests that appointments to the committee should be made by the board on the recommendation of the nomination committee, in consultation with the audit committee chairman. Appointments should be made for a period of up to three years, extendable by no more than two additional three-year periods and so long as the director remains independent.

The UK Corporate Governance Code also states that the board should satisfy itself that at least one member of the committee has 'recent and relevant financial experience'. This individual should ideally have a professional qualification from one of the accountancy bodies, and the degree of financial literacy required from the other committee members will vary according to the nature of the company.

As a matter of good governance practice, the company secretary should act as secretary to the audit committee.

5.3 Legal requirement for an audit committee: UK law

UK listed companies are required to have an audit committee, following the implementation in 2008 of the requirements of the EU Statutory Audit Directive. This statutory requirement is applied through the FSA's Disclosure and Transparency Rules, which also specify the responsibilities of an audit committee. The rules are less onerous and less detailed than the requirements of the UK Corporate Governance Code. However, they are significant because they are an enforceable regulatory requirement implementing an EU Directive.

(Note: national laws vary, and not all countries have a legal requirement for listed or quoted companies to have an audit committee. However, a legal requirement exists throughout the European Union and also in the USA where – under the provisions of the Sarbanes-Oxley Act – national securities exchanges are prohibited from listing the securities of any company unless it has an audit committee and complies with certain audit committee requirements – such as the requirement that all committee members must be independent.)

5.4 The FRC Guidance on audit committees

In the UK, the FRC's Guidance on Audit Committees is not obligatory, and boards of directors are not required to comply with it. However, it is intended to assist boards with the implementation of the requirements on audit committees of the UK Code. (It was originally published in 2003 as the Smith Report, but has since been revised and renamed.)

The introduction to the Guidance makes the following comments.

■ The audit committee arrangements within each company need to be proportionate to the task, and will differ according to the size, complexity and risk profile of the company. However, if the Guidance is followed, audit committees will have 'wide-ranging, time-consuming and sometimes intensive work to do'.

■ All the board directors have a duty to act in the best interests of the company, but the audit committee has a particular role, 'acting independently from the executive, to ensure that the interests of shareholders are properly protected in relation to financial reporting and internal control'.

■ The principle of the unitary board is not affected by the creation of an audit committee. All directors are equally responsible in law for the company's affairs. The audit committee is a committee of the board, and any disagreement within the board, including disagreement between the audit committee members, should be resolved at board level.

■ The UK Corporate Governance Code states that a separate section of the company's annual report should describe the work of the audit committee. 'This deliberately puts the spotlight on the audit committee and gives it an authority it might otherwise lack.'

■ The company's management is under an obligation to make sure that the audit committee is kept properly informed and should take the initiative in providing the committee with information, instead of waiting to be asked. The executive directors should also have regard to their common law duty to provide all directors, including the audit committee members, with all the information they need to discharge their duties as directors of the company. (This guidance is crucial. The audit committee can only do its work properly if it is kept properly informed by the executive management.)

■ The core functions of the audit committee are concerned with 'oversight', 'assessment' and 'review' of other functions and systems in the company. It is not the committee's duty to carry out those functions; for example, management remains responsible for preparing the financial statements and the auditors remain responsible for preparing the audit plan and carrying out the audit.

■ However, the high-level oversight function can sometimes lead to more detailed work. The FRC Guidance gives as an example a situation where the audit committee are unhappy with the explanations of management and the auditors about a particular financial reporting decision, 'there may be no alternative but to grapple with the detail and perhaps seek independent advice'.

■ For groups, the audit committee of the parent company will usually have to review activities relating to subsidiaries within the group. The board of the parent company must ensure that there is adequate co-operation within the group to allow the audit committee of the parent company to do its job properly.

■ The board should decide just what the role of the audit committee should be, and the terms of reference should be tailored to the company's particular circumstances. However, the audit committee should review its terms of reference and effectiveness annually, and recommend any necessary changes to the board. The board should also review the effectiveness of the audit committee annually. (See Chapter 5 for a description of performance evaluation.)

5.5 Remuneration, induction and training of committee members

The FRC Guidance comments that the audit committees have wide-ranging and time-consuming work to do, and companies must make the necessary resources available. This includes making suitable payments to the members of the audit committee, in view of the responsibilities they have and the time they must commit to the work. The amount of remuneration paid to the audit committee members should take account of the remuneration paid to other members of the board. The committee chairman's responsibilities and time commitments will normally be greater than those of the other committee members, and this should be reflected in his/her remuneration.

The committee should have the support of the company secretary and should have access to the services of the company's secretariat.

Audit committee members must also be given suitable induction and training. Ongoing training should include keeping the committee members up to date on developments in financial reporting and related company law. It may, for example, include understanding financial statements, the application of particular accounting standards, the regulatory framework for the company's business, the role of internal and external auditing, and risk management. Both induction and training can take various forms, including attendance at formal courses and conferences, internal company talks and seminars and briefings by external advisers.

5.6 Audit committee meetings

The audit committee chairman should decide the timing and frequency of committee meetings, in consultation with the company secretary, and there should be as many meetings as the role and responsibilities of the committee require. The FRC Guidance suggests the following.

- There should be no fewer than three committee meetings each year, timed to coincide with key dates in the financial reporting and audit calendar. For example, meetings might be held when the audit plans are available for review and when interim statements, preliminary announcements and the full annual report are near completion. Most audit committee chairmen will probably want to call meetings more frequently. (The FRC Guidance is in contrast to the King III Report, which suggests that the audit committee should meet at least twice each year.)
- Sufficient time should be allowed between audit committee meetings and meetings of the main board to allow any work arising out of the committee meeting to be carried out and reported to the board as appropriate.
- Only the audit committee chairman and members are entitled to attend meetings of the committee. It is for the committee to decide whether other individuals should be invited to attend for a particular meeting or a particular agenda item. It is expected that the audit lead partner and the company's finance director will be invited regularly to attend meetings.
- At least once a year, the audit committee should meet the external and internal auditors, without management being present, to discuss matters relating to its responsibilities and issues arising from the audit.

5.7 Financial reporting and the role of the audit committee

It is the responsibility of management, not the audit committee, to prepare complete and accurate financial statements. It is the responsibility of the audit committee to review the significant financial reporting issues and judgements that are made in connection with these statements.

- The audit committee should consider significant accounting policies used to prepare the statements, any changes to them, and any significant estimates or judgements on which the statements have been based.
- Management should inform the committee about the methods they have used to account for significant or unusual transactions, where the accounting treatment is open to different approaches.
- Taking the external auditors' views into consideration, the committee should consider whether the company has adopted appropriate accounting policies and made appropriate estimates and judgements.
- The committee should also consider the clarity and completeness of the disclosures in the financial statements.

If the committee is not satisfied with any aspect of the proposed financial reporting by the company, it should report its views to the board (FRC Guidance). The committee should also review related information presented with the financial statements, including the business review and the corporate governance statements relating to audit and risk management.

5.8 Appointment and removal of external auditors

Under the UK Code, the audit committee is the body responsible for maintaining the company's relations with its external auditors. The Code states that the audit committee has the primary responsibility for making a recommendation to the board on the appointment, reappointment or removal of the external auditors. If the board does not accept this recommendation, it should:

- include in the annual report, and in any papers recommending the appointment or reappointment of the auditors, a statement from the audit committee explaining its recommendation, and
- give reasons why the board has taken a different position.

If the audit committee recommends to the board that new external auditors should be selected, the committee should 'oversee' the selection process (FRC Guidance). The committee's recommendation should be based on the following assessments:

- the qualification and expertise of the auditors
- the resources of the auditors
- the independence of the auditors
- the effectiveness of the audit process.

The assessment should cover all aspects of the audit service provided by the audit firm, and in carrying out the assessment the committee should obtain from the audit firm a report on its own internal quality control procedures (FRC Guidance).

If the external auditors resign, the audit committee should investigate the issues that gave rise to the resignation, and consider whether any action is needed.

Terms and remuneration of the auditors

The audit committee should approve the terms of engagement of the external auditors and the remuneration to be paid to the auditors for their audit services. (The committee should approve the terms and remuneration, but is not required to negotiate them itself.) It should satisfy itself that the amount of the fee payable for the audit services is appropriate, and that an effective audit can be carried out for such a fee. The fee should not be too large, but neither should it be too low. A low audit fee creates a risk that the audit might be of an inadequate scope or quality.

The committee should review and agree the engagement letter issued by the external auditors at the start of each audit, to make sure that it has been updated to reflect any changes in circumstances since the previous year.

The committee should also review the scope of the audit with the auditor. If it is not satisfied that the proposed scope is adequate, the committee should arrange for additional audit work to be undertaken (FRC Guidance).

5.9 Audit committee responsibilities and auditor independence

The UK Corporate Governance Code gives the audit committee the responsibility for monitoring and ensuring the independence of the external auditors. If the external auditors provide non-audit services to the company, the annual report should explain how auditor independence and objectivity are safeguarded.

The audit committee should have procedures for ensuring the independence and objectivity of the external auditors annually. The FRC Guidance suggests various measures for the committee to take.

- The committee should seek reassurance that the auditors and their staff have no family, financial, employment, investment or business relationship with the company other than in the normal course of business.

- The committee should seek from the audit firm, annually, information about the firm's policies and processes for maintaining independence and monitoring compliance with relevant requirements, such as those regarding the rotation of audit partners and staff.
- The committee should agree with the board the company's policy on employing former employees of the external auditor. Particular attention should be given to the company's policy on former employees of the auditor who were members of the audit team and then moved directly to the company. This policy should be drafted, and the audit committee should monitor its application. The committee should monitor the number of former employees of the external auditor who now hold senior positions within the company, and consider in the light of their findings whether there may be some impairment (or appearance of impairment) in the auditors' judgement and independence with regard to the audit.
- The committee should monitor the audit firm's compliance with ethical guidance in the UK about the rotation of audit partners, and the fees the company pays as a proportion of the overall fee income of (1) the firm; (2) the office of the firm responsible for the audit; and (3) the audit partner.
- The audit committee should develop and recommend to the board the company's policy in relation to the provision of non-audit services by the external auditors. The committee's objective should be to ensure that the provision of such services does not impair the independence or objectivity of the auditors.

5.10 Provision of non-audit services

The objective of the audit committee should be to ensure that the provision of non-audit services by the company's audit firm would not impair the objectivity and independence of the auditors. The committee should consider:

- whether the skills and experience of the audit firm make it a suitable supplier of the non-audit services
- whether there are safeguards in place for ensuring that there would be no threat to the objectivity and independence of the auditors arising from the provision of these services
- the nature of the non-audit services and the fees for these services
- the level of fees for individual non-audit services and the fees in aggregate for these services, relative to the size of the audit fee
- the criteria governing the compensation of the individuals who perform the audit.

The audit committee should set and apply a formal policy specifying the types of non-audit work:

- from which the external auditors are excluded
- for which the external auditors can be engaged without referral to the audit committee
- for which a case-by-case decision is necessary. In these cases, it may be appropriate to give a general pre-approval for certain classes of work, subject to a fee limit decided by the audit committee and ratified by the board. If the external auditor subsequently provides any of these services, the engagement of the auditors should then be ratified at the next audit committee meeting.

The policy may also set fee limits generally or for particular classes of non-audit work.

In deciding its policy on the provision of non-audit work by the external auditors, the committee should take into account relevant ethical guidance, but a guiding set of principles should be that the external auditor should not be engaged for non-audit work if the result is that:

- the external auditor would audit work done by its own employees
- the external auditor makes management decisions for the company
- a mutuality of interest is created
- the external auditor is put in the role of advocate for the company (FRC Guidance).

If the external auditors do provide non-financial services, the annual report should explain to shareholders how auditor independence and objectivity is safeguarded (UK Corporate Governance Code).

5.11 The audit committee and the annual audit cycle

The FRC Guidance goes into some detail on the annual audit cycle, and the relationship between the audit committee and the external auditors during this process.

- At the start of each annual audit, the audit committee should ensure that appropriate plans are in place for the audit.
- The committee should consider whether the auditors' overall work plan (including the planned levels of materiality and the proposed resources to carry out the audit) seems consistent with the scope of the audit engagement. This assessment should have regard to the seniority, expertise and experience of the audit team.
- The audit committee should review, with the external auditors, the findings of their work. As a part of this review, the committee should: (1) discuss with the auditors any major issues that arose during the audit (and whether these have been resolved); (2) review key accounting or audit judgements; and (3) review levels of errors identified during the audit and obtain explanations as to why certain errors might remain unadjusted.

The FRC Guidance states that the audit committee should review the following.

- The audit representation letters from management, before they are signed, and consider whether the information provided is complete and appropriate, based on the knowledge the committee has.
- The management letter from the auditors, and the responsiveness of the company's management to the auditors' findings and recommendations.

Management representations

Representation letters from the company's management are a part of the audit evidence collected and considered by the auditors. They contain information from management to the auditors. These deal with matters for which other audit evidence does not exist; therefore, the auditors are relying on what management tell them. Representations are required:

- from the directors, acknowledging their collective responsibility for the financial statements and confirming that they have approved them, and
- with regard to matters where knowledge of the facts is confined to management (e.g. management's intention to sell off a division of the business) or where there is a matter of judgement and opinion (for example, with regard to the trading position of a major customer and debtor, or the likely outcome of litigation in progress).

The audit committee should review these representations from management and assess whether (on the basis of the knowledge of the committee members) the information provided seems complete and appropriate.

Audit review by the audit committee

At the end of the audit cycle, the audit committee should assess the effectiveness of the audit process. As a part of this assessment, the committee should:

- review whether the auditors have met the agreed audit plan and consider the reasons for any changes
- consider the 'robustness and perceptiveness' of the auditors, in their handling of key accounting and audit judgements, and in their commentary on the appropriateness of the company's internal controls
- obtain feedback about the conduct of the auditors from key people within the company, such as the finance director and the head of internal audit
- review the auditor's management letter, to assess whether it is based on a good understanding of the business and to establish whether the auditors' recommendations have been acted on (and if not, why not).

TEST YOUR KNOWLEDGE 7.5

(a) Who should be the members of an audit committee?

(b) According to the FRC Guidance on Audit Committees, what should be the responsibilities of an audit committee in connection with:
- audit committee meetings
- financial reporting
- the provision of non-audit services by the firm of external auditors
- review of the annual audit?

(c) What are the provisions of the UK Code with regard to the appointment, re-appointment or removal of the external auditors?

(d) What is the legal requirement for audit committees in the UK?

(e) What induction or training might be provided for members of an audit committee?

(f) What does the FRC Guidance say about the frequency of audit committee meetings?

(g) What measures might an audit committee take to monitor the independence of the external auditors on a regular basis?

6 Disclosure of governance arrangements

In 2006, the EU adopted a Company Reporting Directive, requiring quoted companies to produce a corporate governance statement in their annual reports. The statement must refer to the corporate governance code applied by the company (for example, the UK Corporate Governance Code) and explain whether, and to what extent, the company complies with that code. The statement must also include a description of the main features of the company's internal control and risk management systems in relation to the financial reporting process, and provide a description of the composition and operation of the board and its committees.

These requirements of the Directive have been introduced into the UK by the FSA's Disclosure and Transparency Rules, and listed companies that apply the 'comply or explain' rule in the UK Listing Rules meet the requirements. In the UK, listed companies were already required to report much of the corporate governance information required by the Company Reporting Directive, because the UK Listing Rules require companies to include in their annual report a statement of how they have applied the principles of the UK Corporate Governance Code. The Code includes requirements for disclosures about governance arrangements, such as reports on the composition of board committees and their work.

However, the Company Reporting Directive requires that the information should be presented in a separate 'corporate governance statement'. The Directive also requires that the statement should include a description of the main features of the company's internal control and risk management systems in relation to the financial reporting process, something not contained in the UK Code.

The compulsory requirements for listed companies in the Disclosure and Transparency Rules, and the provisions of the UK Corporate Governance Code, are briefly summarised in Table 7.1.

TABLE 7.1 Compulsory requirements for listed companies in the Disclosure and Transparency Rules, and the provisions of the UK Corporate Governance Code

Disclosure and Transparency Rules (DTR)	UK Code	Comment
All companies with a premium or standard listing to comply with minimum rules relating to the composition of an audit committee and to disclose the composition and functions of this committee in the annual report.	Sets out provisions relating to the size and composition of the audit committee and disclosures in the annual report about its membership and functions.	Compliance with the UK Code will result in compliance with the DTR requirements.
Company to issue an annual corporate governance statement, describing the main features of the company's internal control and risk management systems for the financial reporting process.	The board must report that it has carried out a review of the risk management and internal control systems. Supplementary recommendations in the **Turnbull Guidance** (see Chapter 10).	The requirements differ, but both can be incorporated into a single internal control statement.
Listed companies should include in their corporate governance statement a description of the composition and operation of the board and its committees.	Annual report to include a statement on how the board operates, to identify the membership of the board and to describe the work of the nomination committee and audit committee. A description of the work of the remuneration committee to be made available.	Compliance with the UK Code provisions will ensure compliance with the DTR requirements, provided that the corporate governance statement also includes a description of the work of the remuneration committee.
	The Preface to the UK Code states that chairmen are encouraged to report personally in their annual statement (in the report and accounts) about how the principles in the Code relating to the role and effectiveness of the board have been applied	

7 Narrative reporting

7.1 Additional financial reporting by listed companies

Listed companies are required to make various announcements about their financial performance or prospects to the stock market, in addition to publishing their annual report and accounts.

- They are required to issue an interim financial statement for the first six months of the financial year. This is not audited.
- They are also required to announce to the stock market relevant information affecting their business (e.g. a profits warning). This information must be issued to the stock market through a Regulated Information Service.
- The Transparency Directive requires listed companies that do not publish quarterly reports to issue two interim management statements, one during the first half and the other during

the second half of the financial year. These should include information on trading performance, financial position and any major transactions or events that have occurred during the relevant period.

Voluntary disclosures

Many listed companies provide a range of voluntary information, either within their annual report and accounts or as separate publications. Much of this voluntary information relates to social and environmental matters. The voluntary disclosure of non-financial information is described in Chapter 12.

7.2 The nature of narrative reporting by companies

Published financial statements are historical in outlook and contain very little non-financial information. Although they can help users to understand the prospects for the company, it has been argued that more information should be provided to improve users understanding.

In addition, it has been argued that international financial reporting standards have possibly made financial statements more difficult for many investors to read and understand. In the attempt to make financial statements more informative and relevant to investors, the accounting standards bodies may have gone the other way and made them more obscure. (This is a matter of argument and debate.)

The result of this debate, however, has been a general agreement that companies should present information about their company's performance, and possibly also about its future prospects, in a way that is clear and which covers non-financial as well as financial aspects of performance and the company's position.

Transparency is a core principle of good governance, and by providing non-financial information and forward-looking information, in addition to historical financial statements, companies make their situation much more apparent and easier to comprehend.

Requirements have been introduced for additional reporting by companies to improve the quality of communications with their shareholders. These combine financial and non-financial information, and should improve corporate governance by enhancing the quality and content of the information provided to shareholders and other stakeholders.

- In the UK, there is a statutory requirement (Companies Act 2006) for an annual business review to be issued by companies: this is usually included in the annual report and accounts.
- The King III Report calls for South African listed companies to publish annual integrated reports, which include both financial information and non-financial information ('sustainability reporting' information).

7.3 The business review

The Companies Act 2006 (section 417) requires companies (with the exception of small companies) to include a business review in their annual report. Companies give a variety of names to this review, including Operating and Financial Review, Business Review or even Directors' Report.

The review should provide a 'balanced and comprehensive analysis' of the development and performance of the business of the company during the financial year and the position of the company's business as at the end of the year. The review should be consistent with the size and complexity of the business. It must contain:

- a fair review of the business of the company, and
- a description of the principal risks and uncertainties that the company faces.

For a quoted company, the review should contain to an extent necessary for an understanding of the company's business:

- trends and factors likely to affect the future development, performance and position of the business

- information on environmental matters (including the company's impact on the environment), employee matters, and social and community matters, including information about the company's policies in relation to these matters and the effectiveness of those policies
- information about persons with whom the company has contractual or other arrangements that are 'essential' to the company's business (except that disclosure is not required if in the opinion of the directors it would be seriously prejudicial to that person or contrary to the public interest). This is not a requirement for a list of major suppliers or customers: the key word is 'essential', and for many companies there may be none.

A business review is mainly in narrative form, but for a quoted company it should also include:

- key financial performance indicators (KPIs), and
- where appropriate, key non-financial performance indicators, including information of environmental and employee matters.

Key non-financial performance risk indicators will vary between companies, according to the businesses they operate in and their strategic targets, and they should not be restricted to performance measures about employees and the environment. For example a non-financial KPI for an insurance company might be customer retention rates. In its 2009 business review Marks and Spencer plc included some environmental KPIs (reduction in CO_2 emissions, reduction in waste sent to landfill sites, energy efficiency improvements in stores) but also measures such as weekly footfall in stores (number of customers visiting stores), market share in clothing and footwear, market share in food, and growth in online sales.

Directors' 'safe harbour provisions'

The auditors must state in their audit report whether in their opinion the information given in the directors' report is consistent with the company's accounts for the financial year. This includes the information in the business review. Directors could be personally liable for incorrect information in the business review. When a director is found liable for an untrue or misleading statement or an omission, he will be liable to compensate the company for any loss it has suffered as a result.

When the requirement for a business review was first introduced into UK law, concerns were expressed about the potential liability of directors for statements they would be required to make in a review, especially statements that are forward-looking and so impossible to make with certainty. To meet general concerns about the potential liability of directors for the contents of reports, the 2006 Act includes so-called **safe harbour provisions** (section 463).

These provisions state that a director can be liable for untrue or misleading statements only if he knew them to be untrue or misleading, or was 'reckless' as to whether they were untrue or misleading. Similarly a director can only be responsible for an omission if he knew the omission to be a 'dishonest' concealment of a material fact.

7.4 The ABI position on narrative reporting

In 2007, the ABI published its views on narrative reporting, following the introduction of the legal requirement for a business review by companies. The ABI stated the following.

- It considered narrative reporting to be an important communication tool, helping investors to understand better the longer-term risks and opportunities facing the companies in which they have invested.
- Social, environmental and ethical (SEE) issues are an important part of this reporting, but strategic, financial and market risks and opportunities should also be an important part.
- The priority for narrative reporting should be for the delivery of forward-looking information and non-financial key performance indicators.

Reporting on SEE issues is described more fully in Chapter 12.

TEST YOUR KNOWLEDGE 7.6

(a) In UK law, which companies must publish an annual business review?
(b) What should be the contents of a business review for a listed company?

CASE QUESTION

Refer to the case study at the beginning of Part Two and answer these questions.

1 What changes will be required in the reporting arrangements of the company, to comply with legal, regulatory and corporate governance requirements?

2 Should the company make changes to its arrangements for the annual external audit, and if so what might those changes be?

CHAPTER SUMMARY

- Financial reporting is an important aspect of corporate governance because it is a means by which the directors of a company are made accountable to the shareholders.
- Shareholders and other investors rely on the reliability of the financial statements when making their investment decisions. Reliable financial reporting helps to maintain investor confidence.
- Concerns of investors about misleading financial statements has been a major factor in the development of corporate governance codes and statutory provisions in recent years. Financial statements can be misleading, due to the selection of inappropriate accounting policies.
- The directors, not the external auditors, are responsible for the financial statements.
- The external auditors provide an opinion on whether the financial accounts appear to provide a true and fair view of the company's performance and financial position.
- Similarly the board of directors, who have a responsibility to safeguard the assets of the company, are responsible for the prevention or detection of fraud within the company. Fraud may take the form of criminal activity by employees or others (such as theft) or deliberate misrepresentation in published financial statements. Measures to prevent or detect fraud should be a part of the internal control system in the company.
- The external auditors do not have a direct responsibility for detecting fraud, but may discover fraud in the course of their annual audit work which should then be reported to senior management (or the authorities, if senior management appear to be responsible themselves for the fraud). However, if the auditors fail to detect fraud when they should reasonably have been expected to do so, they may be liable for negligence.
- To perform their role, the external auditors must be independent from the company.
- Threats to independence can be classified as self-interest threats, self-review threats, advocacy threats, familiarity threats and intimidation threats. Carrying out non-audit work for an audit client may create self-interest threats (concerns about losing the work and the fees). Familiarity threats can be reduced by audit firm rotation (not common) or audit partner rotation.
- Doubts have been expressed about the independence of auditors from the companies to which they provide an audit service. The audit firm (through the ethical codes of the profession) and the company's board of directors both have a responsibility to protect the independence of the auditors.
- Control over the audit profession is therefore a corporate governance issue.
- An audit committee, properly constituted, could provide a valuable role in improving the relationship between a company and its auditors and helping to ensure that the external audit process is satisfactory and that the external auditors remain independent. In Europe, there is now a statutory requirement for quoted companies to have an audit committee.

■ An audit committee should consist entirely of independent non-executive directors. The UK Corporate Governance Code specifies that at least one member should have recent and relevant financial experience.

■ The responsibilities of an audit committee in the UK are set out in detail in the FRC's guidance on the responsibilities of the audit committee.

■ Companies are required to include certain information in their annual report to shareholders. In the UK, this includes a directors' remuneration report (by quoted companies) and a business review (with the exception of small companies).

■ A business review, which is largely in narrative form, should include non-financial information as well as financial information, and should be forward-looking as well as commenting on historical performance. In this way it provides more information to shareholders, and improves both accountability and transparency.

Relations with shareholders

■ **CONTENTS**

■ **INTRODUCTION**

This chapter explores the various aspects of the relationship between a company and its shareholders. Regular and constructive dialogue between a company and its shareholders can help investors understand what the board of directors is planning and how the company intends to set about achieving its objectives. Open communications also help shareholders to understand better the performance and financial position of the company. At the same time, the board of directors should try to learn more about shareholders' expectations and concerns. It is the responsibility of both the board and institutional investors to improve the relationship between them, with a view to improving corporate governance. In the UK, company responsibilities for this relationship are included in the UK Corporate Governance Code, and the responsibilities of institutional investors are set out in the **UK Stewardship Code**. There has been some development towards greater activism by institutional shareholders, and electronic communications may encourage more shareholders to vote at company general meetings.

1   Governance responsibilities of the board and the shareholders

In listed public companies, management is separate from ownership, and the shareholders rely on management to run the company in their interests. Management in return should be able to rely on the support of the shareholders, particularly where new initiatives, such as a proposed takeover, have to be put to a vote at a general meeting. In practice, however, the relationship between shareholders and management can be difficult. Shareholders may suspect management of putting their own interests first or of being incompetent. Management in turn may suspect shareholders of not understanding the business, or not showing enough interest.

In the story *The Forsyte Saga*, the novelist John Galsworthy gave a sharp illustration of the difficult relationship that can exist between a company board and its shareholders. Although set in the late nineteenth century, the insights remain relevant today. Describing an annual general meeting (AGM) of a company where Old Jolyon Forsyte was the chairman, and his nephew Soames was in attendance, he wrote:

'And now old Jolyon rose, to present the report and accounts.

Veiling under a Jove-like serenity that perpetual antagonism deep-seated in the bosom of a director towards his shareholders, he faced them calmly ...

'"If any shareholder has any question to put, I shall be glad to answer it." A soft thump. Old Jolyon had let the report and accounts fall, and stood twisting tortoise-shell glasses between thumb and forefinger.

'The ghost of a smile appeared on Soames' face. They had better hurry up with their questions! He well knew his uncle's method (the ideal one) of at once saying, "I propose, then, that the report and accounts be adopted!" Never let them get their wind – shareholders were notoriously wasteful of time!'

The impression given here is that a chairman, representing the board, regards the shareholders as an irritation whose views are irrelevant, and who can be kept quiet through careful but firm handling. This attitude is perhaps not as old-fashioned or unrealistic as might be supposed.

At the same time, shareholders can be indifferent to their company boards, often failing to attend general meetings or even submit **proxy votes** and seeming to show little interest in the company's affairs, apart from the immediate share price and dividend prospects, until something goes wrong. However, relations between the company's board and its shareholders are an important aspect of corporate governance and both boards of directors and shareholders have responsibilities for improving corporate governance through active engagement with each other.

1.1 Responsibilities of the board for relations with shareholders

From the company's perspective, the directors should recognise that although their legal duties are to the company, the shareholders of the company are its owners. The board should therefore keep the shareholders well informed about what the company is doing and should seek to engage with shareholders and understand what shareholder expectations are. The responsibilities of the board for promoting relations with shareholders should be included in codes of corporate governance. The UK Corporate Governance Code identifies two ways in which relations with shareholders should be developed:

1   through dialogue with shareholders, and
2   through constructive use of the annual general meeting.

These issues are considered in more detail later.

1.2 Responsibilities of shareholders for engagement with companies in which they invest

From the shareholders' perspective, only institutional shareholders normally have the time, as well as the understanding, to monitor the performance of companies and the activities of their boards. Traditionally, institutional investors have taken the view that if they disapprove of a particular company or its management, they can always sell their shares and invest somewhere else. Another view is that many investments by institutional shareholders may be of a long-term nature. Activist shareholders would argue that, over the long term, companies that are better governed will create more value than those that are badly governed. It is therefore in the interest of institutional investors, and the clients or beneficiaries they represent, to encourage companies to adopt best practices in corporate governance.

Principles of shareholder responsibilities have been developed for institutional investors by, among others:

- the **Institutional Shareholder Committee** (ISC) in the UK, whose code of practice was adopted and developed by the Financial Reporting Council into the UK Stewardship Code for institutional investors, and
- the International Corporate Governance Network (ICGN).

1.3 Categories of shareholders

Shareholders in listed companies consist of different types of investor. There are institutional shareholders, small private shareholders, large private shareholders and corporate shareholders. Shareholders may invest for only a short time: speculators, for example, may buy shares in companies in the expectation of being able to make a quick profit from movements in the share price. On the other hand, some shareholders may expect to hold shares as a longer-term investment; although they always have the option of selling their shareholding at any time.

Some shareholders might choose to 'play the stock market', and buy and sell shares regularly. Although they might be long-term investors in some companies, they might treat other shareholdings as short-term investments. If shareholders come and go regularly, a company's board of directors cannot possibly get to know them or develop a relationship with them. Directors should consider the longer-term interest of the company, and their engagement with shareholders should be directed principally to longer-term investors.

1.4 Institutional investors

Institutional shareholders are organisations that have large amounts of funds to invest, and put much of these funds into company shares. In the UK, the institutional investors include pension funds, insurance companies and collective investment institutions such as unit trust funds and open-ended investment companies.

- These operate in the interests of beneficiaries, such as members of pension schemes and holders of life assurance policies.
- They may appoint agents to manage their investments. These investment management firms will be given responsibility for buying and selling investments for their client institution within the framework of investment fund mandates that indicate how the money should be invested and how the shares should be voted.
- Institutional investors may also use the services of proxy voting agencies, which offer research and voting services to institutional clients, and voting advisory services.

All of these different organisations can be classified as 'institutional investors'. There are national associations of institutional investors, such as the Association of British Insurers (ABI) and the National Association of Pension Funds (NAPF) in the UK, but in many countries (including the UK) a large proportion of shares in listed companies are owned by foreign investment institutions. Although there are international organisations such as the ICGN, it is difficult for institutional investors to monitor the governance of all the companies in which they invest in every country. The international nature of investment therefore adds to the difficulties of establishing a good relationship between a company and its shareholders.

 STOP AND THINK **8.1**

In 2010 US group Kraft Foods succeeded with a hostile takeover bid for UK confectioner Cadbury in a deal valued at nearly £12 billion. The board of directors opposed the bid until it became inevitable that the bid would succeed. In the days before a shareholder vote on accepting the terms of the offer it was reported that about a quarter of Cadbury shares were in the hands of speculators hoping to make a quick profit from the deal. It was also reported that Warren Buffet (the 'Sage of Omaha'), head of investment group Berkshire Hathaway and owner at the time of 10 per cent of Kraft shares, opposed the bid because it was a bad deal for Kraft shareholders. In this situation should the Cadbury board have given more consideration to the objectives of its short-term speculative shareholders? Should the Kraft board have given greater consideration to the opposition from its major shareholder? Was this a takeover battle in which the boards of the respective companies did not give sufficient consideration to shareholder interests?

STOP AND THINK 8.2

In the UK, institutional investment organisations that obtain funds for investment include pension funds, life assurance companies and investment trust organisations. These organisations might appoint investment management companies to invest the funds on their behalf ('manage the funds'). The investment managers decide how the money should be invested, possibly with some policy guidance from their client, what investments to buy and whether to sell. The legal owners of the investments are the investment managers, and it is the investment managers (not their clients, the pension funds or life assurance companies) who have the equity voting rights in the companies. Investment managers effectively hold the investments of their clients in a stewardship capacity, on behalf of and in the interests of their clients. Pension funds and other investment organisations may be answerable to their own beneficiaries for the way in which the funds are invested, but to be properly accountable to their beneficiaries, they need to monitor the activities of their investment managers. Investment managers, more so than the pension funds and insurance companies, have the task as shareholders of trying to ensure that best practice in corporate governance is followed by the companies in which they invest.

TEST YOUR KNOWLEDGE 8.1

According to the UK Corporate Governance Code, in what ways should a listed company try to improve relations with its shareholders?

2   Rights and powers of shareholders

Shareholders do not get involved directly in the management of quoted companies, although they may occasionally express their views about corporate strategy to the chairman or other members of the board. The board of directors and management of the company make the strategic and operational decisions. However, as owners of the company, the shareholders should expect their views to be heard by the board of directors, in cases where a substantial proportion of them hold similar opinions.

Shareholders have certain rights in law and under the constitution (articles of association) of their company. For example, they should have a right to receive the annual report and accounts, the right to vote at general meetings and the right to a share of the profits of the company. The powers of shareholders to exercise their rights are limited, and are mainly restricted to:

- voting powers at general meetings, and
- taking legal action in cases where the directors have acted illegally.

2.1 Pre-emption rights and right to approve long-term incentive schemes

In some countries, including the UK, shareholders have pre-emption rights. When a company issues new shares for cash, existing shareholders have the first right of refusal, and should be offered the right to buy new shares in proportion to their existing shareholding. They may agree to waive these rights, e.g. in order to allow a share option scheme to be implemented for employees of senior executives of the company.

In addition to pre-emption rights, shareholders may be given the right to approve any new or amended long-term incentive scheme for the company. (This is a provision of the UK Corporate Governance Code.) Institutional shareholders will normally approve long-term incentive schemes provided the terms are reasonable and the new shares issued as a consequence of the scheme would not result in an increase in share capital by more than a maximum percentage limit.

These rights give shareholders some influence over remuneration schemes for directors and senior executives.

2.2 Election and re-election of directors and auditors

Shareholders could hold individual directors (or the board as a whole) to account for their actions by voting against his re-election. The articles of association of a public company should provide for the directors to retire by rotation, and if they wish submit themselves for re-election at the annual general meeting of the company. In the UK, the articles of most public companies provide for directors to stand for re-election at the AGM following their initial appointment and subsequently every three years. A simple majority is required for the re-election of a director, which means that a simple majority is required to successfully oppose a re-election.

The UK Corporate Governance Code includes a provision that *all* directors of FTSE 350 companies should submit themselves for annual re-election at the company's annual general meeting.

The requirement for directors to stand for periodic re-election offers the shareholders an opportunity to vote a director out of office, or to reject a new director recently appointed by the board. Some activist shareholder groups have occasionally encouraged investment institutions to vote against particular directors. However, most shareholders tend to vote in support of the directors, and it is still difficult for active shareholders to vote successfully against the re-election of any director. Even so, **shareholder activism** or **shareholder engagement** (see section 6.2 later in this chapter) means that shareholder leverage over changes to the board of directors is greater now than it has been in the past.

The shareholders also have the right to approve (or reject) the appointment of the auditors each year.

2.3 Approval of the directors' remuneration report

As explained in Chapter 6, the shareholders of quoted companies have the right to vote to approve the directors' remuneration report at the AGM, but the vote is advisory only and is not binding on the board. Even so, voting against the report has been used occasionally by shareholders to express their strong disapproval of the company's remuneration policies or remuneration packages for directors and senior executives.

2.4 Other voting rights

In UK law, shareholders have a right to:

- call a general meeting of the company, and call for a vote on a resolution that they put to the meeting, or
- propose a resolution to be voted on at the annual general meeting.

The EU Shareholder Rights Directive was introduced into UK law in August 2009 by amendments to the Companies Act 2006.

- Previously, shareholders could require the directors to call an extraordinary general meeting if they held at least 10 per cent of the voting share capital. This has now been reduced to 5 per cent.
- Shareholders were given a new statutory right to include a matter in the business of the AGM of the company provided they hold at least 5 per cent of the voting share capital. The request to include the item in the AGM must be received not later than six weeks before the date of the AGM, and if the request is received before the end of the company's financial year preceding the AGM, the company must bear the costs of circulating the details of the matter to the other shareholders.

In UK law, if the shareholders are dissatisfied with a director, they have the right under the section 168 of the Companies Act 2006 to remove a director by an ordinary resolution in general meeting, before the end of his term of office. In principle, shareholders holding at least 5 per cent of the share capital of their company may therefore call for the removal of the entire board from office, at the AGM or at an extraordinary general meeting called for the purpose.

2.5 Regulatory requirements for shareholder involvement

To a limited extent, the UK Disclosure and Transparency Rules (DTR) give shareholders some rights by obliging a company to keep shareholders informed of certain developments and to obtain shareholder approval for certain transactions. UK listed companies are required to provide certain information to the stock market, such as profit warnings, changes in major shareholdings, changes in directors' shareholdings, and so on. In addition, listed companies must obtain prior approval from the shareholders, by vote in a general meeting, for:

- transactions above a certain size, relative to the size of the company, and
- transactions with related parties.

Large transactions for which prior shareholder approval is required are known as Class 1 transactions; these include major takeovers or the disposal of a large part of the company's business operations. Transactions with related parties are outside the normal commercial business operations of the company between the company and a major shareholder or a director, or someone closely associated with a major shareholder or director (e.g. a relative or business partner). One example of a transaction with a related party is the sale of a company property to one of its directors.

When major transactions or transactions with related parties are planned, the board will have to send out a circular to its shareholders, explaining the reason for the transaction and justifying it, in order to win shareholder approval. In some sense, the company is therefore obliged in these situations to communicate with its shareholders and seek their support. (Legal requirements relating to shareholders' rights to notice of general meetings and to vote at general meetings are described later in this chapter.)

2.6 Limitations of shareholder powers

The powers of shareholders are limited, and for shareholders to exert positive influence on a board of directors, there has to be a positive relationship between them, with constructive dialogue. When there is strong disagreement between the board and some shareholders, it is usually the directors who 'win' and get their way.

 CASE EXAMPLE 8.1

After successfully ousting the chairman of the board of directors, the shareholders of listed UK company SkyePharma requisitioned an extraordinary general meeting at which a proposal would be made for the installation of the nominee of a shareholder group as new chairman. The shareholders requisitioning the EGM also asked for the suspension of any attempts to break up the company before the new chairman was appointed. The shareholder initiative was led by an activist group, North Atlantic Value (NAV), which claimed the support of 37 per cent of the shareholders.

The board of directors defied the shareholders and their demands. In February 2006, it appointed a chairman of its own choice and announced the sale of a US-based subsidiary. NAV accused the directors of 'astonishing arrogance' and stated that it was 'surprised that a board that contains a number of seasoned operators should behave in such a cavalier way towards shareholders. We as shareholders are owners of the company, it is not their company.'

STOP AND THINK 8.3

There has been an increase in shareholder dissent against policies of the board of directors, especially on matters related to remuneration. A large minority vote against a resolution at a general meeting of the company is seen as a 'warning' to the company, but it does not prevent the board from succeeding in getting their resolutions accepted. For example, in 2010 32 per cent of shareholders voted against the remuneration report at the AGM of retailer Tesco and three large shareholders voted against the remuneration report at the AGM of insurance company Prudential (following a failed takeover bid for the AIA insurance group in Asia); and about 20 pe cent of shareholders voted against a proposed new pay scheme at advertising group WPP. At the 2010 AGM of HSBC, nearly 25 per cent of shareholders voted against the remuneration report or abstained; following this protest vote the HSBC chairman announced that the company would review its remuneration policies.

TEST YOUR KNOWLEDGE 8.2

(a) What rights do shareholders have in UK law to approve remuneration arrangements or schemes for executives?

(b) What issues do shareholders have a right to vote on at general meetings of the company?

(c) In the UK, how soon after his appointment and then how frequently may shareholders of a listed company vote to elect or re-elect the company chairman?

(d) In the UK, how could shareholders dismiss the chairman or chief executive of their company?

(e) In UK law, what is the minimum percentage of voting shares that must be held by a group of shareholders to requisition an EGM?

(f) In UK law, what is the minimum percentage of voting shares that must be held by a group of shareholders to add a resolution to the agenda for the AGM?

3 Dialogue between the board and shareholders

Achieving good relations between a company and its shareholders is desirable on a regular and established basis. This calls for measures by both the board and by the shareholders. The UK has developed these ideas a long way, and current thinking on the subject provides a useful framework for study and analysis. Responsibilities of the board of directors are included in the UK Corporate Governance Code; responsibilities for institutional shareholders are set out in the UK Stewardship Code, which was first issued in 2010.

3.1 Board responsibility to maintain a dialogue with institutional shareholders

A principle of the UK Code of Corporate Governance is that:

'There should be a dialogue with shareholders based on the mutual understanding of objectives. The board as a whole has responsibility for ensuring that a satisfactory dialogue with shareholders takes place.'

Dialogue with institutional shareholders calls not just for regular formal announcements by a company to the stock market generally, but also for regular, informal contact with the larger shareholders in the company. In practice, the main point of contact between shareholders and the board is the chairman, the CEO or the finance director. However, the UK Code states as supporting principles that:

- the chairman should ensure that all the directors are made aware of the issues and concerns of the company's major shareholders, and
- the board should keep in touch with shareholder opinion in the most practical and efficient ways, whatever these may be.

The UK Code states a number of practical requirements for maintaining dialogue.

- The chairman should ensure that the views of the shareholders are communicated to the board as a whole.
- The chairman should discuss strategy and governance with the major shareholders.
- Non-executive directors (NEDs) should be given the opportunity to attend existing meetings with major shareholders.
- If requested to attend meetings with major shareholders, NEDs should expect to attend them.
- The senior independent director should attend enough meetings with a range of major shareholders to listen to their views, in order to develop a 'balanced understanding' of their concerns and views.

In the annual report, the board should report on the steps that have been taken to ensure that members of the board, especially the NEDs, develop an understanding of the views of the shareholders, e.g. through face-to-face meetings, analysts' or brokers' briefings or surveys of shareholder opinion.

3.2 Institutional shareholder responsibility for dialogue with companies

In 2009, the Institutional Shareholders Committee (ISC) published a Code on the Responsibilities of Institutional Investors. These were then adopted by the Financial Reporting Council (FRC) and included (with some minor amendments) in the UK Stewardship Code for institutional investors, issued in 2010 and for which the FRC is responsible.

The ISC Code did not comment extensively on dialogue with companies, but stated in its introduction that '[t]he Code aims to enhance the dialogue of institutional investors with companies', in order to:

- help improve long-term returns to shareholders
- reduce the risk that poor strategic decisions will lead to 'catastrophic outcomes', and
- help with the efficient implementation and practice of governance responsibilities.

The Stewardship Code is described in more detail later in this chapter.

TEST YOUR KNOWLEDGE 8.3

According to the UK Code, what practical requirements are needed for a board of directors to maintain a dialogue with major shareholders?

4 Constructive use of the AGM

4.1 AGM: principles and provisions in the UK Code

The UK Corporate Governance Code states that: 'The board should use the AGM to communicate with investors and to encourage their participation.' The provisions in this part of the UK Code are concerned mainly with:

- encouraging attendance by shareholders at the AGM
- giving shareholders an opportunity to ask questions and to hear about the company during the meeting

■ giving shareholders the opportunity to use their vote and greater openness in voting procedures at the annual general meeting.

The Code provisions are as follows.

■ Encouraging attendance. The company should arrange for the notice of the AGM and the related papers to be sent to the shareholders at least 20 working days before the meeting. The minimum notice of an AGM required by the Companies Act 2006 (section 369) is just 21 calendar days.

■ Giving shareholders an opportunity to ask questions. The board chairman should arrange for the chairmen of the audit, nomination and remuneration committees to be available to answer questions at the AGM, and for all directors to attend the meeting.

■ Voting procedures. At the AGM, there should be a separate resolution for each substantially separate issue. This requirement is intended to prevent the practice of combining two or more issues, one 'popular' and the other more controversial, into a single resolution. Each issue will then be voted on separately.

■ Proxy voting forms should include a **vote withheld** box. This is in addition to the 'for' and 'against' boxes for each resolution. The 'vote withheld' box allows shareholders to indicate their displeasure about a company's proposals without actually voting against the resolution in question. However, a vote withheld is not a vote in law and so does not count towards the proportion of votes cast in favour of or against a resolution (for the purpose of deciding whether a resolution has been passed or rejected).

■ Disclosure of information about proxy votes. After a resolution has been dealt with on a show of hands, the company should indicate the level of votes lodged for and against the resolution, including proxy votes, and the number of shares in respect of which there was a specific instruction to withhold a vote. This information should be given at the meeting itself and made available as soon as practicable afterwards on the company's website. By announcing the number of votes including proxy votes, companies will give some recognition to the views of shareholders unable to attend the meeting, and will not be able to pass controversial resolutions simply on a show of hands of shareholders present and attending the meeting, when a vote on a show of hands differs significantly from what the results of a poll vote would have been.

4.2 Voting rights of proxies

Under the provisions of the Companies Act 2006 (section 324) all registered shareholders have the right to nominate one or more proxies, with each proxy having the right to attend and speak at general meetings, demand a poll and vote on any resolution (in both a vote by show of hands and a poll vote).

The right to appoint more than one proxy, with each proxy representing a different part of the shareholder's total shareholdings, might make it easier than in the past for proxies to demand a poll vote on a resolution after the chairman has taken a vote by a show of hands. This would be consistent with the view of many institutional shareholders, including the Shareholder Voting Working Group, that chairmen of companies should use poll votes rather than voting by show of hands for all resolutions at company meetings.

The Companies Act also requires quoted companies to make available on their website details of polls taken at their general meetings, showing the number of votes cast in favour for and against the resolution.

5 Electronic communications and electronic voting

5.1 Benefits of electronic communications with shareholders

Companies and shareholders may communicate electronically.

■ Companies may send out documents and other information to shareholders, either by e-mail to individual shareholders or by posting information on their website.

■ Shareholders may be able to communicate with their companies on some matters, such as appointing proxies for a general meeting (or possibly casting votes in advance of a general meeting).

Some of the benefits of electronic communications for companies should be apparent.

■ It should be much cheaper to produce documents in electronic form, and use e-mails or a website for communicating with shareholders, than it is to print documents and send them out by post.

■ There may also be environmental benefits, for large companies with many shareholders (less wastage of the product of natural resources such as paper).

There are also potential benefits for shareholders.

■ For some shareholders, particularly foreign shareholders, communication should be much faster and possibly more reliable.

■ Companies should also be able to provide more communication, such as posting the results of polls at general meetings on their website, so that shareholders are better informed.

■ Large institutional investors may also benefit, because information sent or notified electronically is more likely to be seen by the key decision makers within large investor institutions: printed copies of annual reports and accounts are more likely to be handled by junior staff.

■ The ability to appoint proxies electronically (or vote electronically, in some countries) may also improve the probability that shareholders will participate in decision-making by submitting proxy votes.

5.2 UK law on electronic communications

In the UK, companies may provide in their articles of association for the company's website to be used for communication with shareholders, and documents (e.g. the annual report and accounts, summary financial statements and notices of meetings) can be sent to shareholders in electronic form, although individual shareholders may opt out of receiving communications from a company through the company website and ask for communications to be sent in written form. However, if a company adopts a system of electronic communications, it is required to notify the shareholders whenever a message has been posted on the website. Companies whose shares are traded on a regular stock market in the UK are also subject to the Financial Services Authority's Disclosure and Transparency Rules, which permit electronic communications.

Shareholders are also permitted to appoint proxies electronically, to vote on their behalf at general meetings, and companies must provide an electronic address for the receipt of any message or instruction relating to proxies at a forthcoming general meeting.

The results of poll votes at general meetings should also be posted on the website of 'traded' companies (most quoted companies), showing the total number of votes cast, the proportion of the issued share capital that the votes represent, and the number of votes for and against the resolution and the number of votes withheld.

In the UK it has been decided that the appointment of proxies electronically is sufficient, but other countries may provide for shareholders to cast their votes electronically in advance of a general meeting, without the need to appoint proxies.

5.3 ICSA guidelines on electronic communications

The ICSA has issued a Guidance Note on Electronic Communications with Shareholders (updated in 2007), which includes practical guidelines for best practice in communication in electronic form. These recommendations are largely a matter of common sense, and include the following suggestions.

■ The facility to communicate in electronic form should be offered to all shareholders on equal terms.

■ Shareholders should be able to retain a copy of any document or information sent to them in electronic form.

■ Any electronic communication sent by a company giving notice of a general meeting and proxy voting should not include any electronic address unless the company intends that this address maybe used by shareholders to respond to their communication.

■ When information or notifications of availability (of information on the website) are sent to shareholders, the company should use a system for producing a list of recipients or a total number of messages sent, as 'proof of sending'.

- Shareholders opting to communicate electronically should be warned that if they file an electronic proxy voting form containing a virus, the company will not accept it.
- The company should alert shareholders to the fact that the company's obligation to communicate electronically ends with the transmission of the message, and the company cannot be responsible for failed transmissions that are outside their control. However, in the case of failed transmissions, the company should send a written communication to the shareholder within 48 hours of the failure.

STOP AND THINK 8.4

In what ways do you think that a public company might use its website to improve relations with its shareholders and other investors?

TEST YOUR KNOWLEDGE 8.4

(a) What are the provisions in the UK code for making constructive use of the AGM?

(a) What are the benefits of electronic communications between a company and its shareholders?

6 Institutional shareholder responsibilities

6.1 Expecting companies to comply with best corporate governance practice

Developing good relations between a company and its shareholders is as much a task for the shareholders as for the board. Institutional investors, as 'professional' shareholders with large investments in public companies, should be particularly responsible for improving the dialogue and conveying the concerns of shareholders to the board. Institutional shareholders, particularly in the USA and UK, express active concern about corporate governance in the companies in which they invest. In the UK, this has been demonstrated largely through the various representative bodies of the institutional investor organisations, particularly the ISC, ABI and NAPF, although in 2010 the FRC took on responsibility for a Stewardship Code for institutional investors. The interests of institutional investors in good corporate governance can be explained as follows.

- Investors expect a return on their investment. Most evidence suggests that well-governed companies deliver reasonable returns over the long term, and shareholders in these companies are less exposed to downside risk than shareholders in companies that are not so well governed.
- Institutional investors also have legal responsibilities (fiduciary duties) to the individuals on whose behalf they invest. For pension funds, these individuals are the beneficiaries of the funds. In fulfilling their responsibilities, institutions should try to ensure that they make a decent return on investment, and promoting good corporate governance is one way of trying to do this.

6.2 Shareholder engagement (shareholder activism)

In response to a suggestion that shareholders should be given more extensive rights under company law, a frequent counter-argument is that shareholders already have sufficient rights, but do not use them constructively enough. Corporate governance would be improved if shareholders were more active in making their views known to their company, and using their votes against the board of directors if the company failed to respond in a satisfactory way to their concerns.

The term 'shareholder activism' refers to activities by institutional investors to influence governance and strategy decisions in companies in which they invest. In most cases activism is constructive, involving dialogue and discussion, and it is only when a board of directors fails to respond in an acceptable and appropriate way to shareholder concerns that more aggressive action may be considered. This further action will often involve withholding a vote at an AGM, or voting against a resolution at a general meeting, including votes against the re-election of certain directors.

Shareholder activism attracts publicity. Its potential strength is that it brings pressure to bear on companies from the negative publicity that shareholder opposition to the board can create.

A problem for effective shareholder activism is that powers over a company are held by the board of directors, and not by the shareholders. In the face of a continuing refusal by the board to listen to their concerns, shareholders can only make their opposition felt by voting against the board's proposals at general meetings. To do this successfully, they need a majority of the votes. Since most shareholders in large public companies hold a relatively small percentage of the total number of shares, organising a group of dissident shareholders into a voting majority is difficult, although voting guidelines on some issues are occasionally issued by institutional investor organisations or voting advisory firms and such guidelines (such as 'red top' notices) may have the effect of persuading shareholders how to vote.

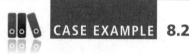

CASE EXAMPLE 8.2

There have been cases where activist shareholders with only a fairly small shareholding in a company have attempted, sometimes successfully, to influence the decisions of company management.

In March 2007 the confectionery and drinks group Cadbury-Schweppes announced its intention to split the drinks division from the confectionery division, with a view to a possible demerger or a sale of the drinks division. This followed an announcement by the company in February that it had no such plans to split the group.

Some City observers believed that the company management had been pushed into a change of mind by the acquisition of 3 per cent of the company's shares by an activist hedge fund that wanted the company to be split up (although the company denied that it had given way to any pressure).

A leading UK fund manager commented in the *Financial Times* in June 2007 that the suspicion that Cadbury-Schweppes had given way to activist pressure 'could represent a come-on to every corporate raider and activist investor'.

In 2010, Cadbury's was subsequently taken over by US food company Kraft.

CASE EXAMPLE 8.3

During 2007, Dutch bank ABN Amro was the target of takeover bids from Barclays Bank and a consortium led by the Royal Bank of Scotland. It was reported that ABN Amro had been forced to break itself up or offer itself for sale as a result of pressure led by The Children's Investment Fund, a 1 per cent shareholder. As the takeover battle progressed, it was also reported in June 2007 that Atticus Capital, holder of a 1 per cent stake in Barclays, had called on the bank to drop its bid for ABN Amro.

Developments such as these raised questions about the extent to which activist investment groups holding a fairly small proportion of the equity shares should be able to bring significant pressure to bear on company management. As events turned out, the decision by Barclays to abandon its pursuit of ABN Amro was a good one; its takeover by a consortium led by the Royal Bank of Scotland (RBS) almost led to the collapse of RBS in 2008 and the acquisition of a controlling stake in the bank by the UK government.

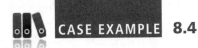

CASE EXAMPLE 8.4

The following episode probably illustrates the problems that occur when shareholders and board cannot get into constructive dialogue with each other than it shows the benefits of shareholder activism.

A bitter dispute developed between the board of UK listed company Mitchells & Butlers (M&B) and some of its largest shareholders following a failed hedging transaction in January 2008 when the company lost hundreds of millions of pounds. Investor Joe Lewis acquired a substantial equity shareholding through an investment company Piedmont, and succeeded in getting some of his representatives appointed as directors of the M&B board. Following continuing disagreements, the chairman of M&B managed to sack four NEDs, including two representatives of Piedmont, and reported Piedmont – unsuccessfully – to the Takeover Panel alleging that it was plotting with other shareholders to seize control of the company. At an AGM in January 2010, the situation was reversed. By a majority of 66 per cent, the chairman of M&B and two other NEDs who were standing for re-election failed to be re-appointed, and another NED stood down from the board. The meeting then appointed as directors three individuals proposed by Piedmont, including a new chairman. However, although there was a large majority in favour of removing the former chairman and two NEDs, most of the votes probably came from Piedmont and six or seven other shareholders, whereas the majority of shareholders by number (rather than size of shareholdings) had supported their re-appointment. A representative of the ABI subsequently commented that it was regrettable that a minority shareholder (Piedmont) had in effect been able to decide the composition of the majority of the M&B board.

6.3 ISC Code on the Responsibilities of Institutional Investors

In 2002, the Institutional Shareholders Committee (ISC) published a statement of principles on the responsibilities of institutional investors, as they should be applied to UK listed companies. In 2009 it was reviewed and re-issued as a Code on the Responsibilities of Institutional Investors. This Code was adopted by the FRC in 2010, and with some small amendments was issued as the UK Stewardship Code.

7 The UK Stewardship Code

7.1 The Stewardship Code and the UK Corporate Governance Code

Both the UK Stewardship Code and the UK Corporate Governance Code are the responsibility of the FRC. The FRC agreed to take on responsibility for the Stewardship Code because it saw an opportunity to build a critical mass of institutional investors who would comply with the Stewardship Code and in doing so commit themselves to high quality dialogue with the companies in which they invest. The FRC has stated that it sees the Stewardship Code as 'complementary' to the UK Corporate Governance Code, in promoting dialogue between institutional investors and UK listed companies.

The concept of stewardship arises from the fact that institutional investors own shares on behalf of beneficiaries, and they are therefore stewards of financial assets for these beneficiaries. As stewards, they have a responsibility to manage these assets and protect them in the best way possible.

7.2 Who should apply the Stewardship Code?

The Stewardship Code is addressed 'in the first instance' to investment managers ('asset managers'), who manage investments on behalf of clients such as pension funds. At the time of writing, the FRC proposed to consider a requirement that authorised investment management organisations in the UK should be required to 'comply or explain' – comply with the Stewardship Code or explain their non-compliance.

However, in a document on Implementation of the Stewardship Code (2010), the FRC states that:

'The responsibility for an effective engagement process does not rest with asset managers alone. The actions of other investors can have a significant beneficial impact on the quality and quantity of engagement with UK companies, and the FRC encourages all institutional investors to report if and how they have applied the Code, on the same basis as asset managers.'

Even if pension funds themselves do not wish to become directly involved in engagement with companies, the FRC argues that they can still support the Code by instructing their investment managers to do so on their behalf and to prepare reports on the nature and extent of their engagement.

Although it is directed primarily at UK institutional investors and their agents in the UK, the FRC hopes that the Stewardship Code will also be adopted by foreign institutional investors, who hold substantial quantities of shares of UK listed companies (and that UK institutions will also apply the principles of the code to their investments outside the UK). The FRC has stated that: 'It is recognised that in practice local institutions usually take the lead in engagement. But support from overseas investors with significant holdings can make a real difference.'

In 2010, the Institutional Shareholders Committee (ISC) responded to Stewardship Code by announcing its intention to establish a new collaborative body, the Institutional Investor Council (IIC), whose terms of reference include working closely with the FRC in promoting the UK Stewardship Code.

7.3 Objectives of the UK Stewardship Code

In an introduction to its consultation on the draft Stewardship Code (in 2009), the FRC commented that directors of UK companies are expected by the Companies Act to pursue 'enlightened shareholder value', and shareholders should take action where they believe that the directors are not serving the interests of the shareholders in the best way. Shareholders should be prepared to be active in the protection of their own interests. 'The concept of active share ownership is central to the regulatory framework for the governance of listed companies in the UK.'

The introduction to the consultation went on:

'While shareholders cannot and should not be involved in the management of their company, they can insist on a high standard of corporate governance as a long-term driver of good investment performance.'

It also suggested that the success of the 'comply or explain' rule for application of the UK Corporate Governance Code by listed companies depends on sufficient institutional investors being willing to put resources into engagement with the companies in which they invest. There are several benefits of active engagement with companies.

- It should improve the governance of listed companies, and this in turn should be expected to improve their longer-term performance.
- Greater clarity about the respective responsibilities of institutional shareholders and their agents should help the shareholders to set the terms of their fund mandates with their investment managers, and make their investment managers more accountable.
- Greater clarity about the respective responsibilities of institutional shareholders and their agents (such as investment managers and voting advisory firms), and better accountability of institutional investment firms to their clients should also improve confidence in the financial system.

The main policy objectives of the Stewardship Code are to:

- set standards for stewardship that institutional investors should try to achieve, and to maintain the quality of these standards through independent input and monitoring by the FRC
- promote a sense of ownership of the Code among UK institutional investors and encourage foreign investors to support it

- ensure that the process of engagement with companies is closely linked to the investment process in firms of institutional investors
- contribute to improved communications between institutional investors and the boards of the companies in which they invest
- ensure sufficient disclosure by investment management firms about how they are engaging with companies, so that this can be taken into account by institutional investors such as pension funds when deciding on which investment managers to appoint to invest their funds.

The main objective of the Stewardship Code is improved engagement by institutional investors, and particularly investment fund managers, with the companies in which they invest. The Preface to the Stewardship Code explains that 'engagement' includes:

- pursuing purposeful dialogue on strategy, performance and the management of risk, as well as
- issues that are the subject of immediate votes at general meetings of the company.

However, it is recognised that not all investment institutions will want to engage directly with companies, e.g. it might not be consistent with the investment strategy of some investment firms. Not all parts of the Code are relevant to smaller investment institutions, and some foreign investment institutions may prefer to follow the requirements of a different code in their own country. The Preface to the Stewardship Code states: 'Institutional investors are free to choose whether or not to engage, but their choice should be a considered one based on their investment approach.'

The UK Stewardship Code is therefore applied on a 'comply or explain' basis. Organisations that adopt the Stewardship Code should provide a statement on their website containing:

- a description of how the principles of the Stewardship Code have been applied
- disclosure of specific information that is required by the Stewardship Code (described later, with regard to Principles 1, 5, 6 and 7 of the Code)
- an explanation of any non-compliance with the Code.

The Code emphasises, however, that compliance with the Stewardship code does *not* constitute an invitation to interfere in the management of companies; nor does it prevent investors from selling their shares, if this is thought to be in the best interests of their end-investors or beneficiaries.

 STOP AND THINK 8.5

The UK Stewardship Code is an attempt to encourage institutional investors to engage more directly with the companies in which they invest, but it is by no means clear that the effort will achieve much success. A doubting voice was raised by commentator Ruth Sunderland in the *Observer* newspaper (4 July 2010). She described the Stewardship Code as an attempt to address the problems of the 'ownerless corporation', where the owners of companies allow directors to do as they please without questioning or challenging their strategies. She argued that the structure of the investment industry is so complex that it may be difficult to improve engagement of investors with company boards. She wrote:

'The chain connecting the end owners – us – to the boards of companies is long, opaque and complicated, involving massed armies of money managers, analysts, brokers and advisers ... The interests of the end-owner – the pensioners on whose behalf all this activity is supposed to take place – are at best seen as a side show, at worst totally ignored. Many pension funds do not even engage with company managements directly, but outsource their judgements to proxy voting agencies. Some are concerned about the costs of becoming more active owners, and fear rivals will hitch a free ride.'

The effectiveness of the UK Stewardship Code will become more apparent over time. It might be unwise, however, to assume that it will have a significant impact in the immediate future.

7.4 The seven principles of the UK Stewardship Code

The Code consists of seven principles, with some guidance for each principle.

Principle 1: Disclosure of policy on discharge of stewardship responsibilities

Institutional investors and their agents should make a public disclosure of their policy on engagement and how they will discharge their stewardship responsibilities. This public disclosure should include the following.

- How they will monitor the companies in which they invest. For monitoring to be effective, it may be necessary to enter into an active dialogue with the company's board of directors.
- The strategy on intervention in the affairs of a company in which they invest.
- The policy on voting, including the policy (if any) on using the services of a proxy voting agency or a voting advisory service.
- The policy on considering explanations by listed companies of non-compliance with the UK Corporate Governance Code.

The FRC also encourages proxy voting services (firms who act as proxies for investor clients, and vote on their behalf at general meetings of companies) to disclose how they carry out the wishes of their clients by applying the principles of the Stewardship Code.

Principle 2: Policy on managing conflicts of interest (and disclosure of policy)

Institutional investors should have a 'robust policy' on managing conflicts of interest in relationship to stewardship, and they should make public disclosure of this policy.

Guidance on this principle comments that institutional investors should act in the interests of their clients or beneficiaries, but conflicts of interest will inevitably arise from time to time. This may occur, for example, when a voting matter arises that affects a parent company or a client. These conflicts of interests must be managed.

Principle 3: Monitoring investee companies

Institutional investors should monitor the companies in which they invest, in order to decide when it is necessary to enter into an active dialogue with their board of directors. They should try to identify problems in a company at an early stage, to minimise the potential loss of shareholder value, and they should make their concerns known to appropriate members of the company's board. Principle 3 encourages investment institutions to:

- meet with the chairman of companies in which they invest (and with other board directors as appropriate) as part of the regular monitoring process, and not just when a matter of concern arises
- maintain a clear audit trail, with records of private meetings with companies, of votes cast at general meetings and reasons for voting against the board, abstaining or voting with the board on a contentious issue
- attend general meetings of companies in which they have a major holding, where appropriate and practicable
- consider carefully the reasons given by an investee company for any departure from the UK Corporate Governance Code and advise the company when they do not agree with its non-compliance (entering into dialogue on the matter, if appropriate).

There is a problem, however, that by engaging in dialogue with a company, an institutional investor may become an insider, and so unable to buy or sell shares. Guidance to the Code suggests:

'Institutional shareholders may not wish to be made insiders. They will expect investee companies ... to ensure that information that could affect their ability to deal in the shares of the company concerned is not conveyed to them without their agreement.'

Principle 4: Escalating shareholder activism

Institutional investors should establish clear guidelines 'on when and how they will escalate their activities as a method of protecting and enhancing shareholder value'. They should set out the circumstances when they will intervene actively, e.g. when they have concerns about the company's strategy, performance, corporate governance or its approach to risks arising from environmental or social matters.

Initial discussions with the company should be on a confidential basis, but if the company's board does not respond constructively, the institutional investor should consider whether to escalate their action, e.g. by:

- holding additional meetings with management to express their concern
- expressing their concern through the company's advisers, e.g. the company's investment bank and sponsor
- meeting with the chairman, or the senior independent director or all the independent NEDs
- intervening jointly with other investment institutions on a particular issue
- making a public statement in advance of an AGM or extraordinary general meeting
- submitting resolutions to general meetings of the company (if sufficient support can be obtained from other shareholders, to get the 5 per cent required)
- requisitioning an extraordinary general meeting, possibly to change the entire board of directors.

Principle 5: Acting with other shareholders

Institutional investors should be willing to act collectively with other investors where appropriate. Collaborative engagement may be particularly appropriate at times when the company is under severe stress, or when risks threaten its ability to continue in operation. Principle 5 also requires institutional investors to disclose their policy on collective engagement.

Principle 6: Policy on voting and disclosure of voting activity

Institutional investors should have a clear policy on voting and should disclose their voting activity. They should not automatically support the board of directors. Where they have been unable to reach a satisfactory outcome through dialogue, they should consider withholding their vote on resolutions at a general meeting, or voting against. It is good practice to notify the company of an intention to vote against a resolution or withhold their vote.

Principle 7: Reporting periodically on stewardship and voting activities

Institutional investors should report periodically on stewardship and voting activities. Investment managers should report to their clients, and institutions that represent the interests of an end-investor or act as principals should report at least annually to those people to whom they are accountable.

The information that is reported may include both qualitative and quantitative information, but the particular information reported (including details of voting) are a matter for agreement between the agent and their client.

Guidance to Principle 7 suggests that asset managers should consider obtaining an independent audit opinion on their engagement and voting processes, but detailed guidance on this matter has not yet been issued.

7.5 Monitoring and review of the UK Stewardship Code

The FRC is responsible for monitoring and review of the UK Stewardship Code. For example, the FRC will monitor the take-up of the Code amongst UK investment institutions and foreign investors. The first review of the Code is expected in 2011.

TEST YOUR KNOWLEDGE 8.5

What are the seven principles of the Stewardship Code?

8   Other guidelines for institutional investors

8.1   ICGN Statement of Principles on Institutional Shareholder Responsibilities

The UK Stewardship Code applies to institutional investors in the UK, although foreign institutional investors are encouraged to adopt it. The ICGN has issued a similar statement of principles (revised 2007) for its own members, who include institutions that invest globally. These do not differ significantly from the UK Stewardship Code. A few extracts from the ICGN Statement of Principles are as follows:

■ 'Successful engagement ... requires more than considered voting. It should also include: maintaining dialogue with the board on governance matters in order to address concerns before they become critical; supporting the company in respect of good governance; and consulting other investors and local investment associations where appropriate.'

■ 'Investors should have a clear approach for dealing with situations where dialogue is failing. This should be communicated to companies as part of their corporate governance policy. Steps that may be taken under such an approach include: expressing concern to the board ...; making a public statement; submitting resolutions to a shareholders' meeting; submitting one or more nominations for election to the board as appropriate; convening a shareholders' meeting; arbitration; and, as a last resort, taking legal actions ...'

■ 'Responsible owners should make use of their voting rights.' 'Institutional investors should ... seek to vote their shares in a considered way ... They should develop and publish a voting policy.'

8.2   NAPF Corporate Governance Policy and Voting Guidelines

Responsible voting was defined in a joint statement (1999) by the ABI and the NAPF:

'Responsible voting involves the application of informed decisions reached within the framework of considered corporate governance policy.'

Institutional shareholders should support the board of directors unless they have good reason not to. When a shareholder thinks that it should vote against the board, it should first make representations to the board in time for the problem to be considered, with a view to reaching a satisfactory solution.

Company law requires some proposals to be approved by the shareholders voting in a general meeting, and specifies the size of majority needed for a resolution to be passed. In the UK, most votes by shareholders require a simple majority (an 'ordinary resolution') but a 75 per cent majority vote is required for a 'special resolution'. For example, in the UK the shareholders have the right to appoint or re-appoint the company's auditors at the AGM and to approve the directors' remuneration report. The most significant voting right for shareholders is probably the right to re-elect directors, in accordance with the company's articles of association and the UK Corporate Governance Code.

In the UK, the NAPF has provided guidelines for a voting policy to its members in its Corporate Governance Policy and Voting Guidelines (2007). Some voting guidelines are shown in Table 8.1 to illustrate how shareholders may decide to vote on governance issues when they have been unable to obtain a satisfactory explanation from the company (under the 'comply or explain' rule). Most of NAPF's voting guidelines are to vote against the re-election of a NED or the company chairman.

TABLE 8.1 Examples of voting guidelines illustrating how shareholders might vote on governance issues

Governance issue	NAPF voting guideline
There are not enough independent NEDs on the board.	Vote against the re-election of the chairman of the nomination committee, or a member of the committee.
The company chairman sits on the audit committee.	Given the broader consequences of voting against the re-election of the chairman, consider abstaining on a vote to re-elect him.
The company chairman was not independent when appointed.	Voting against the election of a company chairman has broad implications for a company; therefore it may be appropriate to consider an 'actively withheld vote' or a vote against the re-election of the chairman of the nomination committee.
The newly appointed chairman was previously the company CEO.	Consider an 'actively withheld vote' or a vote against the re-election of the chairman of the nomination committee. In exceptional circumstances vote against the incoming company chairman.
An NED has a poor record of attendance at board meetings, or there is evidence of poor performance.	In the absence of a sufficient explanation, vote against the re-election of the NED.
There are shortcomings in the annual performance evaluation process for the board and its directors.	Abstain or vote against the re-election of the company chairman or the senior independent director.
The company's remuneration policy contains features that are unacceptable.	Vote against approval of the annual remuneration report.
The annual report fails to provide information about non-audit fees paid to the auditors.	Vote against the re-election of the chairman of the audit committee or any other member of the audit committee.

TEST YOUR KNOWLEDGE 8.6

(a) What is responsible voting? Why is responsible voting recommended by associations of institutional investors (such as the NAPF) to their members?

(b) For what reasons might the NAPF recommend to its members that they should vote against the re-election of the company chairman as a director of the company?

9 Other shareholders: notifications of changes in shareholdings

In terms of corporate governance, institutional investors have the main responsibility for actively engaging with listed companies. However, it is important to be aware of other shareholders in companies, other than institutional investors.

9.1 Small private shareholders

Some individuals own shares directly. In the UK, a share-owning culture is not strong, but even so many individuals have acquired shares. In general, private shareholders hold only small numbers of shares and have very little communication with the company, other than through formal communications from the company. The votes of small shareholders are unlikely to affect the outcome of any shareholder vote at a general meeting of the company, where the block votes of institutional shareholders or large private shareholders carry much more weight. It is easy for a company to overlook the interests of small shareholders, and a corporate governance issue is the extent to which the company should try to establish a relationship.

9.2 Large private shareholders

Occasionally, a large proportion of the shares in a company is held by private shareholders. For example, in a company floating its shares on the stock market for the first time, a large proportion of the shares might be held by individuals who were shareholders when the company was private, and who might still be executive directors. Family shareholders are another example in companies of which, although listed on a stock market, the original family owners continue to hold a position of influence. In these companies, the influence of the large shareholder over decision-making by the board could be fairly strong.

9.3 Corporate shareholders

A significant shareholder in a public company could be another company. Shareholdings by one company in another could be either welcome or a source of concern and mistrust. In some cases, two companies might have cross-shareholdings, so that each holds a block of shares in the other. When cross-shareholdings exist, the companies might have some form of strategic alliance or mutual understanding. In other cases, one company might hold a block of shares in another, possibly with a view to using the investment as a potential base for launching a takeover bid in the future. (A notable example in the UK has been the 17.9 per cent stake in ITV purchased in 2006 by BSkyB, a rival television broadcaster. The UK Competition Commission ordered that the shareholding should be reduced to below 7.5 per cent, on concerns that Sky could influence the output of ITV's news programmes, and BSkyB was eventually obliged to comply with the ruling in 2010.)

9.4 Substantial shareholdings and directors' shareholdings

In the UK, listed companies should be able to identify changes in major shareholdings in the company under the provisions of the FSA's Disclosure and Transparency Rules. These rules require shareholders in listed companies to notify the company when their shareholding reaches 3 per cent of the issued share capital, and then whenever their shareholding changes by 1 per cent or more (up or down). For example, if a shareholder's interest in the share capital of ABC plc reaches 3 per cent, the company must be notified. The company must then be informed each time there is a change, for example, if the shareholding subsequently rises to 4 per cent or more, or drops below 3 per cent. (For listed foreign companies, the disclosure rules are slightly different: changes in shareholdings above 5 per cent should only be made for each additional 5 per cent threshold, rather than every 1 per cent threshold, which is the requirement for UK listed companies.)

 CASE QUESTION

Thinking about the case study of Stenning Tull at the beginning of Part Two, how will the company's relations with its shareholders be affected by the listing?

CHAPTER SUMMARY

- Relations between a company and its shareholders can be poor, particularly when there is a lack of meaningful communication and dialogue.

- However, the UK Corporate Governance Code calls for the creation of good relations between a company and its shareholders through dialogue with institutional investors and constructive use of the annual general meeting (AGM).

- A company might have a majority shareholder, and/or a mix of institutional shareholders and other shareholders. Other shareholders might be corporates or private individuals, and large or small shareholders. The interests and concerns of each type of shareholder, and their relations with the company, will differ.

- The powers of shareholders are limited mainly to voting at general meetings and, in extreme cases, taking a company's directors to court. Voting rights include the right to vote on waiving pre-emption rights when new shares a re issued for cash, approval of new long-term incentive schemes for executives, the election or re-election of directors and approval of the remuneration report (which is only an advisory vote).

- Shareholders could propose resolutions at general meetings, such as a resolution to dismiss one or more directors (provided the resolution is permitted by the company's articles of association). However, shareholders with at least 5 per cent of the company's shares are required to call an extraordinary general meeting or include a resolution to be voted on at the AGM, and a majority of votes at the meeting will be required to pass the resolution. In practice this is a difficult task for shareholders to achieve, unless the situation has become very serious and contentious.

- Companies should make efforts to improve communications with shareholders. The UK Corporate Governance Code encourages companies to enter into constructive dialogue with its institutional shareholders.

- The ISC Code and the Stewardship Code also encourage institutional investors to enter into constructive dialogue with the companies in which they invest.

- The UK Code also requires companies to make constructive use of the AGM to communicate with smaller shareholders and encourage their participation.

- Participation by shareholders can be improved by offering a 'vote withheld' option on proxy forms, the legal entitlement of proxies to vote when a vote is taken by a show of hands, and requirements for a company to report on its website the results of poll votes at general meetings.

- Communications with shareholders are improved by electronic communications. Benefits include faster and more reliable delivery of messages, particularly for foreign shareholders; lower costs due to savings in print and postage costs; a better chance that key decision makers in institutional investor organisations will see messages from a company and act on them; and the likelihood of greater participation by shareholders in the company's affairs due to the convenience of appointing proxies electronically.

- Shareholder activism might be encouraged to bring pressure to bear on companies to pay greater attention to the wishes and concerns of their shareholders. Activism might involve voting against resolutions at general meetings, such as resolutions for the re-election of directors retiring by rotation.

- In the UK the Institutional Shareholders Committee issued a code of practice for UK institutional investors (and inviting foreign shareholders in UK companies to adopt the Code too). This contains seven principles of engagement by investors in companies. This Code was adopted by the FRC in 2010 and issued as a Stewardship Code for institutional investors.

- Associations of institutional investors encourage their members to use responsible voting, generally giving support to the board of directors. Voting guidelines, in the event that shareholders disagree with aspects of a company's performance or decisions, are set out for its members in the NAPF's Corporate Governance Policy and Voting Guidelines

- In the UK, the Disclosure and Transparency Rules require listed companies to report changes in shareholdings of significant shareholders. This should help a company to monitor the identity of its main shareholders.

Risk management and internal control

■ LIST OF CHAPTERS

■ OVERVIEW

The third part of this study text considers risk and risk management as issues in corporate governance. The leaders of companies (and other organisations) are responsible for deciding risk strategies and risk policies, and for ensuring that the internal control system is effective. There are some similarities between a business risk management system and an internal control system, but each has a different purpose and it is important to distinguish between them. The responsibilities of the board of directors for both business risk management and internal control are specified in some corporate governance codes, including the UK Corporate Governance Code and King III Code.

Chapter 9 explains the nature of business risk and the responsibility of the board for deciding how much risk the company should be prepared to accept in order to achieve hoped-for financial returns, and also how much risk the company should be able to tolerate. Exposures to business risk should not exceed the levels determined by the board, and the business risk management system should be effective in ensuring that board strategies and policies are implemented and also reviewed. The chapter describes the elements that may be found in a business risk management system, including the role of a risk committee of the board (or the audit committee) and the measures that may be taken by executive management to implement and monitor risk strategies. The chapter concludes with a brief consideration of how executive remuneration packages might be arranged so that incentive schemes make suitable allowance for risk and risk exposures.

Chapter 10 examines internal control systems. Whereas business risk is an unavoidable aspect of engaging in business activities and is external to a company, internal control risks are internal to a company and so within management control. The chapter describes the nature of internal control risks and internal controls that are applied to prevent adverse events from happening, or identifying them and taking corrective measures when they do happen. A board of directors is responsible for ensuring that the system of internal control is effective, and achieves its purpose. The chapter describes the guidance given to UK listed companies on internal control systems (the Turnbull Guidance). It then goes on to describe several elements of internal control in more detail: the role of internal audit in internal control (and whether companies should have an internal audit function); the benefits of disaster recovery planning; and whistleblowing procedures that enable employees to report suspicions of wrongdoing outside normal lines of reporting through the management hierarchy. The chapter concludes with a description of the statutory measures implemented in the US by the Sarbanes-Oxley Act to ensure more effective internal control within companies.

■ LEARNING OUTCOMES

Part Three should enable you to:

- apply the principles of risk management

- appraise the significance of risk management for good governance

- advise on the appropriate arrangements for an effective risk management system

- advise on the board's responsibility for internal control to meet good governance guidelines

- appraise the effectiveness of an internal control system

- understand and apply the UK principles and guidance in relation to internal audit

- develop appropriate policies and procedures to mitigate the impact of operational disaster and devise a whistleblowing procedure.

 ## PART 3 CASE STUDY

Hunnerware plc is a successful UK listed company whose revenues and profits have been growing at over 20 per cent per year for the past ten years and the company could soon be included in the FTSE 350 list of companies. It operates a large fleet of small aircraft that carry passengers (mainly business passengers) and freight between locations not serviced by larger airlines.

The board of directors is keen to continue with strategies for growth, and a decision has recently been taken to establish a specialised subsidiary company for the maintenance of small aircraft. This maintenance service will be offered to other airline companies as well as Hunnerware's own fleet of planes.

Hunnerware is sponsored by the investment banking division of a large bank, which informed the company chairman that some shareholders were becoming concerned about the risk exposures of the company. They considered that the company is becoming over-exposed to high risks in its pursuit of growth. Some concerns had also been expressed about the company's disputes with government. Twelve months ago the company had been fined by the authorities for allegedly price-fixing on one of its routes: the other company in the price-fixing arrangement had confessed what it had done to the authorities, and its evidence had been used against Hunnerware. Hunnerware was still disputing the fine. The company has also been fined for four breaches of health and safety regulations in the past five years. It has also been accused of tax evasion by the tax authorities, but has denied the charge, claiming that its tax arrangements were entirely tax avoidance measures and within the law.

The chairman discussed the matter of the company's poor reputation for risk management with the chairman of the nomination committee, who agreed

that the board probably gave insufficient attention to risk strategy and lacked board members with experience and knowledge of risk management.

Some time later the nomination committee reported to the board that they were recommending changes to the composition of the board. One of the independent NEDs would not be invited to remain on the board for a further three years when his contract expired soon, and a new appointment to the board was recommended. This was an individual with extensive experience in risk management, at one time as a partner in a risk management consultancy firm.

The change in the board was made, in accordance with the nomination committee recommendations. The new director raised the subject of risk at the first board meeting he attended. The board meeting was held soon after an unusual event had affected the airline industry in Europe generally: a large cloud of volcanic ash from an erupting volcano in Iceland had resulted in the closure of much European air space for several days. As a result the company had lost a substantial amount of business and revenue.

At the meeting, the new director told the other board members that having met and spoken with senior executives in the company, as well as the executive directors, he was unaware of any disaster recovery plan for the company or of any stress testing to assess risk exposures. He recommended that the board should give serious consideration to the development of a risk strategy and the introduction of a risk awareness culture into the company's management and other employees. He also recommended that the company should introduce a system for scenario-based risk identification as an immediate urgent measure.

Risk management and corporate governance

■ CONTENTS

■ INTRODUCTION

The responsibility of the board for effective risk management came under close scrutiny following the banking crisis in 2007–2009. Many banks were criticised for getting into financial difficulty because of reckless business strategies and failing to recognise the business risks that they were taking. Business risks are risks to profitability and financial security that arise from factors in the business environment, including competition, over which management has no direct control. A business must take risks to make profits; but how much risk should it be prepared to tolerate, and would it be able to withstand 'shocks' in the business environment if an unexpected event or development were to occur? The board has the responsibility for strategic decisions on risk, and an important aspect of corporate governance is for the board to recognise its responsibilities and ensure that the risk management system in the company is effective.

1 Risk management and governance

1.1 The relevance of business risk for corporate governance

The board of directors have a responsibility to govern the company in the interests of the shareholders and other stakeholders. A part of this responsibility is to decide the objectives and strategic direction for the company, to approve detailed strategic plans put forward by management, and to monitor and review the implementation of those plans. An important objective of a commercial company is to make a profit, and the company's strategies should be directed towards this. However, any business strategy involves taking risks and actual profits may be higher or lower than expected. When very big risks are taken, a company might even become insolvent and go out of business if actual events turn out much worse than anticipated.

Bad corporate governance can result in the insolvency and collapse of a company, and excessive risk-taking is one aspect of poor governance. The board of directors should take business risk into consideration when it makes strategic business decisions. It should choose policies that are expected to be profitable, but should limit the risks to a level that it considers acceptable. For example, when the board takes major investment decisions itself or decides on corporate strategy, risks as well as expected returns are properly assessed.

The board should also be satisfied that in their decision-making, managers take risk as well as expected returns into account. The Cadbury Report (1992) described risk management as 'the process by which executive management, under board supervision, identifies the risk arising from business ... and establishes the priorities for control and particular objectives'.

The significance of risk management for corporate governance was demonstrated forcibly by the global banking crisis in 2007–2009. In the UK, the government initiated a review into the failures in the banking industry and the resulting Walker Report was published in 2009. It commented that although there were failures in the regulation of the banking industry, much of the blame for the crisis was attributable to poor governance, and in particular inadequate attention to risk management. 'Serious deficiencies in prudential oversight and financial regulation in the period before the crisis were accompanied by major governance failures within banks. These contributed materially to excessive risk-taking and the breadth and depth of the crisis.'

1.2 Risk appetite and risk tolerance

Risk appetite is the level of risk that a company (or any other organisation) is willing to take in the pursuit of its objectives. Risk appetite can be defined as the combination of the desire to take on risk in order to obtain a financial return, risk capacity and risk tolerance.

The 'desire to take on risk' refers to the amount and type of risk that the board of directors would like the company to have exposure to.

■ Risk capacity is the maximum risk exposures that the company can accept without threatening its financial stability.
■ **Risk tolerance** is the amount of risk that the company is prepared to accept in order to achieve its financial objectives. Risk tolerance is therefore the amount of risk that a company's board of directors allows the company to accept.

Risk appetite and risk tolerance are closely related. One is the amount of business risk (and types of business risk) the board would like the company to have and the other is the amount of risk that the board is prepared to tolerate. The Walker Report recommended that the board should consider risk appetite and risk tolerance, and that much more attention should be given to these issues: 'Board-level engagement in risk oversight should be materially increased, with particular attention to the monitoring of risk and discussion leading to decisions on the entity's risk appetite and tolerance.'

The Report went on to state that the board has responsibilities for the determination of risk tolerance and risk appetite through the cycle and in the context of future strategy and, of critical importance, the oversight of risk in real-time in the sense of approving and monitoring appropriate limits on exposures and concentrations. This is largely a forward-looking focus.

Risk appetite should be reviewed regularly by the board, and decisions should be taken about the scale of risk that is desired or acceptable. Risk tolerance could be expressed in numerical terms, such as the maximum loss that the board would be willing to accept on a particular venture if events turn out adversely. This type of risk management is found in banking, for example, where loss limits may be set by a bank for each aspect of its trading activities in the financial markets, and risk measures such as Value at Risk (VaR) are used. Alternatively, risk tolerance could be expressed in terms of a total ban on certain types of business activity or behaviour.

TEST YOUR KNOWLEDGE 9.1

(a) What is the responsibility of a board of directors for business risk
(b) What is risk appetite and risk tolerance?

2   The nature of risk

Risk refers to the possibility that something unexpected or not planned for will happen. In many cases, risk is seen as the possibility that something bad might happen. In everyday life, there is a risk of becoming seriously ill, being involved in a road accident, having a house burgled or flooded, having a motorcar breakdown, and so on. This can be described as downside risk, because it is a risk that something will happen that would not normally be expected.

There is **upside risk** too. This is the possibility that actual events might turn out better than expected. In a business context, an example is the possibility that sales volumes will be higher than planned or that working days lost through industrial action will be lower than anticipated.

Risk management involves making decisions about upside risks as well as downside risks. For example, businesses make investment decisions. Every investment is risky. Actual returns could be lower or higher than expected. In deciding whether or not to undertake an investment, the risks as well as the potential returns should be taken into consideration. Shareholders would like to see their company earning high returns, but might be unwilling to see the management taking excessive investment risks in trying to achieve those returns.

Some risks are easy to recognise, because they are always present and a company may have had many years of experience in dealing with them. For example, financial risks include the risk that customers will not pay what they owe (credit risk), or that interests costs of borrowing will increase or (in the case of an exporting company) that foreign exchange rates will move adversely. Other risks, however, are more difficult to identify and anticipate. The Walker Report commented:

'While a clear continuing responsibility of the board is to ensure that [recognisable financial] risks are indeed appropriately managed and controlled, different and potentially much more difficult issues arise in the identification and measurement of risks where past experience is an uncertain or potentially misleading guide. When risk materialises, it may do so as a risk previously thought to be understood and managed that turns out to be very different indeed ...'

TEST YOUR KNOWLEDGE 9.2

(a) What may be the consequences of failing to consider business risk strategy or establish an effective **business risk management** system?
(b) What is business risk and how could it be measured?

---

3 Business risks and internal control risks

A distinction is made between business risk and internal control risk (sometimes called governance risk).

- Business risks are risks that occur and arise in the external business environment in which a company operates. Business risks are sometimes referred to as strategic risk, because the business risks faced by a company are determined by the strategies that the company pursues.
- Internal control risks are risks of losses that arise through ineffective controls within the processes and systems of a company's business operations. Internal control risk is risk within an organisation; business risk is risk in the external environment.

This chapter is concerned with the management of business risk. Chapter 10 describes **internal control systems** and the management of internal control risks.

3.1 Categories of business risk

The nature and severity of business risks vary from one company to another. Risks also change over time: some become less significant, and new risks emerge.

Business risks are risks that the actual performance of the business could be much worse (or better) than expected, due to unexpected developments in the business environment. For example, when a company develops a new product or service, it will have an expectation of the likely sales demand. Actual demand could be higher or lower than expected. With some new products, the risk that sales demand will differ from expectation could be much more severe than with other new products. There are various reasons why sales demand and profits may be less than expected, or may fall unexpectedly. Competitors may take away some of the company's market share; a company may suffer from bad publicity and so lose customer loyalty; there may be new regulations making the sale of a particular product or service more difficult.

CASE EXAMPLE 9.1

In the early 2000s, there was rapid growth in investment in IT and third generation (3G) telecommunications services. The investments in IT were high risk because huge amounts of money had to be invested to create the service, and there was no certainty that sales demand would achieve the expected levels. Actual demand for the services fell far short of expectation, with the result that many dot.com companies and telecommunications companies collapsed in 2002, resulting in a stock market crash (mainly in the USA).

 CASE EXAMPLE 9.2

In some cases, companies may experience a big fall in sales as a result of bad publicity or acquiring a poor reputation for something. This is reputation risk. In 2010 it was reported that sales of some models of car produced by Toyota had fallen sharply, following the recall of millions of vehicles to rectify a design fault that caused unintended acceleration. There were also suspicions that the company had tried to cover up the scale of the problems. Sales of the cars had been affected by the damage to the company's reputation.

Business risks can be categorised or identified in different ways, but it may help to understand the variety of risks by considering the following sources of risk.

- Reputation risk. The risk of loss in customer loyalty or customer support following an event that damages the company's reputation.
- Competition risk. The risk that business performance will differ from expected performance because of actions taken (or not taken) by business rivals.
- Business environment risks. These are risks of significant changes in the business environment from political and regulatory factors, economic factors, social and environmental factors and technology factors (the so-called 'PEST' factors). For example, business performance may be affected by the introduction of new regulations, political upheaval in a country, economic decline or growth, environmental issues, unexpected changes in social habits, or technological change.
- All companies face financial risks. These are risks that financial conditions may change, with adverse changes in interest rates or exchange rates, higher losses from bad debts or changes in prices in financial markets (such as changes in share prices).
- Liquidity risk is the risk that the company will have insufficient cash to settle all its liabilities on time, and so may be forced out of business. The board of directors should monitor this risk at least annually when they prepare their going concern statement for the annual report and accounts.
- Strategic risks are the risks of taking decisions on strategy that will result in exposures to excessive business risk and so could lead to losses or even business collapse.

 CASE EXAMPLE 9.3

In 2005, the banking group Citigroup Inc took a strategic decision, based partly on advice from outside consultants, to invest more heavily in its 'fixed income' business, which included collateralised debt obligations (CDOs). The bank believed that this new strategic direction offered

(Continued)

CASE EXAMPLE 9.3 *(Continued)*

opportunities for long-term growth. The global banking crisis from 2007 resulted in a collapse in the market value of CDOs. At a hearing of the Financial Crisis Inquiry Commission in Washington in April 2010, former CEO Mr 'Chuck' Prince and former head of the bank's executive committee Mr Robert Rubin said that they did not become aware of the scale of the problem – and its losses – until September 2007. They had been unaware of the scale of the bank's positions in CDOs and the risks surrounding them. Citigroup eventually received a $45 billion bail-out from the Federal government in 2008 to prevent its collapse.

In making the decision to invest more heavily in CDOs, the bank took a strategic risk without being fully aware of the size of the risk it was taking. Risk management systems may also have been ineffective in alerting management to the problems until it was too late to avoid a rescue by the government.

Each industry and each company within an industry faces different risks. The questions that management should ask are as follows.

- What risks does this company face?
- How can these risks be measured? It may be possible to assess the risk in a business in terms of unpredictable variations in key factors such as sales demand or market prices. High volatility is associated with high business risk.
- For each of these risks, how would the company be affected if the worst outcome came about, or if a fairly bad outcome happened?
- What is the likelihood of a bad outcome for that risk item?
- What is the company's risk appetite or risk tolerance?
- What should the company be doing to manage the risk, either by avoiding it altogether or planning to deal with the problems that will arise in the event of a bad outcome?

TEST YOUR KNOWLEDGE 9.3

(a) How might business risks be categorised?
(b) What is the difference between business risk and internal control risk?

4 Responsibilities for risk management

4.1 Responsibilities of the board and executive management

The board is responsible for risk at a 'high level', but responsibilities for the management of risk are delegated to executive management. The board should decide the level of risks that are acceptable at a strategic level, and should ensure that management take risk into consideration in the decisions that they make. The UK Code states: 'The board is responsible for determining the nature and extent of the significant risks it is willing to take in achieving its strategic objectives.'

4.2 UK Corporate Governance Code on risk management

The UK Corporate Governance Code states as a principle that the board should maintain 'sound risk management and internal control systems'.

The board should therefore satisfy itself that appropriate systems are in place to identify, evaluate and manage the significant risks faced by the company.

The UK Code also requires that, at least annually, the board should also carry out a review of the effectiveness of risk management systems in the company. The UK Code therefore includes requirements for:

- a system of risk management, and
- regular reviews of the system (at least annually) by the board.

(Note: The legal requirement for UK companies to include a business review in their annual directors' report was described in Chapter 7. The review should include a description of the principal risks and uncertainties facing the company. However, a requirement to report on significant risks does not necessarily require a formal business risk management system.)

TEST YOUR KNOWLEDGE **9.4**

What are the principles and provisions of the UK Corporate Governance Code with regard to business risk management?

---

5   Risk committees and risk managers

5.1   Risk committees

Responsibilities for risk management vary between companies. An important distinction should be made between the arrangements whereby responsibilities for risk management are fulfilled by:

- the board, and
- executive management.

At board level, responsibility for reviewing the effectiveness of the risk management system may be delegated by the board to the audit committee, which is also likely to have responsibility for reviewing the internal control system. Alternatively, the board may prefer to establish a separate **risk committee** of the board. The advantages of having a separate risk committee are as follows.

- It can focus on risk issues and reviewing the company's risk management system, without having to concern itself with other issues (such as the external auditors). It would give advice to the board on matters such as risk appetite and risk strategy.
- The composition of the board is not restricted by requirements of the corporate governance code. A risk committee should ideally consist mainly of non-executive directors (NEDs) but should also have the finance director as a member. If the audit committee had responsibility for the oversight of risk management, the finance director could not be a committee member (although he could be invited to meetings of the audit committee to give his views).

However, a separate risk committee is probably much more useful for a large public company than for a smaller listed company.

At executive management level, there may be another risk committee consisting of senior executives, chaired by the CEO. This committee would be responsible for risk management at an operational level. The responsibilities of this committee and the board risk committee would be very different. This is explained in the Walker Report (which recommended the establishment of board risk committees in banks):

'The role of the board risk committee is to advise the board on all high-level risk matters and should not extend into operational matters which are for the executive within the overall risk framework determined by the board. The NEDs on the committee cannot be expected to be able to replicate the industry expertise of the executive team nor will their capacity to contribute be enhanced by information overload. The materials presented to them should be in succinct format, highlighting major issues.'

5.2   Risk officers

Some large companies, such as banks and major oil companies, may also appoint specialist executive managers with responsibility for risk. The risk management team would be headed by a chief risk officer (CRO). The Walker Report recommended that the CRO should:

- report directly to the finance director or CEO but also
- have direct access to the board and should be able to provide advice to the board on all risk issues affecting the company.

'Alongside an internal reporting line to the chief executive officer or [Chief Financial Officer CFO], the CRO should report to the board risk committee, with explicit, and what is clearly understood to be, direct access to the chairman of the committee in the event of need, for example, if there is a difference of view with the chief executive officer or CFO ...'

The Report emphasises the need to protect the independence of the CRO from the influence of the CEO or finance director, and it also recommends that (like the company secretary) only the board should be able to appoint or dismiss the CRO, and the remuneration of the CRO should be decided by the company chairman or the remuneration committee.

TEST YOUR KNOWLEDGE 9.5

(a) What is the difference between a risk committee of the board and a **risk management committee**?
(b) What are the responsibilities of the audit committee for business risk and the business risk management system?

---

6 Risk management policies, systems and procedures

To enable the board of directors to carry out its responsibilities for risk management effectively, there are two essential requirements.

1 Board members should have an understanding of risks and risk management.
2 There should be a risk management system in place that the board as a whole or the appropriate board committee can review.

6.1 Risk training for board directors

A requirement of the UK Corporate Governance Code is that directors should have a personal programme for continuing professional development, and this should include where necessary suitable training in risk awareness and risk management systems. This should ensure that they are capable of contributing proactively to board discussions on risk strategy. Training in risk management should be particularly important for members of the board committee (audit committee or risk committee) with responsibility for reviewing the risk management system.

CASE EXAMPLE 9.4

The collapse of Enron has been referred to previously in this text (see, for example, Chapter 1). One of the weaknesses in governance that became apparent after the collapse was the lack of understanding of the risks in the business by the members of the Enron board. Before its collapse, Enron had a good reputation for financial risk management. Because of volatility in prices and supply in the energy industry, Enron used derivative instruments to hedge its long-term exposures to price risk. However, it hedged these risks with special purpose entities (specially created companies) that it owned itself and, as a result, Enron effectively retained the risks itself. These practices were reported to the board, but the board did nothing to stop them or question them, and actually approved resolutions that made some of these dubious 'off balance sheet' hedging transactions possible. After the collapse of the company at the end of 2001, it became apparent that the members of the Enron board, although they had been given information about risk management, did not know enough about derivatives and 'off balance sheet' accounting to understand and assess the risks.

6.2 Basic elements in an effective risk management system

There are four basic elements to a risk management system. (These are the same for both business risk management and internal control systems.)

1 Risk identification.
2 Risk evaluation.
3 Risk management measures.
4 Risk control and review.

These elements are explained here in the context of a business risk management system. They will be described again in Chapter 10 within the context of an internal control system.

Risk identification

A company should have a procedure in place for reviewing and identifying the risks it faces. Risks change over time, and risk reviews should therefore be undertaken regularly.

 CASE EXAMPLE 9.5

After the terrorist attack on the World Trade Center and other US targets on 11 September 2001, the need for a reassessment of the risk from terrorist attacks was all too obvious. The US banks Morgan Stanley and Goldman Sachs, for example, quickly developed new plans to move significant operations out of the lower Manhattan financial district. The terrorist attack had exposed flaws in their contingency plans, because too many of their operations had been located in a 'campus' area, sharing the same telecommunications and power grids. Morgan Stanley moved some operations to the suburbs north of New York City and Goldman Sachs moved its equities business across to New Jersey.

Risk evaluation

The evaluation of risks calls for procedures to assess the potential size of the risk. The expected losses that could occur from adverse events or developments depend on the:

- probability that an adverse outcome will occur
- size of the loss in the event of an adverse outcome.

Where a risk is unlikely to materialise into an adverse outcome, and the loss would in any case be small, no management action might be necessary. Where the risk is higher, measures should be taken to protect the organisation so that the remaining exposure to risk is within the company's tolerance level and consistent with its risk appetite.

Risk management measures

The measures taken to deal with each risk are decided by management, which is accountable to the board for the measures they take. In broad terms, business risks can be dealt with by avoiding them or by taking steps to limit the exposure.

- Some risks can be avoided. For example, a car manufacturer might be concerned about the risk of losses at a subsidiary specialising in car repairs, due to the strength of competition in the car repair industry. It could decide to avoid the risk by selling the subsidiary.
- Many risks have to be accepted as an inevitable feature of business. For significant risks, a company should decide what measures might be necessary to reduce the risk to acceptable proportions. Business risks may be reduced through measures such as a diversification of product range (to avoid over-reliance on a single product), joint ventures (to share new venture risks) and cost reduction measures (to reduce the risks from competition).

From a corporate governance perspective, it should be a responsibility of the board to make sure that risks are reviewed regularly and that management take suitable measures to deal with them.

Risk control and review

Control systems should be established by executive management to monitor risks. There should be a system for identifying situations that are getting out of control or where significant events have developed or are developing.

6.3 Risk register and other risk management processes

A company might use a risk register for:

- recording risks that have been identified
- the evaluation of the risks, and
- the measures that have been taken to deal with them.

The risk register is maintained by executive management, but it can be used by the risk committee of the board (or the audit committee) as a way of reviewing the effectiveness of the risk management system.

The King III Code in South Africa is much more explicit about risk management than the UK Corporate Governance Code. Provisions in the King III Code relating to risk management (both business risks and internal control risks) include the following.

- The board's risk strategy should be executed by management by means of risk management systems and processes.
- The board should ensure that effective and ongoing **risk assessments** are performed by management.
- Risks should be prioritised and ranked, in order to focus on areas where action is most needed.
- The board should regularly receive and review a register of the company's key risks.
- Key risks should be quantified where practicable (for example, in terms of maximum potential loss or expected loss).
- The board should ensure that processes are in place for anticipating unpredictable risks.
- Management should identify and note in the risk register the responses that have been decided upon and taken.
- Management should provide assurances to the board that the risk management plan is integrated into the daily activities of the business.

6.4 Stress testing

Stress testing is widely used by major companies to assess their ability to withstand extreme 'shocks' or unexpected events in the business environment. This can be done by taking the normal business planning or forecasting model used by the company, and altering a key variable, such as the rate of growth (or decline) in economic growth, a very large increase in a major resource such as the cost of oil, loss of access to a key market for purchases or sales, and so on. The purpose of stress testing is to assess whether the company could survive the shock. If there are doubts about this ability, the company should consider measures to reduce the risk, perhaps by developing contingency plans, or taking measures to improve their capital or liquidity.

TEST YOUR KNOWLEDGE 9.6

(a) What are the provisions of the UK Corporate Governance Code with regard to training directors in business risk?
(b) What are the main elements of a business risk management system?
(c) What is a risk register?
(d) What is the purpose of stress testing?

7 Senior executive remuneration: bonuses and risk adjustment

The UK Corporate Governance Code states that remuneration policies should be compatible with risk policies and systems. The purpose of this provision is to reduce the likelihood that executives will be paid large annual bonuses for achieving high levels of performance in the short term, but by taking risks that result in a decline in performance in the following years.

In an original draft of the 2010 Code, it had also been proposed that criteria for paying bonuses should be risk adjusted, but this specific requirement was omitted from the final version of the Code.

A method of adjusting bonus payments for risk is therefore to defer the incentive payments over a number of years, say three to five years. If an executive director is entitled to an annual bonus of £900,000 the incentive scheme could provide for this to be paid over a three-year period. If performance in subsequent years declines, as a consequence of the risks that the company has been exposed to, the amount of the bonus payments could then be reduced in the second and/or third years. For banks, the Walker Report recommended:

'Short-term bonus awards should be paid over a three-year period with not more than one third in the first year. Clawback should be used as the means to reclaim amounts in circumstances of misstatement and misconduct.'

TEST YOUR KNOWLEDGE 9.7

How might executive rewards be adjusted for business risk?

 CASE QUESTION

Refer to the case study at the beginning of Part Three.
1 What significant exposures to business risk are apparent in the case study?
2 Suggest what the newly appointed NED should do to alert his board colleagues to the risk management problems within the company, and try to initiate improvements.

3 In the past Hunnerware has not given as much attention to business risk as it should have done. Outline the areas that the board should consider in developing a better approach to risk management.
4 Explain the nature of scenario-based risk assessment, and suggest how this might be incorporated into the system of risk management within the company.

CHAPTER SUMMARY

- Companies can get into financial difficulty by taking too much business risk. The board of directors has a responsibility for making sure that business risks to which the company is exposed, or might be exposed in the future, are considered acceptable.
- All businesses must accept business risks in order to make a profit. As a general rule, higher risks must be taken to obtain higher returns. The board should decide how much business risk the company wants to accept in order to achieve its financial objectives
- Risk appetite is the amount of exposure to business risk the board wants to take, so that targets for financial performance can be achieved.
- Risk tolerance is the amount of risk that the board is willing to accept. Risk tolerance may be measured quantitatively, so that actual exposures to business risk can be compared with a target or tolerance limit.
- The board should review risk appetite and risk tolerance regularly.

- Business risks are risks that arise from unexpected changes or developments in the business environment that are outside the control of management. These include unexpected initiatives by competitors, unexpected changes in customer demand patterns and changes in the political, regulatory, economic, social, environmental and technological environment. Unexpected changes can be positive as well as negative.

- A measure of high risk is unpredictable variability in key factors such as sales demand or market prices. High volatility is associated with high business risk.

- Business risk should be distinguished from internal control risk. Internal control risk arises from factors within the company (or other organisation) that are within the ability of management to control. Business risks are external and cannot be controlled. However, they should be managed.

- Examples of business risk are reputation risk, competition risk, business environment risk, financial risks in the business environment (such as interest rate risk and foreign exchange rate risk) and liquidity risk.

- Stress testing may be used to assess the ability of a company to withstand unexpected extreme events or developments, so that contingency measures can be planned or risk tolerance levels adjusted.

- The UK Corporate Governance Code includes a requirement for companies to have a system of risk management, with regular reviews (at least annually) of the effectiveness of this system.

- There may be a separate risk committee of the board, with special responsibility for monitoring the risk management system.

- In addition, companies may establish a risk management committee of senior executives, chaired perhaps by the chief executive officer and also including specialist risk officers (or the head of internal audit).

- Directors must understand business risk and risk management systems. It may be necessary to give them suitable training.

- The basic elements of a risk management system are procedures for identifying risks, evaluation the risks that have been identified and assessing their significance, taking measures to manage the risk that are consistent with board policy on risk appetite and risk tolerance, control of the system and regular reviews of the effectiveness of the system.

- The UK Corporate Governance Code states that remuneration policies should be compatible with risk policies and systems, and criteria for paying bonuses should be risk adjusted. One way of doing this is to defer the payment of annual bonuses or spread the payment over several years. Payments can then be reduced or cancelled if it is subsequently found that short-term performance measures were misleading, or that performance levels on which the bonuses were calculated are unsustainable beyond the short term.

10 Internal control systems

■ INTRODUCTION

A company may fail to achieve its objectives because of failures or weaknesses within its systems and operating procedures, or due to human error. These failures and weaknesses could be avoided, or the consequences of failures could be restricted, by means of controls. Internal control risks are the risks of failures in systems and procedures to achieve their intended purpose. Internal controls are measures or arrangements that are intended to prevent failures from happening, limiting their potential effect, or identifying when a failure has occurred so that corrective measures can be taken. This chapter explains the nature of internal control risks and the internal control system, and the responsibilities for internal control within an organisation. Internal control is an aspect of corporate governance, because the board of directors has a responsibility to ensure that the assets of the company are not threatened, and the interests of the shareholders (and other stakeholders) are not damaged, by making sure that an effective system of internal control is in place.

1 Elements of an internal control system

Business risks are risks that arise in the business environment and markets in which a company operates. Internal control risks are risks that arise within an organisation because of weaknesses in its systems, procedures, management or personnel. Unless there are controls to deal with them, internal control risks can lead to losses because of operational failures, errors or fraud. The controls for these risks are 'internal controls' and internal controls are applied within an internal control system.

It is the responsibility of the board of directors of a company to ensure that the internal control system (and the internal controls within this system) is effective in preventing losses from internal control risks, or identifying losses and taking corrective action when they occur.

CASE EXAMPLE 10.1

A small company operated from four separate locations in the same city. At one of these locations, a considerable amount of revenue was received in cash, which was kept in a safe in the manager's office. One day, two uniformed individuals came to the building and said that they had instructions to take the safe to the company's head office, which was in a different building. They were allowed to take the safe and the security guard actually helped them to put it into their vehicle, parked outside the front door of the building. The two individuals drove off with the safe, containing over £100,000, and were not seen again.

It should be apparent that the company lost £100,000 because of basic mistakes, which point to weaknesses in internal controls.

- Why was there was a lot of money in the safe? Why had most of it not been taken to the bank?
- Why were the two individuals allowed to take the safe without checking their authorisation to take it?
- How did they gain access to the building so easily?

There were weaknesses in the procedures for banking cash, building security and authorisation of actions. If suitable internal controls had been in place, the loss of the money should not have occurred.

1.1 Categories of internal control risks

Internal control risks can be categorised into three broad types.

1 Financial risks. These are risks of errors or fraud in accounting systems and accounting and finance activities. Errors or fraud could lead to losses for the organisation, or to incorrect financial statements. Weak controls may also mean that financial assets are not properly protected. Examples of financial risks include the risk of failure to record transactions in the book-keeping system, failure to collect money owed by customers, failure to protect cash and mis-reporting (deliberate or unintentional) in the financial statements.
2 Operational risks. A helpful definition of 'operational risk' is given by the Basel Committee for banking supervision. Although this definition applies to risks in the banking industry, it has a wider application. Operational risk is 'the risk of losses resulting from inadequate or failed internal processes, people and systems, or external events'. Operational risks include the risks of a breakdown in a system due to machine failures or software errors, the risk of losing information from computer files or having confidential information stolen, the risk of a terrorist attack, and losses arising from mistakes or omissions by staff.
3 Compliance risks. These are risk that important laws or regulations will not be complied with properly. Failure to comply with the law could result in legal action against the company and/or fines.

1.2 The purpose of an internal control system and internal controls

An internal control system is the system that an organisation has for identifying internal control risks, applying controls to reduce the risk of losses from these risks and taking corrective action when losses occur.

- There should be controls to ensure that the organisation, its systems and procedures operate in the way that is intended, without disruption or disturbance.
- There should be controls to ensure that assets are safeguarded. For example, there should be controls to ensure that money received is banked and is not stolen, and that operating assets such as items of equipment and computers are not damaged or lost.
- Controls should include measures to reduce the risk of fraud.
- Financial controls should ensure the completeness and accuracy of accounting records, and the timely preparation of financial information.
- Controls should be in place to ensure compliance with key regulations, such as health and safety regulations or, in the case of banks, anti-money laundering regulations.

1.3 Internal control: financial, operational and compliance controls

In the UK, a committee was set up in 1998 to provide guidance on the board's responsibilities for internal control and risk management. This committee produced the Turnbull Report, since revised and re-named the Turnbull Guidance. The Turnbull Report defined an internal control system as 'the policies, processes, tasks, behaviours and other aspects of a company' that, taken together:

- help it to operate effectively and efficiently; these operational controls should allow the company to respond in an appropriate way to significant risks to achieving the company's objectives (this includes the safeguarding of assets from inappropriate use or from loss and fraud and ensuring that liabilities are identified and managed'
- help it to ensure the quality of external and internal financial reporting financial controls
- help to ensure compliance with applicable laws and regulations, and also with internal policies for the conduct of business (compliance controls).

In other words, there should be financial, operational and compliance controls for dealing with financial, operational and compliance risks – preventing losses or adverse events from happening, or detecting and correcting the problem when losses or adverse events do occur.

Financial controls

Financial controls are internal accounting controls that are sufficient to provide reasonable assurance that:

- transactions are made only in accordance with the general or specific authorisation of management
- transactions are recorded so that financial statements can be prepared in accordance with accounting standards and generally accepted accounting principles
- transactions are recorded so that assets can be accounted for
- access to assets is only allowed in accordance with the general or specific authorisation of management
- the accounting records for assets are compared with actual assets at reasonable intervals of time
- appropriate action is taken whenever there are found to be differences.

The maintenance of proper accounting records is an important element of internal control. Effective financial controls should ensure:

- the quality of external and internal financial reporting, so that there are no material errors in the accounting records and financial statements
- that no fraud is committed (or that fraud is detected when it occurs)
- that the financial assets of the company are not stolen, lost or needlessly damaged, or that these risks are reduced.

A useful method of categorising internal financial controls was used in an old guideline issued by the UK Auditing Practices Board, using the mnemonic SPAMSOAP. In this guideline (no longer in issue) internal financial controls are categorised as follows.

- **S**: Segregation of duties. Where possible, duties should be split between two or more people, so that the work done by one person acts as a check on the work done by another. With segregation of duties, it is more difficult for fraud to take place, because several individuals would have to collude in the fraud. It is also more difficult for accidental errors to occur, because when several people are involved in a task, they act as a check on each other.
- **P**: Physical controls. Physical controls are measures to ensure the physical safety of assets, such as putting cash in a safe, banking cash receipts immediately, and preventing unauthorised access to computer systems through the use of passwords and internet firewalls.
- **A**: Authorisation and approval. All financial transactions should require the authorisation or approval of an appropriate responsible person, and there should be an authorisation limit to how much spending each responsible person can approve.
- **M**: Management controls. Management should exercise control over financial systems, for example by preparing a budget and then monitoring actual performance by comparing it with the budget. Management controls can also be exercised by reviewing other financial statements, such as a balance sheet, profit and loss account and cash flow statement.
- **S**: Supervision. The day-to-day work of employees should be properly supervised. Good supervision will reduce the likelihood of errors or fraud.

O: Organisation. Everyone should be fully aware of his responsibilities, and lines of authority, lines of reporting and levels of responsibility should be clear. Errors and fraud are much more likely where it is uncertain who is responsible for what and who should be reporting to whom.

A: Arithmetical and accounting controls. These are procedures in an accounts office to check the accuracy of the records and the numbers. They include the use of control totals and reconciliations.

P: Personnel. The quality of internal controls is dependent on the quality of the individuals working in the organisation, and personnel selected to do a job should have the right personal qualities and be properly trained and/or qualified.

(Note: This list of different types of control is provided as a guide to the nature of financial controls. Corporate governance is concerned with the adequacy of internal controls and the effectiveness of the internal control system; designing and implementing controls is a responsibility of management.)

Operational controls

Operational controls are controls that help to reduce operational risks, or identify failures in operational systems when these occur. They are designed to prevent failures in operational procedures, or to detect and correct operational failures if they do occur. Operational failures may be caused by:

- machine breakdowns
- human error
- failures in the performance of systems (possibly due to human error)
- weaknesses in procedures
- poor management.

Operational controls are measures designed to prevent these failures from happening, or identifying and correcting problems that do occur. Regular equipment maintenance, better training of staff, automation of standard procedures, and reporting systems that make managers accountable for their actions are all examples of operational controls.

Compliance controls

Compliance controls are concerned with making sure that an entity complies with all the requirements of relevant legislation and regulations.

The potential consequences of failure to comply with laws and regulations vary according to the nature of the industry and the regulations. For a manufacturer of food products, for example, food hygiene regulations are important. For a bank, regulations to protect consumers against mis-selling and regulations for detecting and reporting suspicions of money laundering are important.

It can be difficult to understand the nature of internal control risks and internal controls to deal with them. There are many different risks and many controls that are applied. The following are simple examples.

 CASE EXAMPLE 10.2

The owners of a farm located near a major international airport turn some of their land into a car park in the holiday months, and customers can park their cars at the farm and take a taxi service from there to the airport. Customers pay in cash, and the owners of the farm use part-time employees to operate the car park, which remains open for 18 hours each day, and seven days a week. One financial risk is that if fees for parking are charged by the day, customers may pay for the wrong number of days. Another risk is that customers may pay in cash, and employees may keep the cash for themselves, and not report the income to the owners of the farm. Without going into the detail of suitable controls, it may be apparent that to reduce the risk of losses from these risks, there should be a ticketing system based on sequentially numbered tickets for the car park, with the date of the arrival in the car park recorded on each ticket. Other controls would also be necessary to protect the cash from theft. These would be internal financial controls.

CASE EXAMPLE 10.3

A manufacturing company may use large items of machinery that have moving parts, and there is a risk that employees getting too close to the machinery may be injured by a moving part. This is an operational risk. An operational control for this risk would be to surround the machinery with guards or safety rails, with warning signs not to enter inside them.

CASE EXAMPLE 10.4

Another example of operational risk is the risk of a failure in health and safety systems and system controls. A well-publicised example was the series of apparent safety failures (and failures in safety controls) that led to an explosion at the Texas oil refinery of oil company BP in 2005, where 15 people were killed and about 500 injured. In addition to the direct losses suffered by BP, the incident also led to over 1,000 civil legal actions against the company and a federal grand jury investigation into whether criminal charges should be brought against the company.

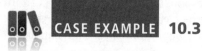

1.4 Elements of an internal control system

Internal controls are an essential part of an internal control system, but an internal control system should also have other elements in order to be effective and achieve its objectives. An internal control system consists of:

- a 'control environment', and
- control procedures.

A useful definition of internal control was given by the US Committee of Sponsoring Organizations of the Treadway Commission (COSO). The COSO Framework defines internal control as 'a process, effected by an entity's board of directors, management and other personnel, designed to provide reasonable assurance regarding the achievement of objectives' in the areas of:

- effectiveness and efficiency of operations (through operational controls)
- the reliability of financial reporting (through financial controls)
- compliance with relevant laws and regulations (through compliance controls).

The COSO Framework identifies five elements to a system of internal control. (These five elements were also recognised in the Turnbull Report.)

1   A control environment. A control environment describes the awareness of (and attitude to) internal controls in the organisation, shown by the directors, management and employees generally. It therefore encompasses corporate culture, management style and employee attitudes to control procedures.
2   Risk identification and assessment. There should be a system or procedures for identifying the risks facing the company (and how these are changing) and assessing their significance. Controls or management initiatives should be devised to deal with significant risks.
3   Internal controls. Controls should be devised and implemented to eliminate, reduce or control risks.
4   Information and communication. All employees who are responsible for the management of risks should receive information that enables them to fulfil this task.
5   Monitoring. The effectiveness of risk controls and the internal control system generally should be monitored regularly. Internal audit is one method of monitoring the internal control system. Internal controls are also monitored by executive management and (as part of their annual audit) by the external auditors. The board of directors also has a responsibility to review the effectiveness of the system.

The nature and extent of the internal controls an organisation has in place will depend to a large extent on its size, what controls it can afford and whether the benefits obtained from any particular control measure are sufficient to justify its cost. The internal control system should, however, be sufficiently robust and effective to minimise the risk of serious losses through error or fraud.

- In a large company, we should expect thousands of different financial operational and compliance controls, each designed to prevent particular financial, operational or compliance failures, or to detect them if they occur.
- An important aspect of corporate governance is to ensure that the system of internal control (and the internal controls within that system) is adequate and effective in preventing or detecting failures in the system. For example, if the system is ineffective, a company may be exposed to a high risk of fraud and also to a high risk that its annual financial statements will not be accurate or reliable.

 CASE EXAMPLE 10.5

In 1995 Barings Bank collapsed as a result of losses incurred in trading in Asia by a 'rogue trader', Nick Leeson. Leeson was sent to the Singapore office of the bank in 1992 as a general manager. He then took an examination that qualified him to trade on the Singapore exchange SIMEX. He acquired a position of considerable authority in the Singapore office, where he became its head trader and the effective head of the 'back office operations' (including settlement of trading transactions), as well as general manager.

There should have been controls within the bank to prevent speculative trades by the bank's traders that would expose the bank to excessive risks. For example, there should have been effective limits on the exposures to risk that Leeson was allowed to take. Because of his powerful position in the office, Leeson was able to ignore and override the controls. He took unauthorised speculative positions by trading on the SIMEX exchange and Japan's Osaka exchange. He had hoped to make large profits on his deals, but he made losses, but by hiding the losses in an unused error account, number 88888, he was able to present figures that made it seem that he was making large profits. The losses hidden in this account rose from £2 million at the end of 1992 to £23 million at the end of 1993 and £208 million at the end of 2004. Leeson was able to fund the losses by borrowing money from other parts of the bank and from client accounts (by falsifying documentation and account records). Senior managers of the bank in London were not aware of what was happening.

Although the losses on his trades were building up, Leeson was able to report profits, partly by cross-trading with account 88888, so that the profits were actually achieved by adding to the losses in account 88888. Leeson and his staff in the Singapore office were paid bonuses on the basis of these reported profits.

The situation could not remain hidden forever, and in February 1995 Leeson fled Singapore, leaving behind losses of £827 million. The bank could not afford losses of this size, and it collapsed soon after.

The collapse of Barings can be explained by severe weaknesses in the internal control system.

- The control environment was poor and the control culture was not strong enough.
- Bonuses were paid for reported profits on trading, regardless of the risks in the trades.
- Internal controls were inadequate. Leeson was general manager, trader and in charge of the settlement of trading transactions in the Singapore office, and there was no segregation of duties whereby one person could act as a check on the activities of someone else. Leeson was inadequately supervised and reporting to management was inaccurate (falsified). Systems of authorisation and approval were inadequate; Leeson was able to borrow large amounts of

money from other offices of the bank, which he could use to pay for his losses, and no one had oversight to stop him from doing this.

■ Monitoring of the internal control system was also inadequate, and the weaknesses in the system were not identified until it was too late.

It might have been thought that the collapse of Barings Bank would provide a lesson about internal control to all other banks, but an even larger scandal rocked the French Bank Société Générale (SocGen) in 2008. The bank's independent directors identified 'weaknesses' in the bank's controls that led to the biggest fraud in banking history. The losses of nearly €5 billion were triggered by junior trader Jérome Kerviel. The independent directors identified 75 'warning signals' on Kerviel's trading that the bank failed to follow up. Kerviel's supervisor accepted explanations that he gave without verifying them, and in spite of warnings about Kerviel from derivatives exchange Eurex. There were also no controls on cancelled or modified trades, which Kerviel used extensively. Within the bank, there may have been a culture of deference by risk managers to successful traders. Subsequent investigations by internal and external auditors for the bank found that traders and their superiors at SocGen frequently flouted the rules, giving Kerviel an opportunity to take €50 billion in unauthorised trades. There was a low appreciation of the risk of fraud, a strong entrepreneurial culture and the emergence of unauthorised practices with trading limits regularly exceeded.

 CASE EXAMPLE   10.6

In April 2010 the UK Financial Services Authority fined the former deputy chief executive officer of Northern Rock bank (Mr DB) over £500,000 and banned him from the industry. It also fined the former managing credit director of Northern Rock (Mr RB) and banned him from holding a senior position. The action against DB arose from a conference call in January 2007, in which he told investors that arrears and repossession levels for Northern Rock mortgages were exceptionally low compared with those of other mortgage lenders, even though he knew that 1,917 loans had been excluded from this total. These loans had been classified into a separate category (loans for which a possession order had been obtained but not yet enforced) that was excluded from the reported total of arrears and repossessions. If they had been included, Northern Rock's reported proportion of overdue loans would have been 50 per cent higher.

DB did not report the correct figures to his CEO in the bank. There was no evidence that he had gained personally from his action. He claimed that his action had been taken in an effort to protect RB, whose wife was seriously ill, and whom he had given another six months to sort out the problem of overdue loans.

The FSA action against Mr RB arose from his failure to take action when he learned of the problems in the process of reporting overdue loans and repossessions by the bank.

The FSA commented that the misreporting of the figures reflected 'pressure' on staff in the bank to keep the reported number of loan arrears below those of competitors in the mortgage market, and also failure to put in place suitable internal controls to prevent this misreporting from happening.

The action by DB explained the surprising apparent success of Northern Rock in the mortgage market at the time. Northern Rock had pursued an aggressive strategy of winning market share by offering large mortgage loans in relation to borrowers' income. Analysts had not been able to understand how Northern Rock could have pursued such an aggressive strategy without suffering from higher mortgage arrears. The answer was that the bank had deceived or misled the market.

This case illustrates how issues in corporate governance and business ethics are inter-connected. DB said that the action he took was to protect a colleague who was going through anxieties in his personal life, but to do this DB had lied to investors. The need to lie resulted from the pressure on staff within the bank and the culture that this pursuit of growth and market share created. Even so, with suitable internal controls, the deception with the reporting of the figures should not have been allowed to happen.

CASE EXAMPLE 10.7

In 2010 the US National Highway Traffic Safety Administration imposed a fine of $16.4 million on car-maker Toyota, the heaviest fine permitted by the law, for failing to notify the US authorities promptly about defective accelerator pedals in about two million of its cars. The company had delayed the recall of 2.3 million cars by almost four months after becoming aware of the problem with the accelerator pedals. Toyota agreed to pay the fine to avoid a protracted dispute, but denied that it had breached the US Safety Act or vehicle safety regulations.

Whatever the reasons, Toyota had not reported the problem to the authorities promptly. The issue raises questions about whether compliance controls within the company were sufficiently robust. Could the problem have been that the company did not have internal controls in place to recognise the need to report to the authorities? Or did internal controls succeed in recognising the problem, but management then decided to ignore it? No doubt Toyota's management looked at the problem in hindsight and took measures to prevent anything similar from happening again. On the same day that the fine was imposed, Toyota announced that it was recalling the 2010 version of another of its models from North America and Europe, to deal with a different safety problem.

 TEST YOUR KNOWLEDGE 10.1

(a) What are the main elements of a system of internal control?
  Give six examples of financial risk within a company.
(b) What might be the main operational risk or compliance risk concerns for a company that operates a chain of family holiday centres and sports centres?
(c) For what reason are procedures for the authorisation of expenditures and approval of payments for expenditures an internal control?
(d) For what reason are procedures for the selection of appropriate applicants to fill job vacancies a part of an internal control system?
(e) Identify two or more examples of significant internal control failings in major companies in the past.

2 The UK corporate governance framework for internal control

In the UK, the connection between good corporate governance and risk management has been recognised for some years, with the inclusion of provisions in the original Combined Code on corporate governance in 1998.

2.1 UK Corporate Governance Code requirements: internal control and risk management systems, and internal audit

A principle of the UK Code is that: 'The board should maintain sound risk management and internal control systems.' The board has overall responsibility for the system of internal control, but the responsibility for designing and implementing the system, and for operating it, is delegated to management. (Responsibility for risk management was explained in Chapter 9.) The UK Code also includes the following principle and provision.

■ Main principle. The board is responsible for determining the nature and extent of the significant risks it is willing to take in achieving its strategic objectives.
■ Provision. The board is required to conduct a review of the effectiveness of the company's system of internal controls at least annually, and should report to the shareholders that they

have done so. 'The review should cover all material controls, including financial, operational and compliance controls.' In other words, the board's responsibility for reviewing internal controls (and risk management) extends beyond financial matters to the business operations and regulatory compliance.

Role of the audit committee

Another principle of the UK Code is that the board should establish 'formal and transparent arrangements' for considering how it should apply the corporate governance principles relating to corporate reporting, risk management and internal control and for maintaining a relationship with the external auditors.

■ An audit committee should have responsibility for corporate governance matters relating to corporate reporting and the company's relationship with its external auditors (as explained in Chapter 7).

■ The board may delegate responsibility for the governance aspects of risk management and internal control to either the audit committee or a risk committee of the board. The board may set up a risk committee to deal with risk management matters and give the responsibilities for review of the internal control system to the audit committee. However, delegated responsibilities to board committees may differ between companies.

The UK Code states that the responsibilities of the audit committee should include:

■ review of the company's internal financial controls
■ review of the rest of the internal control system (and risk management system), unless this responsibility is given to a separate risk committee of the board
■ monitoring and review of the effectiveness of the company's internal audit function
■ review of the company's whistleblowing system.

Internal audit and whistleblowing arrangements are described later in this chapter.

TEST YOUR KNOWLEDGE **10.2**

(a) What are the provisions of the UK Corporate Governance Code relating to internal control?
(b) What are the provisions of the UK Corporate Governance Code relating to internal audit?
(c) What are the responsibilities of an audit committee with respect to internal control and internal audit, as stated in the UK Code?

---

3   The Turnbull Guidance on internal control

When principles and provisions relating to internal control and risk management were first introduced into the UK governance code in 1998, a working party, known as the Turnbull Committee, published guidelines to listed companies on how to apply them. These are now known as the Turnbull Guidance, and are the responsibility of the Financial Reporting Council (FRC). The Guidance applies to the entire system of internal control, including operational and compliance controls as well as financial controls. The introduction to the Guidance makes the following points.

■ Internal control should be embedded in the business and its operating systems. Controls should not be applied occasionally and from an external source. They should be applied regularly and automatically, as part of established procedures.
■ Controls should remain relevant over time. This means that as circumstances change, controls should be altered or adapted to meet the new requirements.
■ The controls that are appropriate to a company should take account of its particular circumstances.

3.1 Maintaining a sound system of internal control

The board of directors is responsible for maintaining a sound system of internal control. The Turnbull Guidance states that the board of directors should:

- set appropriate policies on internal control
- seek regular assurance to satisfy itself that the system is operating effectively
- ensure that the system of internal control is effective in managing risks in the way that it has approved.

In deciding its policies for internal control and assessing what constitutes an effective system of internal control, the board should consider:

- the nature and extent of the risks facing the company
- the amount of risk and types of risk that it regards as acceptable for the company to bear
- the likelihood that the risks will materialise
- the company's ability to reduce the impact on the business of the risks that do materialise
- the costs of operating particular controls relative to the benefits to be obtained from managing the risks they control. Controls are not worth having if they cost more than the expected benefits or savings they will provide.

Having identified the responsibilities of the board for maintaining a sound system of internal control, the Turnbull Guidance adds the following.

- It is the job of management to implement the board's policies on control. To do this management must have procedures for identifying and evaluating the risks faced by the company, and designing, implementing and monitoring a control system to deal with these risks in a way that is consistent with the board's policies.
- In addition all employees have some responsibility for internal control, for example to avoid making mistakes in their work and also to ensure that the control procedures for which they are responsible are properly performed.

3.2 Elements of a sound system of internal control

A sound system of internal control should:

- 'be embedded in the operations of the company and form part of its culture'
- be capable of responding quickly to risks to the business as they emerge and develop
- include procedures for reporting immediately to the management responsible and control failings that have been identified and any corrective action that has been undertaken.

The Turnbull Guidance emphasises that a sound system of internal control cannot provide certain protection against a company suffering losses or breaches of laws or regulations or failing to meet its business objectives. The possibility will always exist of 'poor judgement in decision-making, human error, control processes being deliberately circumvented by employees and others, management overriding controls and the occurrence of unforeseen circumstances'. A sound system of internal control provides reasonable assurance that risks will be suitably controlled, but cannot provide absolute assurance that there will not be any material losses, fraud, errors or breaches of laws and regulations.

3.3 Reviewing the effectiveness of internal control

The UK Corporate Governance Code states that the board of directors (or the audit committee) should carry out, at least annually, a review of the effectiveness of the system of internal control (and risk management). In order to review the effectiveness of the system of internal control, there must be procedures for monitoring and review. The Turnbull Guidance provides some suggestions. It suggests that 'reviewing the effectiveness of internal control is an essential part of the board's responsibilities'. The board or audit committee needs to form its own view about the effectiveness of the system, based on the information and assurances it receives. The sources of information about internal control are:

- management
- the internal auditors, if the company has an internal audit function, and
- the external auditors, who notify management and the audit committee about weaknesses in internal controls that they have discovered in their audit.

The board of directors and the audit committee do not have the time to carry out a detailed review themselves, and they must therefore rely on information provided to them by management and internal auditors. The most regular source of information for the board or audit committee about internal control should be management reports. Additional reporting may be provided, however, by the internal auditors, or by a firm of external accountants or auditors hired to perform a specific internal audit investigation.

In its Guidance on Audit Committees (2008), the FRC states that except where the responsibility is retained by the entire board, or delegated to a risk committee:

'The audit committee should receive reports from management on the effectiveness of the systems they have established and the conclusions of any testing carried out by internal and external auditors.'

Management reports to the audit committee

Management is accountable to the board (or the audit committee) for monitoring the system of internal control and for providing assurances that it has done so. To be effective, monitoring should be on a regular basis, and management should also provide regular reports to the audit committee (or the board). These regular reports should each deal with a specific aspect of operations and:

- provide an assessment of the significance of the risks and the effectiveness of the system of internal control for dealing with them
- report any significant control weaknesses or failings that have been identified, the impact these have had (or may have) on the company and the action that has been taken to deal with the problem.

The board or audit committee may also receive independent reports from the internal auditors. In addition to receiving regular reports from management on internal control, the board (or audit committee) should carry out an annual review of the effectiveness of the internal control system. The annual review should consider the following in particular.

- The changes that have occurred since the previous annual review: in what ways have the significant risks for the company changes, and how successful has the company been in responding to those changes.
- The scope and quality of monitoring of the control system by management.
- The scope and quality of the investigations by the internal audit function, the weaknesses in the system identified by the internal auditors and the measures taken to implement recommendations of the internal auditors.

3.4 The board's statement on internal control

The UK Corporate Governance Code states that the board should report to shareholders each year that it has conducted the annual review of the effectiveness of the systems of internal control and risk management. The Financial Services Authority's Disclosure and Transparency Rules for listed companies also requires companies to report on the main features of their internal control and risk management systems in relation to financial reporting. This information is provided within the annual report as a section on internal control.

Although the review of the effectiveness of internal control may be delegated to the audit committee, the board as a whole is responsible for the statement on internal control in the company's annual report and accounts.

The Turnbull Guidance states: 'The annual report and accounts should include such meaningful, high-level information as the board considers necessary to assist shareholders' understanding of the main features of the company's risk management processes and system of internal control, and should not give a misleading impression.'

- In its statement the board should, as a minimum, disclose that there is a system for identifying, evaluating and managing significant risks.
- The report should acknowledge the board's responsibility for the system of internal control and reviewing its effectiveness. The report should explain that the system is designed to manage risks rather than eliminate them entirely and can only provide reasonable assurance, not absolute assurance against material losses or misstatements in the accounts.

- The report should summarise the process that the board has applied for reviewing the effectiveness of the system of internal control, and confirm that action has been taken to deal with any significant weaknesses or failings identified from the review.
- If a significant problem is disclosed in the company's annual report and accounts, the **internal control report** should disclose the process that has been applied to deal with material internal control aspects of the problem.

3.5 Carrying out an annual evaluation: questions to ask

The Turnbull Guidance includes in an Appendix a list of questions that the board should consider when conducting its annual review of the effectiveness of internal control system. There should be satisfactory answers to each question. The list of questions is not reproduced in full here, but several questions are shown to demonstrate the approach to evaluation that the directors should take.

On risk assessment

- Does the company have clear objectives? Have these been communicated in a way that provides effective direction to employees on risk management and internal control issues?
- Are significant risks assessed regularly? Significant risks are likely to include all the risks identified in the annual business review.
- Do management and others have a clear understanding of what risks are acceptable to the board?

On the control environment and control activities

- Do employees understand what is expected of them, and what is the scope of their freedom to act? The Guidance indicates the scope of this question by stating that it applies to areas such as customer relations, service levels, health safety and environment protection, security of assets, business continuity issues expenditure matters, financial reporting and other reporting.
- Are authority, responsibility and accountability clearly defined, so that decisions are made and actions taken by the appropriate people?
- How are processes and controls adjusted to adapt to new risks or operational deficiencies?

On information and communication

- Do management and the board receive regular and relevant reports on actual performance compared with business objectives and the related risks, suitable for decision-making and management review purposes?
- Are periodic reporting procedures effective in communicating a proper account of the company's performance and prospects?

On monitoring

- Are processes embedded within the company's operations for monitoring the effective application of internal control and risk management?
- Is there appropriate communication to the board (or board committees) on the monitoring of risk and control matters?
- Are there specific arrangements for management monitoring and reporting to the board on risk and control matters of particular importance, including fraud and other illegal acts that could adversely affect the company's reputation or financial position?

3.6 Disclosure of internal control weaknesses

The UK Corporate Governance Code and Turnbull Guidance do not call for disclosures of specific failures in internal controls or the measures that have been taken to deal with them. In this respect, UK governance practice is more limited that reporting requirements in the USA. However, a board of directors should consider its obligations under the Disclosure and Transparency Rules to report significant internal control weaknesses, when they occur, if the company's financial performance or position will be badly affected as a result.

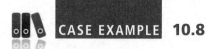

CASE EXAMPLE 10.8

In February 2007, following an internal investigation, accounting irregularities were discovered at a subsidiary company of Alfred McAlpine, a UK support services group. Over a period of about three years, the management of the subsidiary had been deliberately supplying false reports of production volumes and sales. The board was informed, and immediately made an immediate announcement to the stock market information services, reporting the discovery of the accounting irregularities and 'the possibility of fraud'. The statement to the stock market suggested that as a result of the problem, the net assets of the group had been over-stated by about £11 million in the financial statements for the previous financial year and the company would be reducing substantially its profit forecast for the current year. It was also announced that the managers suspected of falsifying the reports had been suspended, and that independent forensic accountants would be appointed to investigate the problem in detail. This would delay publication of the annual report and accounts for 2006.

Following the announcement, the company's share price immediately fell by over 20 per cent. However, the prompt reporting of the problem by the board of directors was a necessary part of good governance – even though the failure to detect the accounting irregularities for three years was a clear indication of skilful fraud or, perhaps more likely, severe weaknesses in internal control.

TEST YOUR KNOWLEDGE 10.3

(a) What are the main recommendations in the Turnbull Guidelines?
(b) How might an audit committee review the effectiveness of the company's system of internal control?

4   Internal audit

The UK Corporate Governance Code states that the audit committee should monitor and review the effectiveness of the activities of the company's internal audit function. If the company does not have an internal audit function:

■ the committee should consider annually whether there is a need for an internal audit function, and make a recommendation to the board, and
■ the reasons why there is no internal audit function should be explained in the 'relevant section' of the annual report.

4.1 Function and scope of internal audit

Internal audit is defined as 'an independent appraisal activity established within an organisation as a service to it. It is a control which functions by examining and evaluating the adequacy and effectiveness of other controls' (CIMA Official Terminology).

'The objective of internal auditing is to assist members of the organisation in the effective discharge of their responsibilities. To this end internal auditing furnishes them with analyses, appraisals, recommendations, counsel and information concerning the activities reviewed' (Institute of Internal Auditors).

An organisation might have an internal audit unit or section, which carries out investigative work.

■ An internal audit function should act independently of executive managers, but normally reports to a senior executive manager such as the finance director.
■ Additionally, internal auditors may report to the board itself or the audit committee. The FRC Guidance on Audit Committees suggests that the audit committee should ensure that

the internal auditor has direct access to the board chairman and the audit committee, and is also responsible to the audit committee.

■ This means that the internal auditors may be in an unusual position within the company. For operational reasons they may have a line reporting responsibility to a senior executive manager such as the finance director. Executive managers may also ask the internal auditors to carry out audits or reviews of the systems or procedures (and internal controls) for which they are responsible. However, the senior internal auditor should have some control over deciding what aspects of the company's systems should be investigated or audited, and also has a responsibility for reporting to the audit committee and the chairman of the board.

The work done by any internal audit unit is not prescribed by regulation, but is decided by management or by the board (or audit committee). The possible tasks of internal audit include the following.

■ Reviewing the internal control system. Traditionally, an internal audit department has carried out independent checks on the financial controls in an organisation, or in a particular process or system. The checks would be to establish whether suitable financial controls exist and if so, whether they are applied properly and are effective. It is not the function of internal auditors to manage risks, only to monitor and report them, and to check that risk controls are efficient and cost-effective.

■ Special investigations. Internal auditors might conduct special investigations into particular aspects of the organisation's operations (systems and procedures), to check the effectiveness of operational controls.

■ Examination of financial and operating information. Internal auditors might be asked to investigate the timeliness of reporting and the accuracy of the information in reports.

■ Value for money (VFM) audits. This is an investigation into an operation or activity to establish whether it is economical, efficient and effective.

■ Reviewing compliance by the organisation with particular laws or regulations. This is an investigation into the effectiveness of compliance controls.

■ Risk assessment. Internal auditors might be asked to investigate aspects of risk management, and in particular the adequacy of the mechanisms for identifying, assessing and controlling significant risks to the organisation, from both internal and external sources.

4.2 Investigation of internal financial controls

Internal auditors are commonly required to check the soundness of internal financial controls. In assessing the effectiveness of individual controls, and of an internal control system generally, the following factors should be considered.

■ Whether the controls are manual or automated. Automated controls are by no means error-proof or fraud-proof, but may be more reliable than similar manual controls.

■ Whether controls are discretionary or non-discretionary. Non-discretionary controls are checks and procedures that must be carried out. Discretionary controls are those that do not have to be applied, either because they are voluntary or because an individual can choose to disapply them. Risks can infiltrate a system, for example, when senior management chooses to disapply controls and allow unauthorised or unchecked procedures to occur.

■ Whether the control can be circumvented easily, because an activity can be carried out in a different way where similar controls do not apply.

■ Whether the controls are effective in achieving their purpose. Are they extensive enough or carried out frequently enough? Are the controls applied rigorously? For example, is a supervisor doing his job properly?

Reports by internal auditors can provide reassurance that internal controls are sound and effective, or might recommend changes and improvements where weaknesses are uncovered.

4.3 The objectivity and independence of internal auditors

The manager of an operation or department should monitor the internal controls within the operation and try to identify and correct weaknesses. He should also report on reviews of the effectiveness of internal control. However, a line manager cannot be properly objective, because he could face 'blame' for control failures in the system or operation for which he is responsible.

In contrast, internal auditors ought to be objective, because they investigate the control systems of other departments and operations. However, they are also employees within the organisation and report to someone on the organisation structure. If the internal auditors report to the finance director, they will find it difficult to be critical of the finance director himself. Similarly, if the internal auditors report to the CEO, they will be reluctant to criticise him. In this respect, their independence could be compromised.

In its Guidance for Audit Committee, the Institute of Chartered Accountants in England and Wales comments that the internal auditors should be separate and independent from line management, but that 'independence' for internal auditors does not have the same meaning as independence for external auditors.

To protect the independence of the internal audit function, the FRC's Guidance on Audit Committees suggests that the audit committee should have the responsibility for the appointment of the head of internal audit, and his removal from office.

4.4 Review of the effectiveness of the internal audit function

The board or audit committee should review the effectiveness of the internal audit function each year. As part of this review, the FRC Guidance on Audit committees suggests that the committee should:

- make sure that the head of internal audit has direct access to the chairman of the board and the audit committee, and is accountable to the audit committee
- review and assess the annual internal audit work plan
- receive reports on the results of work done by the internal auditors
- review and monitor the responses of management to the recommendations made to them by the internal auditors
- meet with the head of internal audit at least once a year without executive management being present.

 TEST YOUR KNOWLEDGE 10.4

(a) What is the purpose of an internal audit function?
(b) What tasks might be carried out by an internal audit department?
(c) What should UK listed companies include in their annual report on internal control?
(d) How can the independence of the head of internal audit be protected?

5 The need for an internal audit function

The UK Corporate Governance Code requires the audit committee to monitor and review the effectiveness of the internal audit function. Where there is no internal audit function, the audit committee should consider annually whether there is a need for one, and make a recommendation to the board.

The FRC's Guidance on Audit Committees suggested that the need for an internal audit function depends on the nature of the company and its activities, and on factors such as company size, diversity and complexity of activities, number of employees, as well as cost-benefit considerations. Some aspects of risk and internal control might be monitored by specialist units (e.g. on health and safety, legal matters and the environment). The Guidance comments:

'In the absence of an internal audit function, management needs to apply other monitoring processes in order to assure itself and the board that the system of internal control is functioning as intended. In these circumstances, the board will need to assess whether such processes provide sufficient and objective assurance.'

6 Disaster recovery plans

As its name suggests, a disaster recovery plan is a plan of what to do in the event of a disaster that is unconnected with the company's business and outside the control of management. Disaster recovery planning goes beyond procedures that should be taken in an emergency, such as a fire or explosion in a building. It is intended to establish what should be done in the event that an extreme disaster that threatens the ability of the company to maintain its operations. Examples of disasters are natural disasters, such as major fires or flooding or storm damage to key installations or offices, and major terrorist attacks.

Disaster recovery plans are most needed in industries where a lengthy or widespread shutdown of operations could be catastrophic, such as in the banking industry, energy supply industry and airline industry. However, all companies should have such plans, which need to be kept under continual review and about which employees need to be kept fully aware and, where appropriate, trained.

Typically a disaster recovery plan should do these things.

- Specify which operations are essential, and must be kept going
- Where operations rely on IT systems, identify the computers or networks to which the system can be transferred in the event of damage to the main system.
- Where operations should be transferred to, if they cannot continue in their normal location.
- Identify key personnel who are needed to maintain the system in operation.
- Identify who should be responsible for keeping the public informed about the impact of the disaster and the recovery measures that are being taken.

A review of disaster recovery plans may therefore be a part of the annual review of the effectiveness of internal control by the board or audit committee.

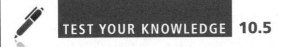

TEST YOUR KNOWLEDGE 10.5

Why should disaster recovery planning be a part of the internal control system of a large company?

7 Whistleblowing procedures

The UK Corporate Governance Code states that the audit committee should 'review arrangements by which staff of the company may, in confidence, raise concerns about possible improprieties in matters of financial reporting or other matters'. In other words, the audit committee should be responsible for review of the provisions and procedures for whistleblowing within the company. The UK Code specifies that the objective of the audit committee should be to ensure that there are satisfactory arrangements in place for:

- the 'proportionate and independent investigation' of allegations by whistleblowers and
- appropriate follow-up action.

The Code is referring to the adequacy of whistleblowing procedures within the company.

7.1 The nature of whistleblowing

A whistleblower is an employee who provides information about his company which he reasonably believes provides evidence of:

- fraud
- a serious violation of a law or regulation by the company or by directors, managers or employees within the company
- a miscarriage of justice
- offering or taking bribes

- price-fixing
- a danger to public health or safety, such as dumping toxic waste in the environment or supplying food that is unfit for consumption
- neglect of people in care
- in the public sector, gross waste or misuse of public funds.

The BSI's 'Whistleblowing Procedures: Code of Practice' provides the following definition:

'Whistleblowing is the popular term used when someone who works in or for an organisation ... raises a concern about a possible fraud, crime, danger or other serious risk that could threaten customers, colleagues, shareholders, the public or the organisation's own reputation.'

It can act as an early warning system to the employer about improper or illegal behaviour within the organisation.

A feature of whistleblowing is that the individual concerned has been unable to get a response from the company's management through normal lines of reporting, which has forced the individual to go to someone else with the information. The whistleblower presumably hopes that this person will take action to deal with the misdemeanour. Whistleblowing can arise in different situations and for different reasons.

- There have been instances in the past where an employee of a company manufacturing defence equipment has passed information to the press about an illegal arms sale. Presumably, the whistleblower in each case disapproved of the transaction and believed that the company was aware that it was in breach of the law, but intended to go through with the sale.
- An employee may have evidence that his superiors are in breach of company regulations and so reports the facts to someone else in a position of seniority within the company, such as a managing director. In these cases, the individual believes the company's senior management is unaware of the problem, but will take action if alerted. This situation arose, for example, with the whistleblowing at Enron in 2001 (see also Chapter 1).

7.2 Whistleblowing and internal control

There is a strong connection between corporate governance and whistleblowing. An employee may honestly believe that there is (or has been or could soon be) serious malpractice by someone within the company, but feel unable to report his concerns in the normal way. This could be because the individual to whom he normally reports is involved in the suspected malpractice. Serious malpractice or a misdemeanour could be damaging to the company.

- It might suffer financial loss if some employees are acting fraudulently.
- It might be incur severe penalties as a consequence of employees breaking the law or regulations.
- There could be damage to the company's reputation if the misdemeanour is made public.

The need for whistleblowing arises when normal procedures and internal controls will not reveal the illicit activity, because the individuals responsible for the activity are somehow able to ignore or get round the normal controls.

However, although whistleblowing procedures are an internal control, they are not an embedded control within the company's regular procedures, and their effectiveness relies on the willingness of genuine whistleblowers to come forward with their allegations. The incidence of illicit or illegal behaviour should be uncommon; therefore whistleblowing should be an occasional event.

7.3 Potential problems with whistleblowing systems

Concerns about whistleblowing have grown in recent years, for the following reasons.

- A huge amount of information about a company is held on computer files, which are accessible to many employees. Individual employees prepared to spend the time to look closely into a matter are likely to discover a large amount of information that they might not 'officially' be supposed to know, or information that no one else has yet become aware of. Companies are now aware, for example, that they could become liable for information held as e-mail messages in the files of employees.

- In many companies, there is a strong culture of loyalty to the company. Employees who question or criticise the actions of management might be considered to be 'traitors'. Despite laws designed to protect them, whistleblowers run the risk of retaliatory action. When they report their suspicions, they may be sacked on the grounds of making false and malicious allegations. It would certainly appear to be the case that whistleblowers are more likely to be dismissed than rewarded. This is particularly the case when the whistleblower passes the information to someone outside the company, such as the media.
- Individual whistleblowers played an important part in uncovering information about financial and accounting mismanagement and corruption at Enron (2001) and WorldCom (2002), and in criticising the handling of security information by the FBI before the September 11 terrorist attacks in New York. The public became aware not only that companies were being mismanaged, but also that honest attempts to reveal the problems were being disregarded by senior management.

As these case examples show, whistleblowers may put their job at risk. An employer taking retaliatory action may claim that sacking the employee had nothing to do with the revelations the employee had made, or claim that the employee was sacked because his statements were vindictive and untrue.

7.4 Whistleblowing: best practice

If an employee has a genuine, honest concern about something happening within the company, which he believes to be dishonest or improper, there should be a way for the employee's concerns to be brought to the attention of management and dealt with in a constructive way. Having a system for listening to employees' concerns should be a part of an effective risk management system within the organisation, because diligent employees can act as an early warning system of problems. However, there are several problems with whistleblowing procedures and policies.

- As stated earlier, experience in many organisations appears to show that an individual who reports concerns about illegal or unethical conduct is often victimised by colleagues and management. If the allegations by the whistleblower are rejected, he might not receive the same salary increases as colleagues, or is overlooked for promotion. The attitude of colleagues and managers might also be hostile, making it difficult for the individual to continue in the job.
- On the other hand, employees may deliberately make false claims about their colleagues or bosses, out of spite or a desire for revenge for some actual or perceived 'wrong'. It would be inappropriate to provide protection for individuals making malicious and intentionally false allegations.

Companies therefore need to establish a whistleblowing system that:

- encourages employees to report of illegal or unethical behaviour, but
- discourages malicious and unfounded allegations.

A company might state its policy on whistleblowing in the following terms.

- An employee is acting correctly if, in good faith, he or he seeks advice about improper behaviour or reports improper behaviour, where it is not possible to resolve the individual's concerns through discussions with colleagues or line management. (Whistleblowing is appropriate if the employee does it in good faith and is not being malicious, and there is no other way to resolve the problem.)
- The company will not tolerate any discrimination by employees or management in the company against an individual who has reported in good faith their concerns about illegal or unethical behaviour. (This is a policy statement that whistleblowers will be protected if they have made their report in good faith.)
- Disciplinary action will be taken against any employee who knowingly makes a false report of illegal or improper behaviour by someone else. (Malicious reporting should not be tolerated.)

In practice, employees may feel obliged to take their concerns (possibly anonymously) to someone outside the company, risking the anger of the employer for breach of proper procedures if he is identified. An employee can be disciplined for making groundless complaints and allegations in bad faith about his employer. On the other hand, there are some 'official' whistleblowing channels that provide a way of reporting concerns to someone outside the employer organisation. An example in the UK is the Whistleblowing Line operated by the FSA for the financial services industry.

7.5 Internal procedures for whistleblowers' allegations

A company should have a fair system for dealing internally with accusations from whistleblowers, so that an honest individual does not feel under threat. Employees ought to know what those procedures are. Since whistleblowing is not a regular event, a company may simply try to deal with each case on its merits when it arises, without any formal procedures or channels of complaint being established. The employee will therefore not know whom to complain to, and will probably go to the most senior manager available – possibly the CEO.

A problem with dealing with whistleblowing incidents on an ad hoc basis is that the accusations may relate to the senior executive directors themselves. An employee who believes the CEO or finance director to be guilty of wrong-doing will have no option other than to resign or take the complaint to an external authority, such as the press or the police.

It may therefore be more appropriate to establish a formal internal channel for dealing with whistleblowers.

- If the company has a culture of ethical conduct, it should be prepared to encourage whistleblowing, and should provide a channel for reporting complaints and allegations by employees about their bosses. At the same time, it should make clear its policy about disciplining employees found to have been malicious in making allegations.
- Although it will often be necessary to involve senior executives in the investigation of allegations, the channel for complaints should not be to senior executive management or the board. One possible arrangement would be for allegations to be made to the company secretary, who would then arrange for the senior independent director (SID) to be notified. The SID, or a committee of non-executive directors could then decide how the allegation should be investigated.
- An allegation might be investigated on behalf of a company by a firm of solicitors, because of the possibility of criminal activity or a misdemeanour that could expose the company to a large civil liability. If so, the solicitors asked to do the work should not have a close relationship with the company, so that their investigation can be independent. For example, the company should not be a large client of the solicitors for other legal work.

However, until every company has adopted an enlightened approach to dealing with employee allegations, and every employee can feel that he is not risking job security by making accusations, many will not trust internal procedures and will prefer to go to an external authority. Anyone making allegations about their company and its management to an external authority could be putting their job at risk. In recognition of the risks taken by honest whistleblowers, the law should offer some protection.

7.6 Establishing whistleblowing procedures

In the UK, the most authoritative guide to whistleblowing procedures is probably now: 'Whistleblowing Arrangements Code of Practice', which was issued by the British Standards Institute (BSI) in 2008. (It is also referred to as 'PAS 1998:2008': PAS stands for publicly Available Specification.)

The Code of Practice states that an internal whistleblowing procedure will be effective only if it has the confidence of the employees, who are its intended users. Confidence in the system will be obtained only if the employer is genuinely committed to the procedure. The Code also recommends that employees' representatives should be involved in establishing the procedure and monitoring its implementation.

The company secretary will often be given an important role in establishing an internal whistleblowing policy and procedures. He needs to ensure that there are trained people in the organisation to operate the procedure so that any matters raised under the internal procedure are dealt with effectively. The Guide adds that if someone does report a genuine concern in good faith, these individuals must be supported. Providing support might be a role for the company secretary.

The Code of Practice suggests that features of an internal whistleblowing policy and procedure should include the following provisions.

- The internal whistleblowing procedures should be documented and a copy should be given to every employee.
- It should set out the key aspects of the procedure, such as the person to whom employees should report their suspicions or concerns. This might be the company secretary or internal audit.
- It should contain a statement that the employer takes malpractice or misconduct seriously, and is committed to a culture of openness in which employees can report legitimate concerns without fear of penalty or punishment.
- It should give examples of the type of misconduct for which employees should use the procedure and set out the level of proof that there should be in an allegation. (Although positive proof might not be required, a whistleblower should be able to provide good reasons for his concern.)
- The document should set out the procedures by which an allegation will be investigated.
- It should make clear that false or malicious allegations will result in disciplinary action against the individual making them.
- It should make clear that no employee will be victimised for raising a genuine concern. Victimisation for raising a qualified disclosure should be a disciplinary offence.
- An external whistleblowing route should be offered, as well as an internal reporting procedure.
- There should be an undertaking that, as far as possible, whistleblowers will be informed about the outcome of their allegations and the action that has been taken.
- Whistleblowers should be promised confidentiality, as far as this is possible.

7.7 Whistleblowing procedures and the Bribery Act 2010

In the UK, the Bribery Act 2010 introduced a new offence of 'failure of commercial organisations to prevent bribery' by a person associated with them (such as an employee or agent). However a company could avoid conviction if it can show that, although bribery may have occurred, it has in place 'adequate processes' to prevent bribery. Having suitable whistle blowing procedures is likely to be a sufficient defence against a criminal charge, provided that the company can demonstrate that the procedures work well in practice. It should not be sufficient simply to have a whistle blowing policy in existence, but which no one uses.

 TEST YOUR KNOWLEDGE 10.6

(a) As company secretary of a public company, you have been asked to develop the appropriate internal procedures for dealing with a whistleblower's allegations. What would you advise?

(b) What are the main problems with systems of whistleblowing in large companies?

8 The Sarbanes-Oxley Act: section 404

Statutory measures relating to risk management and internal control were introduced by the Sarbanes-Oxley Act 2002 following the collapse of Enron and the other US corporate scandals and a stock market collapse in 2002 with the bursting of the so-called 'dotcom bubble'.

Section 404 of the Act directed the Securities and Exchange Commission (SEC) to set rules requiring companies ('SEC registrants') to include an internal control report in their annual report. The Act specified that:

'The Commission shall prescribe rules requiring each annual report ... to contain an internal control report, which shall:

- state the responsibility of management for establishing and maintaining an adequate internal control structure and procedures for financial reporting, and
- contain an assessment, as of the end of the most recent fiscal year of the issuer, of the effectiveness of the internal control structure and procedures of the issuer for financial reporting.'

8.1 SEC regulations relating to section 404

The SEC implemented section 404 and introduced the following regulations.

- 'The management of each ... issuer ... must evaluate, with the participation of the issuer's principal executive and principal finance officers ... the effectiveness, as of the end of each fiscal year, of the issuer's internal control over financial reporting. The framework on which management's evaluation of the issuer's internal control over financial reporting is based must be a suitable, recognized control framework ...'
- 'The management of each issuer ... must evaluate, with the participation of the issuer's principal executive and principal finance officers ... any change in the issuer's internal control over financial reporting that has occurred during each of the issuer's fiscal quarters, or fiscal year in the case of a foreign private issuer, that has materially affected, or is likely to materially affect, the issuer's internal control over financial reporting.'
- Companies should also maintain evidence, including documentation, to provide reasonable support for management's assessment of the effectiveness of internal control over financial reporting.
- Management is required to disclose any material weaknesses in the company's internal control system for financial reporting, and is not permitted to conclude that the internal control is effective if one or more material weaknesses exist.

8.2 Annual statement on internal financial controls and auditors' attestation report

Section 404 requires companies to include in their annual report a report on 'internal control over financial reporting'. This should set out:

- a statement of management's responsibility for establishing and maintaining adequate internal controls over the company's financial reporting
- a statement identifying the framework used by management for evaluating the efficiency and effectiveness of the internal control over financial reporting
- an assessment by management of the effectiveness of the internal control over financial reporting, as at the end of the most recent fiscal year (and any 'material weakness' in internal control)
- disclosure of any material weakness in the company's internal control over financial reporting that management has identified
- a statement that the external auditors have issued an attestation report on management's assessment of the company's internal control over financial reporting. The auditors' attestation report should be filed as part of the company's annual report.

In order to prepare the report on internal control, management must:

- undertake a review of the effectiveness of internal controls over financial reporting (the 'review' requirements'), and
- maintain evidence to provide reasonable support for management's assessment of the effectiveness of internal controls (the 'documentation requirements').

8.3 Review of the section 404 requirements

Section 404 was criticised in the USA, on the grounds that its requirements would take up much valuable management time and resources, and would added substantially to the costs paid to the external auditors for their attestation report. The heavy administrative burdens (and the potential liability that exists for the CEO and the CFO) were blamed for discouraging foreign companies from listing their shares in the USA, and choosing alternative financial centres such as London, where the regulatory burden is much lower.

In December 2006 in response to the continuing criticisms, the SEC issued new guidance for management, allowing management more discretion in how the annual review of internal controls is carried out. It was also intended to free companies from a highly cautious box-ticking approach to compliance, to reduce reliance on advice from external auditors and to reduce the quantities of documentary evidence required. By easing the regulatory and compliance burden of section 404, it was hoped that these changes would restore the attractiveness of New York as an international stock market.

8.4 Comparing SOX, section 404 with the UK Code and Turnbull Guidance

There are significant differences between the requirements of the Sarbanes Oxley Act and the UK Code/Turnbull Guidance. For UK companies without a US listing:

- there is no requirement for management to report on the effectiveness of internal control, only to state each year that they have reviewed the system of control
- there is no requirement for the auditors to report to shareholders on the directors' statement on internal control.

Commenting on its review of the Turnbull Report in 2005, a press release of the Turnbull Review Group commented that 'it would not be appropriate to require boards to make a statement in the annual report about the effectiveness of the company's internal control system'. With its emphasis on a principles-based approach to assessment and review, and the restricted disclosure requirements, the UK regime imposed a much less heavy administrative burden on companies than did section 404. However, section 404 applies to internal control over financial reporting only, whereas the review of internal control in the UK covers all types of internal control – operational controls, compliance controls and risk management generally, in addition to financial controls.

 TEST YOUR KNOWLEDGE 10.7

What are the main requirements of section 404 of the Sarbanes-Oxley Act in the USA?

 CASE QUESTION

1 What internal control risks are evident from the case study and who should be responsible for internal control within the company?

2 How might disaster recovery planning be of value to the company? Use information in the case study to illustrate your argument.

3 What are the potential risks to Hunnerware from ineffective systems of internal control and risk management? What might be the implications for Hunnerware if the board does not respond positively to the concerns expressed by the new NED?

CHAPTER SUMMARY

■ Internal control risk is the risk of losses arising due to failures or weaknesses in the systems, operating procedures and personnel within an organisation.

■ Internal control risks can be categorised into financial risks, operational risks and compliance risks.

■ An internal control system should prevent internal control risks, or reduce the potential impact of internal control risks, or should identify failures when they occur and ensure that corrective measures are taken to deal with them.

■ An internal control system includes internal controls, which may be categorised as financial controls, operational controls or compliance controls, according to the type of risk they are intended to control.

■ An internal control system is not just a larger number of internal controls. There should be an appropriate control environment within the organisation, with leadership from the board. There should also be procedures for identifying and assessing internal control risks, designing and implementing suitable internal controls, communication of control information about monitoring of the effectiveness of controls and the control system as a whole.

■ The board of directors is responsible for ensuring that there is an effective system of internal control. The UK Corporate Governance Code requires the board to review the effectiveness of the systems of internal control and risk management, and report to the shareholders that they have done so.

■ The board may delegate the task of carrying out the review of the internal control system and business risk management system to the audit committee (or a risk committee, in the case of the business risk management system).

■ The UK Corporate Governance Code requires listed companies to include in their annual report and accounts a statement on internal control from the board. The board's responsibility for internal control extends to all types of internal control risk, not just financial risks.

■ In the UK, following publication of the 1998 Combined Code, the Turnbull Committee issued guidelines on how to establish and maintain a sound system of internal controls. The Turnbull Guidance is now the responsibility of the Financial Reporting Council and is periodically reviewed. The Guidance includes a list of questions that should be asked when testing the effectiveness of the system.

■ Internal controls should be embedded within operations and procedures, and many are automated. However, some controls are initiated from 'outside' such as internal audit investigations and whistleblowing.

■ The review of the effectiveness of the internal control system by the audit committee or the board relies mainly on regular risk reports to the committee (or the board) from management, possibly with occasional additional reports from the internal auditors or external auditors (for example, in their end-of-audit report on any weaknesses in internal controls).

■ The UK Code requires the board to state that it is responsible for internal control and has reviewed the effectiveness of the internal control system but does not require weaknesses that have been identified in the system to be disclosed. The Disclosure and Transparency Rules require listed companies to report on the main features of the internal control system for financial reporting (but not operational or compliance controls). Listed companies include an internal control report within their annual report.

■ A company may have an internal audit department or function. Internal audit is audit work carried out at the request of management, for which there is no statutory requirement. The tasks of internal auditors can vary, but can include investigations into aspects of financial, operational or compliance controls in the company's systems and procedures. Internal audit investigations may be carried out at the request of operational management, senior financial management or the audit committee (or board).

■ Internal audit can therefore be used to test the effectiveness of internal controls within a company's systems and operations, and report to management or the audit committee on their findings and recommendations.

■ Internal auditors must be as objective and independent as possible. This is difficult for employees of the company. Although the head of internal audit may have a line reporting responsibility to the finance director, he should also have direct access if required to the audit committee.

■ The UK Code requires companies to review each year the effectiveness of the internal audit function, and if the company does not have an internal audit function to consider the need for one and make a recommendation to the board.

- Companies may have disaster recovery planning as part of their internal control system.
- The UK Code requires the board to assess its whistleblowing procedures.
- There are extensive guidelines on whistleblowing within companies, but whistleblowing procedures are often ineffective.
- In the USA, there is a statutory requirement on companies to include a report on internal control in their annual report to shareholders (Sarbanes-Oxley Act, section 404). The report is restricted to internal controls for financial reporting, and does not cover operational or compliance controls. The Act requires companies to include in the report a statement of management responsibility for internal control, an assessment of the effectiveness of the internal control system, a disclosure of any weaknesses or failures that have been discovered, and a statement that the auditors have produced an attestation report on the assessment of internal control by management.

Corporate social responsibility and sustainability

■ **OVERVIEW**

The fourth part of this study text looks at corporate social responsibility (CSR) as a feature of corporate governance and ways in which companies might report their plans, targets and actual performance to stakeholders on a range of CSR issues. It also considers the significance of CSR issues for companies themselves, for shareholders and for other stakeholders (including the general public).

Chapter 11 explains the nature of CSR and corporate citizenship, and why CSR is an issue for corporate governance. It describes the views of different stakeholder groups, including the government and investors (who might include socially responsible investment within their own organisational objectives). The chapter also explains how companies might benefit from the pursuit of CSR policies, and how these might be implemented. It concludes with some consideration of social and environmental issues for not-for-profit and public sector organisations.

Chapter 12 discusses the reporting of CSR issues by companies to stakeholders. Companies should not only pursue CSR policies; they should also report their intentions and achievements to stakeholders, including the general public. Much of this reporting is on a voluntary basis, but many large public companies recognise its importance. The chapter explains the nature of social and environmental reporting, and the problems with producing meaningful reports in the absence of standardisation and benchmarking. The chapter goes on to explain the nature of sustainability and sustainable business and how the performance of companies might be presented in sustainability reports (triple bottom line reporting). The chapter ends with an explanation of initiatives to create better comparability between companies on CSR issues.

■ LEARNING OUTCOMES

Part Four should enable you to:

- compare the responsibilities of organisations to different stakeholder groups, and advise on the application of principles of corporate responsibility or corporate citizenship

- analyse the benefits of CSR policies to companies

- give advice on developing and implementing a CSR strategy appropriate to your organisation

- apply the principles and guidelines concerning CSR reporting

- explain the significance of and advise on the use of sustainability reporting.

 PART 4 CASE STUDY

MGX Industrial is a large global company with industrial and manufacturing operations on many countries of the world. It has a listing in the UK. Four years ago, the board made its operations director responsible for reporting to the board on social and environmental issues. The company announced that this appointment demonstrated its commitment to acting as a corporate citizen in all parts of the world where it had operations.

The company is subject to various items of environmental legislation and regulation in the countries where it operates. In addition, local site managers are continually under pressure from national governments, local government authorities, regulatory authorities, pressure groups and local communities to improve their social and environmental performance, and to give greater consideration to social and environmental issues. There has been an increase in the past two years of requests by institutional shareholders to discuss environmental issues with the company's board.

The company publishes a social and environmental (SE) report each year, which is produced at the same time as its annual report and accounts. The SE report is produced as a separate document and is also accessible on the company's web site. The main part of the report begins with a list of social and environmental targets, and actual performance to date. Most of the report is a narrative description of these targets, and the reasons for failure to achieve any of them or a description of how a target has been achieved or should be achieved by the target date. An extract from the list of social and environmental reports in the company's most recent SE report is shown opposite.

The director responsible for social and environmental matters is disappointed by the lack of widespread interest in the company's policies or its SE reports. He believes that the problem may be the negative publicity the company received for major environmental contamination at two of its operating sites two or three years ago, and the company's slow response in clearing the pollution and compensating the victims of the accidents.

Case study continued

	Target	Actual performance	Trend	Target date for achievement of target performance
Zero harm	Zero fatalities at operating sites	5 fatalities	Worse than the previous year (3 fatalities)	Ongoing. Target established 4 years ago.
	Zero major environmental incidents	No incidents	Better than previous year (1 incident)	Ongoing. Target established 2 years ago.
Health	25% reduction in the incidence of occupational disease over a 7-year period	21% reduction in the 5 years since the target was established	On track for achievement	2 years' time
Safety	50% reduction in the incidence of recordable injuries at operating sites over a 10-year period	10% reduction in the three years since the target was established	Below expectation in achieving improvements	7 years' time
Environment	10% reduction in greenhouse gas emissions per unit produced	8% reduction in the three years since the target was established	On target for achievement	2 years' time
	15% reduction in carbon-based energy use per unit produced	6% reduction in the three years since the target was established	Target unlikely to be achieved	2 years' time
	12% improvement in ratio of water recycled/ re-used to high-quality water consumed	9% reduction in the three years since the target was established	On target for achievement	2 years' time
Community	1.5% of pre-tax profits to be invested in community projects	1.5% of pre-tax profits were invested	Target achieved	Ongoing

Corporate social responsibility

■ CONTENTS

■ INTRODUCTION

Advocates of an integrated approach or pluralist approach to corporate governance would argue that the board of directors has a responsibility for the formulation of policies on ethical behaviour, employee welfare, social issues and environmental issues. The board should also monitor the effectiveness of these strategies. There is some recognition of the responsibility of the board for **corporate social responsibility** (CSR) issues, although concern for CSR issues varies between countries. This chapter considers the nature of CSR and also sustainability. The following chapter discusses ways in which companies should report to shareholders and other stakeholders on these issues.

1 The nature of corporate social responsibility (CSR)

The European Union has defined corporate social responsibility (CSR) as 'a concept whereby companies integrate social and environmental concerns in their business operations and their interaction with their stakeholders on a voluntary basis'. In a green paper on CSR the EU also stated (2001) that it means 'not only fulfilling legal expectations, but also going beyond compliance and investing more into human capital, the environment and the relations with stakeholders'.

The Business for Social Responsibility has defined CSR as:

'While there is no single, commonly accepted definition of corporate social responsibility, or CSR, it generally refers to business decision-making linked to ethical values, compliance with legal requirements, and respect for people, communities and the environment.'

Business in the Community, a voluntary group of UK companies that promotes CSR, has set out five principles that companies should apply.

1 Treat employees fairly and with respect.
2 Operate in an ethical way and with integrity.
3 Respect basic human rights.
4 Sustain the environment for future generations.
5 Be a responsible neighbour in their communities.

CSR is therefore consistent with a stakeholder approach to corporate governance by companies (or at the very least an enhanced form of 'enlightened shareholder approach' to governance). Several issues come together in a CSR approach to conducting business:

■ an ethical approach to conducting business
■ concern for all stakeholders

- concern for social and environmental issues, but also
- a recognition that a company must be profitable to survive and succeed in the long term.

Although CSR is commonly associated with ethical values and social and environmental issues, it is important to recognise that companies must carry on business in a way that is financially viable and profitable. CSR recognises social, environmental and economic (financial) issues (sometimes known as SEE), and is concerned with how companies can integrate the requirements of each into their business strategies and activities. The EU has stated: 'Through CSR, enterprises of all sizes, in co-operation with their stakeholders, can help to reconcile economic, social and environmental ambitions.'

The ethical element of CSR should not be forgotten either. A socially responsible company should be expected to act in an ethical way, and should not condone the use of unethical practices such as bribery to win contracts.

1.1 Sustainability and sustainable development

The concept of 'sustainability', also called 'sustainable development' or 'sustainable business', is linked to CSR although it focuses more on the environmental aspects of CSR rather than the economic and social aspects. Sustainability has emerged as a social and environmental objective for major companies; however, there is no generally accepted definition of what it actually means. The Brundtland Report (for the World Commission on Environment and Development, 1987) defined sustainable development as 'development that meets the needs of the present without compromising the ability of future generations to meet their own needs'. However, although this definition might seem broadly acceptable, there are difficulties with what it means in practice.

- There can be disagreement about the meaning of 'needs of the present'. Presumably these are more than the bare minimum needs for survival, because in much of the world consumption is well above survival level and affluent societies do not accept the need to reduce consumption to levels in other countries of the world.
- Similarly, it is not clear what the needs of future generations are. If they are just survival needs, there must be an inherent assumption that at some time in the future economic wealth must decline in the more affluent societies.
- It is not clear over what period of time the needs of future generations should be considered and measured. In theory, society's long-term needs should be recognised. However, governments and companies are likely to plan over much shorter timescales. Since companies plan for the future and report their performance within fairly short time frames, reporting for sustainable development by companies is likely to focus on relatively short-term measures of sustainability.
- Should sustainability be measured collectively for all people in all societies of the world, or should sustainability be measured in terms of individual countries or regions?

In general terms, however, sustainability is concerned with conducting business operations in a way that can be continued into the foreseeable future, without using natural resources at such a rate or creating such environmental damage that the continuation of the business will eventually become impossible.

1.2 Social, economic and environmental issues

CSR policies integrate social, economic and environmental objectives. Economic objectives are well understood, and are common to most commercial companies. Economic objectives should be to achieve profitability over the longer term, protect and develop the assets of shareholders and provide shareholders with a satisfactory return on their investment. Objectives can be set in terms of targets for profitability, earnings per share, EPS growth, share price growth, cash flow targets, and so on.

Social and environmental policies are more difficult to define, because these vary between companies and differ according to the industrial sector and the countries in which they operate. Social policies may relate to the company's employees, the employees of major suppliers to the company, local communities or the concerns of wider society. Environmental objectives often relate to issues such as reducing pollution levels, reducing waste and reducing the consumption of non-renewable natural resources, but specific objectives vary between industries because each industry has its own particular forms of pollution and resource consumption.

1.3 King III Code and CSR

The concepts of sustainability and **corporate citizenship** are key elements in the King III Report (2009) on corporate governance for companies in South Africa. The Report states in its introduction:

'Sustainability is the primary moral and economic imperative of the 21st century. It is one of the most important sources of both opportunities and risks for businesses. Nature, society and business are interconnected in complex ways that should be understood by decision-makers.'

The Report also emphasises the concept of corporate citizenship. This is the idea that companies are a 'person' in law and as such are members of the society in which they operate. Like all other members of society, they should be expected to acknowledge the needs and concerns of other citizens, and to act like a good citizen. 'The concept of corporate citizenship ... flows from the fact that the company is a person and should operate in a sustainable manner.'

1.4 The voluntary aspect of CSR

To some extent, companies are required by law and regulation to act in socially responsible ways. For example, there are laws and regulations to protect health and safety, prevent contamination of the environment and protect employees. An important feature of CSR is that CSR policies are largely voluntary and driven by companies themselves, not by external regulation.

NAPF, in a document on CSR and **socially responsible investment** or SRI (2005), suggested that CSR relates to the idea that companies, in addition to their responsibilities to shareholders, also have responsibilities to other stakeholders and to society at large. The document then went on to comment that these responsibilities can be divided into two distinct elements:

- generally accepted responsibilities that the company must fulfil in order to succeed in business or comply with legislation or regulations, and
- functions considered by some groups, including investors, to be responsibilities that go beyond compliance with the law and regulations, and beyond the measures necessary for achieving commercial success.

Whereas it would be widely accepted by directors that companies should comply with the law and should give serious attention to the company's reputation risk, there are probably differences of opinion about the extent to which companies need to go beyond legal, regulatory and commercial requirements in pursuing CSR policies.

1.5 Reasons for developing interest in CSR

The development of concern for CSR by companies has come from several sources, but in particular:

- government
- investors
- companies themselves.

The interests of government, investors and companies in CSR are explained in the following paragraphs.

TEST YOUR KNOWLEDGE 11.1

(a) Define corporate social responsibility and outline some examples of how companies might act in accordance with an awareness of social responsibility.
(b) According to Business in the Community what are the five CSR principles that companies should apply?
(c) Define sustainability.
(d) What is a **corporate citizen**?

2 Corporate social responsibility and government

Many governments are interested in CSR because they want to improve the quality of life of their citizens and to protect the environment, whilst encouraging the successful development of business.

2.1 UK company law and CSR

In the UK, the Companies Act 2006 does not refer specifically to CSR, but it includes as a statutory duty of directors a requirement to promote the success of the company. In fulfilling this duty, directors are required to have regard, amongst other matters, to:

- the interests if the company's employees
- the need to foster relationships with suppliers and customers
- the impact of the company's actions on the community and the environment
- the desirability of maintaining a reputation for high standards of conduct.

This in effect is a requirement that directors should have some regard for CSR issues, and should take an enlightened shareholder approach to governance.

2.2 The European Union and CSR

The European Commission has shown an interest in promoting CSR since 2001 when it issued a green paper on the subject. In 2006 it launched a European Alliance for Corporate Social Responsibility, which is a body with open membership that encourages businesses to promote CSR and raise awareness of it. However, although the European Parliament voted in favour of mandatory reporting on social and environmental issues by companies (in 2006), the approach of the European Commission has so far been to encourage voluntary initiatives and CSR policies by companies.

2.3 The OECD and CSR

In 2001 the Organisation for Economic Cooperation and Development (OECD) issued Guidelines for Multinational Enterprises. (These Guidelines were reviewed in 2010.) The Guidelines were issued by the governments of subscribing countries to multinationals with the aim of encouraging 'the positive contributions that multinational enterprises can make to economic, environmental and social progress and to minimise the difficulties to which their activities may give rise'. The objective of the governments was to encourage multinationals to operate in ways that would improve the welfare and living standards of their peoples, by taking into consideration the stakeholders in the countries where they operate. Although the Guidelines are directed at multinational companies, similar guidelines should apply to local companies. Some of the Guidelines are listed below, to provide an indication of the nature of CSR issues that may affect companies and in which governments may have an interest.

General policies

The OECD Guidelines suggest several general policies that multinationals should adopt. These include having policies that:

- contribute to economic, social and environmental development with a view to achieving sustainable development
- respect the human rights of those people affected by their activities
- encourage the development of local business through cooperation with local communities
- encourage the development of human capital in those communities, by creating employment and providing training
- refrain from seeking or accepting exemptions from local laws on the environment or health
- support and promote good corporate governance practice
- avoid improper involvement in local politics.

Employment policies

The OECD Guidelines include more specific policy guidelines on employment and industrial relations. These include requirements for multinationals to:

- respect the right of employees to be represented by trade unions
- contribute to the abolition of child labour
- contribute to the abolition of forced labour
- avoid discrimination on the grounds of race, gender, religion or political opinion
- observe standards of employment that are not less favourable than those provided by comparable employers in the host country
- take adequate steps to ensure occupational health and safety
- as much as possible, to use local labour and provide them with skills training
- in negotiations with trade union representatives, avoid using the threat of moving all or part of the company's operations to another country or region.

Environment policies

The OECD Guidelines on the environment include requirements for multinationals to:

- establish and maintain a system of environmental management that includes the collection of adequate information about the environmental and health and safety effects of their activities, targets for improvements in environmental performance and regular monitoring of actual performance in comparison with the established targets
- provide the public with adequate information about environmental and health and safety matters, and engage with communities that are directly affected by the environmental and health and safety policies of the company
- consider the long-term environmental, health and safety-related consequences when making decisions
- continually seek to improve environmental performance through encouraging environmentally friendly technologies and developing environmentally friendly products
- maintain contingency plans for dealing with unforeseen environmental, health and safety damage arising from their operations, including accidents and emergencies.

There are other policies in the Guidelines, such as the requirement that multinationals should avoid the use of bribery of officials to obtain contracts and revenue.

TEST YOUR KNOWLEDGE 11.2

(a) What are the general OECD guidelines for multinational companies, and why were these considered necessary?
(b) What are the OECD guidelines to multinational companies on employment policies?

---

3 Corporate social responsibility, investors and SRI

For institutional investors, there is a close connection between SRI and CSR. SRI (also known as ethical investment and sustainable investment) is defined as an approach to investment management that takes into account a proper analysis of the CSR responsibilities of companies to society as a whole and particular stakeholder groups. It is a process whereby the principles of the investor affect their choice of which companies to invest in and how they should exercise their rights as shareholders. It involves both the screening and selection process for investment decision-making and the process of engagement between shareholders and companies. SRI is therefore a method of managing an investment portfolio, whereas CSR relates to the behaviour of companies. Investment institutions each have their own policy towards SRI. Institutional investors have been involved in the development of company attitudes to CSR for three reasons.

- Investors recognise that CSR risks and corporate policies on CSR could affect the long-term prosperity of a company, and boards of directors should be aware of CSR risks for the company. Investors should therefore expect to receive regular disclosures from boards about the CSR risks their company faces, and the policies they have developed and implemented for dealing with them. (Reporting on CSR issues is discussed in Chapter 12.)
- Some institutional investors consider that CSR issues should affect their investment decisions, and the choice of shares for their investment portfolios.
- If institutional investors have a strategy of preferring to invest in companies with sound CSR policies, they may wish to engage with the boards of directors about the CSR policies of their company, and encourage them to develop strategies that are more socially responsible.

Investment institutions are also concerned about the long-term returns on their investments, and may hold the view that companies will perform better in the long term if they have sound CSR policies and also good corporate governance practices. Investors may therefore refer to ESG issues – **environmental, social and governance (ESG) risks** – rather than CSR.

In its Corporate Governance and Voting Guidelines (2007), the NAPF states that it recognises the importance of incorporating ESG considerations into investment decisions by its members and that long-term shareholders should benefit from the application of ESG principles in terms of:

- long-term financial performance
- closer alignment between the interests of institutional investors and society at large, and
- the management of their reputational risk.

3.1 NAPF policy on CSR and SRI

In a 2005 paper on CSR/SRI, the NAPF explained that it had given some consideration to whether it should be active in promoting good CSR practices in companies, in the same way that it had been active in promoting good corporate governance. Its conclusion was that, unlike corporate governance, CSR should be seen as 'a fundamental part of the normal running of the business'.

- CSR is a management responsibility, and management should be allowed to get on with their task without interference from institutional investors.
- Boards should be accountable to shareholders for the way they run the business, including their CSR policies.
- Boards should develop CSR policies as part of their normal business agenda, which they should disclose to shareholders and other stakeholders in the normal process of disclosure by companies.

The NAPF therefore recognised the potential importance of CSR issues, but stated that it did not intend to issue specific guidelines. One of its statements of underlying principles summarised its position:

'At all times the board and Management should be mindful of the wider role of the Company in society, bearing in mind that maximisation of short-term gain in a manner which is deemed unacceptable by society as a whole, can seriously damage the longer term prospects of a Company and lead to real financial losses for shareholders. Such losses may come about as a result of either changing consumer preferences or legislation putting additional cost on the Company, or both.'

In the UK, pension funds are specifically required by law (the SRI Pensions Disclosure Regulations 2000) to state their policy towards social, ethical and environmental in their Statement of Investment Principles. The NAPF has recommended (in its Corporate Governance Policy and Voting Guidelines) that to fulfil this legal requirement and to disclose the extent to which social, environmental and ethical considerations affect its investment strategy, a pension fund may consider applying the UN Principles for Responsible Investment (UNPRI). These Principles are that investors should:

- incorporate ESG issues into their investment analysis and decision-making processes
- be active investors and incorporate ESG issues into their share ownership practices and policies
- seek appropriate disclosures about ESG issues from the companies in which they invest

- promote acceptance of the UN Principles within the investment industry
- work together to improve the effectiveness of the implementation of the UN Principles, and
- report on their progress towards implementing the Principles.

3.2 Pursuing a SRI strategy

There are several different ways in which institutional investors may pursue a SRI strategy:

- engagement
- investment preference
- screening.

With an engagement strategy, the institutional investor acquires shares in which it wants to invest (for financial reasons) but then engages with the board of directors and tries to persuade the company to adopt policies that are socially responsible, or to make improvements in its CSR policies. Engagement may therefore involve expressing the views of the investor about telling what the CSR policies of the company should be and persuading it to change its policies in some areas (through regular meetings with its senior directors). If the company indicates its willingness to make changes, the investor may also offer to help with the formulation of new policies.

With an investment preference strategy, the investor develops a set of guidelines that companies should meet. The investor will then invest only in the shares (or other securities) companies that meet the guidelines, some of which will be social, ethical or environmental in nature. With this strategy is investment decisions need not be based entirely on SRI considerations. The investor can also consider the expected financial returns from an investment, and the selected investment portfolio can be a suitable balance of investments that are ethically sound and those that are not as ethical (or are 'more risky' in social or environmental terms) but should provide better financial returns.

With a screening strategy, investments are restricted to companies that pass a 'screen test' for ethical behaviour. Screening may be positive or negative. Positive screening means that companies must meet certain criteria for ethical and socially responsible behaviour; otherwise the investor will not buy its shares. Negative screening means that an investor will identify companies that fail to meet certain minimum criteria for socially responsible behaviour, and will refuse to buy shares in those companies. The screening process could make use of a published **CSR index** (see also Chapter 12), such as the Dow Jones Sustainability Indices or the FTSE4Good indices, or (in the UK) the Business in the Community Corporate Responsibility Index. These are described in Chapter 12.

Investors that have a SRI strategy need information about the CSR performance of companies in order to assess the success of their investment strategies. Methods of reporting CSR performance are described in Chapter 12.

TEST YOUR KNOWLEDGE 11.3

(a) Define socially responsible investment (SRI) and explain three different approaches to implementing an SRI strategy.
(b) For what reasons might an institutional investor adopt a SRI strategy?

4 Corporate social responsibility and corporate strategy

Government and investor pressure on companies to develop voluntary CSR policies would probably have relatively little effect unless companies themselves saw benefits in the adoption of suitable policies. Perceptions about the benefits of CSR may vary, but have over the past ten years or so it would appear that there has been a growing understanding of how CSR can benefit companies commercially – and possibly financially – to the point where some listed companies now have an ethics and CSR sub-committee of the board.

4.1 The potential benefits of CSR for companies

There are differing views about the extent to which companies benefit commercially from CSR policies. In 2004, the ABI published a research report on CSR and its impact on company performance and investor relations. The key findings of the report were as follows.

■ Some studies had found that companies with active CSR policies benefited financially. The evidence was not conclusive but suggested that companies may benefit in areas such as corporate reputation, consumer acceptance, employee loyalty and environmental management.
■ The benefits of CSR for companies were not uniform across all companies or sectors.
■ The strategic risk aspects of CSR were as important as the effect on short-term profitability. Companies should recognise CSR risks in their strategic planning and management, because they can have important implications for brand value and market acceptability. There was now a greater awareness of the importance of risk as well as returns, including risk to reputation. Social, cultural, demographic and technological changes meant that social and environmental risks were now more significant than in the past.

The potential benefits of CSR policies for companies may be divided broadly into these categories:

■ reduction in reputational risk
■ public relations and marketing benefits, and
■ commercial and financial benefits.

It must be stressed that these benefits may vary between companies, industries and countries.

4.2 CSR policies and reputational risk

Reputation risk is difficult to measure (quantify). It is the risk that a company's reputation with the general public (and customers), or the reputation of its product 'brand', will suffer damage. Damage to reputation can arise in many different ways: incidents that damage reputation are often reported by the media.

There appears to be a link between public attitudes towards a company and the way in which the company presents itself as an organisation concerned with social, ethical and environmental issues. There is a risk to a company's reputation, depending on the CSR policies it adopts. A company's reputation can be damaged by adverse publicity and public comment from incidents such as a serious environmental spillage or a serious accident. Reputational risk exists for many large companies, not just the obvious examples of companies in mining and extracting, pharmaceuticals and food.

■ In the UK the rail system operator Railtrack failed to recover from the damage to its reputation from the safety concerns of the public following the Hatfield rail crash in 2001, and the company collapsed in the following year.
■ Some years ago, a company selling a global brand of leisure footwear suffered damage to its reputation following a report that that one of its footwear suppliers in the Far East used child labour and slave labour. On publication of this news, the company's sales and profits (temporarily) fell. Many Western companies that source their supplies from developing countries have now become alert to the reputational risks of using suppliers whose employment practices are below the standards that their customers would consider morally acceptable.

Managing reputational risk and protecting a company's name or brands against reputational damage is now regarded as a key policy objective for companies with well-known brands. The potential significance of CSR from a financial rather than an ethical perspective are therefore:

■ cost of fines and other legal penalties, payments to victims of environmental damage, cost of defending legal claims
■ cost of rectifying environmental damage or improving environmental and safety features
■ loss of future contracts as a result of damaged reputation.

There are also benefits to be obtained from having a strong reputation for business ethics and CSR policies.

■ Employees may prefer working for ethical organisations.
■ Customers may prefer buying from them and suppliers may prefer dealing with them.
■ Perhaps even more significantly, as discussed previously, investors may prefer holding the shares of ethical companies (and companies with good governance practices).

4.3 Business probity risk

Business probity risk is the risk to a company from a failure to act in an honest or ethical way. Dishonest activity can expose a company not only to reputational risk, but also the risk of regulatory or legal action for breaching rules and laws. Bribery is a well-recognised but seemingly widespread dishonest practice.

In order to win sales in some countries, companies might pay bribes (or 'commissions') to individuals. They might take the view that unless they pay bribes, they will not win major contracts. However, by paying bribes companies act dishonestly, and could be exposed to regulatory action or criminal action by the authorities of evidence of bribery is uncovered. This problem has been reported, for example, in the markets for the sale of military equipment, where the US government authorities in particular have been active in identifying and punishing companies.

Companies should be aware of the risk of unethical practices to their reputation and business. This should extend to avoiding the use of suppliers who make use of child labour or slave labour, and avoiding trading with countries where there are human rights concerns.

 CASE EXAMPLE 11.1

In 2006, the British Jewellers' Association took an ethical stance against the sourcing of diamonds from countries such as the Congo and Sierra Leone, where fighting over diamonds has led to civil war and widespread slaughter. It called these diamonds 'blood diamonds' and attempted to eliminate the trade in the UK.

4.4 Reputation and public relations

Companies that might suffer losses from damage to their reputation need to be vigilant and alert for any incident that could create adverse publicity. CSR policies may therefore be used to create favourable publicity, and PR consultants may be used to publicise ethical or socially responsible activities by companies, including sponsorship of charity events or involvement in community activities.

It may therefore be argued that some CSR policies that companies attempt to publicise are little more than attempts to promote the company and so are similar in many ways to advertising, except at a lower cost.

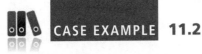 CASE EXAMPLE **11.2**

In 2003 the reputation of the banking group Citigroup was damaged by its associations with companies such as Enron, WorldCom, Adelphia and Parmalat, as a provider of both on-balance sheet and off-balance sheet finance.

The newly appointed CEO Chuck Prince wanted to improve the image and reputation of the bank. He believed that this meant improving its cultural and ethical outlook. He therefore introduced a code

(Continued)

CASE EXAMPLE   11.2 (*Continued*)

of conduct, which stated that the bank should aspire to be a company with the highest standards of ethical conduct and an organisation that people could trust. The bank's executives worldwide were asked to adhere to this code and promote the ethical status of the group.

In 2004, a problem occurred in London on the bank's trading desk for European government bonds. The desk was under pressure to increase its profits, and the management spotted an opportunity to exploit a weakness in MTS, an Italian-based electronic trading system for government bonds. They planned and executed a trade that came to be known as 'Doctor Evil'. They sold a large quantity of bonds early one morning, sufficient to send bond prices falling sharply, then bought the bonds back at much lower prices later the same morning. The trade earned a profit of over €18 million for Citigroup at the expense of other participant banks in the bond market.

The aftermath was that some banks refused to honour their commitment to make a market in government bonds on MTS, and in the next three months daily trading volumes on MTS fell by 30 per cent. Some European governments expressed worries about whether they would be able to continue issuing bonds (to raise new finance) at a reasonable rate of interest. Some governments withdrew business from Citigroup as an expression of their anger. In the UK, the Financial Services Authority fined the bank £14 million for failing to exercise due skill, care and diligence.

The traders responsible for 'Doctor Evil' were suspended. There had been a serious breach of the bank's new code of conduct. Moreover, the incident demonstrated that the change in culture that the code of conduct had intended to introduce had not reached the heart of cultural attitudes within the bank. After a brief suspension, the traders returned to work. The bank admitted to bad ethical behaviour and poor professionalism, but no one within the bank was held responsible.

CASE EXAMPLE   11.3

In the past, oil company BP has promoted itself as a company whose policies and strategies give due regard to its corporate social responsibility and it publicised its 'green credentials'. In spite of some environmental incidents, the company was successful in promoting its reputation as a supporter of CSR. However, in 2010 there was a major oil leak in a BP deep water well in the Gulf of Mexico, causing the biggest environmental damage in US history. In May 2010, President Obama ordered all 33 deep-water rigs in the Gulf of Mexico to stop drilling, and extended by six months an existing moratorium on new deep water wells. He also put on hold planned new drilling off the coast of Alaska and the Virginia coast. As public anger against BP mounted in the USA, the President also stated that the company or companies responsible would be made to pay for 'every cent' of the damage caused. With this incident, the reputation of BP as a CSR company was shattered. It also raised questions about the sincerity of all companies claiming CSR credentials. In an article in the *Financial Times* (28 May 2010) David Scheffer, Professor at Northwestern University School of Law in the USA, wrote: 'BP's catastrophic gusher shows how corporate hype can peddle an illusion at the expense of the oceans.'

4.5 Commercial benefits of CSR policies

Many companies, however, can see commercial and financial benefits from CSR policies. As environmental and social regulations are extended, and governments introduce stricter laws on environmental protection and health and safety, new commercial opportunities for environmentally friendly technologies and environmentally friendly products will emerge. Developing new technologies and new products can take a long time, and require substantial investment, but companies might need to make these investments in order to survive in the long term. The development of renewable energy technology and environmentally friendly cars are perhaps well-known examples.

Many companies have also improved their technology for reducing waste or toxic emissions, in order to avoid fines and penalties.

Although companies may be prepared to develop environmentally friendly products and technologies, they are unlikely to do so unless required by law or regulation, or if a commercial benefit can be obtained by selling more products to earn more profit. Although some consumers may but Fairtrade products, for example, they are unlikely to do so if these products are a lot more expensive than similar products without a Fairtrade label. Similarly companies may voluntarily take measures to reduce waste and pollution, but only if the spending is kept within acceptable limits or, even better, savings can be obtained.

CSR issues vary between companies and industries, but it may be helpful to consider a number of CSR initiatives by major companies in recent years, and the commercial benefits that have been obtained by their actions. These include measures to protecting or sustain supplies of key raw materials for the longer term.

- In 2008 Walmart told 1,000 Chinese suppliers that it would hold them to strict environmental and social standards. It has encouraged companies to cut down on packaging – if suppliers do this, more can be fitted into delivery trucks, and carbon emissions and spending on petrol are reduced. If producers make concentrated laundry detergent, this saves on both packaging and shelf space.

- In 2009, Mars announced that by 2020 its entire cocoa supply will be 'produced in a sustainable manner'. Mars said it would be working with the Rainforest Alliance to encourage farmers in the cocoa-growing regions to preserve their environment.

- Cadbury (prior to its takeover by Kraft in 2010) announced its concern about the sustainability of cocoa supplies, and reported that few children were willing to follow their parents into cocoa farming. It also announced that all the cocoa in Dairy Milk, its biggest-selling brand, would be certified by Fairtrade (which works to ensure a minimum price for farmers). Cadbury was hoping that Fairtrade would encourage the next generation into cocoa production, and sustain supplies into the longer-term future.

- In developing a fuel-efficient propulsion system Norwegian shipping company Wilh. Wilhelmsen found opportunities for using a catalytic converter that injects ammonia to neutralise nitrogen dioxide, a technology for 'sulphur scrubbing' to reduce emissions, a switch to water-based cleaning products instead of chemical-based ones, a better air conditioning system and a cleaning system for ballast water on its ships that reduced the spread of bacteria around the world. The savings in energy costs and the reduced risk of penalties for pollution that the company achieved from these changes justified the new propulsion system financially.

- GlaxoSmithKline (GSK) the pharmaceuticals group, announced in 2009 that it had set a target to cut the waste generated by medicines production at its factories world-wide by two-thirds by 2015. The target was to cut from 100 kg to 30 kg of waste for each 1 kg of 'active pharmaceutical ingredient' (API). The need to cut waste was recognised for both cost-cutting reasons and environmental reasons. The vice president of GSK responsible for the environment is reported to have said: 'It was the idea of sustainability that drove the idea. You make an improvement to the environment and you achieve a reduction in costs.' Another pharmaceuticals company AstraZeneca said that it had succeeded in cutting waste in production by over 50 per cent between 2006 and 2009.

 CASE EXAMPLE 11.4

In 2010 retailer Marks & Spencer announced a new list of ethical and environmental commitments up to 2020, and its intention to become one of the world's most environmentally friendly retailers by 2015. An initial list of 100 five-year ethical and environmental targets had been announced in 2007, including the aim of becoming carbon neutral and eliminating landfill waste, and the company expected to achieve its targets. It had also expected to commit £40 million in expenditure each year to this initiative, but in 2009 it had saved over £50 million. For example, it had achieved a 20 per cent reduction in fuel costs by using aerodynamic lorries for its deliveries. Its new targets for 2020 included sourcing all food, clothing and home items from sustainable or ethical sources such as the Fairtrade scheme and trying to persuade its clothing suppliers, especially in India, to pay a living wage to its employees, but without adding to costs for the consumer.

5 Formulating a CSR policy

The significance of CSR policies varies between companies in different industries, and companies finding themselves subject to the closest scrutiny – and with the biggest potential to benefit commercially – include:

- those with a dominant market position, such as former state-owned utility companies
- those dealing directly with consumers, such as retailers and commercial banks
- those producing essentials, such as food and drugs;
- those exploiting natural resources
- those depending on supply chains in developing counties, such as clothing manufacturers.

However, the responsibility for developing and implementing CSR policies may be split. The company secretary or compliance managers may have responsibility for ensuring compliance with regulations and the application of the company's code of ethics. The PR department may have responsibility for protecting the company against reputation risk and for promoting publicity about the company's CSR policies. Operational managers may have the responsibility for developing environmentally friendly processes and products, and the marketing department may have responsibility for advertising and selling the environmentally friendly products that the company makes. Ideally, there should be someone at board level who has overall responsibility for CSR policies. Companies may therefore appoint a director with specific responsibilities for ethics and CSR policies, or it may establish an ethics and CSR sub-committee of the board. A company formulating a CSR policy should:

- decide on its CSR values (and possibly publish a code of ethics)
- establish the company's current position on these values, and identify the gap between 'where we are' and 'where we want to be'
- obtain board support for the policy and identify responsibilities: nominate board leaders and local 'champions'
- develop realistic strategies and targets
- implement these on a local and global (company-wide) basis
- identify key stakeholders whose views the company wishes to influence (employees, pressure groups, customers)
- communicate the company's targets, policies and activities to its stakeholders, including the general public
- monitor achievements. The company might subscribe to a CSR index or award scheme, such as the schemes operated by Business in the Community (BiTC), a UK-based consortium. Reporting on CSR issues is discussed in Chapter 12.

5.1 CSR and executive remuneration

Companies are more likely to pursue CSR initiatives if senior managers are rewarded for achieving CSR objectives. It is usual for bonus schemes and incentive schemes to be based on the achievement of financial objectives, and possibly also non-financial operational objectives. There has been some progress, however, towards the use of CSR targets in bonus schemes and long-term incentive schemes. This progress is most noticeable in the Netherlands.

■ DSM, a life sciences company that sells chemicals, plastics and nutritional products announced proposals in 2010 that 50 per cent of bonuses and long-term incentives for its senior executives would be linked to targets such as a reduction in greenhouse gas emissions and energy use, introducing new environmentally friendly products and raising employee morale and satisfaction. (The other 50 per cent of bonuses and incentives would be linked to financial targets.)

■ Akzo Nobel, a paints company, has based 50 per cent of the awards under its long-term incentive scheme on the position that the company achieves in the Dow Jones Sustainability Index, an index that ranks comparable companies according to their success in achieving sustainable development.

■ Royal Dutch Shell uses safety targets and the same index as the basis for calculating some bonuses for senior executives.

5.2 Ethical leadership and corporate citizenship: recommendations of King III

The King III Code of governance principles emphasise the ethical and CSR aspects of governance. It states that the board of directors should provide effective leadership based on ethical values and that ethical leaders should:

■ direct strategy and operations to build a sustainable business
■ consider the short-run and long-run impact of decisions on the economy, society and the environment
■ do business ethically
■ avoid compromising the natural environment, and
■ take account of the impact of the company's actions on internal and external stakeholders.

The board should consider not only financial performance, but the impact of its operations on society and the environment. The board of a company should also protect and invest in the well-being of the economy, society and the environment. It should also build and sustain an ethical corporate culture in the company.

The King III Code also requires listed South African companies to issue an integrated report each year that includes both financial reports and information about sustainability performance. (Integrated reports are explained in Chapter 12.)

6 Social responsibility in the public and voluntary sectors

Social responsibility in government and the public sector is more difficult to define and identify than in the corporate sector. This is because many aspects of government policy are directed towards economic, social or environmental well-being of its citizens and, unlike companies, government does not have a profit objective in its policy objectives.

Within government, there may be particular responsibilities for social and environmental policy. In the UK, for example, the Department for the Environment, Food and Rural Affairs (Defra) is responsible for developing government policy on sustainable development and sustainable products. As a major buyer of goods and services from the private sector, the government is also able to pursue a procurement policy that awards supply contracts to companies that meet acceptable CSR standards.

Within the voluntary sector, many charities are established specifically for social or environmental objectives. In the UK, the Good Governance Code for the Voluntary Sector does not specify any guidelines on environmental issues, although it does states that organisations should pursue equal opportunities social policies with regard to:

■ assessing needs to be met
■ allocating resources, providing services and making grants, and
■ staff recruitment and training.

CASE QUESTION

Refer to the case study at the beginning of Part Four.

1 Has the company taken sufficient appropriate measures to restore its reputation on CSR issues? From the information available, does the company seem committed to acting as a corporate citizen?

2 What should be the role of the director who has been given responsibility for SEE issues and what should he be doing to perform this role effectively?

3 What are the risks to the company of failing to address concerns about its social and environmental policies?

CHAPTER SUMMARY

- Corporate social responsibility (CSR) is a concept whereby companies integrate social and environmental concerns into their business strategies, to complement financial concerns.
- CSR policies may be based on the principles of treating employees, fairly, behaving ethically, respecting human rights, sustaining the environment for future generations and being a responsible neighbour in the communities where the company operates.
- The board of directors is responsible for developing CSR strategies and monitoring the effectiveness of their implementation by management.
- CSR policies are usually seen as voluntary measures, in addition to statutory and regulatory requirements imposed by government.
- CSR as a concept is consistent with a stakeholder/pluralist approach to corporate governance, or an enlightened shareholder/integrated approach.
- Sustainability or sustainable development is a possible CSR objective. Sustainability is conducting a business in a way that sustains the environment for future environments and protects environmental resources in a way that will enable the business to continue operating into the foreseeable future. However, sustainability also recognises the need for companies to be profitable and financially secure in order to survive.
- In South Africa the King III Report recognises both sustainability and corporate citizenship as key governance objectives.
- There are several reasons for the development of concerns about and interest in CSR issues. Governments have increased social and environmental regulation, and companies have responded by improving their policies to exceed minimum regulatory requirements. Some major institutional investors have socially responsible investment (SRI) policies. Some companies have seen commercial benefits in the adoption of CSR policies.
- The OECD has issued guidelines for multinational enterprises, encouraging them to pursue CSR policies in the developing countries in which they operate.
- Companies may recognise the need to be seen to adopt CSR policies in order to avoid reputational risk. Some companies use CSR initiatives for PR and marketing purposes. In addition, some companies have identified ways in which environmentally beneficial initiatives can reduce costs or secure long-term supplies of key natural resources. It is recognised that consumers will not pay much extra for environmentally friendly goods; therefore there should also be commercial/financial reasons for CSR initiatives.
- In some countries, some large companies use CSR performance measures as a basis for calculating a large part of bonuses or long-term incentive rewards for senior executives.
- CSR is less clearly developed as an issue in the public sector and voluntary sector. This is because organisations in these sectors do not have a profit objective, and instead have an objective that can be associated with social or environmental issues.

Reporting corporate social responsibility and sustainability

■ CONTENTS

1 Reporting CSR issues to stakeholders
2 Voluntary CSR reporting
3 Sustainability reporting: triple bottom line reporting
4 Benchmarking and corporate social responsibility reporting

■ INTRODUCTION

The previous chapter explained the nature of CSR and sustainable development. Shareholders and other stakeholders have an interest in what a company has been doing and what it plans to do in the future to implement CSR measures. They expect to receive information on these matters, or to have access to information. Reporting by companies on CSR issues (or ESG issues) is a combination of regulatory requirement and voluntary disclosures. This chapter explains the nature and content of such reports.

---

1 Reporting CSR issues to stakeholders

It seems probable that CSR issues will remain as an important aspect of corporate governance. Companies will continue to pursue socially responsible policies, and good corporate governance practice, on a voluntary basis in addition to the requirements of law and regulations. Companies should also be expected to report on their CSR policies, objectives and performance.

■ The government may wish to encourage companies to provide CSR information to shareholders.
■ Investors may wish to know about a company's CSR policies, as well as its corporate governance policies, in order to make their investment decisions. The need for information is particularly important for institutional investors that have their own socially responsible investment (SRI) policies.
■ Other stakeholders, including employees and the general public, may have an interest in the CSR policies, plans and performance of companies.
■ Companies with CSR policies should report internally to management on actual performance. The board of directors may believe that it is good governance practice to provide much of this information to stakeholders. In other words, the impetus to report on CSR issues may come from companies themselves, as well as investors, the public and government.

1.1 Company reporting on social and environmental issues

In the UK, the Companies Act 2006 includes requirements for quoted companies to report on social and environmental issues. The Act states that, to the extent necessary for understanding the development, performance or position of the company's business, the business review should include information about:

SE

- environmental matters (including the impact of the company's business on the environment)
- the company's employees, and
- social and community issues.

To the extent necessary for understanding the development, performance or position of the company's business, a business review should also, where appropriate, include non-financial key performance indicators, including information relating to environmental matters and employee matters.

Although the Act makes it a statutory duty for companies to report on these matters, the decision about what should be reported, and how much should be reported, about social and environmental issues is left largely for the companies themselves to decide.

⊥ Principle risks rel - environ/ sust.

1.2 ABI guidelines to companies on CSR/ESG disclosures

The Association of British Insures (ABI) has issued guidelines (revised in 2007) on the disclosures about CSR issues that they expect companies to provide to their shareholders. These are broad guidelines to all companies about the types of disclosure that institutional investors will expect companies to make about social, ethical and environmental issues.

The guidelines, which are consistent with the UK company law requirements for coverage of ESG issues in the annual business review, state that shareholders place great value on 'narrative reporting which (1) sets environmental, social and governance (ESG) risks in the context of the whole range of risks and opportunities facing a company; (2) contains a forward-looking perspective; and (3) describes the actions of boards in mitigating these risks'.

There are three areas of ESG reporting where companies should make disclosures.

- ESG risk assessment by the board. The annual report should state whether, as a part of its regular assessment of risk, the board takes accounts of significant ESG risks; whether the board has identified any such risks to the company's short- and long-term value (and opportunities to enhance value that may arise by making an appropriate response); and that the company has effective systems in place for mitigating the significant risks.
- ESG risk: policies and procedures. The annual report should include information about significant ESG risks that could affect value and how they might impact on the company, together with a description of the policies and procedures for managing these risks (or a statement that there are no such policies or procedures). The report should also include information about the extent to which the company has complied with its policies and procedures for managing material risks (with key performance indicators (KPIs) where appropriate) and the role of the board in providing oversight.
- Remuneration and ESG issues. In the directors' remuneration report, the company should state whether the remuneration committee is able to consider ESG issues when setting the remuneration of executive directors, and whether the committee has ensured that the incentive structure for senior management does not raise ESG risks by 'inadvertently motivating irresponsible behaviour'.

The ABI commented that if companies provide these disclosures, this should help them to develop appropriate CSR policies and provide a constructive basis for 'engagement' between shareholders and their companies.

  TEST YOUR KNOWLEDGE 12.1

(a) What are the UK statutory requirements for companies to report on social and environmental issues in their annual report and accounts?

(b) What are the main ABI guidelines to companies about ESG reporting?

2 Voluntary CSR reporting

There are no legal requirements for companies to report on social, ethical and environmental (SEE) issues, other than the requirements for the business review. However, many listed companies voluntarily publish a report each year, as a means of communicating with a wider group of stakeholders, including not only shareholders but also employees, investors and the community in general. They may be called social and environmental (SE) reports, corporate social responsibility (CSR) reports, environmental, social and governance (ESG) reports or possibly sustainability reports. ESG reports include disclosures about governance issues as well as social and environmental issues.

These reports are commonly prepared as a separate booklet at the same time as the company's annual report and accounts.

2.1 The reason for social and environmental reports

There are various reasons why companies might want to report voluntarily on SEE issues.

- They might have a genuine concern for social and environmental issues, and consider that they are fulfilling their responsibilities to stakeholders by reporting on these matters.
- The company might recognise that its reputation with the public may be at risk because of the nature of their business activities. Mining companies and oil and gas extraction companies are examples, since the public is aware that they deplete the world's natural resources and pollute the environment. Reporting on social and environmental issues allows the company to demonstrate that it understands the concerns of society and explain how it is addressing them with its social and environmental policies.
- A company might see an opportunity to gain a competitive advantage over rival companies by reporting on its social and environmental policies. A company whose policies are 'greener' and more environmentally friendly than its competitors may hope to build their reputation and attract more customers.
- There might be pressure on companies to report more extensively on ESG issues from major shareholders or bodies representing investment institutions (e.g. the ABI or NAPF).
- Companies might recognise that the general public has lost trust in the ethical behaviour of companies, and reporting on ESG issues is a way of trying to rebuild such trust.

The mining group Xstrata has explained its reasons for publishing annual sustainability reports as follows:

'Our commitment to the principles of sustainable development is based on our belief that operating responsibly and to the highest international standards ... mitigates risk, creates opportunities and enhances our reputation and competitive position. In particular, a strong reputation for operational and environmental excellence and industry-leading community engagement enables us to gain access to new resources, maintain a social licence to operate from the communities associated with our operations, attract and retain the best people and access diverse and low-cost sources of capital.'

2.2 Reasons against voluntary social and environmental reporting

Although many listed companies do publish social and environmental reports, they can control the content of their reports. There might be an inclination to include 'good news' and exclude aspects of the company's social and environmental performance that would attract stakeholder disapproval. For example, a chemical manufacturing company might include a section on health and safety measures at its processing plants without reporting the actual number of accidents and injuries sustained by employees during the year.

There are various reasons why companies might not report social and environmental issues voluntarily.

- The company's directors and senior management might be insufficiently aware of social and environmental issues.
- Companies might be deterred by the cost of obtaining relevant information for reporting, or the difficulty in collecting reliable and useful social and environmental information.

- The company might be reluctant to disclose any information that it is under no legal requirement to provide, possibly to avoid giving sensitive data to competitors or regulators.
- The company might want to avoid the risk of damage to its reputation if it were to present unfavourable information about itself.

 CASE EXAMPLE 12.1

Companies in industries whose operations affect the environment are often very conscious of their SEE responsibilities, but also subject to much more pressure from ethical investors and environmental groups. In 2010, oil group BP was shortlisted for the UK's annual Corporate Responsibility Reporting Awards. At the same time a group of dissident shareholders proposed a resolution at the company's AGM in relation to the company's proposed investment in Canada's oil sands. Oil sands extraction produces more carbon dioxide than 'traditional' oil extraction, and is also damaging to the local environment.

The shareholder resolution proposed that the company should commission a report setting out the assumptions that it has used when deciding on investment in the oil sands, including factors such as the market price of oil, the cost of greenhouse gas emissions and legal and reputation risks arising from environmental damage. BP had already released much of this information, but it opposed the shareholder resolution because it called for commitment (in time and cost) to producing a special report to satisfy a particular shareholder interest group. The company believed that this would be interfering with the right of management to manage the company. At the same time the company acknowledged the environmental concerns and its chief executive officer (CEO) stated his belief that the company would be able to cut emissions more than expected through applications of new technology.

At the AGM there was a vote of only 5.6 per cent in favour of the shareholder resolution and 85.2 per cent against. However, environmental campaigners claimed success in bringing the matter to the attention of the public, and believed that the company would not now be able to ignore their views. The company chairman is reported to have said at the AGM 'This does not mean that we think the resolution is wrong. It only means that we think the concerns raised are in hand.'

This case raises an interesting question about the extent to which special interest groups of shareholders should be able to influence the actions of management. Was it right that the shareholder group tried to force the company to produce a special report, because it should be their right as owners of the company to bring this sort of pressure to bear on management? Or should management be left to manage the company? And if management is given a free hand to manage the company, to what extent should they take social and environmental concerns of shareholders into consideration when making their decisions?

The case of BP is also interesting because shortly after the matter of the Canada oil sands was dealt with, the company faced an even bigger environmental problem in the Gulf of Mexico, referred to in Chapter 11. In April 2010 a deep-sea oil rig exploded, killing 11 men and causing a major oil leak from the deep water well. The oil leak threatened the ecosystems of the Gulf of Mexico, including the shores of Louisiana, Alabama and Florida, and BP became liable for clean-up and legal costs amounting to billions of dollars. It was reported that a shareholder had sued the company, accusing it of putting profits before oil safety and asking for court-enforced changes to BP's corporate governance. The company responded quickly to the disaster, but could not escape accusations that its risk management and safety measures were not as good as company management had supposed.

2.3 Risk society theory of social and environmental reporting

In spite of reasons against social and environmental reporting, it seems probable that voluntary CSR/ESG reporting will increase, because stakeholders in companies want to be given the information that these reports contain.

In her book *Corporate Governance and Accountability* (2007 edition) Jill Solomon makes an interesting reference to risk society theory as a possible explanation of the big changes in society's attitudes to social, ethical and environmental issues. Risk society theory was developed in the early 1990s by Ulrich Beck, a German sociologist. He argued that in today's society there has been an increase in 'high consequence risks' such as global warming and the risk of a major nuclear accident or incident. The whole of society is affected by these risks, at a global level, and although human and corporate behaviour has contributed to these problems, they are largely unmanageable and the blame cannot be placed entirely on specific causes and specific companies. A clear connection between cause and effect does not exist.

As a result, people have lost trust in its leaders and in institutions. They do not believe that companies have genuine ethical, social or environmental concerns, and do believe that companies act unethically and damage society and the environment through their self-centred activities.

Risk society theory can be used to suggest that companies see voluntary social and environmental reporting as an attempt to rebuild public trust in the company. Communicating with stakeholders on these issues is a necessary step towards re-establishing trust.

2.4 The content of social and environmental reports

There are no rules about what CSR reports should contain, or how CSR information should be presented. Some companies produce a separate social and environmental report. Others give information about social, ethical and environmental issues in the chairman's report or report of the CEO in the published annual report and accounts, as well as in the business review. Many CSR reports have consisted largely of a narrative report with some quantitative measures of targets and performance levels achieved.

Reporting on environmental performance: 'Environmental footprints'

A company might report its environmental performance in terms of selected quantitative measures, which are sometimes referred to as its 'environmental footprint'. The measurements for each individual company might vary according to the nature of its business, but it is generally accepted that a company's impact on the environment can be measured in terms of impact on the air, water or land, or 'noise pollution'. Reported environmental performance targets and measurements of actual performance may be:

- the company's use of key resources such as land, and also its consumption of materials subject to depletion (such as quantities of livestock, wild fish or forest timber) and non-renewable resources (such as coal, oil and natural gas, reported perhaps in terms of total energy use for lighting and heating, total fuel use for transport, total water usage)
- pollution caused by the company's activities, measured (for example) in terms of carbon dioxide emissions, chemical waste or spillages of oil
- an assessment in either qualitative or quantitative terms of the broader effect of the company's resource consumption and pollution on the environment.

TEST YOUR KNOWLEDGE 12.2

(a) Why might companies decide to produce voluntary CSR reports?
(b) What might be the arguments against voluntary CSR reporting by companies?

3 Sustainability reporting: triple bottom line reporting

Chapter 11 describes sustainable development as an approach to developing and growing a business that does not put at risk the ability of the business to continue into the foreseeable future. To do this, companies must be profitable, but they must also consider social and environmental issues. Companies that have a policy of sustainable development may produce an annual sustainability report. This is similar to a CSR report but with more quantitative performance measures. Sustainability reports also the importance of financial objectives as well as social and environmental targets, and so are possibly targeted more at shareholders and other investors rather than the general public.

Sustainability reports are also known as **triple bottom line reporting**. The term 'triple bottom line' was coined in 1994 by John Elkington. Its aim is to encourage companies to recognise social and environmental issues in their business reporting systems, as well as financial issues. Its use is encouraged by the Global Reporting Initiative (GRI), an internationally recognised body that promotes sustainability reporting. The term 'triple bottom line' comes from the fact that sustainability reports should provide key measurements for three aspects of performance:

1   economic indicators
2   environmental indicators
3   social indicators.

Triple bottom line reporting is therefore providing a quantitative summary of a company's economic, environmental and social performance over the previous year.

3.1 Economic indicators

Economic indicators in sustainability reports are measures typically associated with financial reporting, such as measurements relating to:

- sales revenue
- profits, earnings and earnings per share
- dividends per share
- global market share (the percentage share of the global market captured by the company's products or services)
- in industries manufacturing standard products, such as car production, units of sale worldwide.

3.2 Social indicators

Social indicators might include measures relating to employment and employees, and measurements relating to society and the community, such as:

- employee diversity (e.g. the percentage of its employees who were female and the percentage who came from minority groups)
- the recordable injury rate per 1,000 employees
- work done by the company in communities of developing countries to provide better standards of education and health.

3.3 Environmental indicators

Environmental indicators might include measurements relating to targets for:

- reducing the consumption of materials in products and services;
- reducing energy use
- minimising the release of toxic materials/pollutants;
- improving the recycling of materials
- maximising the use of renewable resources
- extending the life of a product.

3.4 Limitations of triple bottom line reporting

There are several limitations to triple bottom line reporting.

- There are no widely established standards for triple bottom line reporting, and no standard methods for measuring social and environmental impacts. It is therefore to compare the sustainability of one company with the sustainability of another.
- The GRI is attempting to standardise measurements for the triple bottom line and has published Sustainability Reporting Guidelines since 1999 (see later in this chapter).

■ If the social and environmental measures are not subject to independent audit, there might be doubts about the reliability of the data presented in a company's report. Companies have a vested interest in presenting 'good news' but withholding 'bad news' in any form of voluntary reporting.

3.5 The King III Code in South Africa: integrated reporting

The King III Code in South Africa requires listed companies to produce reports that are similar in concept to sustainability reports. The Code recommends that companies should produce an integrated report each year, that reports on:

■ financial results, and how the company made its money, and
■ environmental, social and governance issues.

Just as financial results are audited, the Code requires that 'sustainability issues' should also be subject to some form of independent assurance. The Code does not comment on how independent assurance should be obtained, except to state that obtaining the assurance should be the responsibility of the audit committee. However, there are firms of independent environmental auditors capable of doing this work.

An important feature of integrated reporting is that 'sustainability reporting and disclosures' (which the King Report defines as reporting on ESG issues) should be integrated with financial reporting into a single report for shareholders (and other stakeholders).

STOP AND THINK 12.1

Use an internet search engine such as Google to locate examples of CSR reports (or social and environmental reports) by large listed companies, and make an assessment of the nature and value of the information that they provide.

TEST YOUR KNOWLEDGE 12.3

(a) What is triple bottom line reporting?
(b) How do triple bottom line reports differ in content from SEE reports?
(c) What are the provisions in the King III Code for reporting on ESG matters?

4 Benchmarking and corporate social responsibility reporting

A major problem with ESG reporting is the diversity of environmental and social issues, and the varying importance of these issues for different companies. Users of reports may want to compare the performance of different companies, but without standards for the content and format of reports, it is difficult to make such comparisons.

Developments in CSR reporting have been assisted by cooperation between companies willing to have their policies and practices assessed and compared with those of other companies, in all industrial sectors. Comparisons provide benchmarks for comparison and standards for attainment. Given suitable data, they can also be used to establish an index for CSR performance measurement.

4.1 CSR indices

There are now several indices that measure and rate companies in terms of their CSR performance. These include the Dow Jones Sustainability Indices and the FTSE4Good Index Series.

The Dow Jones Sustainability Indices, first published in 1999, are indices that track the financial performance of the leading sustainability-driven companies worldwide. The advantage for companies of inclusion in an index is that a number of investment funds base their investment policy on holding a portfolio of shares of companies within a Dow Jones Sustainability Index. Companies must apply to qualify for inclusion in an index, and the selection of companies for inclusion in each index is based on a corporate sustainability assessment. Much of the information for an assessment is supplied by the companies themselves, which complete a questionnaire. External assurance is provided to ensure that the corporate sustainability assessments are completed in accordance with the defined rules.

The FTSE4Good Index Series is similar in purpose to the Dow Jones Sustainability Indices. They are intended to appeal to investors who wish to invest only in companies with good standards in CSR, or who want to minimise the social and environmental risks in their investment portfolios. The criteria for selecting companies for inclusion in the Index Series 'have been designed to identify companies that meet globally recognised and accepted responsible investment criteria'. Companies are not accepted for inclusion unless they meet certain criteria, and companies that fall below the standards required are deleted from their index. To be included in an index, companies need to demonstrate that they are working towards environmental management, climate change mitigation and adaptation, countering bribery and upholding human and labour rights.

4.2 BiTC Corporate Responsibility Index

Another interesting development in the UK has been the Corporate Responsibility Index published annually by Business in the Community (BiTC). The index is derived from over 100 UK companies in different industries that volunteer to be assessed. The assessments are then developed into scores on a 100-point scale relating to:

- each company's CSR strategies
- its success in integrating the strategies into its business operations, and
- the company's management practices that have an impact on four key areas – the community, the environment, the marketplace and the workplace.

The index does not publish the scores for individual companies, but the participating companies are divided into five groups, ranging from a top group whose index scores were above a certain level to those in the bottom group whose scores were below a certain level.

4.3 Conversion factors to standardise measurements and provide comparability

Comparability between companies on environmental performance can be improved by government guidance. In the UK, the Department for the Environment, Forestry and Rural Affairs (Defra) has issued guidelines on the use of conversion factors for environmental reporting. Conversion factors can be used to convert measures of resource consumption, or activities that create emissions or waste, into a small number of standard environmental performance measures. Reporting environmental performance in terms of a limited number of measures (such as carbon dioxide emissions, landfill quantities, water consumption and so on, which are all measured using the same conversion factors) provides comparability that would not otherwise be possible.

For example, a company may wish to report on the quantity of greenhouse gases it has emitted during the year.

- One source of emissions is boilers. Companies can measure their yearly energy consumption from the use of boilers by measuring the kilowatt hours (kWh) and converting this into tonnes of CO_2 emitted using conversion factors provided by defra.
- Another source of emissions is the consumption of fuel by motor vehicles used by a company's employees and vehicle fleets. The distance travelled by vehicles during the year can be measured from employees' expenses claims and annual servicing records of fleet vehicles. The total mileage can be converted into tonnes of CO_2 emitted using conversion factors provided by Defra.

Another measure of environmental performance is the quantity of landfill waste produced. The volume of waste produced by a company can be measured by the number of bins or skips removed for recycling, and this can be converted into landfill quantities using a defra conversion factor.

Other standard measures of environmental performance are also produced by UK companies using defra conversion factors.

4.4 The GRI Reporting Framework: sustainability reporting

The Global Reporting Initiative (GRI) is an organisation that has developed a framework for sustainability reporting. It sets out the principles and indicators that companies can use to report on their economic, social and environmental performance. The GRI reporting framework is based on a number of general guidelines for all companies, together with unique indicators for industry sectors. Reports produced using the GRI framework are similar in format and use similar performance measures (standardised disclosures) calculated on a similar basis.

The framework is currently in its third generation of development and the most recent 'third generation', issued in 2006, is referred to as the 'GRI 3G' guidelines. These guidelines include:

- reporting principles and guidance, which consist of principles and guidance about the content, quality and boundary of sustainability reports, and
- standard disclosures, including standard performance indicators.

The GRI has commented that its Sustainability Reporting Framework is:

'applicable to organisations of any size or type, and from any sector or geographic region, and has been used by thousands of organisations worldwide as the basis for their sustainability reporting. It facilitates transparency and accountability and accountability by organisations, and provides stakeholders a universally applicable, comparable framework from which to understand disclosed information.'

TEST YOUR KNOWLEDGE 12.4

(a) What is the purpose of conversion factors for measuring waste, pollution and the consumption of non-renewable natural resources?
(b) What is the **GRI Sustainability Reporting Framework?**

CASE QUESTION

1 Why might there be limited interest in the company's social and environmental reports?
2 What weaknesses are evident in the company's social and environmental reporting, and what measures could be taken to improve the standard and quality of reporting?

CHAPTER SUMMARY

- Companies provide information on CSR issues to shareholders and other stakeholders, partly because of statutory requirements, partly in response to investor expectations and partly as a result of wanting to publicise the company's CSR performance and policies (possibly for public relations purposes).
- In the UK, quoted companies are required by the Companies Act to include information about environmental, employee and social/community issues in their business review.

- The ABI has issued guidelines to companies on the environmental, social and governance information they should include in reports to shareholders. This should include information about the ESG responsibilities of the board ESG policies and the extent to which ESG performance is used as a basis for deciding executive remuneration (bonuses and long-term incentives).
- Companies may produce voluntary reports on CSR issues for all stakeholders. These reports are generally produced annually at the same time as the annual report and accounts, and published as a separate document. The report may be called a CSR report, a social and environmental (SE) report, a social ethical and environmental (SEE) report, or an environmental, social and governance (ESG) report.
- A problem with these reports is that they do not have a standard format or content, and the directors choose what information to put in and what to keep out. Most CSR reports are not externally checked and approved by specialist 'auditors'; therefore, their objectivity is open to question.
- Sustainability reports are reports that report on three aspects of performance: economic (financial) social and environmental. They include quantitative measures of performance for all three aspects. Unlike CSR reports they do not focus on social and environmental issues, and they recognise that economic performance is important. Producing sustainability reports based on these three aspects of performance is called triple bottom line reporting.
- The King III Report in South Africa calls for listed companies to produce integrated annual reports that combine reporting on financial matters with reporting on CSR issues.
- Companies may produce CSR reports or sustainability reports for marketing or public relations (PR) reasons.
- A problem with CSR reporting is the lack of standardisation in content and quantitative measures of social or environmental performance. It is also difficult for investors to compare the 'CSR credentials' of different companies.
- Comparability is provided to some extent for investors by specialist indices such as the Dow Jones Sustainability Indices and the FTSE4Good Index Series. Companies apply for inclusion in the index but to do so must meet certain requirements. Investors can then make investment decisions based on whether the company is in one of these indices and their position within it.
- Comparability on CSR performance between companies in the same industrial sector is provided in the UK by the BiTC Corporate Responsibility Index. Inclusion in an index for companies is voluntary.
- There are also conversion factors whereby companies can convert measures of pollution or waste creation, or measures of the consumption of non-renewable natural resources, into standard measures of pollution or resource consumption. This improves the comparability of environmental performance reports of companies that use the same conversion factors. In the UK conversion factors are provided by the government.
- On a global basis, a standardised framework for reporting on CSR issues is provided by the GRI Sustainability Reporting Framework.

APPENDIX 1

The UK Corporate Governance Code

June 2010

GOVERNANCE AND THE CODE

1. The purpose of corporate governance is to facilitate effective, entrepreneurial and prudent management that can deliver the long-term success of the company.
2. The first version of the UK Code on Corporate Governance (the Code) was produced in 1992 by the Cadbury Committee. Its paragraph 2.5 is still the classic definition of the context of the Code:

> Corporate governance is the system by which companies are directed and controlled. Boards of directors are responsible for the governance of their companies. The shareholders' role in governance is to appoint the directors and the auditors and to satisfy themselves that an appropriate governance structure is in place. The responsibilities of the board include setting the company's strategic aims, providing the leadership to put them into effect, supervising the management of the business and reporting to shareholders on their stewardship. The board's actions are subject to laws, regulations and the shareholders in general meeting.

3. Corporate governance is therefore about what the board of a company does and how it sets the values of the company, and is to be distinguished from the day to day operational management of the company by full-time executives.
4. The Code is a guide to a number of key components of effective board practice. It is based on the underlying principles of all good governance: accountability, transparency, probity and focus on the sustainable success of an entity over the longer term.
5. The Code has been enduring, but it is not immutable. Its fitness for purpose in a permanently changing economic and social business environment requires its evaluation at appropriate intervals. The reviews preceding this one were in 2005 and 2007. The Preface, which should be regarded as an integral part of the Code, introduces the changes made in the current review.
6. The new Code applies to accounting periods beginning on or after 29 June 2010 and, as a result of the new Listing Regime introduced in April 2010, applies to all companies with a Premium Listing of equity shares regardless of whether they are incorporated in the UK or elsewhere.

PREFACE

1. The financial crisis which came to a head in 2008-09 triggered widespread reappraisal, locally and internationally, of the governance systems which might have alleviated it. In the UK, Sir David Walker was asked to review the governance of banks and other financial institutions, and the FRC decided to bring forward the Code review scheduled for 2010 so that corporate governance in other listed companies could be assessed at the same time.
2. Two principal conclusions were drawn by the FRC from its review. First, that much more attention needed to be paid to following the spirit of the Code as well as its letter. Secondly, that the impact of shareholders in monitoring the Code could and should be enhanced by better interaction between the boards of listed companies and their shareholders. To this end, the FRC has assumed responsibility for a stewardship code that will provide guidance on good practice for investors.

3. Nearly two decades of constructive usage have enhanced the prestige of the Code. Indeed, it seems that there is almost a belief that complying with the Code in itself constitutes good governance. The Code, however, is of necessity limited to being a guide only in general terms to principles, structure and processes. It cannot guarantee effective board behaviour because the range of situations in which it is applicable is much too great for it to attempt to mandate behaviour more specifically than it does. Boards therefore have a lot of room within the framework of the Code to decide for themselves how they should act.

4. To follow the spirit of the Code to good effect, boards must think deeply, thoroughly and on a continuing basis, about their overall tasks and the implications of these for the roles of their individual members. Absolutely key in this endeavour are the leadership of the chairman of a board, the support given to and by the CEO, and the frankness and openness of mind with which issues are discussed and tackled by all directors.

5. The challenge should not be underrated. To run a corporate board successfully is extremely demanding. Constraints on time and knowledge combine with the need to maintain mutual respect and openness between a cast of strong, able and busy directors dealing with each other across the different demands of executive and non-executive roles. To achieve good governance requires continuing and high quality effort.

6. The Code's function should be to help boards discharge their duties in the best interests of their companies. The FRC in this review has focussed on changing the "tone" of the Code by making limited but significant changes to signal the importance of the general principles which should guide board behaviours. It is to be hoped that these changes will promote greater clarity and understanding with regard to the tasks of a board and that communication with shareholders will be more effective as a result.

7. Chairmen are encouraged to report personally in their annual statements how the principles relating to the role and effectiveness of the board (in Sections A and B of the new Code) have been applied. Not only will this give investors a clearer picture of the steps taken by boards to operate effectively but also, by providing fuller context, it may make investors more willing to accept explanations when a company chooses to explain rather than to comply with one or more provisions. Above all, the personal reporting on governance by chairmen as the leaders of boards might be a turning point in attacking the fungus of "boiler-plate" which is so often the preferred and easy option in sensitive areas but which is dead communication.

8. The new Code recommends that, in the interests of greater accountability, all directors of FTSE 350 companies should be subject to annual re-election. As with all other provisions of the Code, companies are free to explain rather than comply if they believe that their existing arrangements ensure proper accountability and underpin board effectiveness, or that a transitional period is needed before they introduce annual re-election. The boards of smaller companies are also encouraged to consider their policy on director re-election.

Financial Reporting Council
June 2010

COMPLY OR EXPLAIN

1. The "comply or explain" approach is the trademark of corporate governance in the UK. It has been in operation since the Code's beginnings and is the foundation of the Code's flexibility. It is strongly supported by both companies and shareholders and has been widely admired and imitated internationally.

2. The Code is not a rigid set of rules. It consists of principles (main and supporting) and provisions. The Listing Rules require companies to apply the Main Principles and report to shareholders on how they have done so. The principles are the core of the Code and the way in which they are applied should be the central question for a board as it determines how it is to operate according to the Code.

3. It is recognised that an alternative to following a provision may be justified in particular circumstances if good governance can be achieved by other means. A condition of doing so is that the reasons for it should be explained clearly and carefully to shareholders[1], who may

---

[1] References to shareholders also apply to intermediaries and agents employed to assist shareholders in scrutinising governance arrangements.

wish to discuss the position with the company and whose voting intentions may be influenced as a result. In providing an explanation, the company should aim to illustrate how its actual practices are both consistent with the principle to which the particular provision relates and contribute to good governance.

4. In their responses to explanations, shareholders should pay due regard to companies' individual circumstances and bear in mind, in particular, the size and complexity of the company and the nature of the risks and challenges it faces. Whilst shareholders have every right to challenge companies' explanations if they are unconvincing, they should not be evaluated in a mechanistic way and departures from the Code should not be automatically treated as breaches. Shareholders should be careful to respond to the statements from companies in a manner that supports the "comply or explain" process and bearing in mind the purpose of good corporate governance. They should put their views to the company and both parties should be prepared to discuss the position.

5. Smaller listed companies, in particular those new to listing, may judge that some of the provisions are disproportionate or less relevant in their case. Some of the provisions do not apply to companies below the FTSE 350. Such companies may nonetheless consider that it would be appropriate to adopt the approach in the Code and they are encouraged to do so. Externally managed investment companies typically have a different board structure which may affect the relevance of particular provisions; the Association of Investment Companies' Corporate Governance Code and Guide can assist them in meeting their obligations under the Code.

6. Satisfactory engagement between company boards and investors is crucial to the health of the UK's corporate governance regime. Companies and shareholders both have responsibility for ensuring that "comply or explain" remains an effective alternative to a rules-based system. There are practical and administrative obstacles to improved interaction between boards and shareholders. But certainly there is also scope for an increase in trust which could generate a virtuous upward spiral in attitudes to the Code and in its constructive use.

THE MAIN PRINCIPLES OF THE CODE

Section A: Leadership

Every company should be headed by an effective board which is collectively responsible for the long-term success of the company.

There should be a clear division of responsibilities at the head of the company between the running of the board and the executive responsibility for the running of the company's business. No one individual should have unfettered powers of decision.

The chairman is responsible for leadership of the board and ensuring its effectiveness on all aspects of its role.

As part of their role as members of a unitary board, non-executive directors should constructively challenge and help develop proposals on strategy.

Section B: Effectiveness

The board and its committees should have the appropriate balance of skills, experience, independence and knowledge of the company to enable them to discharge their respective duties and responsibilities effectively.

There should be a formal, rigorous and transparent procedure for the appointment of new directors to the board.

All directors should be able to allocate sufficient time to the company to discharge their responsibilities effectively.

All directors should receive induction on joining the board and should regularly update and refresh their skills and knowledge.

The board should be supplied in a timely manner with information in a form and of a quality appropriate to enable it to discharge its duties.

The board should undertake a formal and rigorous annual evaluation of its own performance and that of its committees and individual directors.

All directors should be submitted for re-election at regular intervals, subject to continued satisfactory performance.

Section C: Accountability

The board should present a balanced and understandable assessment of the company's position and prospects.

The board is responsible for determining the nature and extent of the significant risks it is willing to take in achieving its strategic objectives. The board should maintain sound risk management and internal control systems.

The board should establish formal and transparent arrangements for considering how they should apply the corporate reporting and risk management and internal control principles and for maintaining an appropriate relationship with the company's auditor.

Section D: Remuneration

Levels of remuneration should be sufficient to attract, retain and motivate directors of the quality required to run the company successfully, but a company should avoid paying more than is necessary for this purpose. A significant proportion of executive directors' remuneration should be structured so as to link rewards to corporate and individual performance.

There should be a formal and transparent procedure for developing policy on executive remuneration and for fixing the remuneration packages of individual directors. No director should be involved in deciding his or her own remuneration.

Section E: Relations with Shareholders

There should be a dialogue with shareholders based on the mutual understanding of objectives. The board as a whole has responsibility for ensuring that a satisfactory dialogue with shareholders takes place.

The board should use the AGM to communicate with investors and to encourage their participation.

SECTION A: LEADERSHIP

A.1 The Role of the Board

Main Principle

Every company should be headed by an effective board which is collectively responsible for the long-term success of the company.

Supporting Principles

The board's role is to provide entrepreneurial leadership of the company within a framework of prudent and effective controls which enables risk to be assessed and managed. The board should set the company's strategic aims, ensure that the necessary financial and human resources are in place for the company to meet its objectives and review management performance. The board should set the company's values and standards and ensure that its obligations to its shareholders and others are understood and met.

All directors must act in what they consider to be the best interests of the company, consistent with their statutory duties[2].

Code Provisions

A.1.1   The board should meet sufficiently regularly to discharge its duties effectively. There should be a formal schedule of matters specifically reserved for its decision. The annual report should include a statement of how the board operates, including a high level statement of which types of decisions are to be taken by the board and which are to be delegated to management.

---

[2] For directors of UK incorporated companies, these duties are set out in the Sections 170 to 177 of the Companies Act 2006.

existence of relationships or circumstances which may appear relevant to its determination, including if the director:

- has been an employee of the company or group within t he last five years;
- has, or has had within the last three years, a material business relationship with the company either directly, or as a partner, shareholder, director or senior employee of a body that has such a relationship with the company;
- has received or receives additional remuneration from the company apart from a director's fee, participates in the company's share option or a performance-related pay scheme, or is a member of the company's pension scheme;
- has close family ties with any of the company's advisers, directors or senior employees;
- holds cross-directorships or has significant links with other directors through involvement in other companies or bodies;
- represents a significant shareholder; or
- has served on the board for more than nine years from the date of their first election.

B.1.2 Except for smaller companies[6], at least half the board, excluding the chairman, should comprise non-executive directors determined by the board to be independent. A smaller company should have at least two independent non-executive directors.

B.2 Appointments to the Board

Main Principle

There should be a formal, rigorous and transparent procedure for the appointment of new directors to the board.

Supporting Principles

The search for board candidates should be conducted, and appointments made, on merit, against objective criteria and with due regard for the benefits of diversity on the board, including gender.

The board should satisfy itself that plans are in place for orderly succession for appointments to the board and to senior management, so as to maintain an appropriate balance of skills and experience within the company and on the board and to ensure progressive refreshing of the board.

Code Provisions

B.2.1 There should be a nomination committee which should lead the process for board appointments and make recommendations to the board. A majority of members of the nomination committee should be independent non-executive directors. The chairman or an independent non-executive director should chair the committee, but the chairman should not chair the nomination committee when it is dealing with the appointment of a successor to the chairmanship. The nomination committee should make available its terms of reference, explaining its role and the authority delegated to it by the board[7].

B.2.2 The nomination committee should evaluate the balance of skills, experience, independence and knowledge on the board and, in the light of this evaluation, prepare a description of the role and capabilities required for a particular appointment.

B.2.3 Non-executive directors should be appointed for specified terms subject to re-election and to statutory provisions relating to the removal of a director. Any term beyond six years for a non-executive director should be subject to particularly rigorous review, and should take into account the need for progressive refreshing of the board.

---

[6] A smaller company is one that is below the FTSE 350 throughout the year immediately prior to the reporting year.

[7] The requirement to make the information available would be met by including the information on a website that is maintained by or on behalf of the company.

B.2.4 A separate section of the annual report should describe the work of the nomination committee[8], including the process it has used in relation to board appointments. An explanation should be given if neither an external search consultancy nor open advertising has been used in the appointment of a chairman or a non-executive director.

B.3 Commitment

Main Principle

All directors should be able to allocate sufficient time to the company to discharge their responsibilities effectively.

Code Provisions

B.3.1 For the appointment of a chairman, the nomination committee should prepare a job specification, including an assessment of the time commitment expected, recognising the need for availability in the event of crises. A chairman's other significant commitments should be disclosed to the board before appointment and included in the annual report. Changes to such commitments should be reported to the board as they arise, and their impact explained in the next annual report.

B.3.2 The terms and conditions of appointment of non-executive directors should be made available for inspection[9]. The letter of appointment should set out the expected time commitment. Non-executive directors should undertake that they will have sufficient time to meet what is expected of them. Their other significant commitments should be disclosed to the board before appointment, with a broad indication of the time involved and the board should be informed of subsequent changes.

B.3.3 The board should not agree to a full time executive director taking on more than one non-executive directorship in a FTSE 100 company nor the chairmanship of such a company.

B.4 Development

Main Principle

All directors should receive induction on joining the board and should regularly update and refresh their skills and knowledge.

Supporting Principles

The chairman should ensure that the directors continually update their skills and the knowledge and familiarity with the company required to fulfil their role both on the board and on board committees. The company should provide the necessary resources for developing and updating its directors' knowledge and capabilities.

To function effectively, all directors need appropriate knowledge of the company and access to its operations and staff.

Code Provisions

B.4.1 The chairman should ensure that new directors receive a full, formal and tailored induction on joining the board. As part of this, directors should avail themselves of opportunities to meet major shareholders.

B.4.2 The chairman should regularly review and agree with each director their training and development needs.

---

[8] This provision overlaps with FSA Rule DTR 7.2.7 R (see Schedule B).

[9] The terms and conditions of appointment of non-executive directors should be made available for inspection by any person at the company's registered office during normal business hours and at the AGM (for 15 minutes prior to the meeting and during the meeting).

B.5 Information and Support

Main Principle

The board should be supplied in a timely manner with information in a form and of a quality appropriate to enable it to discharge its duties.

Supporting Principles

The chairman is responsible for ensuring that the directors receive accurate, timely and clear information. Management has an obligation to provide such information but directors should seek clarification or amplification where necessary.

Under the direction of the chairman, the company secretary's responsibilities include ensuring good information flows within the board and its committees and between senior management and non-executive directors, as well as facilitating induction and assisting with professional development as required.

The company secretary should be responsible for advising the board through the chairman on all governance matters.

Code Provisions

B.5.1   The board should ensure that directors, especially non-executive directors, have access to independent professional advice at the company's expense where they judge it necessary to discharge their responsibilities as directors. Committees should be provided with sufficient resources to undertake their duties.

B.5.2   All directors should have access to the advice and services of the company secretary, who is responsible to the board for ensuring that board procedures are complied with. Both the appointment and removal of the company secretary should be a matter for the board as a whole.

B.6 Evaluation

Main Principle

The board should undertake a formal and rigorous annual evaluation of its own performance and that of its committees and individual directors.

Supporting Principles

The chairman should act on the results of the performance evaluation by recognising the strengths and addressing the weaknesses of the board and, where appropriate, proposing new members be appointed to the board or seeking the resignation of directors.

Individual evaluation should aim to show whether each director continues to contribute effectively and to demonstrate commitment to the role (including commitment of time for board and committee meetings and any other duties).

Code Provisions

B.6.1   The board should state in the annual report how performance evaluation of the board, its committees and its individual directors has been conducted.

B.6.2   Evaluation of the board of FTSE 350 companies should be externally facilitated at least every three years. A statement should be made available of whether an external facilitator has any other connection with the company[10].

B.6.3   The non-executive directors, led by the senior independent director, should be responsible for performance evaluation of the chairman, taking into account the views of executive directors.

B.7 Re-election

Main Principle

All directors should be submitted for re-election at regular intervals, subject to continued satisfactory performance.

---

[10] See footnote 7.

Code Provisions

B.7.1   All directors of FTSE 350 companies should be subject to annual election by shareholders. All other directors should be subject to election by shareholders at the first annual general meeting after their appointment, and to re-election thereafter at intervals of no more than three years. Non-executive directors who have served longer than nine years should be subject to annual re-election. The names of directors submitted for election or re-election should be accompanied by sufficient biographical details and any other relevant information to enable shareholders to take an informed decision on their election.

B.7.2   The board should set out to shareholders in the papers accompanying a resolution to elect a non-executive director why they believe an individual should be elected. The chairman should confirm to shareholders when proposing re-election that, following formal performance evaluation, the individual's performance continues to be effective and to demonstrate commitment to the role.

SECTION C: ACCOUNTABILITY

C.1 Financial and Business Reporting

Main Principle

The board should present a balanced and understandable assessment of the company's position and prospects.

Supporting Principle

The board's responsibility to present a balanced and understandable assessment extends to interim and other price-sensitive public reports and reports to regulators as well as to information required to be presented by statutory requirements.

Code Provisions

C.1.1   The directors should explain in the annual report their responsibility for preparing the annual report and accounts, and there should be a statement by the auditor about their reporting responsibilities[11].

C.1.2   The directors should include in the annual report an explanation of the basis on which the company generates or preserves value over the longer term (the business model) and the strategy for delivering the objectives of the company[12].

C.1.3   The directors should report in annual and half-yearly financial statements that the business is a going concern, with supporting assumptions or qualifications as necessary[13].

C.2 Risk Management and Internal Control[14]

Main Principle

The board is responsible for determining the nature and extent of the significant risks it is willing to take in achieving its strategic objectives. The board should maintain sound risk management and internal control systems.

---

[11] The requirement may be met by the disclosures about the audit scope and the responsibilities of the auditor included, or referred to, in the auditor's report pursuant to the requirements in paragraph 16 of ISA (UK and Ireland) 700, "The Auditor's Report on Financial Statements". Copies are available at: www.frc.org.uk/apb/publications/pub2102.html.

[12] It would be desirable if the explanation were located in the same part of the annual report as the Business Review required by Section 417 of the Companies Act 2006. Guidance as to the matters that should be considered in an explanation of a business model is provided in paragraphs 30 to 32 of the Accounting Standard Board's Reporting Statement: Operating And Financial Review. Copies are available at: www.frc.org.uk/asb/publications/documents.cfm?cat=7.

[13] 'Going Concern and Liquidity Risk: Guidance for Directors of UK Companies 2009' suggests means of applying this part of the Code. Copies are available at: www.frc.org.uk/corporate/goingconcern.cfm.

[14] The Turnbull guidance suggests means of applying this part of the Code. Copies are available at www.frc.org.uk/corporate/internalcontrol.cfm.

Code Provision

C.2.1   The board should, at least annually, conduct a review of the effectiveness of the company's risk management and internal control systems and should report to shareholders that they have done so[15]. The review should cover all material controls, including financial, operational and compliance controls.

C.3 Audit Committee and Auditors[16]

Main Principle

The board should establish formal and transparent arrangements for considering how they should apply the corporate reporting and risk management and internal control principles and for maintaining an appropriate relationship with the company's auditor.

Code Provisions

C.3.1   The board should establish an audit committee of at least three, or in the case of smaller companies[17] two, independent non-executive directors. In smaller companies the company chairman may be a member of, but not chair, the committee in addition to the independent non-executive directors, provided he or she was considered independent on appointment as chairman. The board should satisfy itself that at least one member of the audit committee has recent and relevant financial experience[18].

C.3.2   The main role and responsibilities of the audit committee should be set out in written terms of reference[19] and should include:
- to monitor the integrity of the financial statements of the company and any formal announcements relating to the company's financial performance, reviewing significant financial reporting judgements contained in them;
- to review the company's internal financial controls and, unless expressly addressed by a separate board risk committee composed of independent directors, or by the board itself, to review the company's internal control and risk management systems;
- to monitor and review the effectiveness of the company's internal audit function;
- to make recommendations to the board, for it to put to the shareholders for their approval in general meeting, in relation to the appointment, re-appointment and removal of the external auditor and to approve the remuneration and terms of engagement of the external auditor;
- to review and monitor the external auditor's independence and objectivity and the effectiveness of the audit process, taking into consideration relevant UK professional and regulatory requirements;
- to develop and implement policy on the engagement of the external auditor to supply non-audit services, taking into account relevant ethical guidance regarding the provision of non-audit services by the external audit firm, and to report to the board, identifying any matters in respect of which it considers that action or improvement is needed and making recommendations as to the steps to be taken.

C.3.3   The terms of reference of the audit committee, including its role and the authority delegated to it by the board, should be made available[20]. A separate section of the annual report should describe the work of the committee in discharging those responsibilities[21].

C.3.4   The audit committee should review arrangements by which staff of the company may, in confidence, raise concerns about possible improprieties in matters of financial reporting or other matters. The audit committee's objective should be to ensure that

---

[15] In addition FSA Rule DTR 7.2.5 R requires companies to describe the main features of the internal control and risk management systems in relation to the financial reporting process.

[16] The FRC Guidance on Audit Committees suggests means of applying this part of the Code. Copies are available at: www.frc.org.uk/corporate/auditcommittees.cfm.

[17] See footnote 6.

[18] This provision overlaps with FSA Rule DTR 7.1.1 R (see Schedule B).

[19] This provision overlaps with FSA Rules DTR 7.1.3 R (see Schedule C).

[20] See footnote 7.

[21] This provision overlaps with FSA Rules DTR 7.1.5 R and 7.2.7 R (see Schedule B).

arrangements are in place for the proportionate and independent investigation of such matters and for appropriate follow-up action.

C.3.5   The audit committee should monitor and review the effectiveness of the internal audit activities. Where there is no internal audit function, the audit committee should consider annually whether there is a need for an internal audit function and make a recommendation to the board, and the reasons for the absence of such a function should be explained in the relevant section of the annual report.

C.3.6   The audit committee should have primary responsibility for making a recommendation on the appointment, reappointment and removal of the external auditor. If the board does not accept the audit committee's recommendation, it should include in the annual report, and in any papers recommending appointment or re-appointment, a statement from the audit committee explaining the recommendation and should set out reasons why the board has taken a different position.

C.3.7   The annual report should explain to shareholders how, if the auditor provides non-audit services, auditor objectivity and independence is safeguarded.

SECTION D: REMUNERATION

D.1 The Level and Components of Remuneration

Main Principle

Levels of remuneration should be sufficient to attract, retain and motivate directors of the quality required to run the company successfully, but a company should avoid paying more than is necessary for this purpose. A significant proportion of executive directors' remuneration should be structured so as to link rewards to corporate and individual performance.

Supporting Principle

The performance-related elements of executive directors' remuneration should be stretching and designed to promote the long-term success of the company.

The remuneration committee should judge where to position their company relative to other companies. But they should use such comparisons with caution in view of the risk of an upward ratchet of remuneration levels with no corresponding improvement in performance.

They should also be sensitive to pay and employment conditions elsewhere in the group, especially when determining annual salary increases.

Code Provisions

D.1.1   In designing schemes of performance-related remuneration for executive directors, the remuneration committee should follow the provisions in Schedule A to this Code.

D.1.2   Where a company releases an executive director to serve as a nonexecutive director elsewhere, the remuneration report[22] should include a statement as to whether or not the director will retain such earnings and, if so, what the remuneration is.

D.1.3   Levels of remuneration for non-executive directors should reflect the time commitment and responsibilities of the role. Remuneration for nonexecutive directors should not include share options or other performance-related elements. If, exceptionally, options are granted, shareholder approval should be sought in advance and any shares acquired by exercise of the options should be held until at least one year after the non-executive director leaves the board. Holding of share options could be relevant to the determination of a non-executive director's independence (as set out in provision B.1.1).

D.1.4   The remuneration committee should carefully consider what compensation commitments (including pension contributions and all other elements) their directors' terms of appointment would entail in the event of early termination. The aim should be to avoid rewarding poor performance. They should take a robust line on reducing compensation to reflect departing directors' obligations to mitigate loss.

---

[22] As required for UK incorporated companies under the Large and Medium-Sized Companies and Groups (Accounts and Reports) Regulations 2008.

D.1.5 Notice or contract periods should be set at one year or less. If it is necessary to offer longer notice or contract periods to new directors recruited from outside, such periods should reduce to one year or less after the initial period.

D.2 Procedure

Main Principle

There should be a formal and transparent procedure for developing policy on executive remuneration and for fixing the remuneration packages of individual directors. No director should be involved in deciding his or her own remuneration.

Supporting Principles

The remuneration committee should consult the chairman and/or chief executive about their proposals relating to the remuneration of other executive directors. The remuneration committee should also be responsible for appointing any consultants in respect of executive director remuneration. Where executive directors or senior management are involved in advising or supporting the remuneration committee, care should be taken to recognise and avoid conflicts of interest.

The chairman of the board should ensure that the company maintains contact as required with its principal shareholders about remuneration.

Code Provisions

D.2.1 The board should establish a remuneration committee of at least three, or in the case of smaller companies[23] two, independent non-executive directors. In addition the company chairman may also be a member of, but not chair, the committee if he or she was considered independent on appointment as chairman. The remuneration committee should make available its terms of reference, explaining its role and the authority delegated to it by the board[24]. Where remuneration consultants are appointed, a statement should be made available[25] of whether they have any other connection with the company.

D.2.2 The remuneration committee should have delegated responsibility for setting remuneration for all executive directors and the chairman, including pension rights and any compensation payments. The committee should also recommend and monitor the level and structure of remuneration for senior management. The definition of 'senior management' for this purpose should be determined by the board but should normally include the first layer of management below board level.

D.2.3 The board itself or, where required by the Articles of Association, the shareholders should determine the remuneration of the non-executive directors within the limits set in the Articles of Association. Where permitted by the Articles, the board may however delegate this responsibility to a committee, which might include the chief executive.

D.2.4 Shareholders should be invited specifically to approve all new long-term incentive schemes (as defined in the Listing Rules[26]) and significant changes to existing schemes, save in the circumstances permitted by the Listing Rules.

SECTION E: RELATIONS WITH SHAREHOLDERS

E.1 Dialogue with Shareholders

Main Principle

There should be a dialogue with shareholders based on the mutual understanding of objectives. The board as a whole has responsibility for ensuring that a satisfactory dialogue with shareholders takes place[27].

---

[23] See footnote 6.

[24] This provision overlaps with FSA Rule DTR 7.2.7 R (see Schedule B).

[25] See footnote 7.

[26] Listing Rules LR 9.4; available at http://fsahandbook.info/FSA/html/handbook/LR/9/4.

[27] Nothing in these principles or provisions should be taken to override the general requirements of law to treat shareholders equally in access to information.

Supporting Principles

Whilst recognising that most shareholder contact is with the chief executive and finance director, the chairman should ensure that all directors are made aware of their major shareholders' issues and concerns.

   The board should keep in touch with shareholder opinion in whatever ways are most practical and efficient.

Code Provisions

E.1.1   The chairman should ensure that the views of shareholders are communicated to the board as a whole. The chairman should discuss governance and strategy with major shareholders. Non-executive directors should be offered the opportunity to attend scheduled meetings with major shareholders and should expect to attend meetings if requested by major shareholders. The senior independent director should attend sufficient meetings with a range of major shareholders to listen to their views in order to help develop a balanced understanding of the issues and concerns of major shareholders.

E.1.2   The board should state in the annual report the steps they have taken to ensure that the members of the board, and, in particular, the nonexecutive directors, develop an understanding of the views of major shareholders about the company, for example through direct face-to-face contact, analysts' or brokers' briefings and surveys of shareholder opinion.

E.2 Constructive Use of the AGM

Main Principle

The board should use the AGM to communicate with investors and to encourage their participation.

Code Provisions

E.2.1   At any general meeting, the company should propose a separate resolution on each substantially separate issue, and should, in particular, propose a resolution at the AGM relating to the report and accounts. For each resolution, proxy appointment forms should provide shareholders with the option to direct their proxy to vote either for or against the resolution or to withhold their vote. The proxy form and any announcement of the results of a vote should make it clear that a 'vote withheld' is not a vote in law and will not be counted in the calculation of the proportion of the votes for and against the resolution.

E.2.2   The company should ensure that all valid proxy appointments received for general meetings are properly recorded and counted. For each resolution, where a vote has been taken on a show of hands, the company should ensure that the following information is given at the meeting and made available as soon as reasonably practicable on a website which is maintained by or on behalf of the company:

■ the number of shares in respect of which proxy appointments have been validly made;

■ the number of votes for the resolution;

■ the number of votes against the resolution; and

■ the number of shares in respect of which the vote was directed to be withheld.

E.2.3   The chairman should arrange for the chairmen of the audit, remuneration and nomination committees to be available to answer questions at the AGM and for all directors to attend.

E.2.4   The company should arrange for the Notice of the AGM and related papers to be sent to shareholders at least 20 working days before the meeting.

SCHEDULE A: THE DESIGN OF PERFORMANCE-RELATED REMUNERATION FOR EXECUTIVE DIRECTORS

The remuneration committee should consider whether the directors should be eligible for annual bonuses. If so, performance conditions should be relevant, stretching and designed to promote the long-term success of the company. Upper limits should be set and disclosed. There may be a case for part payment in shares to be held for a significant period.

The remuneration committee should consider whether the directors should be eligible for benefits under long-term incentive schemes. Traditional share option schemes should be weighed against other kinds of long-term incentive scheme. Executive share options should not be offered at a discount save as permitted by the relevant provisions of the Listing Rules.

In normal circumstances, shares granted or other forms of deferred remuneration should not vest, and options should not be exercisable, in less than three years. Directors should be encouraged to hold their shares for a further period after vesting or exercise, subject to the need to finance any costs of acquisition and associated tax liabilities.

Any new long-term incentive schemes which are proposed should be approved by shareholders and should preferably replace any existing schemes or, at least, form part of a well considered overall plan incorporating existing schemes.

The total potentially available rewards should not be excessive. Payouts or grants under all incentive schemes, including new grants under existing share option schemes, should be subject to challenging performance criteria reflecting the company's objectives, including non-financial performance metrics where appropriate. Remuneration incentives should be compatible with risk policies and systems.

Grants under executive share option and other long-term incentive schemes should normally be phased rather than awarded in one large block.

Consideration should be given to the use of provisions that permit the company to reclaim variable components in exceptional circumstances of misstatement or misconduct.

In general, only basic salary should be pensionable. The remuneration committee should consider the pension consequences and associated costs to the company of basic salary increases and any other changes in pensionable remuneration, especially for directors close to retirement.

SCHEDULE B: DISCLOSURE OF CORPORATE GOVERNANCE ARRANGEMENTS

Corporate governance disclosure requirements are set out in three places:

- FSA Disclosure and Transparency Rules sub-chapters 7.1 and 7.2 (which set out certain mandatory disclosures);
- FSA Listing Rules 9.8.6 R, 9.8.7 R, and 9.8.7A R (which includes the 'comply or explain' requirement); and
- The UK Corporate Governance Code (in addition to providing an explanation where they choose not to comply with a provision, companies must disclose specified information in order to comply with certain provisions).

These requirements are summarised below. The full text of Disclosure and Transparency Rules 7.1 and 7.2 and Listing Rules 9.8.6 R, 9.8.7 R and 9.8.7A R are contained in the relevant chapters of the FSA Handbook, which can be found at http://fsahandbook.info/FSA/html/handbook/.

The Disclosure and Transparency Rules sub-chapters 7.1 and 7.2 apply to issuers whose securities are admitted to trading on a regulated market (this includes all issuers with a Premium or Standard listing). The Listing Rules 9.8.6 R, 9.8.7 R and 9.8.7A R and UK Corporate Governance Code apply to issuers of Premium listed equity shares only.

There is some overlap between the mandatory disclosures required under the Disclosure and Transparency Rules and those expected under the UK Corporate Governance Code. Areas of overlap are summarised in the Appendix to this Schedule. In respect of disclosures relating to the audit committee and the composition and operation of the board and its committees, compliance with the relevant provisions of the Code will result in compliance with the relevant Rules.

Disclosure and Transparency Rules

Sub-chapter 7.1 of the Disclosure and Transparency Rules concerns audit committees or bodies carrying out equivalent functions.

- DTR 7.1.1 R to 7.1.3 R set out requirements relating to the composition and functions of the committee or equivalent body:
- DTR 7.1.1 R states than an issuer must have a body which is responsible for performing the functions set out in DTR 7.1.3 R, and that at least one member of that body must be independent and at least one member must have competence in accounting and/or auditing.
- DTR 7.1.2 G states that the requirements for independence and competence in accounting and/or auditing may be satisfied by the same member or by different members of the relevant body.
- DTR 7.1.3 R states that an issuer must ensure that, as a minimum, the relevant body must:
  1) monitor the financial reporting process;
  2) monitor the effectiveness of the issuer's internal control, internal audit where applicable, and risk management systems;
  3) monitor the statutory audit of the annual and consolidated accounts;
  4) review and monitor the independence of the statutory auditor, and in particular the provision of additional services to the issuer.

DTR 7.1.5 R to DTR 7.1.7 G set out what disclosure is required. Specifically:

- DTR 7.1.5 R states that the issuer must make a statement available to the public disclosing which body carries out the functions required by DTR 7.1.3 R and how it is composed.
- DTR 7.1.6 G states that this can be included in the corporate governance statement required under sub-chapter DTR 7.2 (see below).
- DTR 7.1.7 G states that compliance with the relevant provisions of the UK Corporate Governance Code (as set out in the Appendix to this Schedule) will result in compliance with DTR 7.1.1 R to 7.1.5 R.

Sub-chapter 7.2 concerns corporate governance statements. Issuers are required to produce a corporate governance statement that must be either included in the directors' report (DTR 7.2.1 R); or in a separate report published together with the annual report; or on the issuer's website, in which case there must be a cross-reference in the directors' report (DTR 7.2.9 R).

DTR 7.2.2 R requires that the corporate governance statements must contain a reference to the corporate governance code to which the company is subject (for companies with a Premium listing this is the UK Corporate Governance Code). DTR 7.2.3 R requires that, to the extent that it departs from that code, the company must explain which parts of the code it departs from and the reasons for doing so. DTR 7.2.4 G states that compliance with LR 9.8.6 R (6) (the 'comply or explain' rule in relation to the UK Corporate Governance Code) will also satisfy these requirements.

DTR 7.2.5 R to DTR 7.2.10 R set out certain information that must be disclosed in the corporate governance statement:

- DTR 7.2.5 R states that the corporate governance statement must contain a description of the main features of the company's internal control and risk management systems in relation to the financial reporting process. DTR 7.2.10 R states that an issuer which is required to prepare a group directors' report within the meaning of Section 415(2) of the Companies Act 2006 must include in that report a description of the main features of the group's internal control and risk management systems in relation to the process for preparing consolidated accounts.
- DTR 7.2.6 R states that the corporate governance statement must contain the information required by paragraph 13(2)(c), (d), (f), (h) and (i) of Schedule 7 to the Large and Medium-sized Companies and Groups (Accounts and Reports) Regulations 2008 where the issuer is subject to the requirements of that paragraph.
- DTR 7.2.7 R states that the corporate governance statement must contain a description of the composition and operation of the issuer's administrative, management and supervisory bodies and their committees. DTR 7.2.8 G states that compliance with the relevant provisions of the UK Corporate Governance Code (as set out in the Appendix to this Schedule) will satisfy these requirements.

Listing Rules

Listing Rules 9.8.6 R (for UK incorporated companies) and 9.8.7 R (for overseas incorporated companies) state that in the case of a company that has a Premium listing of equity shares, the following items must be included in its annual report and accounts:

- a statement of how the listed company has applied the Main Principles set out in the UK Corporate Governance Code, in a manner that would enable shareholders to evaluate how the principles have been applied;
- a statement as to whether the listed company has:
  - complied throughout the accounting period with all relevant provisions set out in the UK Corporate Governance Code; or
  - not complied throughout the accounting period with all relevant provisions set out in the UK Corporate Governance Code, and if so, setting out:
    i.   those provisions, if any, it has not complied with;
    ii.   in the case of provisions whose requirements are of a continuing nature, the period within which, if any, it did not comply with some or all of those provisions; and
    iii. the company's reasons for non-compliance.

The UK Corporate Governance Code

In addition to the 'comply or explain' requirement in the Listing Rules, the Code includes specific requirements for disclosure which must be provided in order to comply. These are summarised below.

The annual report should include:

- a statement of how the board operates, including a high level statement of which types of decisions are to be taken by the board and which are to be delegated to management (A.1.1);
- the names of the chairman, the deputy chairman (where there is one), the chief executive, the senior independent director and the chairmen and members of the board committees (A.1.2);
- the number of meetings of the board and those committees and individual attendance by directors (A.1.2);
- where a chief executive is appointed chairman, the reasons for their appointment (this only needs to be done in the annual report following the appointment) (A.3.1);
- the names of the non-executive directors whom the board determines to be independent, with reasons where necessary (B.1.1);
- a separate section describing the work of the nomination committee, including the process it has used in relation to board appointments and an explanation if neither external search consultancy nor open advertising has been used in the appointment of a chairman or a non-executive director (B.2.4);
- any changes to the other significant commitments of the chairman during the year (B.3.1);
- a statement of how performance evaluation of the board, its committees and its directors has been conducted (B.6.1);
- an explanation from the directors of their responsibility for preparing the accounts and a statement by the auditors about their reporting responsibilities (C.1.1);
- an explanation from the directors of the basis on which the company generates or preserves value over the longer term (the business model) and the strategy for delivering the objectives of the company (C.1.2);
- a statement from the directors that the business is a going concern, with supporting assumptions or qualifications as necessary (C.1.3);
- a report that the board has conducted a review of the effectiveness of the company's risk management and internal controls systems (C.2.1);
- a separate section describing the work of the audit committee in discharging its responsibilities (C.3.3);
- where there is no internal audit function, the reasons for the absence of such a function (C.3.5);
- where the board does not accept the audit committee's recommendation on the appointment, reappointment or removal of an external auditor, a statement from the audit committee explaining the recommendation and the reasons why the board has taken a different position (C.3.6);

- an explanation of how, if the auditor provides non-audit services, auditor objectivity and independence is safeguarded (C.3.7);
- a description of the work of the remuneration committee as required under the Large and Medium-Sized Companies and Groups (Accounts and Reports) Regulations 2008 including, where an executive director serves as a non-executive director elsewhere, whether or not the director will retain such earnings and, if so, what the remuneration is (D.1.2);
- the steps the board has taken to ensure that members of the board, in particular the non-executive directors, develop an understanding of the views of major shareholders about their company (E.1.2).

The following information should be made available (which may be met by placing the information on a website that is maintained by or on behalf of the company):

- the terms of reference of the nomination, audit and remuneration committees, explaining their role and the authority delegated to them by the board (B.2.1, C.3.3 and D.2.1);
- the terms and conditions of appointment of non-executive directors (B.3.2) (see footnote 9);
- where performance evaluation has been externally facilitated, a statement of whether the facilitator has any other connection with the company (B.6.2); and
- where remuneration consultants are appointed, a statement of whether they have any other connection with the company (D.2.1).

The board should set out to shareholders in the papers accompanying a resolution to elect or re-elect directors:

- sufficient biographical details to enable shareholders to take an informed decision on their election or re-election (B.7.1);
- why they believe an individual should be elected to a non-executive role (B.7.2); and
- on re-election of a non-executive director, confirmation from the chairman that, following formal performance evaluation, the individual's performance continues to be effective and to demonstrate commitment to the role (B.7.2).

The board should set out to shareholders in the papers recommending appointment or reappointment of an external auditor:

- if the board does not accept the audit committee's recommendation, a statement from the audit committee explaining the recommendation and from the board setting out reasons why they have taken a different position (C.3.6).

Additional guidance

The Turnbull Guidance and FRC Guidance on Audit Committees contain further suggestions as to information that might usefully be disclosed in the internal control statement and the report of the audit committee respectively. Both sets of guidance are available on the FRC website at: www.frc.org.uk/corporate/ukcgcode.cfm

APPENDIX

OVERLAP BETWEEN THE DISCLOSURE AND TRANSPARENCY RULES AND THE UK CORPORATE GOVERNANCE CODE

DISCLOSURE AND TRANSPARENCY RULES	UK CORPORATE GOVERNANCE CODE
D.T.R 7.1.1 R Sets out minimum requirements on composition of the audit committee or equivalent body.	**Provision C.3.1** Sets out recommended composition of the audit committee.
D.T.R 7.1.3 R Sets out minimum functions of the audit committee or equivalent body.	**Provision C.3.2** Sets out the recommended minimum terms of reference for the audit committee.
D.T.R 7.1.5 R The composition and function of the audit committee or equivalent body must be disclosed in the annual report *DTR 7.1.7 R states that compliance with Code provisions A.1.2, C.3.1, C.3.2 and C.3.3 will result in compliance with DTR 7.1.1 R to DTR 7.1.5 R.*	**Provision A.1.2** The annual report should identify members of the board committees. **Provision C.3.3** The annual report should describe the work of the audit committee. Further recommendations on the content of the audit committee report are set out in the FRC Guidance on Audit Committees.
D.T.R 7.2.5 R The corporate governance statement must include a description of the main features of the company's internal control and risk management systems in relation to the financial reporting process. *While this requirement differs from the requirement in the UK Corporate Governance Code, it is envisaged that both could be met by a single internal control statement.*	**Provision C.2.1** The Board must report that a review of the effectiveness of the risk management and internal control systems has been carried out. Further recommendations on the content of the internal control statement are set out in the Turnbull Guidance.
DTR 7.2.7 R The corporate governance statement must include a description of the composition and operation of the administrative, management and supervisory bodies and their committees. *DTR 7.2.8 R states that compliance with Code provisions A.1.1, A.1.2, A.4.6, B.2.1 and C.3.3 will result in compliance with DTR 7.2.7 R.*	This requirement overlaps with a number of different provisions of the Code: **A.1.1:** the annual report should include a statement of how the board operates. **A.1.2:** the annual report should identify members of the board and board committees. **B.2.4:** the annual report should describe the work of the nomination committee. **C.3.3:** the annual report should describe the work of the audit committee. **D.2.1:** a description of the work of the remuneration committee should be made available. *[Note: in order to comply with DTR 7.2.7 R this information will need to be included in the corporate governance statement.]*

APPENDIX 2

OECD Principles of Corporate Governance

Part One   The OECD Principles of Corporate Governance

I.   Ensuring the Basis for an Effective Corporate Governance Framework

The corporate governance framework should promote transparent and efficient markets, be consistent with the rule of law and clearly articulate the division of responsibilities among different supervisory, regulatory and enforcement authorities.

A.   The corporate governance framework should be developed with a view to its impact on overall economic performance, market integrity and the incentives it creates for market participants and the promotion of transparent and efficient markets.

B.   The legal and regulatory requirements that affect corporate governance practices in a jurisdiction should be consistent with the rule of law, transparent and enforceable.

C.   The division of responsibilities among different authorities in a jurisdiction should be clearly articulated and ensure that the public interest is served.

D.   Supervisory, regulatory and enforcement authorities should have the authority, integrity and resources to fulfil their duties in a professional and objective manner. Moreover, their rulings should be timely, transparent and fully explained.

II.   The Rights of Shareholders and Key Ownership Functions

The corporate governance framework should protect and facilitate the exercise of shareholders' rights.

A.   Basic shareholder rights should include the right to: 1) secure methods of ownership registration; 2) convey or transfer shares; 3) obtain relevant and material information on the corporation on a timely and regular basis; 4) participate and vote in general shareholder meetings; 5) elect and remove members of the board; and 6) share in the profits of the corporation.

B.   Shareholders should have the right to participate in, and to be sufficiently informed on, decisions concerning fundamental corporate changes such as: 1) amendments to the statutes, or articles of incorporation or similar governing documents of the company; 2) the authorisation of additional shares; and 3) extraordinary transactions, including the transfer of all or substantially all assets, that in effect result in the sale of the company.

C.   Shareholders should have the opportunity to participate effectively and vote in general shareholder meetings and should be informed of the rules, including voting procedures, that govern general shareholder meetings:

   1.   Shareholders should be furnished with sufficient and timely information concerning the date, location and agenda of general meetings, as well as full and timely information regarding the issues to be decided at the meeting.

2. Shareholders should have the opportunity to ask questions to the board, including questions relating to the annual external audit, to place items on the agenda of general meetings, and to propose resolutions, subject to reasonable limitations.

3. Effective shareholder participation in key corporate governance decisions, such as the nomination and election of board members, should be facilitated. Shareholders should be able to make their views known on the remuneration policy for board members and key executives. The equity component of compensation schemes for board members and employees should be subject to shareholder approval.

4. Shareholders should be able to vote in person or in absentia, and equal effect should be given to votes whether cast in person or in absentia.

D. Capital structures and arrangements that enable certain shareholders to obtain a degree of control disproportionate to their equity ownership should be disclosed.

E. Markets for corporate control should be allowed to function in an efficient and transparent manner.

1. The rules and procedures governing the acquisition of corporate control in the capital markets, and extraordinary transactions such as mergers, and sales of substantial portions of corporate assets, should be clearly articulated and disclosed so that investors understand their rights and recourse. Transactions should occur at transparent prices and under fair conditions that protect the rights of all shareholders according to their class.

2. Anti-take-over devices should not be used to shield management and the board from accountability.

F. The exercise of ownership rights by all shareholders, including institutional investors, should be facilitated.

1. Institutional investors acting in a fiduciary capacity should disclose their overall corporate governance and voting policies with respect to their investments, including the procedures that they have in place for deciding on the use of their voting rights.

2. Institutional investors acting in a fiduciary capacity should disclose how they manage material conflicts of interest that may affect the exercise of key ownership rights regarding their investments.

G. Shareholders, including institutional shareholders, should be allowed to consult with each other on issues concerning their basic shareholder rights as defined in the Principles, subject to exceptions to prevent abuse.

III. The Equitable Treatment of Shareholders

The corporate governance framework should ensure the equitable treatment of all shareholders, including minority and foreign shareholders. All shareholders should have the opportunity to obtain effective redress for violation of their rights.

A. All shareholders of the same series of a class should be treated equally.

1. Within any series of a class, all shares should carry the same rights. All investors should be able to obtain information about the rights attached to all series and classes of shares before they purchase. Any changes in voting rights should be subject to approval by those classes of shares which are negatively affected.

2. Minority shareholders should be protected from abusive actions by, or in the interest of, controlling shareholders acting either directly or indirectly, and should have effective means of redress.

3. Votes should be cast by custodians or nominees in a manner agreed upon with the beneficial owner of the shares.

4. Impediments to cross border voting should be eliminated.

5. Processes and procedures for general shareholder meetings should allow for equitable treatment of all shareholders. Company procedures should not make it unduly difficult or expensive to cast votes.

B. Insider trading and abusive self-dealing should be prohibited.

C. Members of the board and key executives should be required to disclose to the board whether they, directly, indirectly or on behalf of third parties, have a material interest in any transaction or matter directly affecting the corporation.

IV. The Role of Stakeholders in Corporate Governance

The corporate governance framework should recognise the rights of stakeholders established by law or through mutual agreements and encourage active co-operation between corporations and stakeholders in creating wealth, jobs, and the sustainability of financially sound enterprises.

A. The rights of stakeholders that are established by law or through mutual agreements are to be respected.

B. Where stakeholder interests are protected by law, stakeholders should have the opportunity to obtain effective redress for violation of their rights.

C. Performance-enhancing mechanisms for employee participation should be permitted to develop.

D. Where stakeholders participate in the corporate governance process, they should have access to relevant, sufficient and reliable information on a timely and regular basis.

E. Stakeholders, including individual employees and their representative bodies, should be able to freely communicate their concerns about illegal or unethical practices to the board and their rights should not be compromised for doing this.

F. The corporate governance framework should be complemented by an effective, efficient insolvency framework and by effective enforcement of creditor rights.

V. Disclosure and Transparency

The corporate governance framework should ensure that timely and accurate disclosure is made on all material matters regarding the corporation, including the financial situation, performance, ownership, and governance of the company.

A. Disclosure should include, but not be limited to, material information on:
1. The financial and operating results of the company.
2. Company objectives.
3. Major share ownership and voting rights.
4. Remuneration policy for members of the board and key executives, and information about board members, including their qualifications, the selection process, other company directorships and whether they are regarded as independent by the board.
5. Related party transactions.
6. Foreseeable risk factors.
7. Issues regarding employees and other stakeholders.
8. Governance structures and policies, in particular, the content of any corporate governance code or policy and the process by which it is implemented.

B. Information should be prepared and disclosed in accordance with high quality standards of accounting and financial and non-financial disclosure.

C. An annual audit should be conducted by an independent, competent and qualified, auditor in order to provide an external and objective assurance to the board and shareholders that the financial statements fairly represent the financial position and performance of the company in all material respects.

D. External auditors should be accountable to the shareholders and owe a duty to the company to exercise due professional care in the conduct of the audit.

E. Channels for disseminating information should provide for equal, timely and cost- efficient access to relevant information by users.

F. The corporate governance framework should be complemented by an effective approach that addresses and promotes the provision of analysis or advice by analysts, brokers, rating agencies and others, that is relevant to decisions by investors, free from material conflicts of interest that might compromise the integrity of their analysis or advice.

VI. The Responsibilities of the Board

The corporate governance framework should ensure the strategic guidance of the company, the effective monitoring of management by the board, and the board's accountability to the company and the shareholders.

A. Board members should act on a fully informed basis, in good faith, with due diligence and care, and in the best interest of the company and the shareholders.

B. Where board decisions may affect different shareholder groups differently, the board should treat all shareholders fairly.

C. The board should apply high ethical standards. It should take into account the interests of stakeholders.

D. The board should fulfil certain key functions, including:

1. Reviewing and guiding corporate strategy, major plans of action, risk policy, annual budgets and business plans; setting performance objectives; monitoring implementation and corporate performance; and overseeing major capital expenditures, acquisitions and divestitures.

2. Monitoring the effectiveness of the company's governance practices and making changes as needed.

3. Selecting, compensating, monitoring and, when necessary, replacing key executives and overseeing succession planning.

4. Aligning key executive and board remuneration with the longer term interests of the company and its shareholders.

5. Ensuring a formal and transparent board nomination and election process.

6. Monitoring and managing potential conflicts of interest of management, board members and shareholders, including misuse of corporate assets and abuse in related party transactions.

7. Ensuring the integrity of the corporation's accounting and financial reporting systems, including the independent audit, and that appropriate systems of control are in place, in particular, systems for risk management, financial and operational control, and compliance with the law and relevant standards.

8. Overseeing the process of disclosure and communications.

E. The board should be able to exercise objective independent judgement on corporate affairs.

1. Boards should consider assigning a sufficient number of non-executive board members capable of exercising independent judgement to tasks where there is a potential for conflict of interest. Examples of such key responsibilities are ensuring the integrity of financial and non-financial reporting, the review of related party transactions, nomination of board members and key executives, and board remuneration.

2. When committees of the board are established, their mandate, composition and working procedures should be well defined and disclosed by the board.

3. Board members should be able to commit themselves effectively to their responsibilities.

F. In order to fulfil their responsibilities, board members should have access to accurate, relevant and timely information.

APPENDIX 3

The King Code of Governance Principles (KING III)

September 2009

1. ETHICAL LEADERSHIP AND CORPORATE CITIZENSHIP

Responsible leadership

1.1. The board should provide effective leadership based on an ethical foundation

Ethical leaders should:

1.1.1. direct the strategy and operations to build a sustainable business;
1.1.2. consider the short- and long-term impacts of the strategy on the economy, society and the environment;
1.1.3. do business ethically;
1.1.4. do not compromise the natural environment; and
1.1.5. take account of the company's impact on internal and external stakeholders.

The board's responsibilities

The board should:

1.1.6. be responsible for the strategic direction of the company and for the control of the company;
1.1.7. set the values to which the company will adhere formulated in its code of conduct;
1.1.8. ensure that its conduct and that of management aligns to the values and is adhered to in all aspects of its business; and
1.1.9. promote the stakeholder-inclusive approach of governance.

Ethical foundation

The board should:

1.1.10. ensure that all deliberations, decisions and actions are based on the four values underpinning good governance; and
1.1.11. ensure that each director adheres to the duties of a director.

1.2. The board should ensure that the company is and is seen to be a responsible corporate citizen

The board should:

1.2.1. consider not only on financial performance but also the impact of the company's operations on society and the environment;
1.2.2. protect, enhance and invest in the wellbeing of the economy, society and the environment;
1.2.3. ensure that the company's performance and interaction with its stakeholders is guided by the Constitution and the Bill of Rights;
1.2.4. ensure that collaborative efforts with stakeholders are embarked upon to promote ethical conduct and good corporate citizenship;

1.2.5. ensure that measurable corporate citizenship programmes are implemented; and

1.2.6. ensure that management develops corporate citizenship policies.

1.3. The board should ensure that the company's ethics are managed effectively

The board should ensure that:

1.3.1. it builds and sustains an ethical corporate culture in the company;

1.3.2. it determines the ethical standards which should be clearly articulated and ensures that the company takes measures to achieve adherence to them in all aspects of the business;

1.3.3. adherence to ethical standards is measured;

1.3.4. internal and external ethics performance is aligned around the same ethical standards;

1.3.5. ethical risks and opportunities are incorporated in the risk management process;

1.3.6. a code of conduct and ethics-related policies are implemented;

1.3.7. compliance with the code of conduct is integrated in the operations of the company; and

1.3.8. the company's ethics performance should be assessed, monitored, reported and disclosed.

2. BOARDS AND DIRECTORS

Role and function of the board

2.1. The board should act as the focal point for and custodian of corporate governance

The board should:

2.1.1. have a charter setting out its responsibilities;

2.1.2. meet at least four times per year;

2.1.3. monitor the relationship between management and the stakeholders of the company; and

2.1.4. ensure that the company survives and thrives.

2.2. The board should appreciate that strategy, risk, performance and sustainability are Inseparable.

The board should:

2.2.1. inform and approve the strategy;

2.2.2. ensure that the strategy is aligned with the purpose of the company, the value drivers of its business and the legitimate interests and expectations of its stakeholders;

2.2.3. satisfy itself that the strategy and business plans are not encumbered by risks that have not been thoroughly examined by management; and

2.2.4. ensure that the strategy will result in sustainable outcomes taking account of people, planet and profit.

2.3. The board should provide effective leadership based on an ethical foundation
Refer principle 1.1

2.4. The board should ensure that the company is and is seen to be a responsible corporate citizen
Refer principle 1.2

2.5. The board should ensure that the company's ethics are managed effectively
Refer principle 1.3

2.6. The board should ensure that the company has an effective and independent audit committee
Refer to chapter 3

2.7. The board should be responsible for the governance of risk
Refer to chapter 4

2.8. The board should be responsible for information technology (IT) governance
Refer to chapter 5

2.9. The board should ensure that the company complies with applicable laws and considers adherence to non-binding rules, codes and standards
Refer to chapter 6

2.10. The board should ensure that there is an effective risk-based internal audit
Refer to chapter 7

2.11. The board should appreciate that stakeholders' perceptions affect the company's reputation
Refer to chapter 8

2.12. The board should ensure the integrity of the company's integrated report
Refer to chapter 9

2.13. The board should report on the effectiveness of the company's system of internal controls
Refer to chapters 7 and 9

2.14. The board and its directors should act in the best interests of the company
2.14.1. The board must act in the best interests of the company.
2.14.2. Directors must adhere to the legal standards of conduct.
2.14.3. Directors or the board should be permitted to take independent advice in connection with their duties following an agreed procedure.
2.14.4. Real or perceived conflicts should be disclosed to the board and managed.
2.14.5. Listed companies should have a policy regarding dealing in securities by directors, officers and selected employees.

2.15. The board should consider business rescue proceedings or other turnaround mechanisms as soon as the company is financially distressed as defined in the Act The board should ensure that:
2.15.1. the solvency and liquidity of the company is continuously monitored;
2.15.2. its consideration is fair to save a financially distressed company either by way of workouts, sale, merger, amalgamation, compromise with creditors or business rescue;
2.15.3. a suitable practitioner is appointed if business rescue is adopted; and
2.15.4. the practitioner furnishes security for the value of the assets of the company.

2.16. The board should elect a chairman of the board who is an independent non-executive director. The CEO of the company should not also fulfil the role of chairman of the board
2.16.1. The members of the board should elect a chairman on an annual basis.
2.16.2. The chairman should be independent and free of conflict upon appointment.
2.16.3. A lead independent director should be appointed in the case where an executive chairman is appointed or where the chairman is not independent or conflicted.
2.16.4. The appointment of a chairman, who is not independent, should be justified in the integrated report.
2.16.5. The role of the chairman should be formalised.
2.16.6. The chairman's ability to add value, and his performance against what is expected of his role and function, should be assessed every year.
2.16.7. The CEO should not become the chairman until 3 years have lapsed.
2.16.8. The chairman together with the board, should consider the number of outside chairmanships held.
2.16.9. The board should ensure a succession plan for the role of the chairman.

2.17. The board should appoint the chief executive officer and establish a framework for the delegation of authority

The board should:

2.17.1. appoint the CEO;
2.17.2. provide input regarding senior management appointments;
2.17.3. define its own level of materiality and approve a delegation of authority framework;
2.17.4. ensure that the role and function of the CEO is formalised and the performance of the CEO is evaluated against the criteria specified; and
2.17.5. ensure succession planning for the CEO and other senior executives and officers is in place.

Composition of the board

2.18.   The board should comprise a balance of power, with a majority of non-executive directors. The majority of non-executive directors should be independent

2.18.1.   The majority of board members should be non-executive directors.

2.18.2.   The majority of the non-executive directors should be independent.

2.18.3.   When determining the number of directors serving on the board, the knowledge, skills and resources required for conducting the business of the board should be considered.

2.18.4.   Every board should consider whether its size, diversity and demographics make it effective.

2.18.5.   Every board should have a minimum of two executive directors of which one should be the CEO and the other the director responsible for finance.

2.18.6.   At least one third of the non-executive directors should rotate every year.

2.18.7.   The board, through its nomination committee, should recommend the eligibility of prospective directors.

2.18.8.   Any independent non-executive directors serving more than 9 years should be subjected to a rigorous review of his independence and performance by the board.

2.18.9.   The board should include a statement in the integrated report regarding the assessment of the independence of the independent non-executive directors.

2.18.10.   The board should be permitted to remove any director without shareholder approval.

Board appointment process

2.19.   Directors should be appointed through a formal process

2.19.1.   A nomination committee should assist with the process of identifying suitable members of the board.

2.19.2.   Background and reference checks should be performed before the nomination and appointment of directors.

2.19.3.   The appointment of non-executive directors should be formalised through a letter of appointment.

2.19.4.   The board should make full disclosure regarding individual directors to enable shareholders to make their own assessment of directors.

Director development

2.20.   The induction of and ongoing training and development of directors should be conducted through formal processes

The board should ensure that:

2.20.1.   a formal induction programme is established for new directors;

2.20.2.   inexperienced directors are developed through mentorship programmes;

2.20.3.   continuing professional development programmes are implemented; and

2.20.4.   directors receive regular briefings on changes in risks, laws and the environment.

Company secretary

2.21.   The board should be assisted by a competent, suitably qualified and experienced company secretary

2.21.1.   The board should appoint and remove the company secretary.

2.21.2.   The board should empower the individual to enable him to properly fulfil his duties. The company secretary should:

2.21.3.   have an arms-length relationship with the board;

2.21.4.   not be a director of the company;

2.21.5.   assist the nominations committee with the appointment of directors;

2.21.6.   assist with the director induction and training programmes;

2.21.7. provide guidance to the board on the duties of the directors and good governance;

2.21.8. ensure board and committee charters are kept up to date;

2.21.9. prepare and circulate board papers;

2.21.10. elicit responses, input, feedback for board and board committee meetings;

2.21.11. assist in drafting yearly work plans;

2.21.12. ensure preparation and circulation of minutes of board and committee meetings; and

2.21.13. assist with the evaluation of the board, committees and individual directors.

Performance assessment

2.22   The evaluation of the board, its committees and the individual directors should be performed every year

2.22.1. The board should determine its own role, functions, duties and performance criteria as well as that for directors on the board and board committees to serve as a benchmark for the performance appraisal.

2.22.2. Yearly evaluations should be performed by the chairman or an independent provider.

2.22.3. The results of performance evaluations should identify training needs for directors.

2.22.4. An overview of the appraisal process, results and action plans should be disclosed in the integrated report.

2.22.5. The nomination for the re-appointment of a director should only occur after the evaluation of the performance and attendance of the director.

Board committees

2.23.   The board should delegate certain functions to well-structured committees but without abdicating its own responsibilities

2.23.1. Formal terms of reference should be established and approved for each committee of the board.

2.23.2. The committees' terms of reference should be reviewed yearly.

2.23.3. The committees should be appropriately constituted and the composition and the terms of reference should be disclosed in the integrated report.

2.23.4. Public and state-owned companies must appoint an audit committee.

2.23.5. All other companies should establish an audit committee and define its composition, purpose and duties in the memorandum of incorporation.

2.23.6. Companies should establish risk, nomination and remuneration committees.

2.23.7. Committees, other than the risk committee, should comprise a majority of nonexecutive directors of which the majority should be independent.

2.23.8. External advisers and executive directors should attend committee meetings by invitation.

2.23.9. Committees should be free to take independent outside professional advice at the cost of the company subject to an approved process being followed.

Group boards

2.24.   A governance framework should be agreed between the group and its subsidiary boards

2.24.1. Listed subsidiaries must comply with the rules of the relevant stock exchange in respect of insider trading.

2.24.2. The holding company must respect the fiduciary duties of the director serving in a representative capacity on the board of the subsidiary.

2.24.3. The implementation and adoption of policies, processes or procedures of the holding company should be considered and approved by the subsidiary company.

2.24.4. Disclosure should be made on the adoption of the holding company's policies in the integrated report of the subsidiary company.

Remuneration of directors and senior executives

2.25. Companies should remunerate directors and executives fairly and responsibly
 2.25.1. Companies should adopt remuneration policies aligned with the strategy of the company and linked to individual performance.
 2.25.2. The remuneration committee should assist the board in setting and administering remuneration policies.
 2.25.3. The remuneration policy should address base pay and bonuses, employee contracts, severance and retirement benefits and share-based and other long-term incentive schemes.
 2.25.4. Non-executive fees should comprise a base fee as well as an attendance fee per meeting.

2.26. Companies should disclose the remuneration of each individual director and certain senior executives

The remuneration report, included in the integrated report, should include:

 2.26.1. all benefits paid to directors;
 2.26.2. the salaries of the three most highly-paid employees who are not directors;
 2.26.3. the policy on base pay;
 2.26.4. participation in share incentive schemes;
 2.26.5. the use of benchmarks;
 2.26.6. incentive schemes to encourage retention;
 2.26.7. justification of salaries above the median;
 2.26.8. material payments that are ex-gratia in nature;
 2.26.9. policies regarding executive employment; and
 2.26.10. the maximum expected potential dilution as a result of incentive awards.

2.27. Shareholders should approve the company's remuneration policy
 2.27.1. Shareholders should pass a non-binding advisory vote on the company's yearly remuneration policy.
 2.27.2. The board should determine the remuneration of executive directors in accordance with the remuneration policy put to shareholder's vote.

3. AUDIT COMMITTEES

3.1. The board should ensure that the company has an effective and independent audit committee
 3.1.1. Listed and state-owned companies must establish an audit committee.
 3.1.2. All other companies should establish an audit committee and define its composition, purpose and duties in the memorandum of incorporation.
 3.1.3. The board should approve the terms of reference of the audit committee.
 3.1.4. The audit committee should meet as often as is necessary to fulfil its functions but at least twice a year.
 3.1.5. The audit committee should meet with internal and external auditors at least once a year without management being present.

Membership and resources of the audit committee

3.2. Audit committee members should be suitably skilled and experienced independent non-executive directors
 3.2.1. All members of the audit committee should be independent non-executive directors.
 3.2.2. The audit committee should consist of at least three members.
 3.2.3. The chairman of the board should not be the chairman or member of the audit committee.
 3.2.4. The committee collectively should have sufficient qualifications and experience to fulfil its duties.
 3.2.5. The audit committee members should keep up-to-date with developments affecting the required skill-set.

3.2.6. The committee should be permitted to consult with specialists or consultants subject to a board-approved process.

3.2.7. The board must fill any vacancies on the audit committee.

3.3. The audit committee should be chaired by an independent non-executive director

3.3.1. The board should elect the chairman of the audit committee.

3.3.2. The chairman of the audit committee should participate in setting and agreeing the agenda of the committee.

3.3.3. The chairman of the audit committee should be present at the AGM.

Responsibilities of the audit committee

3.4. The audit committee should oversee integrated reporting

3.4.1. The audit committee should have regard to all factors and risks that may impact on the integrity of the integrated report.

3.4.2. The audit committee should review and comment on the financial statements included in the integrated report.

3.4.3. The audit committee should review the disclosure of sustainability issues in the integrated report to ensure that it is reliable and does not conflict with the financial information.

3.4.4. The audit committee should recommend to the board to engage an external assurance provider on material sustainability issues.

3.4.5. The audit committee should consider the need to issue interim results.

3.4.6. The audit committee should review the content of the summarised information.

3.4.7. The audit committee should engage the external auditors to provide assurance on the summarised financial information.

3.5. The audit committee should ensure that a combined assurance model is applied to provide a coordinated approach to all assurance activities

3.5.1. The audit committee should ensure that the combined assurance is received is appropriate to address all the significant risks facing the company.

3.5.2. The relationship between the external assurance providers and the company should be monitored by the audit committee.

Internal assurance providers

3.6. The audit committee should satisfy itself of the expertise, resources and experience of the company's finance function

3.6.1. Every year a review of the finance function should be performed by the audit committee.

3.6.2. The results of the review should be disclosed in the integrated report.

3.7. The audit committee should be responsible for overseeing of internal audit

3.7.1. The audit committee should be responsible for the appointment, performance assessment and/or dismissal of the CAE.

3.7.2. The audit committee should approve the internal audit plan.

3.7.3. The audit committee should ensure that the internal audit function is subject to an independent quality review as and when the committee determines it appropriate.

3.8. The audit committee should be an integral component of the risk management process

3.8.1. The charter of the audit committee should set out its responsibilities regarding risk management.

3.8.2. The audit committee should specifically have oversight of:

3.8.2.1. financial reporting risks;

3.8.2.2. internal financial controls;

3.8.2.3. fraud risks as it relates to financial reporting; and

3.8.2.4. IT risks as it relates to financial reporting.

External assurance providers

3.9. The audit committee is responsible for recommending the appointment of the external auditor and overseeing the external audit process

The audit committee:

3.9.1. must nominate the external auditor for appointment;

3.9.2. must approve the terms of engagement and remuneration for the external audit engagement;

3.9.3. must monitor and report on the independence of the external auditor;

3.9.4. must define a policy for non-audit services provided by the external auditor and must approve the contracts for non-audit services;

3.9.5. should be informed of any Reportable Irregularities identified and reported by the external auditor; and

3.9.6. should review the quality and effectiveness of the external audit process.

Reporting

3.10. The audit committee should report to the board and shareholders on how it has discharged its duties

3.10.1. The audit committee should report internally to the board on its statutory duties and duties assigned to it by the board.

3.10.2. The audit committee must report to the shareholders on its statutory duties:

3.10.2.1. how its duties were carried out;

3.10.2.2. if the committee is satisfied with the independence of the external auditor;

3.10.2.3. the committee's view on the financial statements and the accounting practices; and

3.10.2.4. whether the internal financial controls are effective.

3.10.3. The audit committee should provide a summary of its role and details of its composition, number of meetings and activities, in the integrated report.

3.10.4. The audit committee should recommend the integrated report for approval by the board.

4.   THE GOVERNANCE OF RISK

The board's responsibility for risk governance

4.1. The board should be responsible for the governance of risk

4.1.1. A policy and plan for a system and process of risk management should be developed.

4.1.2. The board should comment in the integrated report on the effectiveness of the system and process of risk management.

4.1.3. The board's responsibility for risk governance should be expressed in the board charter.

4.1.4. The induction and ongoing training programmes of the board should incorporate risk governance.

4.1.5. The board's responsibility for risk governance should manifest in a documented risk management policy and plan.

4.1.6. The board should approve the risk management policy and plan.

4.1.7. The risk management policy should be widely distributed throughout the company.

4.1.8. The board should review the implementation of the risk management plan at least once a year.

4.1.9. The board should ensure that the implementation of the risk management plan is monitored continually.

4.2. The board should determine the levels of risk tolerance

4.2.1. The board should set the levels of risk tolerance once a year.

4.2.2. The board may set limits for the risk appetite.

4.2.3. The board should monitor that risks taken are within the tolerance and appetite levels.

4.3. The risk committee or audit committee should assist the board in carrying out its risk responsibilities

4.3.1. The board should appoint a committee responsible for risk.

4.3.2. The risk committee should:
  4.3.2.1. consider the risk management policy and plan and monitor the risk management process;
  4.3.2.2. have as its members executive and non-executive directors, members of senior management and independent risk management experts to be invited, if necessary;
  4.3.2.3. have a minimum of three members; and
  4.3.2.4. convene at least twice per year.
4.3.3. The performance of the committee should be evaluated once a year by the board.

Management's responsibility for risk management

4.4. The board should delegate to management the responsibility to design, implement and monitor the risk management plan
  4.4.1. The board's risk strategy should be executed by management by means of risk management systems and processes.
  4.4.2. Management is accountable for integrating risk in the day-to-day activities of the company.
  4.4.3. The CRO should be a suitably experienced person who should have access and interact regularly on strategic matters with the board and/or appropriate board committee and executive management.

Risk assessment

4.5. The board should ensure that risk assessments are performed on a continual basis
  4.5.1. The board should ensure effective and ongoing risk assessments are performed.
  4.5.2. A systematic, documented, formal risk assessment should be conducted at least once a year.
  4.5.3. Risks should be prioritised and ranked to focus responses and interventions.
  4.5.4. The risk assessment process should involve the risks affecting the various income streams of the company, the critical dependencies of the business, the sustainability and the legitimate interests and expectations of stakeholders.
  4.5.5. Risk assessments should adopt a top-down approach.
  4.5.6. The board should regularly receive and review a register of the company's key risks.
  4.5.7. The board should ensure that key risks are quantified where practicable.

4.6. The board should ensure that frameworks and methodologies are implemented to increase the probability of anticipating unpredictable risks
  4.6.1. The board should ensure that a framework and processes are in place to anticipate unpredictable risks.

Risk response

4.7. The board should ensure that management considers and implements appropriate risk responses
  4.7.1. Management should identify and note in the risk register the risk responses decided upon.
  4.7.2. Management should demonstrate to the board that the risk response provides for the identification and exploitation of opportunities to improve the performance of the company.

Risk monitoring

4.8. The board should ensure continual risk monitoring by management
  4.8.1. The board should ensure that effective and continual monitoring of risk management takes place.
  4.8.2. The responsibility for monitoring should be defined in the risk management plan.

Risk assurance

4.9. The board should receive assurance regarding the effectiveness of the risk management process

    4.9.1. Management should provide assurance to the board that the risk management plan is integrated in the daily activities of the company.

    4.9.2. Internal audit should provide a written assessment of the effectiveness of the system of internal controls and risk management to the board.

Risk disclosure

4.10. The board should ensure that there are processes in place enabling complete, timely, relevant, accurate and accessible risk disclosure to stakeholders

    4.10.1. Undue, unexpected or unusual risks should be disclosed in the integrated report.

    4.10.2. The board should disclose its view on the effectiveness of the risk management process in the integrated report.

5. THE GOVERNANCE OF INFORMATION TECHNOLOGY

5.1. The board should be responsible for information technology (IT) governance

    5.1.1. The board should assume the responsibility for the governance of IT and place it on the board agenda.

    5.1.2. The board should ensure that an IT charter and policies are established and implemented.

    5.1.3. The board should ensure promotion of an ethical IT governance culture and awareness and of a common IT language.

    5.1.4. The board should ensure that an IT internal control framework is adopted and implemented.

    5.1.5. The board should receive independent assurance on the effectiveness of the IT internal controls.

5.2. IT should be aligned with the performance and sustainability objectives of the company

    5.2.1. The board should ensure that the IT strategy is integrated with the company's strategic and business processes.

    5.2.2. The board should ensure that there is a process in place to identity and exploit opportunities to improve the performance and sustainability of the company through the use of IT.

5.3. The board should delegate to management the responsibility for the implementation of an IT governance framework

    5.3.1. Management should be responsible for the implementation of the structures, processes and mechanisms for the IT governance framework.

    5.3.2. The board may appoint an IT steering committee of similar function to assist with its governance of IT.

    5.3.3. The CEO should appoint a Chief Information Officer responsible for the management of IT.

    5.3.4. The CIO should be a suitably qualified and experienced person who should have access and interact regularly on strategic IT matters with the board and/or appropriate board committee and executive management.

5.4. The board should monitor and evaluate significant IT investments and expenditure

    5.4.1. The board should oversee the value delivery of IT and monitor the return on investment from significant IT projects.

    5.4.2. The board should ensure that intellectual property contained in information systems are protected.

    5.4.3. The board should obtain independent assurance on the IT governance and controls supporting outsourced IT services.

5.5. IT should form an integral part of the company's risk management
- 5.5.1. Management should regularly demonstrate to the board that the company has adequate business resilience arrangements in place for disaster recovery.
- 5.5.2. The board should ensure that the company complies with IT laws and that IT related rules, codes and standards are considered.

5.6. The board should ensure that information assets are managed effectively
- 5.6.1. The board should ensure that there are systems in place for the management of information which should include information security, information management and information privacy.
- 5.6.2. The board should ensure that all personal information is treated by the company as an important business asset and is identified.
- 5.6.3. The board should ensure that an Information Security Management System is developed and implemented.
- 5.6.4. The board should approve the information security strategy and delegate and empower management to implement the strategy.

5.7. A risk committee and audit committee should assist the board in carrying out its IT responsibilities
- 5.7.1. The risk committee should ensure that IT risks are adequately addressed.
- 5.7.2. The risk committee should obtain appropriate assurance that controls are in place and effective in addressing IT risks.
- 5.7.3. The audit committee should consider IT as it relates to financial reporting and the going concern of the company.
- 5.7.4. The audit committee should consider the use of technology to improve audit coverage and efficiency.

6. COMPLIANCE WITH LAWS RULES CODES AND STANDARDS

6.1. The board should ensure that the company complies with applicable laws and considers adherence to nonbinding rules, codes and standards
- 6.1.1. Companies must comply with all applicable laws.
- 6.1.2. Exceptions permitted in law, shortcomings and proposed changes expected should be handled ethically.
- 6.1.3. Compliance should be an ethical imperative.
- 6.1.4. Compliance with applicable laws should be understood not only in terms of the obligations that they create, but also for the rights and protection that they afford.
- 6.1.5. The board should understand the context of the law, and how other applicable laws interact with it.
- 6.1.6. The board should monitor the company's compliance with applicable laws, rules, codes and standards.
- 6.1.7. Compliance should be a regular item on the agenda of the board.
- 6.1.8. The board should disclose details in the integrated report on how it discharged its responsibility to establish an effective compliance framework and processes.

6.2. The board and each individual director should have a working understanding of the effect of the applicable laws, rules, codes and standards on the company and its business
- 6.2.1. The induction and ongoing training programmes of directors should incorporate an overview of and any changes to applicable laws, rules, codes and standards.
- 6.2.2. Directors should sufficiently familiarise themselves with the general content of applicable laws, rules, codes and standards to discharge their legal duties.

6.3. Compliance risk should form an integral part of the company's risk management process
- 6.3.1. The risk of non-compliance should be identified, assessed and responded to through the risk management processes.
- 6.3.2. Companies should consider establishing a compliance function.

6.4. The board should delegate to management the implementation of an effective compliance framework and processes

    6.4.1. The board should ensure that a legal compliance policy, approved by the board, has been implemented by management.

    6.4.2. The board should receive assurance on the effectiveness of the controls around compliance with laws, rules, codes and standards.

    6.4.3. Compliance with laws, rules, codes and standards should be incorporated in the code of conduct of the company.

    6.4.4. Management should establish the appropriate structures, educate and train, and communicate and measure key performance indicators relevant to compliance.

    6.4.5. The integrated report should include details of material or often repeated instances of non-compliance by either the company or its directors in their capacity as such.

    6.4.6. An independent, suitably skilled compliance officer may be appointed.

    6.4.7. The compliance officer should be a suitably skilled and experienced person who should have access and interact regularly on strategic compliance matters with the board and/or appropriate board committee and executive management.

    6.4.8. The structuring of the compliance function, its role and its position in terms of reporting lines should be a reflection of the company's decision on how compliance is to be integrated with its ethics and risk management.

    6.4.9. The compliance function should have adequate resources to fulfil its function.

7. INTERNAL AUDIT

The need for and role of internal audit

7.1. The board should ensure that there is an effective risk based internal audit

    7.1.1. Companies should establish an internal audit function.

    7.1.2. Internal audit should perform the following functions:

        7.1.2.1. evaluate the company's governance processes;

        7.1.2.2. perform an objective assessment of the effectiveness of risk management and the internal control framework;

        7.1.2.3. systematically analyse and evaluating business processes and associated controls; and

        7.1.2.4. provide a source of information as appropriate, regarding instances of fraud, corruption, unethical behaviour and irregularities.

    7.1.3. An internal audit charter should be defined and approved by the board.

    7.1.4. The internal audit function should adhere to the IIA Standards and code of ethics.

Internal audit's approach and plan

7.2. Internal audit should follow a risk based approach to its plan

    7.2.1. The internal audit plan and approach should be informed by the strategy and risks of the company.

    7.2.2. Internal audit should be independent from management.

    7.2.3. Internal audit should be an objective provider of assurance that considers:

        7.2.3.1. the risks that may prevent or slow down the realisation of strategic goals;

        7.2.3.2. whether controls are in place and functioning effectively to mitigate these; and

        7.2.3.3. the opportunities that will promote the realisation of strategic goals that are identified, assessed and effectively managed by the company's management team.

7.3. Internal audit should provide a written assessment of the effectiveness of the company's system of internal controls and risk management

    7.3.1. Internal audit should form an integral part of the combined assurance model as internal assurance provider.

    7.3.2. Internal controls should be established not only over financial matters, but also operational, compliance and sustainability issues.

7.3.3. Companies should maintain an effective governance, risk management and internal control framework.

7.3.4. Management should specify the elements of the control framework.

7.3.5. Internal audit should provide a written assessment of the system of internal controls and risk management to the board.

7.3.6. Internal audit should provide a written assessment of internal financial controls to the audit committee.

7.4. The audit committee should be responsible for overseeing internal audit

7.4.1. The internal audit plan should be agreed and approved by the audit committee.

7.4.2. The audit committee should evaluate the performance of the internal audit function.

7.4.3. The audit committee should ensure that the internal audit function is subjected to an independent quality review.

7.4.4. The CAE should report functionally to the audit committee chairman.

7.4.5. The audit committee should be responsible for the appointment, performance assessment and dismissal of the CAE.

7.4.6. The audit committee should ensure that the internal audit function is appropriately resourced and has appropriate budget allocated to the function.

7.4.7. Internal audit should report at all audit committee meetings.

Internal audit's status in the company

7.5. Internal audit should be strategically positioned to achieve its objectives

7.5.1. The internal audit function should be independent and objective.

7.5.2. The internal audit function should report functionally to the audit committee.

7.5.3. The CAE should have a standing invitation to attend executive committee meetings.

7.5.4. The internal audit function should be skilled and resourced as is appropriate for the complexity and volume of risk and assurance needs.

7.5.5. The CAE should develop and maintain a quality assurance and improvement programme.

8. GOVERNING STAKEHOLDER RELATIONSHIPS

Code of governance principles

8.1. The board should appreciate that stakeholders' perceptions affect a company's reputation

8.1.1. The gap between stakeholder perceptions and the performance of the company should be managed and measured to enhance or protect the company's reputation.

8.1.2. The company's reputation and its linkage with stakeholder relationships should be a regular board agenda item.

8.1.3. The board should identify important stakeholder groupings.

8.2. The board should delegate to management to proactively deal with stakeholder relationships

8.2.1. Management should develop a strategy and formulate policies for the management of relationships with each stakeholder grouping.

8.2.2. The board should consider whether it is appropriate to publish its stakeholder policies.

8.2.3. The board should oversee the establishment of mechanisms and processes that support stakeholders in constructive engagement with the company.

8.2.4. The board should encourage shareholders to attend AGM's.

8.2.5. The board should consider not only formal, but also informal, processes for interaction with the company's stakeholders.

8.2.6. The board should disclose in its integrated report the nature of the company's dealings with stakeholders and the outcomes of these dealings.

8.3. The board should strive to achieve the appropriate balance between its various stakeholder groupings, in the best interests of the company

    8.3.1. The board should take account of the legitimate interests and expectations of its stakeholders in its decision-making in the best interests of the company.

8.4. Companies should ensure the equitable treatment of shareholders

    8.4.1. There must be equitable treatment of all holders of the same class of shares issued.

    8.4.2. The board should ensure that minority shareholders are protected.

8.5. Transparent and effective communication with stakeholders is essential for building and maintaining their trust and confidence

    8.5.1. Complete, timely, relevant, accurate, honest and accessible information should be provided by the company to its stakeholders whilst having regard to legal and strategic considerations.

    8.5.2. Communication with stakeholders should be in clear and understandable language.

    8.5.3. The board should adopt communication guidelines that support a responsible communication programme.

    8.5.4. The board should consider disclosing in the integrated report the number and reasons for refusals of requests of information that were lodged with the company in terms of the Promotion of Access to Information Act, 2000.

Dispute resolution

8.6. The board should ensure that disputes are resolved as effectively, efficiently and expeditiously as possible

    8.6.1. The board should adopt formal dispute resolution processes for internal and external disputes.

    8.6.2. The board should select the appropriate individuals to represent the company in ADR.

9. INTEGRATED REPORTING AND DISCLOSURE

Transparency and accountability

9.1. The board should ensure the integrity of the company's integrated report

    9.1.1. A company should have controls to enable it to verify and safeguard the integrity of its integrated report.

    9.1.2. The board should delegate to the audit committee to evaluate sustainability disclosures.

9.2. Sustainability reporting and disclosure should be integrated with the company's financial reporting

    9.2.1. The board should include commentary on the company's financial results.

    9.2.2. The board must disclose if the company is a going concern.

    9.2.3. The integrated report should describe how the company has made its money.

    9.2.4. The board should ensure that the positive and negative impacts of the company's operations and plans to improve the positives and eradicate or ameliorate the negatives in the financial year ahead are conveyed in the integrated report.

9.3. Sustainability reporting and disclosure should be independently assured

    9.3.1. General oversight and reporting of sustainability should be delegated by the board to the audit committee.

    9.3.2. The audit committee should assist the board by reviewing the integrated report to ensure that the information contained in it is reliable and that it does not contradict the financial aspects of the report.

    9.3.3. The audit committee should over see the provision of assurance over sustainability issues

APPENDIX 4

The UK Stewardship Code

July 2010

PREFACE

The Stewardship Code aims to enhance the quality of engagement between institutional investors and companies to help improve long-term returns to shareholders and the efficient exercise of governance responsibilities. Engagement includes pursuing purposeful dialogue on strategy, performance and the management of risk, as well as on issues that are the immediate subject of votes at general meetings.

The Code sets out good practice on engagement with investee companies to which the FRC believes institutional investors should aspire. It provides an opportunity to build a critical mass of UK and overseas investors committed to the high quality dialogue with companies needed to underpin good governance. By creating a sound basis of engagement it should create a much needed stronger link between governance and the investment process, and lend greater substance to the concept of "comply or explain" as applied by listed companies. The FRC therefore sees it as complementary to the UK Corporate Governance Code for listed companies, as revised in June 2010.

Institutional shareholders are free to choose whether or not to engage but their choice should be a considered one based on their investment approach. Their managers or agents are then responsible for ensuring that they comply with the terms of the mandate as agreed.

Disclosures made by institutions under the Code should assist companies to understand the approach and expectations of their major shareholders. They should also assist those issuing mandates to institutional fund managers to make a better informed choice, thereby improving the functioning of the market and facilitating the exercise of responsibility to end-investors.

As with the UK Corporate Governance Code, the Code should be applied on a "comply or explain" basis. In reporting terms this entails providing a statement on the institution's website that contains:

- a description of how the principles of the Code have been applied, and
- disclosure of the specific information listed under Principles 1, 5, 6 and 7; or
- an explanation if these elements of the Code have not been complied with.

It should be noted that compliance with the Code does not constitute an invitation to manage the affairs of investee companies or preclude a decision to sell a holding, where this is considered in the best interest of end-investors.

The Code is addressed in the first instance to firms who manage assets on behalf of institutional shareholders such as pension funds, insurance companies, investment trusts and other collective investment vehicles. The FRC expects those firms to disclose on their websites how they have applied the Code. Institutions that manage several types of fund need to make only one statement.

However the responsibility for monitoring company performance does not rest with fund managers alone. Pension fund trustees and other owners can do so either directly or indirectly through the mandates given to fund managers. Their actions can have a significant impact on the quality and quantity of engagement with UK companies. The FRC therefore strongly encourages all institutional investors to report if and how they have complied with the Code.

Principle 1 of the Code states that institutional investors that make use of proxy voting and other advisory services should disclose how they are used. The FRC encourages those service providers in turn to disclose how they carry out the wishes of their clients by applying the principles of the Code that are relevant to their activities.

The FRC recognises that not all parts of the Code will be relevant to all institutional investors, while smaller institutions may judge that some of its principles and guidance are disproportionate in their case. In these circumstances, they should take advantage of the "comply or explain" approach and set out why this is the case.

Specifically, the "explain" option means that overseas investors who follow other national or international standards that have similar objectives should not feel application of the Code duplicates or confuses their responsibilities. Disclosures made in respect of those standards can also be used to demonstrate the extent to which they have complied with the Code. In a similar spirit, UK institutions that apply the Code should use their best efforts to apply its principles to overseas holdings.

The FRC will retain on its website a list of those investors that have published a statement on their compliance or otherwise with the Code, and requests that they notify the FRC when they have done so. The FRC also considers that it would be good practice for each institution to name in its statement an individual who can be contacted for further information and by those interested in collective engagement.

The FRC will carry out regular monitoring of the take-up and application of the Code.

The FRC expects the content of the Code to evolve over time to reflect developments in good engagement practice, in the structure and operation of the market, and the broader regulatory framework, and it will need to give further consideration to issues raised in response to the consultation on this Code in the same light. A decision on the timing of the first review of the content of the Code will be taken in the second half of 2011.

Financial Reporting Council July 2010

THE PRINCIPLES OF THE CODE

Institutional investors should:

- publicly disclose their policy on how they will discharge their stewardship responsibilities.
- have a robust policy on managing conflicts of interest in relation to stewardship and this policy should be publicly disclosed.
- monitor their investee companies.
- establish clear guidelines on when and how they will escalate their activities as a method of protecting and enhancing shareholder value.
- be willing to act collectively with other investors where appropriate.
- have a clear policy on voting and disclosure of voting activity.
- report periodically on their stewardship and voting activities.

THE UK STEWARDSHIP CODE

Principle 1

Institutional investors should publicly disclose their policy on how they will discharge their stewardship responsibilities.

Guidance

The disclosure should include:
how investee companies will be monitored. In order for monitoring to be effective an active dialogue may, where necessary, need to be entered into with the investee company's board;

- the strategy on intervention;
- internal arrangements, including how stewardship is integrated with the wider investment process;
- the policy on voting and the use made of, if any, proxy voting or other voting advisory service, including information on how they are used; and
- the policy on considering explanations made in relation to the UK Corporate Governance Code.

Principle 2

Institutional investors should have a robust policy on managing conflicts of interest in relation to stewardship and this policy should be publicly disclosed.

Guidance

An institutional investor's duty is to act in the interests of all clients and/or beneficiaries when considering matters such as engagement and voting.

Conflicts of interest will inevitably arise from time to time, which may include when voting on matters affecting a parent company or client.

Institutional investors should put in place and maintain a policy for managing conflicts of interest.

Principle 3

Institutional investors should monitor their investee companies.

Guidance

Investee companies should be monitored to determine when it is necessary to enter into an active dialogue with their boards. This monitoring should be regular, and the process clearly communicable and checked periodically for its effectiveness.

As part of this monitoring, institutional investors should:

■ seek to satisfy themselves, to the extent possible, that the investee company's board and committee structures are effective, and that independent directors provide adequate oversight, including by meeting the chairman and, where appropriate, other board members;
■ maintain a clear audit trail, for example, records of private meetings held with companies, of votes cast, and of reasons for voting against the investee company's management, for abstaining, or for voting with management in a contentious situation; and
■ attend the General Meetings of companies in which they have a major holding, where appropriate and practicable.

Institutional investors should consider carefully explanations given for departure from the UK Corporate Governance Code and make reasoned judgements in each case. They should give a timely explanation to the company, in writing where appropriate, and be prepared to enter a dialogue if they do not accept the company's position.

Institutional investors should endeavour to identify problems at an early stage to minimise any loss of shareholder value. If they have concerns they should seek to ensure that the appropriate members of the investee company's board are made aware of them.

Institutional investors may not wish to be made insiders. They will expect investee companies and their advisers to ensure that information that could affect their ability to deal in the shares of the company concerned is not conveyed to them without their agreement.

Principle 4

Institutional investors should establish clear guidelines on when and how they will escalate their activities as a method of protecting and enhancing shareholder value.

Guidance

Institutional investors should set out the circumstances when they will actively intervene and regularly assess the outcomes of doing so. Intervention should be considered regardless of whether an active or passive investment policy is followed. In addition, being underweight is not, of itself, a reason for not intervening. Instances when institutional investors may want to intervene include when they have concerns about the company's strategy and performance, its governance or its approach to the risks arising from social and environmental matters.

Initial discussions should take place on a confidential basis. However, if boards do not respond constructively when institutional investors intervene, then institutional investors will consider whether to escalate their action, for example, by:

■ holding additional meetings with management specifically to discuss concerns;
■ expressing concerns through the company's advisers;
■ meeting with the chairman, senior independent director, or with all independent directors;
■ intervening jointly with other institutions on particular issues;
■ making a public statement in advance of the AGM or an EGM;
■ submitting resolutions at shareholders' meetings; and
■ requisitioning an EGM, in some cases proposing to change board membership.

Principle 5

Institutional investors should be willing to act collectively with other investors where appropriate.

Guidance

At times collaboration with other investors may be the most effective manner in which to engage.

Collaborative engagement may be most appropriate at times of significant corporate or wider economic stress, or when the risks posed threaten the ability of the company to continue.

Institutional investors should disclose their policy on collective engagement.

When participating in collective engagement, institutional investors should have due regard to their policies on conflicts of interest and insider information.

Principle 6

Institutional investors should have a clear policy on voting and disclosure of voting activity.

Guidance

Institutional investors should seek to vote all shares held. They should not automatically support the board.

If they have been unable to reach a satisfactory outcome through active dialogue then they should register an abstention or vote against the resolution. In both instances, it is good practice to inform the company in advance of their intention and the reasons why.

Institutional investors should disclose publicly voting records and if they do not explain why.

Principle 7

Institutional investors should report periodically on their stewardship and voting activities.

Guidance

Those that act as agents should regularly report to their clients details of how they have discharged their responsibilities. Such reports will be likely to comprise qualitative as well as quantitative information. The particular information reported, including the format in which details of how votes have been cast are presented, should be a matter for agreement between agents and their principals.

Transparency is an important feature of effective stewardship. Institutional investors should not, however, be expected to make disclosures that might be counterproductive. Confidentiality in specific situations may well be crucial to achieving a positive outcome.

Those that act as principals, or represent the interests of the end-investor, should report at least annually to those to whom they are accountable on their policy and its execution.

Those that sign up to this Code should consider obtaining an independent audit opinion on their engagement and voting processes having regard to the standards in AAF 01/06[1] and SAS 70[2]. The existence of such assurance certification should be publicly disclosed.

---

[1] Assurance reports on internal controls of service organisations made available to third parties.

[2] Statement on Auditing Standards No.70: Reports on the processing of transactions by service organizations.

APPENDIX 5

Financial Reporting Council guidance on audit committees

CONTENTS

1. Introduction

1.1. This guidance is designed to assist company boards in making suitable arrangements for their audit committees, and to assist directors serving on audit committees in carrying out their role. While boards are not required to follow this guidance, it is intended to assist them when implementing the relevant provisions of the Combined Code.

1.2. The paragraphs in bold are taken from the Combined Code (Section C3). Listed companies that do not comply with those provisions should include an explanation as to why they have not complied in the statement required by the Listing Rules.

1.3. Best practice requires that every board should consider in detail what arrangements for its audit committee are best suited for its particular circumstances. Audit committee arrangements need to be proportionate to the task, and will vary according to the size, complexity and risk profile of the company.

1.4. While all directors have a duty to act in the interests of the company the audit committee has a particular role, acting independently from the executive, to ensure that the interests of shareholders are properly protected in relation to financial reporting and internal control.

1.5. Nothing in the guidance should be interpreted as a departure from the principle of the unitary board. All directors remain equally responsible for the company's affairs as a matter of law. The audit committee, like other committees to which particular responsibilities are delegated (such as the remuneration committee), remains a committee of the board. Any disagreement within the board, including disagreement between the audit committee's members and the rest of the board, should be resolved at board level.

1.6. The Code provides that a separate section of the annual report should describe the work of the committee. This deliberately puts the spotlight on the audit committee and gives it an authority that it might otherwise lack. This is not incompatible with the principle of the unitary board.

1.7. The guidance contains recommendations about the conduct of the audit committee's relationship with the board, with the executive management and with internal and external auditors. However, the most important features of this relationship cannot be drafted as guidance or put into a code of practice: a frank, open working relationship and a high level of mutual respect are essential, particularly between the audit committee chairman and the board chairman, the chief executive and the finance director. The audit committee must be prepared to take a robust stand, and all parties must be prepared to make information freely available to the audit committee, to listen to their views and to talk through the issues openly.

1.8. In particular, the management is under an obligation to ensure the audit committee is kept properly informed, and should take the initiative in supplying information rather than waiting to be asked. The board should make it clear to all directors and staff that they must cooperate with the audit committee and provide it with any information it requires. In addition, executive board members will have regard to their duty to provide all directors, including those on the audit committee, with all the information they need to discharge their responsibilities as directors of the company.

1.9. Many of the core functions of audit committees set out in this guidance are expressed in terms of 'oversight', 'assessment' and 'review' of a particular function. It is not the duty of audit committees to carry out functions that properly belong to others, such as the company's management in the preparation of the financial statements or the auditors in the planning or conducting of audits. To do so could undermine the responsibility of management and auditors. Audit committees should, for example, satisfy themselves that there is a proper system and allocation of responsibilities for the day-to-day monitoring of financial controls but they should not seek to do the monitoring themselves.

1.10. However, the high-level oversight function may lead to detailed work. The audit committee must intervene if there are signs that something may be seriously amiss. For example, if the audit committee is uneasy about the explanations of management and auditors about a particular financial reporting policy decision, there may be no alternative but to grapple with the detail and perhaps to seek independent advice.

1.11. Under this guidance, audit committees have wide-ranging, time-consuming and sometimes intensive work to do. Companies need to make the necessary resources available. This includes suitable payment for the members of audit committees themselves. They – and particularly the audit committee chairman-bear a significant responsibility and they need to commit a significant extra amount of time to the job. Companies also need to make provision for induction and training for new audit committee members and continuing training as may be required.

1.12. This guidance applies to all companies to which the Code applies – i.e. UK registered companies listed on the Main Market of the London Stock Exchange. For groups, it will usually be necessary for the audit committee of the parent company to review issues that relate to particular subsidiaries or activities carried on by the group. Consequently, the board of a UK-listed parent company should ensure that there is adequate cooperation within the group (and with internal and external auditors of individual companies within the group) to enable the parent company audit committee to discharge its responsibilities effectively.

2. Establishment and role of the audit committee; membership, procedures and resources

Establishment and role

2.1. The board should establish an audit committee of at least three, or in the case of smaller companies two, members.

2.2. The main role and responsibilities of the audit committee should be set out in written terms of reference and should include:

- to monitor the integrity of the financial statements of the company and any formal announcements relating to the company's financial performance, reviewing significant financial reporting judgements contained in them;
- to review the company's internal financial controls and, unless expressly addressed by a separate board risk committee composed of independent directors or by the board itself, the company's internal control and risk management systems;
- to monitor and review the effectiveness of the company's internal audit function;
- to make recommendations to the board, for it to put to the shareholders for their approval in general meeting, in relation to the appointment of the external auditor and to approve the remuneration and terms of engagement of the external auditor;
- to review and monitor the external auditor's independence and objectivity and the effectiveness of the audit process, taking into consideration relevant UK professional and regulatory requirements;
- to develop and implement policy on the engagement of the external auditor to supply non-audit services, taking into account relevant ethical guidance regarding the provision of non-audit services by the external audit firm; and
- to report to the board, identifying any matters in respect of which it considers that action or improvement is needed, and making recommendations as to the steps to be taken.

Membership and appointment

2.3. The board should establish an audit committee of at least three, or in the case of smaller companies two, independent non-executive directors. In smaller companies the company chairman may be a member of, but not chair, the committee in addition to the independent non-executive directors, provided he or she was considered independent on appointment as chairman. The board should satisfy itself that at least one member of the audit committee has recent and relevant financial experience.

2.4. Appointments to the audit committee should be made by the board on the recommendation of the nomination committee (where there is one), in consultation with the audit committee chairman.

2.5. Appointments should be for a period of up to three years, extendable by no more than two additional three-year periods, so long as members continue to be independent.

Meetings of the audit committee

2.6. It is for the audit committee chairman, in consultation with the company secretary, to decide the frequency and timing of its meetings. There should be as many meetings as the audit committee's role and responsibilities require. It is recommended there should be not fewer than three meetings during the year, held to coincide with key dates within the financial reporting and audit cycle.[1] However, most audit committee chairmen will wish to call more frequent meetings.

2.7. No one other than the audit committee's chairman and members is entitled to be present at a meeting of the audit committee. It is for the audit committee to decide if non-members should attend for a particular meeting or a particular agenda item. It is to be expected that the external audit lead partner will be invited regularly to attend meetings as well as the finance director. Others may be invited to attend.

2.8. Sufficient time should be allowed to enable the audit committee to undertake as full a discussion as may be required. A sufficient interval should be allowed between audit committee meetings and main board meetings to allow any work arising from the audit committee meeting to be carried out and reported to the board as appropriate.

2.9. The audit committee should, at least annually, meet the external and internal auditors, without management, to discuss matters relating to its remit and any issues arising from the audit.

---

[1] For example, when the audit plans (internal and external) are available for review and when interim statements, preliminary announcements and the full annual report are near completion.

2.10. Formal meetings of the audit committee are the heart of its work. However, they will rarely be sufficient. It is expected that the audit committee chairman, and to a lesser extent the other members, will wish to keep in touch on a continuing basis with the key people involved in the company's governance, including the board chairman, the chief executive, the finance director, the external audit lead partner and the head of internal audit.

Resources

2.11. The audit committee should be provided with sufficient resources to undertake its duties.

2.12. The audit committee should have access to the services of the company secretariat on all audit committee matters including: assisting the chairman in planning the audit committee's work, drawing up meeting agendas, maintenance of minutes, drafting of material about its activities for the annual report, collection and distribution of information and provision of any necessary practical support.

2.13. The company secretary should ensure that the audit committee receives information and papers in a timely manner to enable full and proper consideration to be given to the issues.

2.14. The board should make funds available to the audit committee to enable it to take independent legal, accounting or other advice when the audit committee reasonably believes it necessary to do so.

Remuneration

2.15. In addition to the remuneration paid to all non-executive directors, each company should consider the further remuneration that should be paid to members of the audit committee to recompense them for the additional responsibilities of membership. Consideration should be given to the time members are required to give to audit committee business, the skills they bring to bear and the onerous duties they take on, as well as the value of their work to the company. The level of remuneration paid to the members of the audit committee should take into account the level of fees paid to other members of the board. The chairman's responsibilities and time demands will generally be heavier than the other members of the audit committee and this should be reflected in his or her remuneration.

Skills, experience and training

2.16. It is desirable that the committee member whom the board considers to have recent and relevant financial experience should have a professional qualification from one of the professional accountancy bodies. The need for a degree of financial literacy among the other members will vary according to the nature of the company, but experience of corporate financial matters will normally be required. The availability of appropriate financial expertise will be particularly important where the company's activities involve specialised financial activities.

2.17. The company should provide an induction programme for new audit committee members. This should cover the role of the audit committee, including its terms of reference and expected time commitment by members; and an overview of the company's business, identifying the main business and financial dynamics and risks. It could also include meeting some of the company staff.

2.18. Training should also be provided to members of the audit committee on an ongoing and timely basis and should include an understanding of the principles of and developments in financial reporting and related company law. In appropriate cases, it may also include, for example, understanding financial statements, applicable accounting standards and recommended practice; the regulatory framework for the company's business; the role of internal and external auditing and risk management.

2.19. The induction programme and ongoing training may take various forms, including attendance at formal courses and conferences, internal company talks and seminars, and briefings by external advisers.

3.   Relationship with the board

3.1. The role of the audit committee is for the board to decide and to the extent that the audit committee undertakes tasks on behalf of the board, the results should be reported to, and considered by, the board. In doing so it should identify any matters in respect of which it considers that action or improvement is needed, and make recommendations as to the steps to be taken.

3.2. The terms of reference should be tailored to the particular circumstances of the company.

3.3. The audit committee should review annually its terms of reference and its own effectiveness and recommend any necessary changes to the board.

3.4. The board should review the audit committee's effectiveness annually.

3.5. Where there is disagreement between the audit committee and the board, adequate time should be made available for discussion of the issue with a view to resolving the disagreement. Where any such disagreements cannot be resolved, the audit committee should have the right to report the issue to the shareholders as part of the report on its activities in the annual report.

4.   Role and responsibilities

Financial reporting

4.1. The audit committee should review the significant financial reporting issues and judgements made in connection with the preparation of the company's financial statements, interim reports, preliminary announcements and related formal statements.

4.2. It is management's, not the audit committee's, responsibility to prepare complete and accurate financial statements and disclosures in accordance with financial reporting standards and applicable rules and regulations. However the audit committee should consider significant accounting policies, any changes to them and any significant estimates and judgements. The management should inform the audit committee of the methods used to account for significant or unusual transactions where the accounting treatment is open to different approaches. Taking into account the external auditor's view, the audit committee should consider whether the company has adopted appropriate accounting policies and, where necessary, made appropriate estimates and judgements. The audit committee should review the clarity and completeness of disclosures in the financial statements and consider whether the disclosures made are set properly in context.

4.3. Where, following its review, the audit committee is not satisfied with any aspect of the proposed financial reporting by the company, it shall report its views to the board.

4.4. The audit committee should review related information presented with the financial statements, including the operating and financial review, and corporate governance statements relating to the audit and to risk management. Similarly, where board approval is required for other statements containing financial information (for example, summary financial statements, significant financial returns to regulators and release of price sensitive information), whenever practicable (without being inconsistent with any requirement for prompt reporting under the Listing Rules) the audit committee should review such statements first.

Internal controls and risk management systems

4.5. The audit committee should review the company's internal financial controls (that is, the systems established to identify, assess, manage and monitor financial risks); and unless expressly addressed by a separate board risk committee comprised of independent directors or by the board itself, the company's internal control and risk management systems.

4.6. The company's management is responsible for the identification, assessment, management and monitoring of risk, for developing, operating and monitoring the system of internal control and for providing assurance to the board that it has done so. Except where the board or a risk committee is expressly responsible for reviewing the effectiveness of the internal control and risk management systems, the audit committee should receive reports from management on the effectiveness of the systems they have established and the conclusions of any testing carried out by internal and external auditors.

4.7.   Except to the extent that this is expressly dealt with by the board or risk committee, the audit committee should review and approve the statements included in the annual report in relation to internal control and the management of risk.

Whistleblowing

4.8.   The audit committee should review arrangements by which staff of the company may, in confidence, raise concerns about possible improprieties in matters of financial reporting or other matters. The audit committee's objective should be to ensure that arrangements are in place for the proportionate and independent investigation of such matters and for appropriate follow-up action.

The internal audit process

4.9.   The audit committee should monitor and review the effectiveness of the company's internal audit function. Where there is no internal audit function, the audit committee should consider annually whether there is a need for an internal audit function and make a recommendation to the board, and the reasons for the absence of such a function should be explained in the relevant section of the annual report.

4.10. The need for an internal audit function will vary depending on company specific factors including the scale, diversity and complexity of the company's activities and the number of employees, as well as cost/benefit considerations. Senior management and the board may desire objective assurance and advice on risk and control. An adequately resourced internal audit function (or its equivalent where, for example, a third party is contracted to perform some or all of the work concerned) may provide such assurance and advice. There may be other functions within the company that also provide assurance and advice covering specialist areas such as health and safety, regulatory and legal compliance and environmental issues.

4.11. When undertaking its assessment of the need for an internal audit function, the audit committee should also consider whether there are any trends or current factors relevant to the company's activities, markets or other aspects of its external environment, that have increased, or are expected to increase, the risks faced by the company. Such an increase in risk may also arise from internal factors such as organisational restructuring or from changes in reporting processes or underlying information systems. Other matters to be taken into account may include adverse trends evident from the monitoring of internal control systems or an increased incidence of unexpected occurrences.

4.12. In the absence of an internal audit function, management needs to apply other monitoring processes in order to assure itself, the audit committee and the board that the system of internal control is functioning as intended. In these circumstances, the audit committee will need to assess whether such processes provide sufficient and objective assurance.

4.13. The audit committee should review and approve the internal audit function's remit, having regard to the complementary roles of the internal and external audit functions. The audit committee should ensure that the function has the necessary resources and access to information to enable it to fulfil its mandate, and is equipped to perform in accordance with appropriate professional standards for internal auditors[2].

4.14. The audit committee should approve the appointment or termination of appointment of the head of internal audit.

4.15. In its review of the work of the internal audit function, the audit committee should, inter alia:
  - ensure that the internal auditor has direct access to the board chairman and to the audit committee and is accountable to the audit committee;
  - review and assess the annual internal audit work plan;
  - receive a report on the results of the internal auditors' work on a periodic basis;
  - review and monitor management's responsiveness to the internal auditor's findings and recommendations;

---

[2] Further guidance can be found in the Institute of Internal Auditors' Code of Ethics and the International Standards for the Professional Practice of Internal Auditing.

- meet with the head of internal audit at least once a year without the presence of management; and
- monitor and assess the role and effectiveness of the internal audit function in the overall context of the company's risk management system.

The external audit process

4.16. The audit committee is the body responsible for overseeing the company's relations with the external auditor.

Appointment

4.17. The audit committee should have primary responsibility for making a recommendation on the appointment, reappointment and removal of the external auditors. If the board does not accept the audit committee's recommendation, it should include in the annual report, and in any papers recommending appointment or reappointment, a statement from the audit committee explaining its recommendation and should set out reasons why the board has taken a different position.

4.18. The audit committee's recommendation to the board should be based on the assessments referred to below. If the audit committee recommends considering the selection of possible new appointees as external auditors, it should oversee the selection process.

4.19. The audit committee should assess annually the qualification, expertise and resources, and independence (see below) of the external auditors and the effectiveness of the audit process. The assessment should cover all aspects of the audit service provided by the audit firm, and include obtaining a report on the audit firm's own internal quality control procedures and consideration of audit firms' annual transparency reports, where available. It might also be appropriate for the audit committee to consider whether there might be any benefit in using firms from more than one audit network[3].

4.20. If the external auditor resigns, the audit committee should investigate the issues giving rise to such resignation and consider whether any action is required.

4.21. The audit committee should consider the need to include the risk of the withdrawal of their auditor from the market in their risk evaluation and planning.

4.22. The audit committee section of the annual report should explain to shareholders how it reached its recommendation to the board on the appointment, reappointment or removal of the external auditors. This explanation should normally include supporting information on tendering frequency, the tenure of the incumbent auditor, and any contractual obligations that acted to restrict the audit committee's choice of external auditors.

Terms and Remuneration

4.23. The audit committee should approve the terms of engagement and the remuneration to be paid to the external auditor in respect of audit services provided.

4.24. The audit committee should review and agree the engagement letter issued by the external auditor at the start of each audit, ensuring that it has been updated to reflect changes in circumstances arising since the previous year. The scope of the external audit should be reviewed by the audit committee with the auditor. If the audit committee is not satisfied as to its adequacy it should arrange for additional work to be undertaken.

4.25. The audit committee should satisfy itself that the level of fee payable in respect of the audit services provided is appropriate and that an effective audit can be conducted for such a fee.

Independence, including the provision of non-audit services

4.26. The audit committee should assess the independence and objectivity of the external auditor annually, taking into consideration relevant UK law, regulation and professional requirements. This assessment should involve a consideration of all relationships between the company and the audit firm (including the provision of non-audit services)

---

[3] Guidance on the considerations relevant to the use of firms from more than one audit network can be found in the Appendix.

and any safeguards established by the external auditor. The audit committee should consider whether, taken as a whole and having regard to the views, as appropriate, of the external auditor, management and internal audit, those relationships appear to impair the auditor's independence and objectivity.

4.27. The audit committee should seek reassurance that the auditors and their staff have no financial, business, employment or family and other personal relationship with the company which could adversely affect the auditor's independence and objectivity, taking account of relevant Ethical Standards. The audit committee should seek from the audit firm, on an annual basis, information about policies and processes for maintaining independence and monitoring compliance with relevant requirements, including current requirements regarding the rotation of audit partners and staff.

4.28. The audit committee should agree with the board the company's policy for the employment of former employees of the external auditor, paying particular attention to the policy regarding former employees of the audit firm who were part of the audit team and moved directly to the company. This should be drafted taking into account the relevant Ethical Standards governing the accounting profession. The audit committee should monitor application of the policy, including the number of former employees of the external auditor currently employed in senior positions in the company, and consider whether in the light of this there has been any impairment, or appearance of impairment, of the auditor's independence and objectivity in respect of the audit.

4.29. The audit committee should monitor the external audit firm's compliance with relevant Ethical Standards relating to the rotation of audit partners, the level of fees that the company pays in proportion to the overall fee income of the firm, or relevant part of it[4], and other related regulatory requirements.

4.30. The audit committee should develop and recommend to the board the company's policy in relation to the provision of non-audit services by the auditor. The audit committee's objective should be to ensure that the provision of such services does not impair the external auditor's independence or objectivity. In this context, the audit committee should consider:
- whether the skills and experience of the audit firm make it a suitable supplier of the non-audit service;
- whether there are safeguards in place to eliminate or reduce to an acceptable level any threat to objectivity and independence in the conduct of the audit resulting from the provision of such services by the external auditor;
- the nature of the non-audit services, the related fee levels and the fee levels individually and in aggregate relative to the audit fee; and
- the criteria which govern the compensation of the individuals performing the audit.

4.31. The audit committee should set and apply a formal policy specifying the types of non-audit work:
- from which the external auditors are excluded;
- for which the external auditors can be engaged without referral to the audit committee; and
- for which a case-by-case decision is necessary.
- In addition, the policy may set fee limits generally or for particular classes of work.

4.32. In the third category, if it is not practicable to give approval to individual items in advance, it may be appropriate to give a general pre-approval for certain classes for work, subject to a fee limit determined by the audit committee and ratified by the board. The subsequent provision of any service by the auditor should be ratified at the next meeting of the audit committee.

4.33. In determining the policy, the audit committee should take into account relevant Ethical Standards regarding the provision of non-audit services by the external audit firm, and in principle should not agree to the auditor providing a service if, having regard to the ethical guidance, the result is that:
- the external auditor audits its own firm's work;
- the external auditor makes management decisions for the company;

---

[4] Where the audit firm's profits are not shared on a firm-wide basis, the relevant part of the firm is that by reference to which the audit engagement partner's profit share is calculated.

- a mutuality of interest is created;
- the external auditor develops close personal relationships with the company's personnel; or
- the external auditor is put in the role of advocate for the company.

The audit committee should satisfy itself that any safeguards required by Ethical Standards are implemented.

4.34. The annual report should explain to shareholders how, if the auditor provides non-audit services, auditor objectivity and independence is safeguarded.

Annual audit cycle

4.35. At the start of each annual audit cycle, the audit committee should ensure that appropriate plans are in place for the audit.

4.36. The audit committee should consider whether the auditor's overall work plan, including planned levels of materiality, and proposed resources to execute the audit plan appears consistent with the scope of the audit engagement, having regard also to the seniority, expertise and experience of the audit team.

4.37. The audit committee should review, with the external auditors, the findings of their work. In the course of its review, the audit committee should:
- discuss with the external auditor major issues that arose during the course of the audit and have subsequently been resolved and those issues that have been left unresolved;
- review key accounting and audit judgements; and
- review levels of errors identified during the audit, obtaining explanations from management and, where necessary, the external auditors as to why certain errors might remain unadjusted.

4.38. The audit committee should also review the audit representation letters before signature by management and give particular consideration to matters where representation has been requested that relate to non-standard issues[5]. The audit committee should consider whether the information provided is complete and appropriate based on its own knowledge.

4.39. As part of the ongoing monitoring process, the audit committee should review the management letter (or equivalent). The audit committee should review and monitor management's responsiveness to the external auditor's findings and recommendations.

4.40. At the end of the annual audit cycle, the audit committee should assess the effectiveness of the audit process. In the course of doing so, the audit committee should:
- review whether the auditor has met the agreed audit plan and understand the reasons for any changes, including changes in perceived audit risks and the work undertaken by the external auditors to address those risks;
- consider the robustness and perceptiveness of the auditors in their handling of the key accounting and audit judgements identified and in responding to questions from the audit committees, and in their commentary where appropriate on the systems of internal control;
- obtain feedback about the conduct of the audit from key people involved, e.g. the finance director and the head of internal audit; and
- review and monitor the content of the external auditor's management letter, in order to assess whether it is based on a good understanding of the company's business and establish whether recommendations have been acted upon and, if not, the reasons why they have not been acted upon.

5. Communication with shareholders

5.1. The terms of reference of the audit committee, including its role and the authority delegated to it by the board, should be made available. A separate section in the annual report should describe the work of the committee in discharging those responsibilities.

5.2. The audit committee section should include, inter alia:
- a summary of the role of the audit committee;
- the names and qualifications of all members of the audit committee during the period;

---

[5] Further guidance can be found in the Auditing Practices Board's International Standard on Auditing (UK and Ireland) 580: "Management Representations".

- the number of audit committee meetings;
- a report on the way the audit committee has discharged its responsibilities; and
- the explanations provided for in paragraphs 4.22 and 4.34 above.

5.3. The chairman of the audit committee should be present at the AGM to answer questions, through the chairman of the board, on the report on the audit committee's activities and matters within the scope of the audit committee's responsibilities.

APPENDIX

Revised guidance on use of firms from more than one network

Introduction

This guidance has been produced in response to a recommendation made by the Markets Participants Group (MPG) that advised the FRC on the Choice in the Audit Market project.

The MPG recommended that: "The FRC should provide independent guidance for audit committees and other market participants on considerations relevant to the use of firms from more than one network".

The MPG intended that the guidance would provide audit committees of growing companies using non-Big Four firms with relevant factors they may wish to consider when their activities expand geographically beyond the perceived capacity of their existing firm.

More generally, it was expected that the guidance could also help audit committees to select auditors for individual components of the group financial statements based on how best to achieve audit quality for that particular component and for the group as a whole.

To assist users to compare different group audit arrangements, the guidance includes a description of considerations relevant to the use of firms from one audit network as well as those relevant to the use of firms from more than one network.

Drivers of audit quality for group audits

Under UK auditing standards, the group auditor has sole responsibility for the audit opinion on the group accounts, the group auditor cannot limit its responsibility by referring to the work of another firm.

For the group auditor's work to be effective there are key quality drivers that need to be in place, including:

- A well structured and efficient methodology;
- Arrangements to safeguard auditor integrity, objective and independence;
- Arrangements to ensure partners and staff understand their client's business and staff performing detailed "on-site" audit work have sufficient experience;
- Effective, understood and applied quality control procedures;
- Effective communication between the group auditor and the parent company's audit committee covering the key risks identified and judgements made in reaching the group audit opinion.

Achieving each of these drivers on a group audit presents some challenges to the auditor where there are international components. The extent of this challenge will vary by group depending on factors that may include the:

- Extent to which the group has international operations and subsidiary undertakings;
- Countries and regions in which the group has international components;
- Extent to which the components of the group transact with each other;
- Diversity of the groups operations including the industries in which it operates;
- Extent to which the finance function of the firm is centralised;
- Extent to which the components require local statutory audits.

Use of firms from a single network

It is common practice to appoint one firm to audit the parent group and the consolidated group accounts. This firm then uses other firms from within its international network to carry out audit work on components that are needed for group audit purposes. It is common for the same firms to carry out statutory audits of subsidiaries where these are needed.

The 'single network' arrangement is common because firms from a single network may have:

- Common audit methodology that is generally seen as well-structured, efficient and effective;
- Effective inter-office communication arrangements;
- Partners and staff in network firms internationally that understand the group's business and have staff available to perform detailed 'on¬site' audit work with that experience;
- Common quality control policies and monitoring arrangements across the network that are effective, understood and applied.

In assessing the use of firms from a single network, audit committees may wish to consider:

- Do each of the network's member firms that will be involved in the group audit have partners and staff that understand the group's business?
- Will each of the network's member firms select a staff with sufficient experience to perform detailed "on-site" audit work?
- In considering the findings of each of the other firms from within its network, will the group auditor review the degree to which the firm has followed the network's common audit methodology and associated procedures?
- What quality checks and inspections are carried out by the network organisation on its member firms?
- What information is available to the group auditor on the results of these quality inspections and on any follow-up actions?

Use of firms from more than one network

In some circumstances it may be appropriate to use a firm from more than one network to achieve a high quality and cost-effective audit. The group would still appoint a single firm to audit the parent company and the group's consolidated financial statements. However, the group would agree with the group auditor that for some components the audit work that is needed for group audit purposes will be carried out by one or more firms from other networks.

However, where consideration is given to using firms from more than one network, groups should be mindful that the firm appointed to audit the parent company and group's consolidated financial statements must be able to demonstrate that they can satisfy the principal auditor requirements as set out in ISA600 (UK and Ireland).

It is likely that the same firms will be used to carry out audits of subsidiaries where these are needed for local statutory purposes.

- Groups for which this arrangement may be useful include:
- Groups that consider their current auditor delivers high quality audits but have growing or new subsidiaries in locations not well served by their current auditor's network;
- Groups wishing to give subsidiaries the option of which audit firm to use for local audits;
- Groups wishing to have the flexibility to select the firms in each country with the most suitable capabilities to carry out audit work on the relevant subsidiary.

In assessing the use of firms from more than one network, audit committees may wish to consider:

- How will the group auditor assess the independence and professional competence of the firms from other networks?
- How the group auditor will ensure that they are familiar with the methodology of the other firms, in order to enable them to evaluate the audit evidence obtained?
- The arrangements the group auditor will make with different networks to ensure that they communicate effectively with each other.
- The overall costs and benefits associated with using firms from more than one network.
- What costs will be attached to the group auditor assessing firms from other networks evaluating audit evidence obtained by them and addressing any issues?

Use of joint auditors

This is a special case of use of firms from more than one audit network. The group appoints two firms who are expected to reach a single group audit opinion for which they are jointly responsible. Audit work that is needed for group audit purposes would normally be carried out by firms from the joint auditors' networks.

The groups may find this arrangement useful if they:

- Have completed a merger and wish to maintain audit experience and knowledge by keeping the auditors involved in each of the merged entities;
- Wish to have the benefits of an audit opinion from two firms;
- Wish to reduce the scope for close relationships to build up with the auditor or for the auditor to become complacent;
- Wish to facilitate the rotation of audit firms by maintaining audit knowledge and experience;
- Wish to have a safeguard against the withdrawal from the market of their auditor.

In assessing the uses of joint auditors, audit committees may wish to consider:

- How effectively will the two joint auditors coordinate their work and cooperate with each other in reviewing findings?
- How effectively will the joint auditors ensure that all key issues are addressed?
- How effectively will the joint auditors conclude on highly judgemental matters?
- Balancing the benefits of a joint opinion with the underlying costs.

© The Financial Reporting Council Limited 2008

APPENDIX 6

Guidance on Internal Control (The Turnbull Guidance)

PREFACE

Internal Control: Guidance for Directors on the Combined Code (The Turnbull guidance) was first issued in 1999.

In 2004, the Financial Reporting Council established the Turnbull Review Group to consider the impact of the guidance and the related disclosures and to determine whether the guidance needed to be updated.

In reviewing the impact of the guidance, our consultations revealed that it has very successfully gone a long way to meeting its original objectives. Boards and investors alike indicated that the guidance has contributed to a marked improvement in the overall standard of risk management and internal control since 1999.

Notably, the evidence gathered by the Review Group demonstrated that respondents considered that the substantial improvements in internal control instigated by application of the Turnbull guidance have been achieved without the need for detailed prescription as to how to implement the guidance. The principles-based approach has required boards to think seriously about control issues and enabled them to apply the principles in a way that appropriately dealt with the circumstances of their business. The evidence also supported the proposition that the companies which have derived most benefit from application of the guidance were those whose boards saw embedded risk management and internal control as an integral part of running the business.

Accordingly, the Review Group strongly endorsed retention of the flexible, principles-based approach of the original guidance and has made only a small number of changes.

This however does not mean that there is nothing new for boards to do or that some companies could not make more effective use of the guidance. Establishing an effective system of internal control is not a one-off exercise. No such system remains effective unless it develops to take account of new and emerging risks, control failures, market expectations or changes in the company's circumstances or business objectives. The Review Group reiterates the view of the vast majority of respondents in emphasising the importance of regular and systematic assessment of the risks facing the business and the value of embedding risk management and internal control systems within business processes. It is the board's responsibility to make sure this happens.

Boards should review whether they can make more of the communication opportunity of the internal control statement in the annual report. Investors consider the board's attitude towards risk management and internal control to be an important factor when making investment decisions about a company. Taken together with the Operating and Financial Review, the internal control statement provides an opportunity for the board to help shareholders understand the risk and control issues facing the company, and to explain how the company maintains a framework of internal controls to address these issues and how the board has reviewed the effectiveness of that framework.

It is in this spirit that directors need to exercise their responsibility to review on a continuing basis their application of the revised guidance.

Turnbull Review Group
October 2005

One – Introduction

The importance of internal control and risk management

1. A company's system of internal control has a key role in the management of risks that are significant to the fulfilment of its business objectives. A sound system of internal control contributes to safeguarding the shareholders' investment and the company's assets.

2. Internal control (as referred to in paragraph 19) facilitates the effectiveness and efficiency of operations, helps ensure the reliability of internal and external reporting and assists compliance with laws and regulations.

3. Effective financial controls, including the maintenance of proper accounting records, are an important element of internal control. They help ensure that the company is not unnecessarily exposed to avoidable financial risks and that financial information used within the business and for publication is reliable. They also contribute to the safeguarding of assets, including the prevention and detection of fraud.

4. A company's objectives, its internal organisation and the environment in which it operates are continually evolving and, as a result, the risks it faces are continually changing. A sound system of internal control therefore depends on a thorough and regular evaluation of the nature and extent of the risks to which the company is exposed. Since profits are, in part, the reward for successful risk-taking in business, the purpose of internal control is to help manage and control risk appropriately rather than to eliminate it.

Objectives of the guidance

5. This guidance is intended to:
   - reflect sound business practice whereby internal control is embedded in the business processes by which a company pursues its objectives;
   - remain relevant over time in the continually evolving business environment; and
   - enable each company to apply it in a manner which takes account of its particular circumstances.

The guidance requires directors to exercise judgement in reviewing how the company has implemented the requirements of the Combined Code relating to internal control and reporting to shareholders thereon.

6. The guidance is based on the adoption by a company's board of a risk-based approach to establishing a sound system of internal control and reviewing its effectiveness. This should be incorporated by the company within its normal management and governance processes. It should not be treated as a separate exercise undertaken to meet regulatory requirements.

Internal control requirements of the Combined Code

7. Principle C.2 of the Code states that 'The board should maintain a sound system of internal control to safeguard shareholders' investment and the company's assets'.

8. Provision C.2.1 states that 'The directors should, at least annually, conduct a review of the effectiveness of the group's system of internal control and should report to shareholders that they have done so. The review should cover all material controls, including financial, operational and compliance controls and risk management systems'.

9. Paragraph 9.8.6 of the UK Listing Authority's Listing Rules states that in the case of a listed company incorporated in the United Kingdom, the following items must be included in its annual report and accounts:
   - a statement of how the listed company has applied the principles set out in Section 1 of the Combined Code, in a manner that would enable shareholders to evaluate how the principles have been applied;
   - a statement as to whether the listed company has:
     - complied throughout the accounting period with all relevant provisions set out in Section 1 of the Combined Code; or
     - not complied throughout the accounting period with all relevant provisions set out in Section 1 of the Combined Code and if so, setting out:

(i) those provisions, if any, it has not complied with;

(ii) in the case of provisions whose requirements are of a continuing nature, the period within which, if any, it did not comply with some or all of those provisions; and

(iii) the company's reasons for non-compliance.

10. The Preamble to the Code makes it clear that there is no prescribed form or content for the statement setting out how the various principles in the Code have been applied. The intention is that companies should have a free hand to explain their governance policies in the light of the principles, including any special circumstances which have led to them adopting a particular approach.

11. The guidance in this document applies for accounting periods beginning on or after 1 January 2006, and should be followed by boards of listed companies in:

- assessing how the company has applied Code Principle C.2;
- implementing the requirements of Code Provision C.2.1; and
- reporting on these matters to shareholders in the annual report and accounts.

12. For the purposes of this guidance, internal controls considered by the board should include all types of controls including those of an operational and compliance nature, as well as internal financial controls.

Groups of companies

13. Throughout this guidance, where reference is made to 'company' it should be taken, where applicable, as referring to the group of which the reporting company is the parent company. For groups of companies, the review of effectiveness of internal control and the report to the shareholders should be from the perspective of the group as a whole.

The Appendix

14. The Appendix to this document contains questions which boards may wish to consider in applying this guidance.

Two – Maintaining a sound system of internal control

Responsibilities

15. The board of directors is responsible for the company's system of internal control. It should set appropriate policies on internal control and seek regular assurance that will enable it to satisfy itself that the system is functioning effectively. The board must further ensure that the system of internal control is effective in managing those risks in the manner which it has approved.

16. In determining its policies with regard to internal control, and thereby assessing what constitutes a sound system of internal control in the particular circumstances of the company, the board's deliberations should include consideration of the following factors:

- the nature and extent of the risks facing the company;
- the extent and categories of risk which it regards as acceptable for the company to bear;
- the likelihood of the risks concerned materialising;
- the company's ability to reduce the incidence and impact on the business of risks that do materialise; and
- the costs of operating particular controls relative to the benefit thereby obtained in managing the related risks.

17. It is the role of management to implement board policies on risk and control. In fulfilling its responsibilities management should identify and evaluate the risks faced by the company for consideration by the board and design, operate and monitor a suitable system of internal control which implements the policies adopted by the board.

18. All employees have some responsibility for internal control as part of their accountability for achieving objectives. They, collectively, should have the necessary knowledge, skills, information, and authority to establish, operate and monitor the system of internal control. This will require an understanding of the company, its objectives, the industries and markets in which it operates, and the risks it faces.

Elements of a sound system of internal control

19. An internal control system encompasses the policies, processes, tasks, behaviours and other aspects of a company that, taken together:
    - facilitate its effective and efficient operation by enabling it to respond appropriately to significant business, operational, financial, compliance and other risks to achieving the company's objectives. This includes the safeguarding of assets from inappropriate use or from loss and fraud and ensuring that liabilities are identified and managed;
    - help ensure the quality of internal and external reporting. This requires the maintenance of proper records and processes that generate a flow of timely, relevant and reliable information from within and outside the organisation;
    - help ensure compliance with applicable laws and regulations, and also with internal policies with respect to the conduct of business.

20. A company's system of internal control will reflect its control environment which encompasses its organisational structure. The system will include:
    - control activities;
    - nformation and communications processes; and
    - processes for monitoring the continuing effectiveness of the system of internal control.

21. The system of internal control should:
    - be embedded in the operations of the company and form part of its culture;
    - be capable of responding quickly to evolving risks to the business arising from factors within the company and to changes in the business environment; and
    - include procedures for reporting immediately to appropriate levels of management any significant control failings or weaknesses that are identified together with details of corrective action being undertaken.

22. A sound system of internal control reduces, but cannot eliminate, the possibility of poor judgement in decision-making; human error; control processes being deliberately circumvented by employees and others; management overriding controls; and the occurrence of unforeseeable circumstances.

23. A sound system of internal control therefore provides reasonable, but not absolute, assurance that a company will not be hindered in achieving its business objectives, or in the orderly and legitimate conduct of its business, by circumstances which may reasonably be foreseen. A system of internal control cannot, however, provide protection with certainty against a company failing to meet its business objectives or all material errors, losses, fraud, or breaches of laws or regulations.

Three – Reviewing the effectiveness of internal control

Responsibilities

24. Reviewing the effectiveness of internal control is an essential part of the board's responsibilities. The board will need to form its own view on effectiveness based on the information and assurances provided to it, exercising the standard of care generally applicable to directors in the exercise of their duties. Management is accountable to the board for monitoring the system of internal control and for providing assurance to the board that it has done so.

25. The role of board committees in the review process, including that of the audit committee, is for the board to decide and will depend upon factors such as the size and composition of the board; the scale, diversity and complexity of the company's operations; and the nature of the significant risks that the company faces. To the extent that designated board committees carry out, on behalf of the board, tasks that are attributed in this guidance document to the board, the results of the relevant committees' work should be reported to, and considered by, the board. The board takes responsibility for the disclosures on internal control in the annual report and accounts.

The process for reviewing effectiveness

26. Effective monitoring on a continuous basis is an essential component of a sound system of internal control. The board cannot, however, rely solely on the embedded monitoring processes within the company to discharge its responsibilities. It should regularly receive and review reports on internal control. In addition, the board should undertake an annual assessment for the purposes of making its public statement on internal control to ensure that it has considered all significant aspects of internal control for the company for the year under review and up to the date of approval of the annual report and accounts.

27. The board should define the process to be adopted for its review of the effectiveness of internal control. This should encompass both the scope and frequency of the reports it receives and reviews during the year, and also the process for its annual assessment, such that it will be provided with sound, appropriately documented, support for its statement on internal control in the company's annual report and accounts.

28. The reports from management to the board should, in relation to the areas covered by them, provide a balanced assessment of the significant risks and the effectiveness of the system of internal control in managing those risks. Any significant control failings or weaknesses identified should be discussed in the reports, including the impact that they have had, or may have, on the company and the actions being taken to rectify them. It is essential that there be openness of communication by management with the board on matters relating to risk and control.

29. When reviewing reports during the year, the board should:
    - consider what are the significant risks and assess how they have been identified, evaluated and managed;
    - assess the effectiveness of the related system of internal control in managing the significant risks, having regard in particular to any significant failings or weaknesses in internal control that have been reported;
    - consider whether necessary actions are being taken promptly to remedy any significant failings or weaknesses; and
    - consider whether the findings indicate a need for more extensive monitoring of the system of internal control.

30. Additionally, the board should undertake an annual assessment for the purpose of making its public statement on internal control. The assessment should consider issues dealt with in reports reviewed by it during the year together with any additional information necessary to ensure that the board has taken account of all significant aspects of internal control for the company for the year under review and up to the date of approval of the annual report and accounts.

31. The board's annual assessment should, in particular, consider:
    - the changes since the last annual assessment in the nature and extent of significant risks, and the company's ability to respond to changes in its business and the external environment;
    - the scope and quality of management's ongoing monitoring of risks and of the system of internal control, and, where applicable, the work of its internal audit function and other providers of assurance;
    - the extent and frequency of the communication of the results of the monitoring to the board (or board committee(s)) which enables it to build up a cumulative assessment of the state of control in the company and the effectiveness with which risk is being managed;
    - the incidence of significant control failings or weaknesses that have been identified at any time during the period and the extent to which they have resulted in unforeseen outcomes or contingencies that have had, could have had, or may in the future have, a material impact on the company's financial performance or condition; and
    - the effectiveness of the company's public reporting processes.

32. Should the board become aware at any time of a significant failing or weakness in internal control, it should determine how the failing or weakness arose and reassess the effectiveness of management's ongoing processes for designing, operating and monitoring the system of internal control.

Four – The board's statement on internal control

33. The annual report and accounts should include such meaningful, high-level information as the board considers necessary to assist shareholders' understanding of the main features of the company's risk management processes and system of internal control, and should not give a misleading impression.

34. In its narrative statement of how the company has applied Code Principle C.2, the board should, as a minimum, disclose that there is an ongoing process for identifying, evaluating and managing the significant risks faced by the company, that it has been in place for the year under review and up to the date of approval of the annual report and accounts, that it is regularly reviewed by the board and accords with the guidance in this document.

35. The disclosures relating to the application of Principle C.2 should include an acknowledgement by the board that it is responsible for the company's system of internal control and for reviewing its effectiveness. It should also explain that such a system is designed to manage rather than eliminate the risk of failure to achieve business objectives, and can only provide reasonable and not absolute assurance against material misstatement or loss.

36. In relation to Code Provision C.2.1, the board should summarise the process it (where applicable, through its committees) has applied in reviewing the effectiveness of the system of internal control and confirm that necessary actions have been or are being taken to remedy any significant failings or weaknesses identified from that review. It should also disclose the process it has applied to deal with material internal control aspects of any significant problems disclosed in the annual report and accounts.

37. Where a board cannot make one or more of the disclosures in paragraphs 34 and 36, it should state this fact and provide an explanation. The Listing Rules require the board to disclose if it has failed to conduct a review of the effectiveness of the company's system of internal control.

38. Where material joint ventures and associates have not been dealt with as part of the group for the purposes of applying this guidance, this should be disclosed.

Five – Appendix

Assessing the effectiveness of the company's risk and control processes

Some questions which the board may wish to consider and discuss with management when regularly reviewing reports on internal control and when carrying out its annual assessment are set out below. The questions are not intended to be exhaustive and will need to be tailored to the particular circumstances of the company.

This Appendix should be read in conjunction with the guidance set out in this document.

Risk assessment

- Does the company have clear objectives and have they been communicated so as to provide effective direction to employees on risk assessment and control issues? For example, do objectives and related plans include measurable performance targets and indicators?
- Are the significant internal and external operational, financial, compliance and other risks identified and assessed on an ongoing basis? These are likely to include the principal risks identified in the Operating and Financial Review.
- Is there a clear understanding by management and others within the company of what risks are acceptable to the board?

Control environment and control activities

- Does the board have clear strategies for dealing with the significant risks that have been identified? Is there a policy on how to manage these risks?
- Do the company's culture, code of conduct, human resource policies and performance reward systems support the business objectives and risk management and internal control system?

- Does senior management demonstrate, through its actions as well as it policies, the necessary commitment to competence, integrity and fostering a climate of trust within the company?
- Are authority, responsibility and accountability defined clearly such that decisions are made and actions taken by the appropriate people? Are the decisions and actions of different parts of the company appropriately co-ordinated?
- Does the company communicate to its employees what is expected of them and the scope of their freedom to act? This may apply to areas such as customer relations; service levels for both internal and outsourced activities; health, safety and environmental protection; security of tangible and intangible assets; business continuity issues; expenditure matters; accounting; and financial and other reporting.
- Do people in the company (and in its providers of outsourced services) have the knowledge, skills and tools to support the achievement of the company's objectives and to manage effectively risks to their achievement?
- How are processes/controls adjusted to reflect new or changing risks, or operational deficiencies?

Information and communication

- Do management and the board receive timely, relevant and reliable reports on progress against business objectives and the related risks that provide them with the information, from inside and outside the company, needed for decision-making and management review purposes? This could include performance reports and indicators of change, together with qualitative information such as on customer satisfaction, employee attitudes etc.
- Are information needs and related information systems reassessed as objectives and related risks change or as reporting deficiencies are identified?
- Are periodic reporting procedures, including half-yearly and annual reporting, effective in communicating a balanced and understandable account of the company's position and prospects?
- Are there established channels of communication for individuals to report suspected breaches of law or regulations or other improprieties?

Monitoring

- Are there ongoing processes embedded within the company's overall business operations, and addressed by senior management, which monitor the effective application of the policies, processes and activities related to internal control and risk management? (Such processes may include control self-assessment, confirmation by personnel of compliance with policies and codes of conduct, internal audit reviews or other management reviews).
- Do these processes monitor the company's ability to re-evaluate risks and adjust controls effectively in response to changes in its objectives, its business, and its external environment?
- Are there effective follow-up procedures to ensure that appropriate change or action occurs in response to changes in risk and control assessments?
- Is there appropriate communication to the board (or board committees) on the effectiveness of the ongoing monitoring processes on risk and control matters? This should include reporting any significant failings or weaknesses on a timely basis.
- Are there specific arrangements for management monitoring and reporting to the board on risk and control matters of particular importance? These could include, for example, actual or suspected fraud and other illegal or irregular acts, or matters that could adversely affect the company's reputation or financial position.

Glossary

'Apply or explain' rule Similar to the 'comply or explain' rule. Companies should apply the principles of a code or explain why they have not done so.

Accountability The requirement for a person in a position of responsibility to justify, explain or account for the exercise of his authority and his performance or actions. Accountability is to the person or persons from whom the authority is derived.

Agency theory Theory based on the separation of ownership from control in a large organisation and the conflict of interests between the individuals who direct the organisation and the people who own it. In a company, the directors act as agents for the shareholders, and the conflict of interests between them should be controlled.

Aggressive accounting Accounting policies by a company that are just within accepted accounting practice, but which have the effect of making the company's performance seem better that it would if more conservative accounting policies were used. For example, accounting policies might be used that recognise income at an early stage in a transaction process, or defer the recognition of expenses.

Audit committee Committee of the board, consisting entirely of independent non-executive directors, with responsibility (amongst other things) of monitoring the reliability of the financial statements, the quality of the external audit and the company's relationship with its external auditors.

Audit firm rotation Changing the firm of external auditors on a regular basis, say every seven years. Not common in practice.

Audit partner rotation Changing the lead partner (and possibly other partners) involved with a company audit on a regular basis, typically every five or seven years.

Audit report Report for shareholders produced by the external auditors on completion of the annual audit, and included in the company's published annual report and accounts. The report gives the opinion of the auditors on whether the financial statements present a true and fair view of the company's financial performance and position.

Balance of power A situation in which power is shared out more or less evenly between a number of different individuals or groups, so that no single individual or group is in a position to dominate.

Bear phase The conditions in a stock market when share prices in general are declining. On the other hand, a 'bull phase' indicates that share prices in general are rising.

Board committee A committee established by the board of directors, with delegated responsibility for a particular aspect of the board's affairs. For example, audit committee, remuneration/compensation committee and nominations committee.

Board succession The replacement of a senior director (typically the chairman or chief executive officer) when he or she retires or resigns.

Bond credit ratings Ratings given to issues of bonds by agencies such as Standard & Poor's and Moody's, that give an assessment of the credit risk for investors in the bonds, i.e. the risk of default by the credit issuer.

Box-ticking approach An approach to compliance based on following all the specific rules or provisions in a code, and not considering the principles that should be applied and circumstances where the principles are best applied by not following the detailed provisions.

Business risk The risk from unexpected events or developments in a business or in the business environment, which are outside the control of management. Business risks should be managed and kept within acceptable limits.

Business risk management The management of business risks within a strategy based on risk appetite and risk tolerance. The board his responsible for business risk strategy and management is responsible for implementing the strategy within a business risk management system. The board is also responsible for monitoring the effectiveness of the business risk management system, at least annually according to the UK Corporate Governance Code.

Cadbury Code A code of corporate governance, published by the Cadbury Committee in the UK in 1992 (and since superseded).

Chairman Leader of the board of directors. Often referred to as the 'company chairman' in companies and 'chair' in public bodies and voluntary organisations.

Chief executive officer (CEO) The executive director who is head of the executive management team in an organisation.

Close period A period of time during which directors should not (in normal circumstances) buy or sell shares in their company.

Combined Code The UK code on corporate governance for listed companies from 1998 to 2010. It was revised in 2010 and re-named the UK Corporate Governance Code.

Compliance risk Risk of a failure to comply with laws or regulations, and the consequences of such a failure if discovered.

Compliance statement A statement by a listed company of whether it has complied with the requirements of the national (UK) code of corporate governance, and if not, in what ways has it failed to do so. In the UK, listed companies are required by the Listing Rules to include a compliance statement in their annual report and accounts.

'Comply or explain' rule Requirement (e.g. in the UK, a requirement of the Listing Rules) for a company to comply with a voluntary code of corporate governance (in the UK, the UK Corporate Governance Code) or explain any non-compliance.

Corporate citizen/citizenship A company acting with due regard for its responsibilities as a member of the society in which it operates. Corporate citizenship is demonstrated through CSR policies.

Corporate ethics Standards of business behaviour, sometimes set out by companies in a code of corporate ethics.

Corporate governance The system by which a company is directed, so as to achieve its overall objectives. It is concerned with relationships, structures, processes, information flows, controls, decision-making and accountability at the highest level in a company.

Corporate social responsibility (CSR) Responsibility shown by a company (or other organisations) for matters of general concern to the society in which it operates, such as protection of the environment, health and safety, and social welfare.

CSR index/indices An index that measures and rates companies in terms of their CSR performance. Produced by publishers of stock market indices (Dow Jones, FTSE). Used by institutional investors.

Deferred annual bonus scheme An element in a remuneration package for a directors or senior executives whereby the individuals are allowed to use some or all of their annual cash bonus entitlement to acquire shares in the company, which are then matched after several years (typically three years) by the award of additional free shares.

Derivative action Legal action taken against a director by shareholders in the name of the company, alleging negligence or breach of duty.

Directors' report The 'report' in the annual report and accounts of a company. A report by the board of directors to the shareholders, contained in the annual report and accounts of the company and containing a variety of reports and information disclosures, such as the business review and remuneration report.

Disaster recovery plan Plans to be implemented, in the event of a disaster that puts normal operational systems out of action, to restore operational capability as quickly as possible. The need for many companies to have a disaster recovery plan was highlighted by the terrorist attack on the USA on 11 September 2001.

Disclosure and Transparency Rules In the UK, rules on disclosures that listed companies are required to comply with. The rules (like the Listing Rules) are issued and enforced by the UK financial markets regulator.

Downside risk A risk that actual events will turn out worse than expected. Downside risk can be measure in terms of the amount by which profits could be worse than expected. The expected outcome is the forecast or budget expectation.

Duty of skill and care A duty owed by a director to the company. In the UK, this has been a common law duty, but became a statutory duty under the provisions of the Companies Act 2006. A question can be raised, however, about what level of skill and care should be expected from a director.

Enlightened shareholder approach Approach to corporate governance based on the view that the objective of its directors should be to meet the needs of shareholders, whilst also showing concern for other major stakeholders. Also called an inclusive approach to governance.

Environmental, social and governance (ESG) risks Environmental, social and governance risks. These are risks of adverse consequences to a company from circumstances or events relating to environmental, social or corporate governance issues.

EU Directive An instruction, devised by the European Commission and approved by the European Council and European Parliament. The contents of a Directive must be introduced into national law or regulations by all member states of the European Union. Some Directives, such as the Shareholder Rights Directive, deal wholly or partly with corporate governance issues.

European Commission The managing and administrative body of the European Union.

Executive director A director who also has executive responsibilities in the management structure. Usually a full-time employee with a contract of employment.

External audit Statutory annual audit of a company by independent external auditors.

Fairness Impartiality, a lack of bias. In a corporate governance context, the quality of fairness refers to things that are done or decided in a reasonable manner, and with sense of justice, avoiding bias.

Fiduciary duty A duty of a trustee. The directors of a company are given their powers in trust by the company, and have fiduciary duties towards the company.

Financial risk A risk of a failure or error, deliberate (fraud) or otherwise, in the systems or procedures for recording financial transactions and reporting financial performance and position, or the risk of a failure to safeguard financial assets such as cash and accounts receivable.

Financial statement A statement containing financial information. The main financial statements by a company are the balance sheet (statement of financial position) and income statement (profit and loss account) in the annual report and accounts. Other financial statements include a cashflow statement and the balance sheets and

profit and loss account in a company's published interim or quarterly accounts.

Fixed pay The elements in a remuneration package that are a fixed amount each year, such as basic salary.

FTSE This is a stock market index. The FTSE 100 is the index of the 100 most highly capitalised companies listed on the London Stock Exchange; the FTSE 350 is the 350 most highly capitalised companies.

General meeting A meeting of the equity shareholders of a company. Public companies are required to hold an annual general meeting (AGM).

Going concern statement A requirement of some corporate governance codes, such as the UK Corporate Governance Code. A statement by the board of directors that in their view the company will remain as a going concern for the next financial year.

Greenbury Report Report in the UK in 1995 by the Greenbury Committee, focusing mainly on corporate governance issues related to directors' remuneration.

GRI Sustainability Reporting Framework A voluntary framework for standardising the content of, and measurements, in sustainability reports.

Hampel Committee Committee set up in the UK to continue the review of corporate governance practices in the UK, following the Cadbury and Greenbury Committee Reports. The Hampel Committee suggested that the recommendations of all three committees should be integrated into a single code of corporate governance, which was published in 1998 as the Combined Code.

Higgs Report The 2003 UK government-commissioned review into the role and effectiveness of non-executive directors.

Induction Process of introducing a newly appointed director into his or her role, by providing appropriate information, site visits, meetings with management and (where necessary) training.

Insider dealing Dealing in the shares of a company by an individual who has knowledge of undisclosed 'insider information' (price-sensitive information) that comes from an 'inside source'. In the UK insider dealing is a criminal offence under Part V of the Criminal Justice Act 1993.

Institutional investor An organisation or institution that invests funds of clients, savers or depositors. The main institutional investors in the UK are pension funds, insurance/life assurance companies, investment trust companies and mutual organisations such as unit trusts and open-ended investment companies ('OEICs'). Institutional investors are the main investors in shares in the leading stock markets of the world. In the UK, most institutional investors are members of an 'industry association', such as the Association of British Insurers (ABI) and the National Association of Pension Funds (NAPF).

Institutional Shareholders Committee (ISC) A collective body representing the associations of institutional investors in the UK, including the ABI and NAPF.

Internal audit Investigations and checks carried out by internal auditors of an organisation. Internal audit is a function rather than a specific activity. However, work programme of the internal audit team might reduce the amount of work the external auditors need to carry out in their annual audit, provided the internal and external auditors collaborate properly.

Internal control A procedure or arrangement that is implemented to prevent an internal control risk, reduce the potential impact of such a risk, or detect a failure of internal control when it occurs (and initiate remedial action).

Internal control report A statement by the board of directors of a listed company to the shareholders on internal control, and contained in the company's annual report and accounts. This statement is a requirement of the UK Corporate Governance Code and the Disclosure and Transparency Rules.

Internal control risk A risk of failure in a system or procedure due to causes that are within the control of management. They can be categorised as financial risks, operational risk and compliance risks.

Internal control system A system of internal controls within an organisation. The system should have a suitable control environment, and should provide for the identification and assessment of internal control risks, the design and implementation of internal controls, communication and information and monitoring. In the UK, the board of directors of a listed company has responsibility for the system of internal control.

International Corporate Governance Network (ICGN) A voluntary association of institutional investors which has the objective of raising standards of corporate governance globally, to meet the requirements and expectations of global investors.

King Code Also called the King Report and King III (because it is the third version of the Code/Report, issued in 2009). The corporate governance code for listed companies in South Africa.

Majority shareholder A shareholder holding a majority of the equity shares in a company and so having a controlling interest in the company. A majority shareholder has the voting power to remove directors from the board, and so can control the board.

Management board A board of executive managers, chaired by the CEO, within a two-tier board structure. The chairman of the management board reports to the chairman of the supervisory board. The management board has responsibility for the operational performance of the business.

Market abuse Market abuse occurs when an individual distorts a market in investments, creates a false or misleading impression of the value or price of an investment, or misuses relevant information before it is published. Although it is similar to insider dealing, which is a criminal offence, this is a civil offence under the Financial Services and Markets Act.

Minority shareholders Shareholders holding a fairly small proportion of the total equity shares in a company who could be at risk of having their interests ignored in favour of a controlling shareholder or group of large shareholders.

Model articles of association In the context of UK company law, a company may adopt standard articles of association (company constitution) and amend these as necessary to meet the requirements and particular circumstances of the individual company. In practice, the articles of association of most UK companies formed under the Companies Act 1985 are based on the Table A Articles. Different model articles apply to companies formed under the Companies Act 2006.

Model Code A code of conduct for directors of listed companies, stating when they should (in normal circumstances) avoid buying or selling shares in their company.

Modified audit report Audit report in which the auditors express some reservations about the financial statements of the company, because of insufficient information to reach an opinion or disagreement with the figures in the statements.

Money laundering The process of transferring or using money obtained from criminal activity, so as to make it seem to have come from legitimate (non-criminal) sources. Companies are often used as a cover for money laundering.

Myners Report A UK report into the role and responsibilities of institutional investors.

Nasdaq/NASDAQ A screen-based electronic market for dealing in equities, mainly in the USA. NASDAQ originally stood for National Association of Securities Dealers Automated Quotations, but the full name is now obsolete.

Nomination committee A committee of the board of directors, with responsibility for identifying potential new members for the board of directors. Suitable candidates are recommended to the main board, which then makes a decision about their appointment.

Non-audit work Work done by a firm of auditors for a client company, other than work on the annual audit, such as consultancy services and tax advice. In the context of corporate governance, the independence of the auditors might be questionable when they earn high fees for non-audit work.

Non-executive director (NEDs) A director who is not an employee of the company and who does not have any responsibilities for executive management in the company.

OECD Principles of Corporate Governance General principles of corporate governance issued by the Organisation for Economic Co-operation and Development, which all countries are encouraged to adopt.

Operational risk Risk of an error, deliberate or otherwise, in operating systems or procedures within an organisation; the risk of failure in equipment or system design; the risk of failures due to weak organisational structure; or risks due to human error including inefficient management. Includes health and safety risks, environmental risks.

Out-of-the-money Term that describes share options whose exercise price is higher than the current market value of the shares they can purchase.

Performance-related incentives Incentives to an individual, typically to an executive director and in the form of a cash bonus, that are payable if certain performance targets are achieved. Performance targets might be related to a rise in the share price, growth in sales or profits, growth in earnings per share, or to non-financial performance criteria.

Premium listing One of two categories of listing for companies in the UK. Companies with a premium listing are required to meet the highest standards of regulation and corporate governance.

Price-sensitive information Undisclosed information that, if generally known, would be likely to have an effect on the share price of the company concerned.

Principles-based code of governance A code based on general principles of best governance practice, rather than detailed rules and guidelines. A principles-based code may include some practical provisions or guidelines, but these are not comprehensive.

Proxy A person appointed by a shareholder to vote on the shareholder's behalf at a general meeting. In the UK shareholders can appoint proxies electronically. They can either instruct a proxy how to vote on each resolution at a meeting, or can give the proxy freedom to decide how to vote on each resolution.

Proxy vote A vote delivered by an individual (a proxy) on behalf of a shareholder, in the shareholder's absence.

Red top alert/warning A notice sent out by an institutional investor organisation to its members, advising the members who are shareholders to vote against a particular resolution at an approaching general meeting of a company.

Related party transaction A transaction by a company with a 'related party' such as a major shareholder, a director, a company in which a director has a major interest or a member of a director's family.

Remuneration committee A committee of the board of directors, with responsibility for deciding remuneration policy for top executives and the individual remuneration packages of certain senior executives, for example all the executive directors.

Reputation risk Risk to the reputation of a company or other organisation in the mind of the public (including customers and suppliers) when a particular matter becomes public knowledge.

Responsibility Having power and authority over something. A person in a position of responsibility should be held accountable for the exercise of that authority.

Responsible voting Voting by a shareholder in a way that fulfils the shareholder's responsibilities to another group, typically the shareholder's clients. The term is used in connection with voting by institutional shareholders. It is increasingly accepted that institutional shareholders should vote responsibly in the interests of their clients. Responsible voting is associated with upholding best practice in corporate governance.

Risk appetite The amount and type of business risk that the board of directors would like their company to have exposure to. Identifying risk appetite should be a part of strategic planning.

Risk assessment An assessment of risks faced by an organisation. Typically, risks are assessed according to how probable or how frequent an adverse outcome is likely to be in the planning period and the potential size of the losses of an adverse outcome occurs. The greatest risks are those with a high probability of an adverse outcome combined with the likelihood of a large loss if this were to happen.

Risk committee A committee of the board that a company may establish, with the responsibility of monitoring the risk management system within the company, instead of the audit committee. A risk committee may be established when the audit committee has too many other responsibilities to handle.

Risk management committee A committee of senior executive managers and risk managers, whose responsibility is to implement the risk management strategy of the board.

Risk tolerance The amount of business risk that the board is willing to let their company be exposed to. Alternatively, the amount of risk that the company is able to accept without serious threat to its stability (which may also be called risk capacity).

Safe harbour provisions Provisions in the UK Companies Act whereby directors are not liable for incorrect or misleading statements (or omissions) in a report to shareholders, unless they knew the statements or omissions to be incorrect or misleading. These provisions reduced concern about directors ' liability for the information provided by their company in its business review.

Sarbanes-Oxley Act Legislation, largely on corporate governance issues, introduced in the USA in 2002 following a series of corporate scandals such as Enron and WorldCom.

Secret profit A profit that is not revealed. In the context of corporate governance, a director should not make a secret profit for his/her personal benefit and at the expense of the company.

Senior independent director A non-executive director (NED) who is the nominal head of all the non-executive directors on the board. The SID may act as a channel of communication between the NEDs and the chairman, or (in some situations) between major shareholders and the board.

Severance payment Payment to a director (or other employee) on being required to resign (or otherwise leave the company).

Share options Rights given to an individual giving him (or her) the right but not the obligation to buy new shares in the company at a fixed price (the exercise price), not earlier than a specified date and not later than a specified date in the future (typically not earlier than three years after the options are granted and not later than ten years respectively).

Shareholder activism A term that refers to: (1) the considered use by institutional investors of their rights as shareholders, by voting against the board of directors at general meetings (or threatening to vote against the board); and (2) active dialogue with the boards of companies, to influence decisions by the board.

Shareholder engagement Similar in meaning to shareholder activism, except that the term is associated more with active and constructive dialogue rather than opposition to the board.

Shareholder value approach Approach to corporate governance based on the view that the objective of its directors should be to maximise benefits for shareholders.

Socially responsible investment Investment by institutional investors that takes into consideration the CSR policies of companies when deciding which companies to invest in or whether to hold on to investments.

Stakeholder A stakeholder group is an identifiable group of individuals or organisations with a vested interest. Stakeholder groups in a company include the shareholders, the directors, senior executive management and other employees, customers, suppliers, the general public and (in the case of many companies) the government. Stakeholders may be categorised as financial or non-financial stakeholders, and as external or internal stakeholders (depending on whether they work in the company). The nature of their interests differs between stakeholder groups.

Stakeholder approach Approach to governance based on the view that the organisation should aim to satisfy the needs of all stakeholders. Also called a 'pluralist approach'.

Stakeholder theory The view that the purpose of corporate governance should be to satisfy, as far as possible, the objectives of all key stakeholders.

Statutory duties Duties imposed by statute law.

Stress testing Testing the ability of a business to withstand the effects of extreme adverse events or developments in the business environment.

Succession planning Planning for the eventual replacement of a senior member of the board (chairman, CEO and possibly finance director) by his or her successor.

Supervisory board A board of non-executive directors, found in a company with a two-tier board structure. The supervisory board reserves some responsibilities to itself. These include oversight of the management board.

Sustainability Conducting business operations in a way that can be continued into the foreseeable future, without using natural resources at such a rate or creating such environmental damage that the continuation of the business will eventually become impossible.

Sustainability report Report on the economic, social and environmental performance of a company.

Total shareholder return The total returns in a period earned by the company's shareholders, consisting normally of the dividends received and the gain (or minus the fall) in the share price during the period. The returns might be expressed as a percentage of the share value, e.g. the share price at the start of the period.

Transaction cost theory A theory about organisations that includes the view that management are opportunistic and may take opportunities that arise to pursue their personal interests.

Transparency Openness. Being clear about historical performance and future intentions, and not trying to hide information.

Triple bottom line reporting Reporting on the economic, social and environmental performance of a company.

Turnbull Guidance Initially a report of the Turnbull Committee in the UK, giving listed companies guidance on how the directors should carry out their responsibility for the internal control system, as required by the UK corporate governance code. Now the responsibility of the FRC.

Two-tier board Board structure in which responsibilities are divided between a supervisory board of non-executive directors led by the chairman, and a management board of executives led by the CEO.

UK Corporate Governance Code The code of corporate governance issued by the Financial Reporting Council in the UK, which is applied to UK listed companies. Formerly (until 2010) called the Combined Code.

UK Listing Rules Rules that apply to all listed companies in the UK. They include the 'comply or explain' rule on compliance with the UK Corporate Governance Code.

UK Stewardship Code A set of principles and guidelines for behaviour by institutional investors in their dealings with a company, issued by the FRC. This Code is based on a code previously issued by the Institutional Shareholders Committee.

Under water Term that describes share options whose exercise price is higher than the market value of the shares they can purchase.

Unitary board Board structure in which decisions are taken by a single group of executive and non-executive directors, led by the company chairman.

Upside risk A risk that actual events will turn out better than expected and will provide unexpected profits. Some risks, such as the risk of a change in foreign exchange rates, or a change in interest rates, or a change in consumer buying patterns could be 'two-way' with both upside and downside potential.

Variable pay The elements in a remuneration package that vary each year according to the individual's performance, such as annual bonuses, and the grant of shares or share options.

Voluntary code of governance A code of governance that is not enforced by law or regulation. However, as in the UK and South Africa, listed companies may be encouraged to adopt a voluntary code by means of a 'comply or explain' or 'apply or explain' regulation.

Vote withheld A voting option for shareholders who appoint a proxy, as an alternative to voting for or against a resolution, or not voting at all. The proxy may be instructed to abstain on a particular resolution at the general meeting. Votes withheld are 'positive abstentions' and the number of votes withheld should be counted and recorded.

Walker Report A report published in the UK in 2009 about corporate governance in banks and other financial services organisations, following the banking crisis of 2007–2008.

Window dressing (of accounts, and financial reports and performance) Applying accounting policies that are just within the limits of permissible accounting practice, but which have the effect of making the company's performance or financial position seem better than it would if more conservative accounting policies were used. For example, accounting policies might be used that recognise income at an early stage in a transaction process, or defer the recognition of expenses.

Wrongful trading Wrongful trading occurs when a company continues to trade when the directors are aware that the company had gone into (or would soon go into) insolvent liquidation.

Directory

Further Reading

General

Cassley, V. and Mensley, D., *The ICSA Corporate Governance Planner* (ICSA Publishing, 2006).

Chambers, A., *Corporate Governance Handbook*, 4th edition (Bloomsbury Professional 2008)

Charkham, J., *Keeping Better Company: Corporate Governance Ten Years On* 2nd edition (Oxford University Press, 2008)

Clarke, T., *Theories of Corporate Governance* (Routledge, 2004)

Barber, B., ICSA's *Corporate Governance Handbook* (ICSA Publishing, 2010)

Dattani, R., *The ICSA Directors' Handbook* (ICSA Publishing, 2009)

Herbert Smith LLP, *A Practical Guide to the UK Listing Regime* (ICSA Publishing, 2008)

Keasey, K. (ed), *Corporate Governance: Accountability, Enterprise and International Comparisons* (John Wiley and Sons, 2005)

Mallin, C., *Corporate Governance* 3rd edition (Oxford University Press, 2009)

Monks, A. G. and Minow, N. (eds), *Corporate Governance* 3rd edition (Blackwell, 2007)

Solomon, J. F. *Corporate Governance and Accountability*, 3rd edition (John Wiley & Sons Inc, 2010)

Tricker, R.I., *Corporate Governance: Principles, Policies and Practices* (OUP, 2008)

Wearing, R., *Cases in Corporate Governance* (Sage, 2005)

Yew, J and Grant, A., *Boardroom Employment Law: From Recruitment to Dismissal* (ICSA Publishing, 2008)

Not-for-Profit/Public Sector

Carver, J. and Shrader, A., *Boards That Make a Difference: A New Design for Leadership in Nonprofit and Public Organizations* 3rd edition (Jossey-Bass, 2006)

Charity Commission, *The Hallmarks of an Effective Charity* (2010)

CIPFA, *Approaches to Corporate Governance in the Public Sector* (2000)

Cornforth, C., *The Governance of Public and Non-Profit Organisations – What Do Boards Do?* (Routledge, 2005)

Dyer, P. and Ramrayka, L. (eds), *The Good Trustee Guide* 5th edition (NCVO Publications, 2008)

National Housing Federation, *Competence and Accountability 2004 Code of Governance* (2004)

Corporate Social Responsibility

Hoskins, T., *The ICSA Corporate Social Responsibility Handbook: Making CSR Work for Your Business*, 2nd edition (ICSA Publishing, 2008)

OECD guidelines for multinational companies. See www.oecd.org.

Whistleblowing

ICSA, *Establishing a Whistleblowing Procedure* 2nd edition (ICSA, 2007)

Directors, Boards and Committees

Executive Remuneration: Guidelines on Policies and Practices (ABI, 2009). Available at www.ivis.co.uk.

Bruce, M., *The ICSA Director's Guide*, 4th edition (ICSA Publishing, 2010)

Bruce, M., *Rights and Duties of Directors*, 10th edition (Bloomsbury Professional, 2010)

Cadbury, A., *Corporate Governance and Chairmanship: A Personal View* (Oxford University Press, 2002)

Charon, R., *Boards that Deliver* (Jossey-Bass, 2005)

Copnell, T., *The ICSA Audit Committee Guide* 2nd edition (ICSA Publishing, 2010)

Dunne, P., *Running Board Meetings* 3rd edition (Kogan Page, 2007)

Garrett, R., *Thin on Top* (Nicholas Brealey Publishing, 2006)

Leblanc, R. and Gillies, J., *Inside the Boardroom* (John Wiley and Sons, 2005)

Nadler, D.A., *Building Better Boards* (Pfeiffer Wiley, 2006)

O'Hare, S., *The ICSA Remuneration Committee Guide* (ICSA Publishing, 2006)

Stiles, P. and Taylor, B., *Boards at Work* (Oxford University Press, 2002)

UK Listing Authority, *The Model Code* (Appendix to the UK Listing Rules) (FSA, updated annually).

Shareholder relations

ABI/NAPF Statement on Responsible Voting (ABI/NAPF, 1999). Available at www.ivis.co.uk.

Developments in Narrative Reporting: An ABI Position Paper, ABI, 2006,

Charkham, J. and Simpson, A., *Fair Shares: The Future of Shareholder Power and Responsibility* (Oxford University Press, 1999)

Copnell, T and Ray, S., *ICSA Shareholder Questions and the AGM* (ICSA Publishing, 2007)

Hermes, *Hermes Statement on Corporate Governance and Voting Policy* (Hermes, 1998, updated 2001). Available at www.hermes.co.uk.

Hermes, *The Hermes Responsible Ownership Principles* (Hermes, 2010). Available at www.hermes.co.uk.

Hoskins, T., *The ICSA Company Reporting Handbook* (ICSA Publishing, 2007)

NAPF, Corporate Governance Policy (NAPF, revised 2007).

PIRC, *Shareholder Voting Guidelines* (PIRC, 2008)

Reports, Codes of Practice and Guidelines

Boardroom Behaviours: A Report prepared for Sir David Walker by the Institute of Chartered Secretaries and Administrators, ICSA 2009

Report of the Committee on the Financial Aspects of Corporate Governance: The Code of Best Practice (Cadbury Code)

Directors' Remuneration: Report of a Study Group chaired by Sir Richard Greenbury (Greenbury Committee Report)

Executive Remuneration – ABI Guidelines on Policies and Practices, (ABI 2009)

Committee on Corporate Governance: Final Report (Hampel Committee report).

Investor Relations best practice guides, available from Investor Relations Society, www.ir-soc.org.uk

Key Principles of Good Governance 2010 Available from the Charity Commission www.charitycommission.gov.uk. Revises the principles first published in *Good Governance: A Code for the Voluntary and Community Sector* (2005) by the National Governance Hub (see below)

Myners, P., *Institutional Investment in the UK: A Review* (HM Treasury, 2001, updated 2007)

Sarbanes-Oxley Act of 2002, H.R. 3763.

The European Commission's Action Plan for Company Law and Corporate Governance (2003)

The Stewardship Code, (Financial Reporting Council (FRC) 2010)

The Tyson Report on the Recruitment and Development of Non-Executive Directors (2003)

The UK Corporate Governance Code Financial Reporting Council 2010. The FRC also holds previous versions of the UK Combined Codes and related reviews and consultations. See also the FRC's Associated Guidance (*Turnbull and FRC Guidance on Audit Committees and Suggestions for Good Practice from the Higgs Report*). All available to download from www.frc.org.uk

Walker, Sir David, *A Review of Corporate Governance in UK Banks and Other Financial Industry Entities (Walker Review)*, HM Treasury 2009, www.hm-treasury.gov.uk

National Hub of Expertise in Governance, *Good Governance: A Code for the Voluntary and Community Sector* (2005). The National Governance Hub has now been disbanded and their publications are available from the National Council for Voluntary Organisations (NCVO).

ICSA Guidance Notes

The ICSA Policy Unit produces a range of Guidance Notes on Corporate Governance topics, including electronic communications and committee terms of reference. These are available at www.icsa.org.uk/policy-guidance

Magazines, journals and newsletters

Boardroom Update

A bi-monthly ICSA newsletter that provides directors, company secretaries and in-house legal teams with news and case law coverage on corporate governance, company law and other issues.

Chartered Secretary

The ICSA monthly magazine carries regular updates and articles on a variety of corporate governance topics and issues. The magazine's companion website, www.charteredsecretary.net has a searchable archive of recent features and daily news updates.

The magazines published by ICSA Divisions in Malaysia, Singapore, Hong Kong and elsewhere also cover a broad range of corporate governance issues.

Chartered Secretary Newswire

A new weekly e-mail service which provides a round-up of key industry news and events. To register, go to www.charteredsecretary. net.

Corporate Governance: An International Review

An academic research journal with particular emphasis on international issues.
Global Proxy Watch
Monthly e-mail or fax newsletter from Davis Global Advisors

Governance

An independent monthly newsletter, which is particularly strong on international developments. Available in print, electronically or both. Governance Publications www.governance.co.uk

Investor Relations

Monthly review with strong international coverage.

Web resources

A regular review the key websites listed below will help to keep you up to date with current debates and issues.
Accounting Standards Board www.frc.org.uk/asb
Asian Corporate Governance Association www.acga-asia.org
Association of British Insurers www.abi.org.uk
Association of British Insurers remuneration guidelines: www.ivis.co.uk
Business for Social Responsibility www.bsr.org
Business in the Community www.bitc.org.uk

Calpers www.calpers.org
Charity Commission www.charitycommission.gov.uk
Committee on Standards in Public Life, UK www.public-standards.gov.uk
Council of Institutional Investors, USA www.cii.org
Davis Global Advisors www.davisglobal.com
Deminor (scorecards) www.deminor.com
EIRIS (Ethical Investment Research Service) www.eiris.org
European Corporate Governance Institute www.ecgi.org
Financial Reporting Council www.frc.org.uk. This website includes the UK Corporate Governance Code and the Stewardship Code.
Financial Services Authority www.fsa.gov.uk
Global Corporate Governance Forum www.gcgf.org
Hermes www.hermes.co.uk
International Organization of Securities Commissions www.iosco.org
Institutional Shareholder Services (ISS) www.issproxy.com
International Corporate Governance Network www.icgn.org
Investor Relations Society www.ir-soc.org.uk
London Stock Exchange www.stockex.com
National Association of Pension Funds (NAPF) www.napf.co.uk
National Council for Voluntary Organisations (NCVO) www.ncvo-vol.org.uk
OECD Principles of Corporate Governance www.oecd.org
Pensions & Investment Research Consultants Limited www.pirc.co.uk
Public Concern at Work (Whistleblowing) www.pcaw.co.uk
Quoted Companies Alliance (QCA) www.qcanet.co.uk
Standard and Poors (ratings) www.standardandpoors.com
Sustainability at Work, www.sustainabilityatwork.org.uk
The Corporate Library www.thecorporatelibrary.com
The Department for Business, Innovation and Skills (BIS) www.bis.gov.uk
The Institute of Business Ethics www.ibe.org.uk
The Institute of Chartered Secretaries and Administrators (ICSA) www.icsa.org.uk
The Institute of Directors www.iod.co.uk
The Investor Responsibility Research Centre www.irrc.org
The National Association of Corporate Directors, USA www.nacdonline.org
US Securities and Exchange Commission www.sec.gov

Index